P9-DEO-862

Using R for Introductory Econometrics

Florian Heiss

Using R for Introductory Econometrics
© Florian Heiss 2016. All rights reserved.

Companion website: `http://www.URfIE.net`

Address:
Universitätsstraße 1, Geb. 24.31.01.24
40225 Düsseldorf, Germany

ISBN: 978-1523285136
ISBN-10: 1523285133

Contents

List of Tables

List of Figures

Preface

R is a powerful programming language that is especially well-suited for statistical analyses and the creation of graphics. In many areas of applied statistics, R is the most widely used software package. In other areas, such as econometrics, it is quickly catching up to commercial software packages. R is constantly adjusted and extended by a large user community so that many state-of-the-art econometric methods are available very quickly. R is powerful and versatile for the advanced user and is also quite easy for a beginner to learn and use.

The software package R is completely free and available for most operating systems. When using it in econometrics courses, students can easily download a copy to their own computers and use it at home (or their favorite cafés) to replicate examples and work on take-home assignments. This hands-on experience is essential for the understanding of the econometric models and methods. It also prepares students to conduct their own empirical analyses for their theses, research projects, and professional work.

Several excellent books introduce R and its application to statistics; for example, Dalgaard (2008); Field, Miles, and Field (2012); Hothorn and Everitt (2014); and Verzani (2014). The books of Kleiber and Zeileis (2008) and Fox and Weisberg (2011) not only introduce applied econometrics with R but also provide their own extensions to R, which we will make use of here. A problem I encountered when teaching introductory econometrics classes is that the textbooks that also introduce R do not discuss econometrics in the breadth and depth required to be used as the main text. Conversely, my favorite introductory econometrics textbooks do not cover R. Although it is possible to combine a good econometrics textbook with an unrelated introduction to R, this creates substantial hurdles because the topics and order of presentation are different, and the terminology and notation are inconsistent.

This book does not attempt to provide a self-contained discussion of econometric models and methods. It also does not give an independent general introduction to R. Instead, it builds on the excellent and popular textbook "Introductory Econometrics" by Wooldridge (2016). It is compatible in terms of topics, organization, terminology, and notation, and is designed for a seamless transition from theory to practice.

The first chapter provides a gentle introduction to R, covers some of the topics of basic statistics and probability presented in the appendix of Wooldridge (2016), and introduces Monte Carlo simulation as an additional tool. The other chapters have the same names and cover the same material as the respective chapters in Wooldridge (2016). Assuming the reader has worked through the material discussed there, this book explains and demonstrates how to implement everything in R and replicates many textbook examples. We also open some black boxes of the built-in functions for estimation and inference by directly applying the formulas known from the textbook to reproduce the results. Some supplementary analyses provide additional intuition and insights.

The book is designed mainly for students of introductory econometrics who ideally use Wooldridge (2016) as their main textbook. It can also be useful for readers who are familiar with econometrics and possibly other software packages. For them, it offers an introduction to R and can be used to look up the implementation of standard econometric methods.

Because we are explicitly building on Wooldridge (2016), it is useful to have a copy at hand while working through this book. The fifth edition of Wooldridge (2013) can be used as well; older editions are not perfectly compatible with regard to references to sections and examples. The stripped-down textbook sold only in Europe, the Middle East, and Africa (Wooldridge, 2014) is mostly consistent, but lacks, among other things, the appendices on fundamental math, probability, and statistics.

All computer code used in this book can be downloaded to make it easier to replicate the results and tinker with the specifications. The companion website also provides the full text of this book for online viewing and additional material. It is located at

<code>http://www.URfIE.net.</code>

1. Introduction

Learning to use *R* is straightforward but not trivial. This chapter prepares us for implementing the actual econometric analyses discussed in the following chapters. First, we introduce the basics of the software system *R* in Section 1.1. In order to build a solid foundation we can later rely on, Chapters 1.2 through 1.4 cover the most important concepts and approaches used in *R* like working with objects, dealing with data, and generating graphs. Sections 1.5 through 1.7 quickly go over the most fundamental concepts in statistics and probability and show how they can be implemented in *R*. More advanced *R* topics like conditional execution, loops, and functions are presented in Section 1.8. They are not really necessary for most of the material in this book. An exception is Monte Carlo simulation which is introduced in Section 1.9.

1.1. Getting Started

Before we can get going, we have to find and download the relevant software, figure out how the examples presented in this book can be easily replicated and tinkered with, and understand the most basic aspects of *R*. That is what this section is all about.

1.1.1. Software

R is a free and open source software. Its homepage is `http://www.r-project.org/`. There, a wealth of information is available as well as the software itself. Most of the readers of this book will not want to compile the software themselves, so downloading the pre-compiled binary distributions is recommended. They are available for Windows, Mac, and Linux systems.

After downloading, installing, and running *R*, the program window will look similar to the screen shot in Figure 1.1. It provides some basic information on *R* and the installed version. Right to the > sign is the prompt where the user can type commands for *R* to evaluate.

We can type whatever we want here. After pressing the return key (⏎), the line is terminated, *R* tries to make sense out of what is written and gives an appropriate answer. In the example shown in Figure 1.1, this was done four times. The texts we typed are shown next to the ">" sign, *R* answers under the respective line next to the "[1]".

Our first attempt did not work out well: We have got an error message. Unfortunately, *R* does not comprehend the language of Shakespeare. We will have to adjust and learn to speak *R*'s less poetic language. The other experiments were more successful: We gave *R* simple computational tasks and got the result (next to a "[1]"). The syntax should be easy to understand – apparently, *R* can do simple addition, deals with the parentheses in the expected way, can calculate square roots (using the term **sqrt**) and knows the number π.

R is used by typing commands such as these. Not only Apple users may be less than impressed by the design of the user interface and the way the software is used. There are various approaches to make it more user friendly by providing a different user interface added on top of plain *R*. Notable examples include R commander, Deducer, RKWard, and RStudio. In the following, we will use the latter which can be downloaded free of charge for the most common operating systems at `http://www.rstudio.com/`.

Figure 1.1. Plain *R* user interface with some text entered

A screen shot of the user interface is shown in Figure 1.2. There are several sub-windows. The big one on the left named "Console" looks very similar and behaves exactly the same as the plain R window. In addition, there are other windows and tabs some of which are obvious (like "Help"). The usefulness of others will become clear soon. We will show some RStudio-specific tips and tricks below, but all the calculations can be done with any user interface and plain *R* as well.

Here are a few quick tricks for working in the Console of Rstudio:

- When starting to type a command, press the tabulator key ⇥ to see a list of suggested commands along with a short description. Typing **sq** followed by ⇥ gives a list of all *R* commands starting with **sq**.

- The F1 function key opens the full help page for the current command in the help window (bottom right by default).[1] The same can be achieved by typing **?commmand**.

- With the ↑ and ↓ arrow keys, we can scroll through the previously entered commands to repeat or correct them.

- With Ctrl pressed, ↑ will give you a list of all previous commands. This list is also available in the "History" window (top right by default).

1.1.2. R Scripts

As already seen, we will have to get used to interacting with our software using written commands. While this may seem odd to readers who do not have any experience with similar software at this point, it is actually very common for econometrics software and there are good reasons for this. An important advantage is that we can easily collect all commands we need for a project in a text file called *R* script.

An *R* script contains all commands including those for reading the raw data, data manipulation, estimation, post-estimation analyses, and the creation of graphs and tables. In a complex project, these tasks can be divided into separate *R* scripts. The point is that the script(s) together with the raw data generate the output used in the term paper, thesis, or research paper. We can then ask *R* to evaluate all or some of the commands listed in the *R* script at once.

---

[1]On some computers, the function keys are set to change the display brightness, volume, and the like by default. This can be changed in the system settings.

Figure 1.2. RStudio user interface

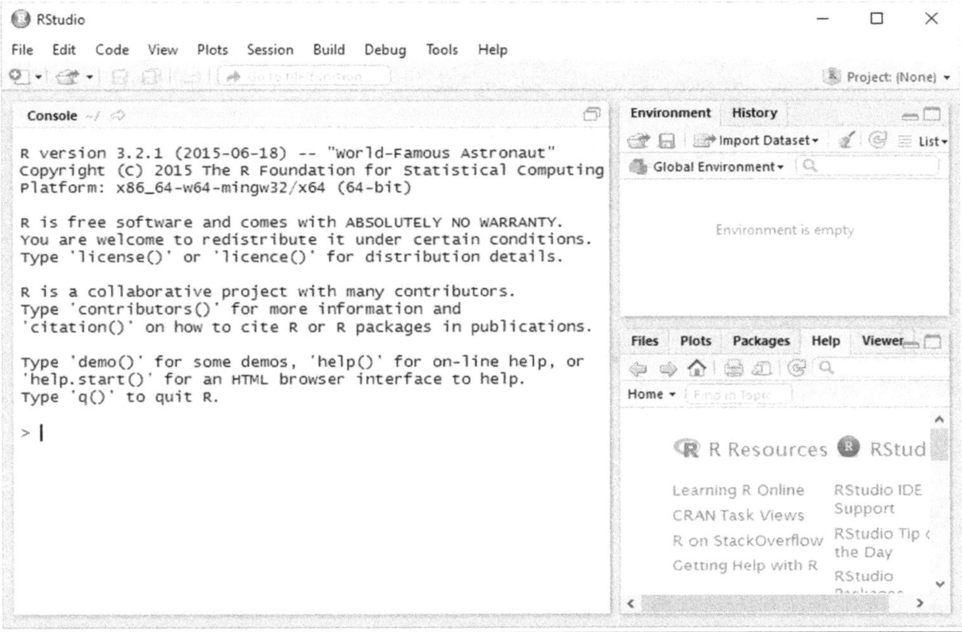

This is important since a key feature of the scientific method is reproducibility. Our thesis adviser as well as the referee in an academic peer review process or another researcher who wishes to build on our analyses must be able to fully understand where the results come from. This is easy if we can simply present our *R* script which has all the answers.

Working with *R* scripts is not only best practice from a scientific perspective, but also very convenient once we get used to it. In a nontrivial data analysis project, it is very hard to remember all the steps involved. If we manipulate the data for example by directly changing the numbers in a spreadsheet, we will never be able to keep track of everything we did. Each time we make a mistake (which is impossible to avoid), we can simply correct the command and let *R* start from scratch by a simple mouse click if we are using scripts. And if there is a change in the raw data set, we can simply rerun everything and get the updated tables and figures instantly.

Using *R* scripts is straightforward: We just write our commands into a text file and save it with a ".R" extension. When using a user interface like RStudio, working with scripts is especially convenient since it is equipped with a specialized editor for script files. To open the editor for creating a new *R* script, use the menu File→New→R Script, or click on the symbol in the top left corner, or press the buttons Ctrl + Shift ⇧ + N simultaneously.

The window that opens in the top left part is the script editor. We can type arbitrary text, begin a new line with the return key, and navigate using the mouse or the ↑ ↓ ← → arrow keys. Our goal is not to type arbitrary text but sensible *R* commands. In the editor, we can also use tricks like code completion that work in Console window as described above. A new command is generally started in a new line, but also a semicolon ";" can be used if we want to cram more than one command into one line – which is often not a good idea in terms of readability.

An extremely useful tool to make *R* scripts more readable are comments. These are lines beginning with a **#**. These lines are not evaluated by *R* but can (and should) be used to structure the script and

Figure 1.3. RStudio with the script `First-R-Script.R`

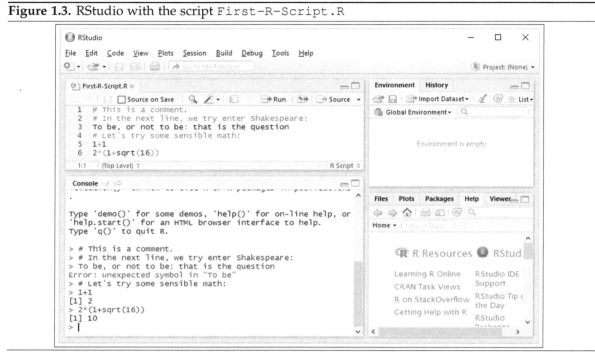

explain the steps. In the editor, comments are by default displayed in green to further increase the readability of the script. R Scripts can be saved and opened using the `File` menu.

Given an *R* script, we can send lines of code to *R* to be evaluated. To run the line in which the cursor is, click on the `Run` button on top of the editor or simply press `Ctrl` + `←`. If we highlight multiple lines (with the mouse or by holding `Shift ↑` while navigating), all are evaluated. The whole script can be highlighted by pressing `Ctrl` + `A`.

Figure 1.3 shows a screenshot of RStudio with an *R* script saved as "First-R-Script.R". It consists of six lines in total including three comments. It has been executed as can be seen in the Console window: The lines in the scripts are repeated next to the > symbols and the answer of *R* (if there is any) follows as though we had typed the commands directly into the Console.

In what follows, we will do everything using *R* scripts. All these scripts are available for download to make it easy and convenient to reproduce all contents in real time when reading this book. As already mentioned, the address is

`http://www.URfIE.net`

They are also printed in Appendix IV. In the text, we will usually only show the results since they also include the commands. Input is printed in **bold** with the **>** at the beginning of the line similar to the display in the Console window. *R*'s response (if any) follows in `standard font`. Script 1.1 (`R-as-a-Calculator.R`) is an example in which *R* is used for simple tasks any basic calculator can do. The *R* script and output are:

———————————— Script 1.1: `R-as-a-Calculator.R` ————————————
```
1+1
5*(4−1)^2
sqrt( log(10) )
```

—————————— **Output of Script 1.1:** `R-as-a-Calculator.R` ——————————

```
> 1+1
[1] 2

> 5*(4-1)^2
[1] 45

> sqrt( log(10) )
[1] 1.517427
```

We will discuss some additional hints for efficiently working with *R* scripts in Section 19.

1.1.3. Packages

The functionality of *R* can be extended relatively easily by advanced users. This is not only useful those who are able and willing to do this, but also for a novice user who can easily make use of a wealth of extensions generated by a big and active community. Since these extensions are mostly programmed in *R*, everybody can check and improve the code submitted by a user, so the quality control works very well.

These extensions are called packages. The standard distribution of *R* already comes with a number of packages. In RStudio, the list of currently installed packages can be seen in the "Packages" window (bottom right by default). A click on the package name opens the corresponding help file which describes what functionality it provides and how it works.

In the Packages window, next to the names we find check boxes, some of which are already activated by default. In order to be able to use a package, we have to make sure it is activated by clicking on the check box.[2] Instead of having to click on a number of check boxes before we can run an *R* script (and having to know which ones), it is much more elegant to automatically activate the required packages by lines of code within the script. This is done with the command `library(package name)`.[3] After activating a package, nothing obvious happens immediately, but *R* understands more commands.

On top of the packages that come with the standard installation, there are countless packages available for download. If they meet certain quality criteria, they can be published on the official "Comprehensive R Archive Network" (CRAN) servers at `http://cran.r-project.org`. Downloading and installing these packages is especially simple: In the Packages window of RStudio, click on "Install Packages", enter the name of the package and click on "Install". If you prefer to do it using code, here is how it works: `install.packages("package name")`. In both cases, the package is added to our list and ready to be activated using `library(package name)`.

There are thousands of packages provided at the CRAN. Here is a list of those we will use throughout this book:

- **AER** ("Applied Econometrics with R"): Provided with the book with the same name by Kleiber and Zeileis (2008). Provides some new commands, e.g. for instrumental variables estimation and many interesting data sets.
- **car** ("Companion to Applied Regression"): A comprehensive package that comes with the book of Fox and Weisberg (2011). Provides many new commands and data sets.
- **censReg**: Censored regression/tobit models.

---

[2]The reason why not all installed packages are loaded automatically is that *R* saves valuable start-up time and system resources and might be able to avoid conflicts between some packages.

[3]The command `require` does almost the same as `library`.

- *dummies*: Automatically generating dummy/indicator variables.
- *dynlm*: Dynamic linear regression for time series.
- *effects*: Graphical and tabular illustration of partial effects, see Fox (2003).
- *ggplot2*: Advanced and powerful graphics, see Wickham (2009) and Chang (2012).
- *knitr*: Combine *R* and LaTeX code in one document, see Xie (2015).
- *lmtest* ("Testing Linear Regression Models"): Includes many useful tests for the linear regression model.
- *maps*: Draw geographical maps.
- *mfx*: Marginal effects, odds ratios and incidence rate ratios for GLMs.
- *orcutt*: Cochrane-Orcutt estimator for serially correlated errors.
- *pdfetch*: Fetch economic and financial time series data from public sources.
- *plm* ("Linear Models for Panel Data"): A large collection of panel data methods, see Croissant and Millo (2008).
- *quantreg*: Quantile regression, especially least absolute deviation (LAD) regression, see Koenker (2012).
- *rmarkdown*: Convert *R* Markdown documents into HTML, MS Word, and PDF.
- *sampleSelection*: Sample selection models, see Toomet and Henningsen (2008).
- *sandwich*: Different "robust" covariance matrix estimators, see Zeileis (2004).
- *stargazer*: Formatted tables of regression results, see Hlavac (2013).
- *survival*: Survival analysis and censored regression models, see Therneau and Grambsch (2000).
- *systemfit*: Estimation of simultaneous equations models, see Henningsen and Hamann (2007).
- *truncreg*: Truncated Gaussian response models.
- *tseries*: Time series analysis and computational finance.
- *urca*: Unit root and cointegration tests for time series data.
- *vars*: (Structural) vector autoregressive and error correction models, see Pfaff (2008).
- *xtable*: Export tables to LaTeX or HTML.
- *xts* ("eXtensible Time Series"): Irregular time series , see Ryan and Ulrich (2008).
- *zoo* ("Zeileis' Ordered Observations"): Irregular time series, see Zeileis and Grothendieck (2005).

Script 1.2 (`Install-Packages.R`) named `Install-Packages.R` installs all these packages. Of course, it only has to be run once per computer/user and needs an active internet connection.

1.1.4. File names and the Working Directory

There are several possibilities for *R* to interact with files. The most important ones are to load, save, import, or export a data file. We might also want to save a generated figure as a graphics file or store regression tables as text, spreadsheet, or LaTeX files.

Whenever we provide *R* with a file name, it can include the full path on the computer. Note that the path separator has to be the forward slash **/** instead of the backslash **** which is common on MS Windows computers. So the full (i.e. "absolute") path to a script file might be something like
`C:/Users/MyUserName/Documents/MyRProject/MyScript.R`
(or equivalently `~/MyRProject/MyScript.R`) on a Windows system or

```
~/MyRProject/MyScript.R
```
on a Mac or Linux system.

If we do not provide any path, R will use the current "working directory" for reading or writing files. It can be obtained by the command **getwd()**. In RStudio, it is also displayed on top of the Console window. To change the working directory, use the command **setwd(path)**.

If we provide a relative path, it is interpreted relative to the current working directory. For a neat file organization, best practice is to generate a directory for each project (say `MyRProject`) with several sub-directories (say `Rscripts`, `data`, and `figures`). At the beginning of our script, we can use **setwd(~/MyRProject)** and afterwards refer to a data set in the respective sub-directory as `data/MyData.RData` and to a graphics files as `figures/MyFigure.png`.[4]

1.1.5. Errors and Warnings

Something you will experience very soon when starting to work with R (or any other similar software package) is that you will make mistakes. The main difference to learning to ride a bicycle is that when learning to use R, mistakes will not hurt. Another difference is that even people who have been using R for years make mistakes all the time.

Many mistakes will cause R to complain in the form of error messages or warnings displayed in red. An important part of learning R is to roughly get an idea of what went wrong from these messages. Here is a list of frequent error messages and warnings you might get:

- **Error: object 'x' not found**: We have tried to use a variable **x** that isn't defined (yet). Could also be due to a typo in the variable name.
- **Error: could not find function "srot"**: We have used the expression **srot(...)** so R assumes we want to call a function. But it doesn't know a function with that name. Could be a typo (we actually wanted to type **sort**). Or the function is defined in a package we haven't loaded yet, see Section 1.1.3.
- **[...] there is no package called 'foreing'**: We mistyped the package name. Or the required package is not installed on the computer. In this case, install it using **install.packages**, see Section 1.1.3.
- **Error in download.file [...] cannot open URL [...]**: R wasn't able to download a file. Maybe we don't have a working internet connection? Or there is a typo in the address? Or the server is down? ...?
- **Error: '\U' used without hex digits in character string starting "C:\U"**: Most likely, you're using a Windows machine and gave R a file path like **"C:\Users\..."** Remember not to use the backslash \ in file paths. Instead, write **"C:/Users/..."**, see Section 1.1.4.

There are countless other error messages and warnings you may encounter. Some of them are easy to interpret such as **In log(-1) : NaNs produced**. Others might require more investigative prowess. Often, the search engine of your choice will be helpful.

1.1.6. Other Resources

There are many useful resources helping to learn and use R. Useful books on R in general include Matloff (2011), Teetor (2011), and many others. Dalgaard (2008), Field, Miles, and Field (2012), Hothorn and Everitt (2014), and Verzani (2014) all introduce statistics with R. General econometrics with R is covered by Kleiber and Zeileis (2008) and Fox and Weisberg (2011).

---

[4]For working with data sets, see Section 1.3.

There are also countless specialized books. Specific book series are published by

- O'Reilly: `http://shop.oreilly.com/category/browse-subjects/programming/r.do`
- Springer: `http://www.springer.com/series/6991`
- Chapman & Hall/CRC: `http://www.crcpress.com/browse/series/crctherser`

Since *R* has a very active user community, there is also a wealth of information available for free on the internet. Here are some suggestions:

- The *R* manuals available at the Comprehensive R Archive Network
  `http://www.r-project.org`
- Quick-R: A nice introduction to *R* with simple examples
  `http://www.statmethods.net`
- Cookbook for R: Useful examples for all kinds of *R* problems
  `http://www.cookbook-r.com`
- R-bloggers: News and blogs about *R*
  `http://www.r-bloggers.com`
- Planet R: Site aggregator, all the latest news around *R*
  `http://planetr.stderr.org`
- RSeek: Search engine for *R* topics
  `http://rseek.org`
- r4stats.com: Articles, blogs and other resources for doing statistics with *R*
  `http://r4stats.com`
- Stack Overflow: A general discussion forum for programmers, including many *R* users
  `http://stackoverflow.com`
- Cross Validated: Discussion forum on statistics and data analysis with an active *R* community
  `http://stats.stackexchange.com`

1.2. Objects in *R*

R can work with numbers, vectors, matrices, texts, data sets, graphs, functions, and many more objects of different types. This sections covers the most important ones we will frequently encounter in the remainder of this book.

1.2.1. Basic Calculations and Objects

We have already observed *R* doing some basic arithmetic calculations. From script 1.1 (`R-as-a-Calculator.R`), the general approach of *R* should be self-explanatory. Fundamental operators include `+`, `-`, `*`, `/` for the respective arithmetic operations and parentheses `(` and `)` that work as expected. The symbol `^` indicates taking powers, for example 3^2 is `3^2` in *R*.

We already used the *R* function **sqrt** to take a square root of a number. Table 1.1 lists other important *R* functions that mostly work as expected. The reader is strongly encouraged to play around to get used to them and to *R* more generally.

We will often want to store results of calculations to reuse them later. For this, we can work with basic **objects**. An object has a name and a content. We can freely choose the name of an object given certain rules – they have to start with a (small or capital) letter and include only letters, numbers, and some special characters such as "`.`" and "`_`". *R* is case sensitive, so x and X are different object names.

Table 1.1. *R* functions for important arithmetic calculations

`abs(v)`	Absolute value $|v|$
`sqrt(v)`	Square root of v
`exp(v)`	Exponential function e^v
`log(v)`	Natural logarithm $\ln(v)$
`log(v,b)`	Logarithm to base b: $\log_b(v)$
`round(v,s)`	Round v to s digits
`factorial(n)`	Factorial $n!$
`choose(n,k)`	Binomial coefficient $\binom{n}{k}$

The content of an object is assigned using **<-** which is supposed to resemble an arrow and is simply typed as the two characters "less than" and "minus".[5] In order to assign the value 5 to the object x, type (the spaces are optional)

x <- 5

A new object x is created and has the value 5. If there was an object with this name before, its content is overwritten. From now on, we can use x in our calculations. Assigning a value to an object will not produce any output. The simplest shortcut for immediately displaying the result is to put the whole expression into parentheses as in **(x <- 5)**. Script 1.3 (`Objects.R`) shows simple examples using the three objects x, y, and z.

─────── **Output of Script 1.3: `Objects.R`** ───────

```
> # generate object x (no output):
> x <- 5

> # display x & x^2:
> x
[1] 5

> x^2
[1] 25

> # generate objects y&z with immediate display using ():
> (y <- 3)
[1] 3

> (z <- y^x)
[1] 243
```

A list of all currently defined object names can be obtained using **ls()**. In RStudio, it is also shown in the "Workspace" window (top right by default). The command **exists**("name") checks whether an object with the name "name" is defined and returns either **TRUE** or **FALSE**, see Section 1.2.3 for this type of "logical" object. Removing a previously defined object (for example x) from the workspace is done using **rm(x)**. All objects are removed with **rm(list = ls())**.

─────────────

[5]Consistent with other programming languages, the assignment can also be done using x=5. *R* purists frown on this syntax. It makes a lot of sense to distinguish the mathematical meaning of an equality sign from the assignment of a value to an object. Mathematically, the equation $x = x + 1$ does not make any sense, but the assignment x<-x+1 does – it increases the previous value of x by 1. We will stick to the standard *R* syntax using <- throughout this text.

1.2.2. Vectors

For statistical calculations, we obviously need to work with data sets including many numbers instead of scalars. The simplest way we can collect many numbers (or other types of information) is called a vector in *R* terminology. To define a vector, we can collect different values using **c(value1,value2,...)**. All the operators and functions used above can be used for vectors. Then they are applied to each of the elements separately.[6] The examples in Script 1.4 (Vectors.R) should help to understand the concept and use of vectors.

—————————— **Output of Script 1.4: Vectors.R** ——————————

```
> # Define a with immediate output through parantheses:
> (a <- c(1,2,3,4,5,6))
[1] 1 2 3 4 5 6

> (b <- a+1)
[1] 2 3 4 5 6 7

> (c <- a+b)
[1]  3  5  7  9 11 13

> (d <- b*c)
[1]  6 15 28 45 66 91

> sqrt(d)
[1] 2.449490 3.872983 5.291503 6.708204 8.124038 9.539392
```

There are also specific functions to create, manipulate and work with vectors. The most important ones are shown in Table 1.2. Script 1.5 (Vector-Functions.R) provides examples to see them in action. We will see in section 1.5 how to obtain descriptive statistics for vectors.

Table 1.2. *R* functions specifically for vectors

length(v)	Number of elements in v
max(v), min(v)	Largest/smallest value in v
sort(v)	Sort the elements of vector v
sum(v),prod(v)	Sum/product of the elements of v
numeric(n)	Vector with n zeros
rep(z,n)	Vector with n equal elements z
seq(t)	Sequence from 1 to t: $\{1, 2, ..., t\}$, alternative: **1:t**
seq(f,t)	Sequence from f to t: $\{f, f + 1, ..., t\}$, alternative: **f:t**
seq(v,b,s)	Sequence from f to t in steps s: $\{f, f + s, ..., t\}$

---

[6]Note that also the multiplication of two vectors using the $*$ operator performs element-wise multiplication. For vector and matrix algebra, see Section 1.2.5 on matrices.

--- **Output of Script 1.5:** `Vector-Functions.R` ---

```
> # Define vector
> (a <- c(7,2,6,9,4,1,3))
[1] 7 2 6 9 4 1 3

> # Basic functions:
> sort(a)
[1] 1 2 3 4 6 7 9

> length(a)
[1] 7

> min(a)
[1] 1

> max(a)
[1] 9

> sum(a)
[1] 32

> prod(a)
[1] 9072

> # Creating special vectors:
> numeric(20)
 [1] 0 0 0 0 0 0 0 0 0 0 0 0 0 0 0 0 0 0 0 0

> rep(1,20)
 [1] 1 1 1 1 1 1 1 1 1 1 1 1 1 1 1 1 1 1 1 1

> seq(50)
 [1]  1  2  3  4  5  6  7  8  9 10 11 12 13 14 15 16 17 18 19 20 21 22
[23] 23 24 25 26 27 28 29 30 31 32 33 34 35 36 37 38 39 40 41 42 43 44
[45] 45 46 47 48 49 50

> 5:15
 [1]  5  6  7  8  9 10 11 12 13 14 15

> seq(4,20,2)
[1]  4  6  8 10 12 14 16 18 20
```

Table 1.3. Logical Operators

x==y	x is equal to y	**x!=y**	x is NOT equal to y
x<y	x is less than y	**!b**	NOT b (i.e. b is **FALSE**)
x<=y	x is less than or equal to y	**a|b**	Either a or b is **TRUE** (or both)
x>y	x is greater than y	**a&b**	Both a and b are **TRUE**
x>=y	x is greater than or equal to y		

1.2.3. Special Types of Vectors

The contents of *R* vectors do not need to be numeric. A simple example of a different type are **character** vectors. For handling them, the contents simply need to be enclosed in quotation marks:

```
> cities <- c("New York","Los Angeles","Chicago")

> cities
[1] "New York"      "Los Angeles" "Chicago"
```

Another useful type are **logical** vectors. Each element can only take one of two values: **TRUE** or **FALSE**. The easiest way to generate them is to state claims which are either true or false and let *R* decide. Table 1.3 lists the main logical operators.

It should be noted that internally, **FALSE** is equal to **0** and **TRUE** is equal to **1** and we can do calculations accordingly. Script 1.6 (Logical.R) demonstrates the most important features of logical vectors and should be pretty self-explanatory.

──────── **Output of Script 1.6: Logical.R** ────────

```
> # Basic comparisons:
> 0 == 1
[1] FALSE

> 0 < 1
[1] TRUE

> # Logical vectors:
> ( a <- c(7,2,6,9,4,1,3) )
[1] 7 2 6 9 4 1 3

> ( b <- a<3 | a>=6 )
[1]  TRUE  TRUE  TRUE  TRUE FALSE  TRUE FALSE
```

Many economic variables of interest have a qualitative rather than quantitative interpretation. They only take a finite set of values and the outcomes don't necessarily have a numerical meaning. Instead, they represent **qualitative** information. Examples include gender, academic major, grade, marital status, state, product type or brand. In some of these examples, the order of the outcomes has a natural interpretation (such as the grades), in others, it does not (such as the state).

As a specific example, suppose we have asked our customers to rate our product on a scale between 1 (="bad"), 2 (="okay"), and 3 (="good"). We have stored the answers of our ten respondents in terms of the numbers 1,2, and 3 in a vector. We could work directly with these numbers, but often, it is convenient to use so-called **factors**. One advantage is that we can attach labels to the outcomes. Given a vector x with a finite set of values, a new factor xf can be generated using the command

```
xf <- factor(x, labels=mylabels )
```

The vector `mylabels` includes the names of the outcomes, we could for example state **xf <- factor(x, labels=c("bad","okay","good"))**. In this example, the outcomes are ordered, so the labeling is not arbitrary. In cases like this, we should add the option **ordered=TRUE**. This is done for a simple example with ten ratings in Script 1.7 (`Factors.R`).

──────────── **Output of Script 1.7: `Factors.R`** ────────────

```
> # Original ratings:
> x <- c(3,2,2,3,1,2,3,2,1,2)

> xf <- factor(x, labels=c("bad","okay","good"))

> x
 [1] 3 2 2 3 1 2 3 2 1 2

> xf
 [1] good okay okay good bad  okay good okay bad  okay
Levels: bad okay good
```

1.2.4. Naming and Indexing Vectors

The elements of a vector can be named which can increase the readability of the output. Given a vector `vec` and a string vector `namevec` of the same length, the names are attached to the vector elements using **names(vec) <- namevec**.

If we want to access a single element or a subset from a vector, we can work with indices. They are written in square brackets next to the vector name. For example **myvector[4]** returns the 4th element of `myvector` and **myvector[6] <- 8** changes the 6th element to take the value 8. For extracting more than one element, the indices can be provided as a vector themselves. If the vector elements have names, we can also use those as indices like in **myvector["elementname"]**.

Finally, logical vectors can also be used as indices. If a general vector `vec` and a logical vector `b` have the same length, then **vec[b]** returns the elements of `vec` for which `b` has the value **TRUE**.

These features are demonstrated in Script 1.8 (`Vector-Indices.R`).

──────────── **Output of Script 1.8: `Vector-Indices.R`** ────────────

```
> # Create a vector "avgs":
> avgs <- c(.366, .358, .356, .349, .346)

> # Create a string vector of names:
> players <- c("Cobb","Hornsby","Jackson","O'Doul","Delahanty")

> # Assign names to vector and display vector:
> names(avgs) <- players

> avgs
     Cobb   Hornsby   Jackson    O'Doul Delahanty
    0.366     0.358     0.356     0.349     0.346

> # Indices by number:
> avgs[2]
Hornsby
  0.358
```

```
> avgs[1:4]
  Cobb Hornsby Jackson  O'Doul
  0.366   0.358   0.356   0.349

> # Indices by name:
> avgs["Jackson"]
Jackson
  0.356

> # Logical indices:
> avgs[ avgs>=0.35 ]
  Cobb Hornsby Jackson
  0.366   0.358   0.356
```

1.2.5. Matrices

Matrices are important tools for econometric analyses. Appendix D of Wooldridge (2016) introduces the basic concepts of matrix algebra.[7] *R* has a powerful matrix algebra system. Most often in applied econometrics, matrices will be generated from an existing data set. We will come back to this below and first look at three different ways to define a matrix object from scratch:

- **matrix(vec,nrow=m)** takes the numbers stored in vector vec and put them into a matrix with m rows.
- **rbind(r1,r2,...)** takes the vectors r1,r2,... (which obviously should have the same length) as the rows of a matrix.
- **cbind(c1,c2,...)** takes the vectors c1,c2,... (which obviously should have the same length) as the columns of a matrix.

Script 1.9 (Matrices.R) first demonstrates how the same matrix can be created using all three approaches. A close inspection of the output reveals the technical detail that the rows and columns of matrices can have names. The functions **rbind** and **cbind** automatically assign the names of the vectors as row and column names, respectively. As demonstrated in the output, we can manipulate the names using the commands **rownames** and **colnames**. This has only cosmetic consequences and does not affect our calculations.

────────────── **Output of Script 1.9: Matrices.R** ──────────────

```
> # Generating matrix A from one vector with all values:
> v <- c(2,-4,-1,5,7,0)

> ( A <- matrix(v,nrow=2) )
     [,1] [,2] [,3]
[1,]    2   -1    7
[2,]   -4    5    0

> # Generating matrix A from two vectors corresponding to rows:
> row1 <- c(2,-1,7); row2 <- c(-4,5,0)

> ( A <- rbind(row1, row2) )
     [,1] [,2] [,3]
row1    2   -1    7
row2   -4    5    0
```

---

[7]The strippped-down European and African textbook Wooldridge (2014) does not include the Appendix on matrix algebra.

```
> # Generating matrix A from three vectors corresponding to columns:
> col1 <- c(2,-4); col2 <- c(-1,5); col3 <- c(7,0)

> ( A <- cbind(col1, col2, col3) )
     col1 col2 col3
[1,]    2   -1    7
[2,]   -4    5    0

> # Giving names to rows and columns:
> colnames(A) <- c("Alpha","Beta","Gamma")

> rownames(A) <- c("Aleph","Bet")

> A
      Alpha Beta Gamma
Aleph     2   -1     7
Bet      -4    5     0

> # Diaginal and identity matrices:
> diag( c(4,2,6) )
     [,1] [,2] [,3]
[1,]    4    0    0
[2,]    0    2    0
[3,]    0    0    6

> diag( 3 )
     [,1] [,2] [,3]
[1,]    1    0    0
[2,]    0    1    0
[3,]    0    0    1

> # Indexing for extracting elements (still using A from above):
> A[2,1]
[1] -4

> A[,2]
Aleph   Bet
   -1     5

> A[,c(1,3)]
      Alpha Gamma
Aleph     2     7
Bet      -4     0
```

We can also create **special matrices** as the examples in the output show:

- **diag(vec)** (where vec is a vector) creates a **diagonal matrix** with the elements on the main diagonal given in vector vec.
- **diag(n)** (where n is a scalar) creates the $n \times n$ **identity matrix**.

If instead of a vector or scalar, a matrix M is given as an argument to the function **diag**, it will return the main diagonal of M.

Finally, Script 1.9 (Matrices.R) shows how to access a **subset** of matrix elements. This is straightforward with indices that are given in brackets much like indices can be used for vectors as already discussed. We can give a row and then a column index (or vectors of indices), separated by a comma:

- **A[2,3]** is the element in row 2, column 3
- **A[2,c(1,2)]** is a vector consisting of the elements in row 2, columns 1 and 2
- **A[2,]** is a vector consisting of the elements in row 2, all columns

Basic matrix algebra includes:

- Matrix addition using the operator **+** as long as the matrices have the same dimensions.
- The operator ***** does <u>not</u> do matrix multiplication but rather element-wise multiplication.
- Matrix multiplication is done with the somewhat clumsy operator **%*%** (yes, it consists of three characters!) as long as the dimensions of the matrices match.
- Transpose of a matrix X: as **t(X)**
- Inverse of a matrix X: as **solve(X)**

The examples in Script 1.10 (Matrix-Operators.R) should help to understand the workings of these basic operations. In order to see how the OLS estimator for the multiple regression model can be calculated using matrix algebra, see Section 3.2. Standard *R* is capable of many more matrix algebra methods. Even more advanced methods are available in the ***Matrix*** package.

--------- **Output of Script 1.10: Matrix-Operators.R** ---------

```
> A <- matrix( c(2,-4,-1,5,7,0), nrow=2)

> B <- matrix( c(2,1,0,3,-1,5), nrow=2)

> A
     [,1] [,2] [,3]
[1,]    2   -1    7
[2,]   -4    5    0

> B
     [,1] [,2] [,3]
[1,]    2    0   -1
[2,]    1    3    5

> A*B
     [,1] [,2] [,3]
[1,]    4    0   -7
[2,]   -4   15    0

> # Transpose:
> (C <- t(B) )
     [,1] [,2]
[1,]    2    1
[2,]    0    3
[3,]   -1    5

> # Matrix multiplication:
> (D <- A %*% C )
     [,1] [,2]
[1,]   -3   34
[2,]   -8   11

> # Inverse:
> solve(D)
           [,1]        [,2]
[1,] 0.0460251 -0.1422594
[2,] 0.0334728 -0.0125523
```

1.2.6. Lists

In *R*, a **list** is a generic collection of objects. Unlike vectors, the components can have different types. Each component can (and in the cases relevant for us will) be named. Lists can be generated with a command like

```
mylist <- list( name1=component1, name2=component2, ... )
```

The names of the components are returned by **names(mylist)**. A component can be addressed by name using **mylist$name**. These features are demonstrated in Script 1.11 (Lists.R).

We will encounter special classes of lists in the form of analysis results: Commands for statistical analyses often return a list that contains characters (like the calling command), vectors (like the parameter estimates), and matrices (like variance-covariance matrices). But we're getting ahead of ourselves – we will encounter this for the first time in Section 1.7.4.

─────── **Output of Script 1.11:** `Lists.R` ───────

```
> # Generate a list object:
> mylist <- list( A=seq(8,36,4), this="that", idm = diag(3))

> # Print whole list:
> mylist
$A
[1]   8 12 16 20 24 28 32 36

$this
[1] "that"

$idm
     [,1] [,2] [,3]
[1,]    1    0    0
[2,]    0    1    0
[3,]    0    0    1


> # Vector of names:
> names(mylist)
[1] "A"    "this" "idm"

> # Print component "A":
> mylist$A
[1]   8 12 16 20 24 28 32 36
```

1.3. Data Frames and Data Files

For *R* users, it is important to make the distinction between a data set (= data frame in *R* terminology) which is a collection of variables on the same observational units and a data file which can include several data sets and other objects.

1.3.1. Data Frames

A data frame is an object that collects several variables and can be thought of as a rectangular shape with the rows representing the observational units and the columns representing the variables. As such, it is similar to a matrix. For us, the most important difference to a matrix is that a data frame can contain variables of different types (like numerical, logical, string and factor), whereas matrices can only contain numerical values. Unlike some other software packages, we can work with several data sets stored as data frame objects simultaneously.

Like a matrix, the rows can have names. Unlike a matrix, the columns always contain names which represent the variables. We can define a data frame from scratch by using the command `data.frame` or `as.data.frame` which transform inputs of different types (like a matrix) into a data frame. Script 1.12 (`Data-frames.R`) presents a simple example where a matrix with row and column names is created and transformed into a data frame called `sales`.

Output of Script 1.12: `Data-frames.R`

```
> # Define one x vector for all:
> year      <- c(2008,2009,2010,2011,2012,2013)

> # Define a matrix of y values:
> product1<-c(0,3,6,9,7,8); product2<-c(1,2,3,5,9,6); product3<-c(2,4,4,2,3,2)

> sales_mat <- cbind(product1,product2,product3)

> rownames(sales_mat) <- year

> # The matrix looks like this:
> sales_mat
     product1 product2 product3
2008        0        1        2
2009        3        2        4
2010        6        3        4
2011        9        5        2
2012        7        9        3
2013        8        6        2

> # Create a data frame and display it:
> sales <- as.data.frame(sales_mat)

> sales
     product1 product2 product3
2008        0        1        2
2009        3        2        4
2010        6        3        4
2011        9        5        2
2012        7        9        3
2013        8        6        2
```

The outputs of the matrix `sales_mat` and the data frame `sales` look exactly the same, but they behave differently. In RStudio, the difference can be seen in the Workspace window (top right by default). It reports the content of `sales_mat` to be a "`6x3 double matrix`" whereas the content of `sales` is "`6 obs. of 3 variables`".

We can address a single variable `var` of a data frame `df` using the matrix-like syntax **df[, "var"]** or by stating **df$var**.[8] This can be used for extracting the values of a variable but also for creating new variables. Sometimes, it is convenient not to have to type the name of the data frame several times within a command. The function **with(df, some expression using vars of df)** can help. Yet another method for conveniently working with data frames is to **attach** them before doing several calculations using the variables stored in them. It is important to **detach** them later. Script 1.13 (`Data-frames-vars.R`) demonstrates these features.

——————— **Output of Script 1.13: `Data-frames-vars.R`** ———————

```
> # Accessing a single variable:
> sales$product2
[1] 1 2 3 5 9 6

> # Generating a new  variable in the data frame:
> sales$totalv1 <- sales$product1 + sales$product2 + sales$product3

> # The same but using "with":
> sales$totalv2 <- with(sales, product1+product2+product3)

> # The same but using "attach":
> attach(sales)

> sales$totalv3 <- product1+product2+product3

> detach(sales)

> # Result:
> sales
     product1 product2 product3 totalv1 totalv2 totalv3
2008        0        1        2       3       3       3
2009        3        2        4       9       9       9
2010        6        3        4      13      13      13
2011        9        5        2      16      16      16
2012        7        9        3      19      19      19
2013        8        6        2      16      16      16
```

1.3.2. Subsets of Data

Sometimes, we do not want to work with a whole data set but only with a subset. This can be easily achieved with the command **subset(df, criterion)**, where `criterion` is a logical expression which evaluates to **TRUE** for the rows which are to be selected. Script 1.14 (`Data-frames-subsets.R`) shows how to select a sub sample of the data frame `sales` from above.

---

[8]Technically, a data frame is just a special class of a list of variables. This is the reason why the $ syntax is the same as for general list, see Section 1.2.6

Output of Script 1.14: `Data-frames-subsets.R`

```
> # Full data frame (from Data-frames.R, has to be run first)
> sales
     product1 product2 product3
2008        0        1        2
2009        3        2        4
2010        6        3        4
2011        9        5        2
2012        7        9        3
2013        8        6        2

> # Subset: all years in which sales of product 3 were >=3
> subset(sales, product3>=3)
     product1 product2 product3
2009        3        2        4
2010        6        3        4
2012        7        9        3
```

1.3.3. *R* Data Files

R has its own data file format. The usual extension of the file name is `.RData`. It can contain one or more objects of arbitrary type (scalars, vectors, matrices, data frames, ...). If the objects `v1, v2, ...` are currently in the workspace, they can be saved to a file named `mydata.RData` by

```
save(v1,v2,..., file="mydata.RData")
```

Of course, the file name can also contain an absolute or relative path, see Section 1.1.4. To save all currently defined objects, use **`save(list=ls(), file="mydata.RData")`** instead. All objects stored in `mydata.RData` can be loaded into the workspace with

```
load("mydata.RData")
```

1.3.4. Basic Information on a Data Set

After loading a data set into a data frame, it is often useful to get a quick overview of the variables it contains. There are several possibilities. Suppose we seek information on a data frame `df`.

- **`head(df)`** displays the first few rows of data.
- **`str(df)`** lists the `structure`, i.e. the variable names, variable types (numeric, string, logical, factor,...), and the first few values.
- **`colMeans(df)`** reports the averages of all variables and **`summary(df)`** shows summary statistics, see Section 1.5.4.

Script 1.15 (`RData-Example.R`) demonstrates these commands for the `sales` data frame generated in Script 1.12 (`Data-frames.R`). We save it in a file `"oursalesdata.RData"` (in the current working directory), delete from memory, load it again, and produce a vector of variable averages.

—— **Output of Script 1.15:** `RData-Example.R` ——

```
> # Note: "sales" is defined in Data-frames.R, so it has to be run first!
> # save data frame as RData file (in the current working directory)
> save(sales, file = "oursalesdata.RData")

> # remove data frame "sales" from memory
> rm(sales)

> # Does variable "sales" exist?
> exists("sales")
[1] FALSE

> # Load data set  (in the current working directory):
> load("oursalesdata.RData")

> # Does variable "sales" exist?
> exists("sales")
[1] TRUE

> sales
     product1 product2 product3 totalv1 totalv2 totalv3
2008        0        1        2       3       3       3
2009        3        2        4       9       9       9
2010        6        3        4      13      13      13
2011        9        5        2      16      16      16
2012        7        9        3      19      19      19
2013        8        6        2      16      16      16

> # averages of the variables:
> colMeans(sales)
 product1  product2  product3   totalv1   totalv2   totalv3
 5.500000  4.333333  2.833333 12.666667 12.666667 12.666667
```

1.3.5. Import and Export of Text Files

Probably all software packages that handle data are capable of working with data stored as text files. This makes them a natural way to exchange data between different programs and users. Common file name extensions for such data files are RAW, CSV or TXT.

The *R* command **read.table** provides possibilities for reading many flavors of text files which are then stored as a data frame.[9] The general command is

```
newdataframe <- read.table(filename, ...)
```

For the general rules on the file name, once again consult Section 1.1.4. The optional arguments that can be added, separated by comma, include but are not limited to:

- **header=TRUE**: The text file includes the variable names as the first line
- **sep=","**: Instead of spaces or tabs, the columns are separated by a comma. Instead, an arbitrary other character can be given. **sep=";"** might be another relevant example of a separator.
- **dec=","**: Instead of a decimal point, a decimal comma is used. For example, some international versions of MS Excel produce these sorts of text files.

---

[9]The commands **read.csv** and **read.delim** work very similarly but have different defaults for options like **header** and **sep**.

Figure 1.4. Examples of text data files

year product1 product2 product3
2008 0 1 2
2009 3 2 4
2010 6 3 4
2011 9 5 2
2012 7 9 3
2013 8 6 2

2008,0,1,2
2009,3,2,4
2010,6,3,4
2011,9,5,2
2012,7,9,3
2013,8,6,2

(a) `sales.txt`   (b) `sales.csv`

- **row.names=number**: The values in column number `number` are used as row names instead of variables.

RStudio provides a graphical user interface for importing text files which also allows to preview the effects of changing the options: In the Workspace window, click on "Import Dataset".

Figure 1.4 shows two flavors of a raw text file containing the same data. The file `sales.txt` contains a header with the variable names. It can be imported with

```
mydata <- read.table("sales.txt", header=TRUE)
```

In file `sales.csv`, the columns are separated by a comma. The correct command for the import would be

```
mydata <- read.table("sales.csv", sep=",")
```

Since this data file does not contain any variable names, they are set to their default values `V1` through `V4` in the resulting data frame `mydata`. They can be changed manually afterward, e.g. by **colnames(mydata) <- c("year","prod1","prod2","prod3")**.

Given some data in a data frame `mydata`, they can be exported to a text file using similar options as for **read.table** using

```
write.table(mydata, file = "myfilename", ...)
```

1.3.6. Import and Export of Other Data Formats

Just as *R*, most statistics and spreadsheet programs come with their own file format to save and load data. While its is basically always possible to exchange data via text files, it might be convenient to be able to directly read or write data in the native format of some other software. The package *foreign* provides the possibility for importing data from the programs

- Stata (DTA) with **read.dta**,
- SPSS (SAV,SYS,POR) with **read.spss**,
- SAS (XPORT,SSD) with **read.xport** and **read.ssd**,
- Systat (SYSTAT) with **read.systat**
- Minitab (MTP) with **read.mtp**

and more. The export to some formats like Stata files is also supported. Excel spreadsheets are not the best format for storing data, so exporting to a text file from the spreadsheet program and importing the result in *R* often is the best solution if the data are stored in such a format. Nevertheless, there are several possibilities for directly importing Excel files into *R*. A notable example is the package *gdata* with its command **read.xls**.

1.3.7. Data Sets in the Examples

We will reproduce many of the examples from Wooldridge (2016). The companion web site of the textbook provides the sample data sets in different formats, including RData files. If you have an access code that came with the textbook, they can be downloaded free of charge.[10]

The Stata data sets are also made available online at the "Instructional Stata Datasets for econometrics" collection from Boston College, maintained by Christopher F. Baum.[11] Instead of worrying about downloading the data first, we can ask *R* to directly download them from the internet and store them as a data frame using a command like

```
require(foreign)
affairs <- read.dta("http://fmwww.bc.edu/ec-p/data/wooldridge/affairs.dta")
```

This is the approach taken by the Example *R* scripts in this book. Script 1.16 (Example-Data.R) demonstrates this approach. The downside is that we depend on a working internet connection and servers at Boston college. On a machine without internet connection, we can manually save the data sets and then change the code in the example scripts to load from the local file system instead of from the internet.

─────── **Output of Script 1.16: Example-Data.R** ───────

```
> # load package for dealing with Stata files:
> library(foreign)

> # download data and create data frame "affairs":
> affairs<-read.dta("http://fmwww.bc.edu/ec-p/data/wooldridge/affairs.dta")

> # first six rows:
> head(affairs)
   id male age yrsmarr kids relig educ occup ratemarr naffairs affair
1   4    1  37    10.0    0     3   18     7        4        0      0
2   5    0  27     4.0    0     4   14     6        4        0      0
3   6    1  27     1.5    0     3   18     4        4        3      1
4  11    0  32    15.0    1     1   12     1        4        0      0
5  12    0  27     4.0    1     3   17     1        5        3      1
6  16    1  57    15.0    1     5   18     6        5        0      0
  vryhap hapavg avgmarr unhap vryrel smerel slghtrel notrel
1      0      1       0     0      0      0        1      0
2      0      1       0     0      0      1        0      0
3      0      1       0     0      0      0        1      0
4      0      1       0     0      0      0        0      0
5      1      0       0     0      0      0        1      0
6      1      0       0     0      1      0        0      0

> #averages:
> colMeans(affairs)
          id         male          age      yrsmarr         kids
1059.7221298    0.4758735   32.4875208    8.1776955    0.7154742
        relig         educ        occup     ratemarr     naffairs
   3.1164725   16.1663894    4.1946755    3.9317804    1.4559068
       affair        vryhap       hapavg      avgmarr        unhap
   0.2495840    0.3860233    0.3227953    0.1547421    0.1098170
       vryrel       smerel     slghtrel       notrel
   0.1164725    0.3161398    0.2146423    0.2728785
```

─────────────────

[10] The address is http://wooldridge-datasets.swlearning.com.

[11] The address is http://econpapers.repec.org/paper/bocbocins/.

Figure 1.5. Examples of function plots using `curve`

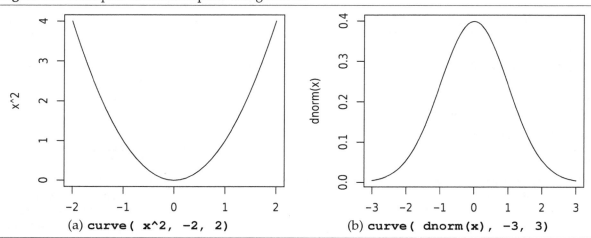

(a) `curve( x^2, -2, 2)`   (b) `curve( dnorm(x), -3, 3)`

1.4. Graphics

R is a versatile tool for producing all kinds of graphs. We can only scratch the surface. In this section we discuss the overall approach for producing graphs and the most important general types of graphs. We will look at some specific graphs used for descriptive statistics in Section 1.5.

1.4.1. Basic Graphs

One very general type is two-way graphs with an abscissa and an ordinate that typically represent two variables like x and y. An obvious example is a **function plot** in which the function values $y = f(x)$ are plotted against x. In *R*, a function plot can be generated using the command

```
curve( function(x), xmin, xmax )
```

where **function(x)** is the function to be plotted in general *R* syntax involving x and `xmin` and `xmax` are the limits for the x axis. For example, the command **curve(x^2, -2, 2)** generated Figure 1.5(a) and **curve(dnorm(x), -3, 3)** produced Figure 1.5(b).[12]

If we have data or other points in two vectors x and y, we can easily generate scatter plots, line plots or similar two-way graphs. The command **plot** is a generic plotting command that is capable of these types of graphs and more. We will see some of the more specialized uses later on. We define two short vectors and simply call **plot** with the vectors as arguments:

```
x <- c(1,3,4,7,8,9)
y <- c(0,3,6,9,7,8)
plot(x,y)
```

This will generate Figure 1.6(a). The most fundamental option of these plots is the **type**. It can take the values **"p"** (the default), **"l"**, **"b"**, **"o"**, **"s"**, **"h"**, and more. The resulting plots are shown in Figure 1.6.

---

[12]The function **dnorm(x)** is the standard normal density, see Section 1.6.

Figure 1.6. Examples of point and line plots using `plot(x,y)`

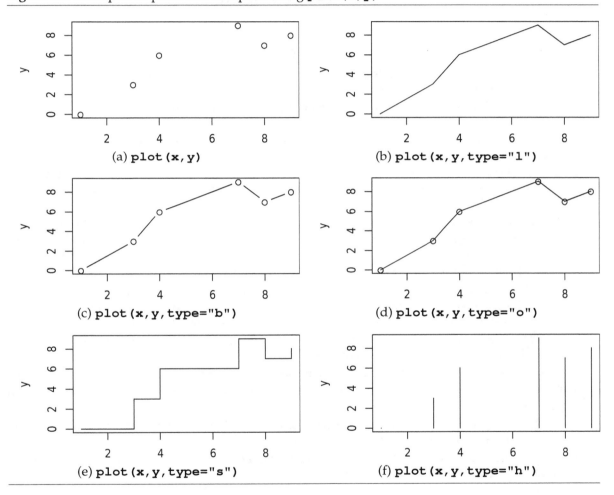

(a) `plot(x,y)`

(b) `plot(x,y,type="l")`

(c) `plot(x,y,type="b")`

(d) `plot(x,y,type="o")`

(e) `plot(x,y,type="s")`

(f) `plot(x,y,type="h")`

1.4.2. Customizing Graphs with Options

These plots as well as those created by **curve** can be adjusted very flexibly. A few examples:

- The point symbol can be changed using the option **pch**. It can take a single character such as **pch="B"** where this character is used as a marker. Or it can take predefined values which are chosen by number such as **pch=3**. Here is a list of the symbols associated with numbers 1–18:

  □   ○   △   +   ×   ◇   ▽   ⊠   ✳   ⊕   ⊕   ⋈   ⊞   ⊠   ◪   ■   ●   ▲   ◆
  0   1   2   3   4   5   6   7   8   9   10 11 12 13 14 15 16 17 18

- The line type can be changed using the option **lty**. It can take (among other specifications) the values 1 through 6:

  1   2   3   4   5   6

- The size of the points and texts can be changed using the option **cex**. It represents a factor (standard: **cex=1**).

- The width of the lines can be changed using the option **lwd**. It represents a factor (standard: **lwd=1**).

- The color of the lines and symbols can be changed using the option **col=value**. It can be specified in several ways:

  - By name: A list of available color names can be obtained by **colors()** and will include several hundred color names from the obvious **"black"**, **"blue"**, **"green"** or **"red"** to more exotic ones like **"papayawhip"**.
  - By a number corresponding to a list of colors (**palette**) that can be adjusted.
  - Gray scale: **gray(level)** with **level**=0 indicating black and **level**=1 indicating white.
  - By RGB values with a string of the form **"#RRGGBB"** where each of the pairs RR, GG, BB consist of two hexadecimal digits.[13] This is useful for fine-tuning colors.
  - Using the function **rgb(red, green, blue)** where the arguments represent the RBG values, normalized between 0 and 1 by default. They can also be normalized e.g. to be between 0 and 255 with the additional option **maxColorValue = 255**.
  - The **rgb** function can also define transparency with the additional option **alpha=value**, where **alpha=0** means fully transparent (i.e. invisible) and **alpha=1** means fully opaque.

- A main title and a subtitle can be added using **main="My Title"** and **sub="My Subtitle"**.

- The horizontal and vertical axis can be labeled using **xlab="My x axis label"** and **ylab="My y axis label"**.

- The limits of the horizontal and the vertical axis can be chosen using **xlim=c(min,max)** and **ylim=c(min,max)**, respectively.

- The axis labels can be set to be parallel to the axis (**las=0**), horizontal (**las=1**), perpendicular to the axis (**las=2**), or vertical (**las=3**).

Some additional options should be set *before* the graph is created using the command **par(option1=value1, option2=value2, ...)**. For some options, this is the only possibility. An important example is the margin around the plotting area. It can be set either in inches using **mai=c(bottom, left, top, right)** or in lines of usual text using **mar=c(bottom, left, top, right)**. In both cases, they are simply set to a numerical vector with four elements. Another example is the possibility to easily put several plots below or next to each other in one graph using the options **mfcol** or **mfrow**.

---

[13]The RGB color model defines colors as a mix of the components red, green, and blue.

Figure 1.7. Overlayed plots

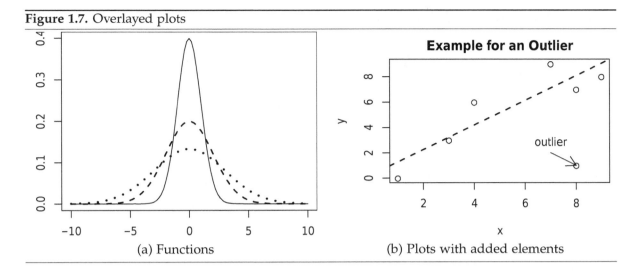

(a) Functions   (b) Plots with added elements

1.4.3. Overlaying Several Plots

Often, we want to plot more than one function or set of variables. We can use several **curve** and/or **plot** commands sequentially. By default, each plot replaces the previous one. To avoid this and overlay the plots instead, use the **add=TRUE** option. Here is an example that also demonstrates the options **lwd** and **lty**.[14] Its result is shown in Figure 1.7(a):

```
curve( dnorm(x,0,1), -10, 10, lwd=1, lty=1 )
curve( dnorm(x,0,2),add=TRUE, lwd=2, lty=2 )
curve( dnorm(x,0,3),add=TRUE, lwd=3, lty=3 )
```

There are also useful specialized commands for adding elements to an existing graph each of which can be tweaked with the same formatting options presented above:

- **points(x,y,...)** and **lines(x,y,...)** add point and line plots much like **plot** with the **add=TRUE** option.
- **text(x,y,"mytext",...)** adds text to coordinates **(x,y)**. The option **pos=number** positions the text below, to the left of, above or to the right of the specified coordinates if **pos** is set to 1, 2, 3, or 4, respectively.
- **abline(a=value,b=value,...)** adds a line with intercept a and slope b
- **abline(h=value(s),...)** adds one or more horizontal line(s) at position h (which can be a vector).
- **abline(v=value(s),...)** adds one or more vertical line(s) at position v (which can be a vector).
- **arrows(x0, y0, x1, y1, ...)** adds an arrow from point x0,y0 to point x1,y1.

An example is shown in Script 1.17 (Plot-Overlays.R). It combines different plotting commands and options to generate Figure 1.7(b).

---

[14]The function **dnorm(x,0,2)** is the normal density with mean 0 and standard deviation 2, see Section 1.6.

Figure 1.8. Graph generated by `matplot`

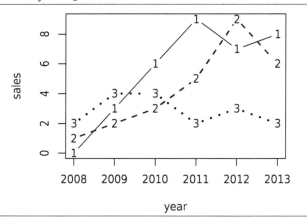

_____ Script 1.17: `Plot-Overlays.R` _____

```
plot(x,y, main="Example for an Outlier")
points(8,1)
abline(a=0.31,b=0.97,lty=2,lwd=2)
text(7,2,"outlier",pos=3)
arrows(7,2,8,1,length=0.15)
```

A convenient alternative for specifying the plots separately is to use the command `matplot`. It expects several y variables as a matrix and x either as a vector or a matrix with the same dimensions. We can use all formatting options discussed above which can be set as vectors. Script 1.18 (`Plot-Matplot.R`) demonstrates this command. The result is shown in Figure 1.8.

_____ Script 1.18: `Plot-Matplot.R` _____

```
# Define one x vector for all:
year     <- c(2008,2009,2010,2011,2012,2013)
# Define a matrix of y values:
product1 <- c(0,3,6,9,7,8)
product2 <- c(1,2,3,5,9,6)
product3 <- c(2,4,4,2,3,2)
sales <- cbind(product1,product2,product3)
# plot
matplot(year,sales, type="b", lwd=c(1,2,3), col="black" )
```

1.4.4. Legends

If we combine several plots into one, it is often useful to add a legend to a graph. The command is `legend(position,labels,formats,...)` where

- **`position`** determines the placement. It can be a set of x and y coordinates but usually it is more convenient to use one of the self-explanatory keywords `"bottomright"`, `"bottom"`, `"bottomleft"`, `"left"`, `"topleft"`, `"top"`, `"topright"`, `"right"`, or `"center"`.
- **`labels`** is a vector of strings that act as labels for the legend. It should be specified like `c("first label","second label",...)`.

Figure 1.9. Using legends

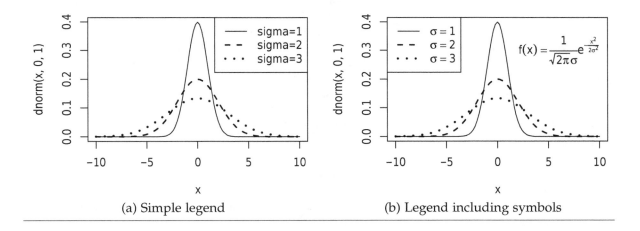

(a) Simple legend   (b) Legend including symbols

- **formats** is supposed to reproduce the line and marker styles used in the plot. We can use the same options listed in Section 1.4.2 like **pch** and **lty**.

Script 1.19 (`Plot-Legend.R`) adds a legend to the plot of the different density functions. The result can be seen in Figure 1.9(a).

```
──────── Script 1.19: Plot-Legend.R ────────
curve( dnorm(x,0,1), -10, 10, lwd=1, lty=1)
curve( dnorm(x,0,2),add=TRUE, lwd=2, lty=2)
curve( dnorm(x,0,3),add=TRUE, lwd=3, lty=3)
# Add the legend
legend("topright",c("sigma=1","sigma=2","sigma=3"), lwd=1:3, lty=1:3)
```

In the legend, but also everywhere within a graph (title, axis labels, texts, ...) we can also use Greek letters, equations, and similar features in a relatively straightforward way. This is done using the command **expression(specific syntax)**. A complete list of that syntax can be found in the help files somewhat hidden under **plotmath**. Instead of trying to reproduce this list, we just give an example in Script 1.20 (`Plot-Legend2.R`). Figure 1.9(b) shows the result.

```
──────── Script 1.20: Plot-Legend2.R ────────
curve( dnorm(x,0,1), -10, 10, lwd=1, lty=1)
curve( dnorm(x,0,2),add=TRUE, lwd=2, lty=2)
curve( dnorm(x,0,3),add=TRUE, lwd=3, lty=3)
# Add the legend with greek sigma
legend("topleft",expression(sigma==1,sigma==2,sigma==3),lwd=1:3,lty=1:3)
# Add the text with the formula, centered at x=6 and y=0.3
text(6,.3,
     expression(f(x)==frac(1,sqrt(2*pi)*sigma)*e^{-frac(x^2,2*sigma^2)}))
```

1.4.5. Exporting to a File

By default, a graph generated in one of the ways we discussed above will be displayed in its own window. For example, RStudio has a Plots window (bottom right by default). This window also has an Export button which allows to save the generated plot in different graphics formats. Obviously, it is inconvenient to export graphics manually this way when we are working with scripts, especially if one script generates several figures. Not surprisingly, *R* offers the possibility to export the generated plots automatically using specific commands within the script.

Among the different graphics formats, the PNG (Portable Network Graphics) format is very useful for saving plots to use them in a word processor and similar programs. For LaTeX users, PS, EPS, and SVG files are available and PDF is very useful. Exporting works in three steps:

1. Start the graphics file and give some options:
   - For a PNG file, the command is:
     png(filename="myfilename.png",width=value,height=value,...)
     For the **filename**, the general rules for working with paths and the working directory apply, see Section 1.1.4. The **width** and **height** are specified in *pixels* and both are equal to 480 by default. The same approach works for BMP, JPEG and TIFF formats accordingly.
   - For a PDF file, the command is:
     pdf(file = "myfilename.pdf", width=value, height=value,...)
     The difference is that the file name is specified as **file** and that the **width** and **height** are specified in *inches* and are both are equal to 7 by default.
2. Create the graph using the commands we looked at above. If we want to set options using **par**, do that first. We can use as many lines of code as we like to generate complicated overlayed plots.
3. Tell *R* that we are finished with the current graphics file by using the command **dev.off()**. This is important and will create problems with the file if forgotten.

To create a 4×3 inch PDF file distributions.pdf in the sub-directory figures of the working directory (which must exist), the code to exactly reproduce Figure 1.7(a) including the specified margins would be

```
pdf(file = "figures/distributions.pdf"), width = 4, height = 3)
par(mar=c(2,2,0,0))
curve( dnorm(x,0,1), -10, 10)
curve( dnorm(x,0,2),add=TRUE, col="blue" )
curve( dnorm(x,0,3),add=TRUE, col="red" )
dev.off()
```

Figure 1.10. Maps example: unemployment by county in the U.S.

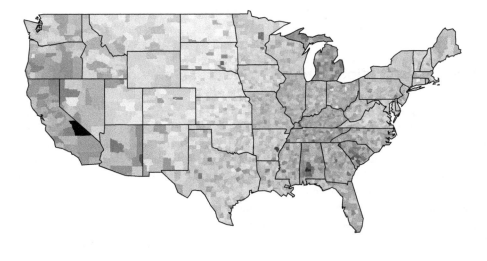

1.4.6. Advanced Graphs

R has incredibly rich possibilities to create useful and pretty graphs. We covered only the basics here. A different and powerful approach to generating graphs is provided by the package *ggplot2*. Many resources explain the package. Important ones are Wickham (2009) and Chang (2012).

Because a comprehensive treatment would be infeasible, we look at just one other arbitrary (yet nice) example. The package *maps* provides possibilities for drawing maps in a straightforward manner. The package already contains the relevant geographic information for the most important maps, others are freely available as additional packages or can be imported. These maps can be filled with colors to represent economic information. Figure 1.10 shows an example illustrating the geographical distribution of unemployment by county in the U.S. The main line of code that generated the graph is as simple as

```
map("county", col=plotcol, fill=TRUE,resolution=0,lty = 0)
```

The name of the (predefined) map with the geographical information is **"county"**. We give a few self-explanatory options for **fill**, **resolution**, and **lty**. And we provide a vector of color codes **plotcol** for each of the counties. The main other work we need to do is generate this vector of color codes. The full script creating this plot is shown in Appendix IV as Script 1.21 (Maps-Example.R) (p. 288).

1.5. Descriptive Statistics

Obviously, as a statistics program *R* offers many commands for descriptive statistics. In this section, we cover the most important ones for our purpose.

1.5.1. Discrete Distributions: Frequencies and Contingency Tables

Suppose we have a sample of the random variables *X* and *Y* stored in the *R* vectors x and y, respectively. For discrete variables, the most fundamental statistics are the frequencies of outcomes. The command **table(x)** gives such a table of counts. If we provide two arguments like **table(x,y)**, we get the contingency table, i.e. the counts of each combination of outcomes for variables x and y. For getting the sample *shares* instead of the *counts*, we can request **prop.table(table(x))**. For the two-way tables, we can get a table of

*   the overall sample share: **prop.table(table(x,y))**
*   the share within x values (row percentages): **prop.table(table(x,y),margin=1)**
*   the share within y values (column percentages): **prop.table(table(x,y),margin=2)**

As an example, we look at the data set affairs.dta. It contains two variables we look at in Script 1.22 (Descr-Tables.R) to demonstrate the workings of the **table** and **prop.table** commands:

*   kids = 1 if the respondent has at least one child
*   ratemarr = Rating of the own marriage (1=very unhappy, 5=very happy)

Output of Script 1.22: `Descr-Tables.R`

```
> # load data set
> library(foreign)

> affairs<-read.dta("http://fmwww.bc.edu/ec-p/data/wooldridge/affairs.dta")

> # Generate "Factors" to attach labels
> haskids <- factor(affairs$kids,labels=c("no","yes"))

> mlab <- c("very unhappy","unhappy","average","happy", "very happy")

> marriage <- factor(affairs$ratemarr, labels=mlab)

> # Frequencies for having kids:
> table(haskids)
haskids
 no yes
171 430

> # Marriage ratings (share):
> prop.table(table(marriage))
marriage
very unhappy        unhappy        average        happy     very happy
   0.0266223      0.1098170      0.1547421    0.3227953      0.3860233
```

```
> # Contigency table: counts (display & store in var.)
> (countstab <- table(marriage,haskids))
             haskids
marriage        no yes
  very unhappy   3  13
  unhappy        8  58
  average       24  69
  happy         40 154
  very happy    96 136

> # Share within "marriage" (i.e. within a row):
> prop.table(countstab, margin=1)
             haskids
marriage            no        yes
  very unhappy 0.1875000 0.8125000
  unhappy      0.1212121 0.8787879
  average      0.2580645 0.7419355
  happy        0.2061856 0.7938144
  very happy   0.4137931 0.5862069

> # Share within "haskids"  (i.e. within a column):
> prop.table(countstab, margin=2)
             haskids
marriage             no         yes
  very unhappy 0.01754386 0.03023256
  unhappy      0.04678363 0.13488372
  average      0.14035088 0.16046512
  happy        0.23391813 0.35813953
  very happy   0.56140351 0.31627907
```

In the *R* script, we first generate **factor** versions of the two variables of interest. In this way, we can generate tables with meaningful labels instead of numbers for the outcomes, see Section 1.2.3. Then different tables are produced. Of the 601 respondents, 430 (=71.5%) have children. Overall, 2.66% report to be very unhappy with their marriage and 38.6% are very happy. In the contingency table with counts, we see for example that 136 respondents are very happy and have kids.

The table reporting shares within the rows tell us that for example 81.25% of very unhappy individuals have children and only 58.6% of very happy respondents have kids. The last table reports the distribution of marriage ratings separately for people with and without kids: 56.1% of the respondents without kids are very happy, whereas only 31.6% of those with kids report to be very happy with their marriage. Before drawing any conclusions for your own family planning, please keep on studying econometrics at least until you fully appreciate the difference between correlation and causation!

There are several ways to graphically depict the information in these tables. Figure 1.11 demonstrates the creation of basic pie and bar charts using the commands **pie** and **barplot**, respectively. These figures can of course be tweaked in many ways, see the help pages and the general discussions of graphics in section 1.4. We create vertical and horizontal (**horiz=TRUE**) bars, align the axis labels to be horizontal (**las=1**) or perpendicular to the axes (**las=2**), include and position the legend, and add a main title. The best way to explore the options is to tinker with the specification and observe the results.

Figure 1.11. Pie and bar plots

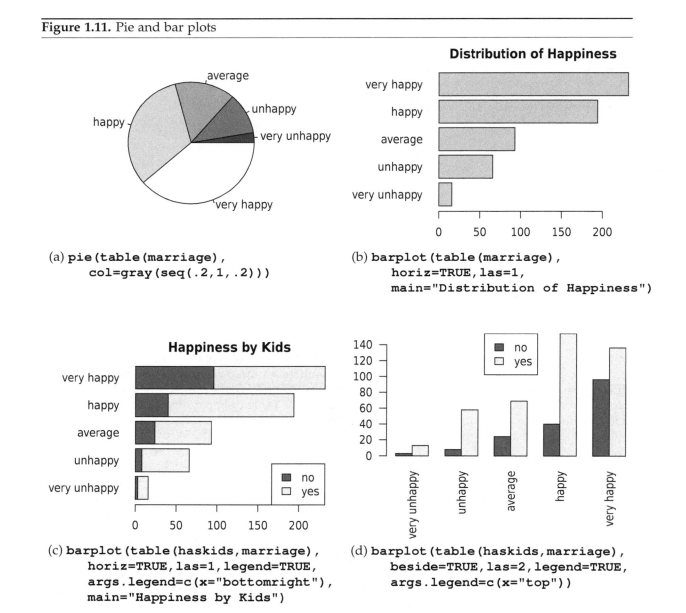

(a) `pie(table(marriage),`
`   col=gray(seq(.2,1,.2)))`

(b) `barplot(table(marriage),`
`    horiz=TRUE,las=1,`
`    main="Distribution of Happiness")`

(c) `barplot(table(haskids,marriage),`
`    horiz=TRUE,las=1,legend=TRUE,`
`    args.legend=c(x="bottomright"),`
`    main="Happiness by Kids")`

(d) `barplot(table(haskids,marriage),`
`    beside=TRUE,las=2,legend=TRUE,`
`    args.legend=c(x="top"))`

1.5.2. Continuous Distributions: Histogram and Density

For continuous variables, every observation has a distinct value. In practice, variables which have many (but not infinitely many) different values can be treated in the same way. Since each value appears only once (or a very few times) in the data, frequency tables or bar charts are not useful. Instead, the values can be grouped into intervals. The frequency of values within these intervals can then be tabulated or depicted in a histogram.

In *R*, the function **hist(x, options)** assigns observations to intervals which can be manually set or automatically chosen and creates a histogram which plots values of x against the count or density within the corresponding bin. The most relevant options are

- **breaks=...**: Set the interval boundaries:
    - no **breaks** specified: let *R* choose number and position
    - **breaks=n** for a scalar n: select the *number* of bins, but let *R* choose the position.
    - **breaks=v** for a vector v: explicitly set the boundaries
    - a function of name of algorithm for automatically choosing the breaks
- **freq=FALSE**: do not use the count but the density on the vertical axis. Default if **breaks** are not equally spaced.
- We can use the general options for graphs like **lwd** or **ylim** mentioned in Section 1.4.2 to adjust the appearance.

Let's look at the data set CEOSAL1.dta which is described and used in Wooldridge (2016, Example 2.3). It contains information on the salary of CEOs and other information. We will try to depict the distribution of the return on equity (ROE), measured in percent. Script 1.23 (Histogram.R) generates the graphs of Figure 1.12. In Sub-figure (b), the **breaks** are manually chosen and not equally spaced. Therefore, we automatically get the densities on the horizontal axis: The sample share of observations within a bin is therefore reflected by the *area* of the respective rectangle, not the height.

_____ Script 1.23: **Histogram.R** _____

```
# Load data
library(foreign)
ceosal1<-read.dta("http://fmwww.bc.edu/ec-p/data/wooldridge/ceosal1.dta")

# Extract ROE to single vector
ROE <- ceosal1$roe

# Subfigure (a): histogram (counts)
hist(ROE)

# Subfigure (b): histogram (densities, explicit breaks)
hist(ROE, breaks=c(0,5,10,20,30,60) )
```

A kernel density plot can be thought of as a more sophisticated version of a histogram. We cannot go into detail here, but an intuitive (and oversimplifying) way to think about it is this: We could create a histogram bin of a certain width, centered at an arbitrary point of x. We will do this for many points and plot these x values against the resulting densities. Here, we will not use this plot as an estimator of a population distribution but rather as a pretty alternative to a histogram for the descriptive characterization of the sample distribution. For details, see for example Silverman (1986).

In *R*, generating a kernel density plot is straightforward: **plot(density(x))** will automatically choose appropriate parameters of the algorithm given the data and often produce a useful result. Of course, these parameters (like the kernel and bandwidth for those who know what that is) can be set manually. Also general **plot** options can be used.

Figure 1.12. Histograms

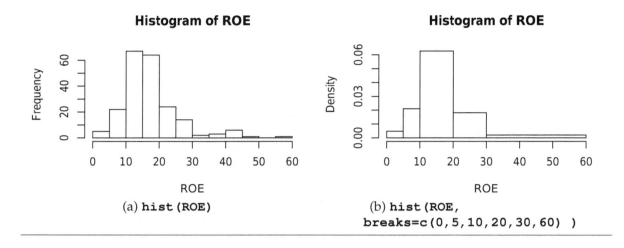

(a) `hist(ROE)`

(b) `hist(ROE,`
`breaks=c(0,5,10,20,30,60) )`

Script 1.24 (`KDensity.R`) generates the graphs of Figure 1.13. In Sub-figure (b), a histogram is overlayed with a kernel density plot by using the **lines** instead of the **plot** command for the latter. We adjust the **ylim** axis limits and increase the line width using **lwd**.

Script 1.24: **KDensity.R**

```
# Subfigure (c): kernel density estimate
plot( density(ROE) )

# Subfigure (d): overlay
hist(ROE, freq=FALSE, ylim=c(0,.07))
lines( density(ROE), lwd=3 )
```

1.5.3. Empirical Cumulative Distribution Function (ECDF)

The ecdf is a graph of all values x of a variable against the share of observations with a value less than or or equal to x. A straightforward way to plot the ecdf for a variable x is **plot(ecdf(x))**. We will just give a simple example and refer the interested reader to the help page or the internet for further refinements. For our ROE variable, the ecdf created by the command **plot(density(ROE))** is shown in Figure 1.14.

For example, the value of the ecdf for point ROE= 15.5 is 0.5. Half of the sample is less or equal to a ROE of 15.5%. In other words: the median ROE is 15.5%.

Figure 1.13. Kernel Density Plots

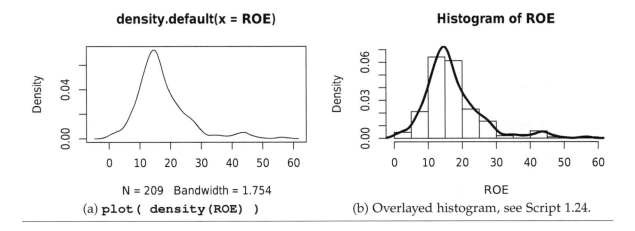

(a) `plot( density(ROE) )`

(b) Overlayed histogram, see Script 1.24.

Figure 1.14. Empirical CDF

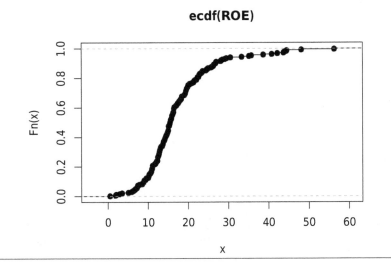

Table 1.4. *R* functions for descriptive statistics

`mean(x)`	Sample average $\bar{x} = \frac{1}{n}\sum_{i=1}^{n} x_i$
`median(x)`	sample median
`var(x)`	Sample variance $s_x^2 = \frac{1}{n-1}\sum_{i=1}^{n}(x_i - \bar{x})^2$
`sd(x)`	Sample standard deviation $s_x = \sqrt{s_x^2}$
`cov(x,y)`	Sample covariance $c_{xy} = \frac{1}{n-1}\sum_{i=1}^{n}(x_i - \bar{x})(y_i - \bar{y})$
`cor(x,y)`	Sample correlation $r_{xy} = \frac{s_{xy}}{s_x \cdot s_y}$
`quantile(x,q)`	q quantile = $100 \cdot q$ percentile, e.g. `quantile(x,0.5)` = sample median

1.5.4. Fundamental Statistics

The functions for calculating the most important descriptive statistics are listed in Figure 1.4. The command **summary** is a generic command that accepts many different object types and reports appropriate summary information. For numerical vectors, **summary** displays the mean, median, quartiles and extreme values. Script 1.25 (`Descr-Stats.R`) demonstrates this using the `CEOSAL1.dta` data set we already introduced in Section 1.5.2.

summary(df) shows the summary statistics for all variables if `df` is a data frame. To calculate all averages within rows or columns of matrices or data frames, consider the commands **colSums**, **rowSums**, **colMeans**, and **rowMeans**.

-------- Output of Script 1.25: `Descr-Stats.R` --------

```
> library(foreign)

> ceosal1<-read.dta("http://fmwww.bc.edu/ec-p/data/wooldridge/ceosal1.dta")

> # sample average:
> mean(ceosal1$salary)
[1] 1281.12

> # sample median:
> median(ceosal1$salary)
[1] 1039

> #standard deviation:
> sd(ceosal1$salary)
[1] 1372.345

> # summary information:
> summary(ceosal1$salary)
   Min. 1st Qu.  Median    Mean 3rd Qu.    Max.
    223     736    1039    1281    1407   14820

> # correlation with ROE:
> cor(ceosal1$salary, ceosal1$roe)
[1] 0.1148417
```

A box plot displays the median (the bold line), the upper and lower quartile (the box) and the extreme points graphically. Figure 1.15 shows two examples. 50% of the observations are within the interval covered by the box, 25% are above and 25% are below. The extreme points are marked by the "whiskers" and outliers are printed as separate dots. In *R*, box plots are generated using the **boxplot** command. We have to supply the data vector and can alter the design flexibly with numerous options.

Figure 1.15. Box Plots

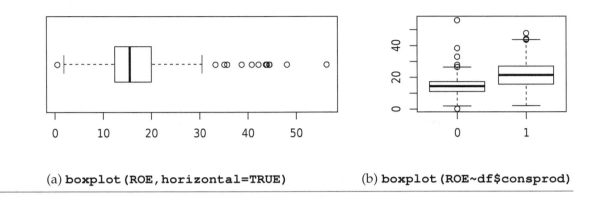

(a) `boxplot(ROE,horizontal=TRUE)`   (b) `boxplot(ROE~df$consprod)`

Figure 1.15(a) shows how to get a horizontally aligned plot and Figure 1.15(b) demonstrates how to produce different plots by sub group defined by a second variable. The variable `consprod` from the data set `ceosall` is equal to 1 if the firm is in the consumer product business and 0 otherwise. Apparently, the ROE is much higher in this industry.[15]

1.6. Probability Distributions

Appendix B of Wooldridge (2016) introduces the concepts of random variables and their probability distributions.[16] *R* has built in many functions for conveniently working with a large number of statistical distributions. The commands for evaluating the probability density function (pdf) for continuous, the probability mass function (pmf) for discrete, and the cumulative distribution function (cdf) as well as the quantile function (inverse cdf) for the most relevant distributions are shown in Table 1.5 together with the commands to generate a (pseudo-) random sample from the respective distributions. We will now briefly discuss each of these function types.

1.6.1. Discrete Distributions

Discrete random variables can only take a finite (or "countably infinite") set of values. The pmf $f(x) = P(X = x)$ gives the probability that a random variable X with this distribution takes the given value x. For the most important of those distributions (Bernoulli, Binomial, Hypergeometric, Poisson, and Geometric), Table 1.5 lists the *R* functions that return the pmf for any value x given the parameters of the respective distribution.

For a specific example, let X denote the number of white balls we get when drawing with re-placement 10 balls from an urn that includes 20% white balls. Then X has the Binomial distribution

---

[15]The data set is loaded in Script 1.25 (`Descr-Stats.R`) which therefore has to be executed before we can work with it.

[16]The stripped-down textbook for Europe and Africa Wooldridge (2014) does not include this appendix. But the material is pretty standard.

Table 1.5. *R functions for statistical distributions*

Distribution	Param.	pmf/pdf	cdf	Quantile	Random numbers
Discrete distributions:					
Bernoulli	p	$\texttt{dbinom}(x,1,p)$	$\texttt{pbinom}(x,1,p)$	$\texttt{qbinom}(q,1,p)$	$\texttt{rbinom}(R,1,p)$
Binomial	n,p	$\texttt{dbinom}(x,n,p)$	$\texttt{pbinom}(x,n,p)$	$\texttt{qbinom}(q,n,p)$	$\texttt{rbinom}(R,n,p)$
Hypergeom.	S,W,n	$\texttt{dhyper}(x,S,W,n)$	$\texttt{phyper}(x,S,W,n)$	$\texttt{qhyper}(q,S,W,n)$	$\texttt{rhyper}(R,S,W,n)$
Poisson	λ	$\texttt{dpois}(x,\lambda)$	$\texttt{ppois}(x,\lambda)$	$\texttt{qpois}(q,\lambda)$	$\texttt{rpois}(R,\lambda)$
Geometric	p	$\texttt{dgeom}(x,p)$	$\texttt{pgeom}(x,p)$	$\texttt{qgeom}(q,p)$	$\texttt{rgeom}(R,p)$
Continuous distributions:					
Uniform	a,b	$\texttt{dunif}(x,a,b)$	$\texttt{punif}(x,a,b)$	$\texttt{qunif}(q,a,b)$	$\texttt{runif}(R,a,b)$
Logistic	—	$\texttt{dlogis}(x)$	$\texttt{plogis}(x)$	$\texttt{qlogis}(q)$	$\texttt{rlogis}(R)$
Exponential	λ	$\texttt{dexp}(x,\lambda)$	$\texttt{pexp}(x,\lambda)$	$\texttt{qexp}(q,\lambda)$	$\texttt{rexp}(R,\lambda)$
Std. normal	—	$\texttt{dnorm}(x)$	$\texttt{pnorm}(x)$	$\texttt{qnorm}(q)$	$\texttt{rnorm}(R)$
Normal	μ,σ	$\texttt{dnorm}(x,\mu,\sigma)$	$\texttt{pnorm}(x,\mu,\sigma)$	$\texttt{qnorm}(q,\mu,\sigma)$	$\texttt{rnorm}(R,\mu,\sigma)$
Lognormal	m,s	$\texttt{dlnorm}(x,m,s)$	$\texttt{plnorm}(x,m,s)$	$\texttt{qlnorm}(q,m,s)$	$\texttt{rlnorm}(R,m,s)$
χ^2	n	$\texttt{dchisq}(x,n)$	$\texttt{pchisq}(x,n)$	$\texttt{qchisq}(q,n)$	$\texttt{rchisq}(R,n)$
t	n	$\texttt{dt}(x,n)$	$\texttt{pt}(x,n)$	$\texttt{qt}(q,n)$	$\texttt{rt}(R,n)$
F	m,n	$\texttt{df}(x,m,n)$	$\texttt{pf}(x,m,n)$	$\texttt{qf}(q,m,n)$	$\texttt{rf}(R,m,n)$

with the parameters $n = 10$ and $p = 20\% = 0.2$. We know that the probability to get exactly $x \in \{0, 1, \ldots, 10\}$ white balls for this distribution is[17]

$$f(x) = \mathrm{P}(X = x) = \binom{n}{x} \cdot p^x \cdot (1-p)^{n-x} = \binom{10}{x} \cdot 0.2^x \cdot 0.8^{10-x} \qquad (1.1)$$

For example, the probability to get exactly $x = 2$ white balls is $f(2) = \binom{10}{2} \cdot 0.2^2 \cdot 0.8^8 = 0.302$. Of course, we can let *R* do these calculations using basic *R* commands we know from Section 1.1. More conveniently, we can also use the built-in function for the Binomial distribution from Table 1.5 $\texttt{dbinom}(x,n,p)$:

```
> # Pedestrian approach:
> choose(10,2) * 0.2^2 * 0.8^8
[1] 0.3019899

> # Built-in function:
> dbinom(2,10,0.2)
[1] 0.3019899
```

We can also give vectors as one or more arguments to $\texttt{dbinom}(x,n,p)$ and receive the results as a vector. Script 1.26 (PMF-example.R) evaluates the pmf for our example at all possible values for x (0 through 10). It displays a table of the probabilities and creates a bar chart of these probabilities which is shown in Figure 1.16(a). Note that the option $\texttt{type="h"}$ of the command $\texttt{plot}$ draws vertical lines instead of points, see Section 1.4. As always: feel encouraged to experiment!

---

[17] see Wooldridge (2016, Equation (B.14))

Figure 1.16. Plots of the pmf and pdf

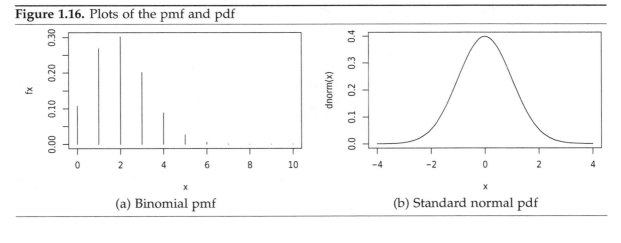

(a) Binomial pmf   (b) Standard normal pdf

———————— Output of Script 1.26: **PMF-example.R** ————————

```
> # Values for x: all between 0 and 10
> x <- seq(0,10)

> # pmf for all these values
> fx <- dbinom(x, 10, 0.2)

> # Table(matrix) of values:
> cbind(x, fx)
        x          fx
 [1,]   0  0.1073741824
 [2,]   1  0.2684354560
 [3,]   2  0.3019898880
 [4,]   3  0.2013265920
 [5,]   4  0.0880803840
 [6,]   5  0.0264241152
 [7,]   6  0.0055050240
 [8,]   7  0.0007864320
 [9,]   8  0.0000737280
[10,]   9  0.0000040960
[11,]  10  0.0000001024

> # Plot
> plot(x, fx, type="h")
```

1.6.2. Continuous Distributions

For continuous distributions like the uniform, logistic, exponential, normal, t, χ^2, or F distribution, the probability density functions $f(x)$ are also implemented for direct use in R. These can for example be used to plot the density functions using the **curve** command (see Section 1.4). Figure 1.16(b) shows the famous bell-shaped pdf of the standard normal distribution. It was created using the command **curve(dnorm(x), -4,4)**.

1.6.3. Cumulative Distribution Function (CDF)

For all distributions, the cdf $F(x) = P(X \leq x)$ represents the probability that the random variable X takes a value of *at most* x. The probability that X is between two values a and b is $P(a < X \leq b) = F(b) - F(a)$. We can directly use the built-in functions in the second column of Table 1.5 to do these calculations. In our example presented above, the probability that we get 3 or fewer white balls is $F(3)$ using the appropriate cdf of the Binomial distribution. It amounts to 87.9%:

```
> pbinom(3, 10, 0.2)
[1] 0.8791261
```

The probability that a standard normal random variable takes a value between -1.96 and 1.96 is 95%:

```
> pnorm(1.96) - pnorm(-1.96)
[1] 0.9500042
```

Wooldridge, Example B.6: Probabilities for a normal random variable

We assume $X \sim \text{Normal}(4, 9)$ and want to calculate $P(2 < X \leq 6)$. We can rewrite the problem so it is stated in terms of a standard normal distribution as shown by Wooldridge (2016): $P(2 < X \leq 6) = \Phi(\frac{2}{3}) - \Phi(-\frac{2}{3})$. We can also spare ourselves the transformation and work with the non-standard normal distribution directly. Be careful that the third argument in the R commands for the normal distribution is not the variance $\sigma^2 = 9$ but the standard deviation $\sigma = 3$. $P(|X| > 2) = \underbrace{1 - P(X \leq 2)}_{P(X>2)} + P(X < -2)$:

```
> # Using the transformation:
> pnorm(2/3) - pnorm(-2/3)
[1] 0.4950149

> # Working directly with the distribution of X:
> pnorm(6,4,3) - pnorm(2,4,3)
[1] 0.4950149
```

Note that we get a slightly different answer than the one given in Wooldridge (2016) since we're working with the exact $\frac{2}{3}$ instead of the rounded .67. The same approach can be used for the second problem:

```
> 1 - pnorm(2,4,3) + pnorm(-2,4,3)
[1] 0.7702576
```

The graph of the cdf is a step function for discrete distributions and can therefore be best created using the **type="s"** option of **plot**, see Section 1.4. For the urn example, the cdf is shown in Figure 1.17(a). It was created using the following code:

```
x <- seq(-1,10)
Fx <- pbinom(x, 10, 0.2)
plot(x, Fx, type="s")
```

The cdf of a *continuous* distribution can very well be plotted using the **curve** command. The S-shaped cdf of the normal distribution is shown in Figure 1.17(b). It was simply generated with **curve(pnorm(x), -4, 4)**.

Figure 1.17. Plots of the cdf of discrete and continuous RV

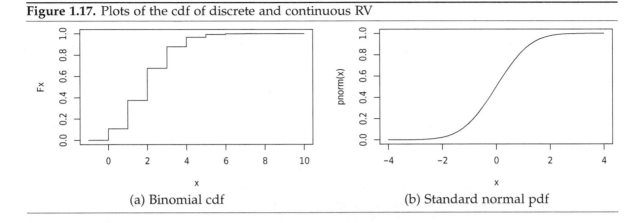

(a) Binomial cdf	(b) Standard normal pdf

Quantile function

The q-quantile $x[q]$ of a random variable is the value for which the probability to sample a value $x \leq x[q]$ is just q. These values are important for example for calculating critical values of test statistics.

To give a simple example: Given X is standard normal, the 0.975-quantile is $x[0.975] \approx 1.96$. So the probability to sample a value less or equal to 1.96 is 97.5%:

```
> qnorm(0.975)
[1] 1.959964
```

1.6.4. Random Draws from Probability Distributions

It is easy to simulate random outcomes by taking a sample from a random variable with a given distribution. Strictly speaking, a deterministic machine like a computer can never produce any truly random results and we should instead refer to the generated numbers as *pseudo-random* numbers. But for our purpose, it is enough that the generated samples look, feel and behave like true random numbers and so we are a little sloppy in our terminology here. For a review of sampling and related concepts see Wooldridge (2016, Appendix C.1).

Before we make heavy use of generating random samples in Section 1.9, we introduce the mechanics here. Table 1.5 shows the R commands to draw a random sample from the most important distributions. We could for example simulate the result of flipping a fair coin 10 times. We draw a sample of size $n = 10$ from a Bernoulli distribution with parameter $p = \frac{1}{2}$. Each of the 10 generated numbers will take the value 1 with probability $p = \frac{1}{2}$ and 0 with probability $1 - p = \frac{1}{2}$. The result behaves the same way as though we had actually flipped a coin and translated heads as 1 and tails as 0 (or vice versa). Here is the code and a sample generated by it:

```
> rbinom(10,1,0.5)
 [1] 1 1 0 0 0 0 1 0 1 0
```

Translated into the coins, our sample is heads-heads-tails-tails-tails-tails-heads-tails-heads-tails. An obvious advantage of doing this in R rather than with an actual coin is that we can painlessly increase the sample size to 1,000 or 10,000,000. Taking draws from the standard normal distribution is equally simple:

```
> rnorm(10)
 [1]  0.83446013  1.31241551  2.50264541  1.16823174 -0.42616558
 [6] -0.99612975 -1.11394990 -0.05573154  1.17443240  1.05321861
```

Working with computer-generated random samples creates problems for the reproducibility of the results. If you run the code above, you will get different samples. If we rerun the code, the sample will change again. We can solve this problem by making use of how the random numbers are actually generated which is, as already noted, not involving true randomness. Actually, we will always get the same sequence of numbers if we reset the random number generator to some specific state ("seed"). In *R*, this is done with **set.seed(number)**, where number is some arbitrary number that defines the state but has no other meaning. If we set the seed to some arbitrary number, take a sample, reset the seed to the same state and take another sample, both samples will be the same. Also, if I draw a sample with that seed it will be equal to the sample you draw if we both start from the same seed.

Script 1.27 (Random-Numbers.R) demonstrates the workings of **set.seed**.

———————————— **Output of Script 1.27: Random-Numbers.R** ————————————

```
> # Sample from a standard normal RV with sample size n=5:
> rnorm(5)
[1]  0.05760597 -0.73504289  0.93052842  1.66821097  0.55968789

> # A different sample from the same distribution:
> rnorm(5)
[1] -0.75397477  1.25655419  0.03849255  0.18953983  0.46259495

> # Set the seed of the random number generator and take two samples:
> set.seed(6254137)

> rnorm(5)
[1]  0.6601307  0.5123161 -0.4616180 -1.3161982  0.1811945

> rnorm(5)
[1] -0.2933858 -0.9023692  1.8385493  0.5652698 -1.2848862

> # Reset the seed to the same value to get the same samples again:
> set.seed(6254137)

> rnorm(5)
[1]  0.6601307  0.5123161 -0.4616180 -1.3161982  0.1811945

> rnorm(5)
[1] -0.2933858 -0.9023692  1.8385493  0.5652698 -1.2848862
```

1.7. Confidence Intervals and Statistical Inference

Wooldridge (2016) provides a concise overview over basic sampling, estimation, and testing. We will touch on some of these issues below.[18]

1.7.1. Confidence Intervals

Confidence intervals (CI) are introduced in Wooldridge (2016, Appendix C.5). They are constructed to cover the true population parameter of interest with a given high probability (before a sample is drawn).

CI are easy to compute. For a normal population with unknown mean μ and variance σ^2, the $100(1 - \alpha)\%$ confidence interval for μ is given in Wooldridge (2016, Equations C.24 and C.25):

$$\left[\bar{y} - c_{\frac{\alpha}{2}} \cdot se(\bar{y}), \quad \bar{y} + c_{\frac{\alpha}{2}} \cdot se(\bar{y}) \right] \tag{1.2}$$

where $\bar{y}$ is the sample average, $se(\bar{y}) = \frac{s}{\sqrt{n}}$ is the standard error of $\bar{y}$ (with s being the sample standard deviation of y), n is the sample size and $c_{\frac{\alpha}{2}}$ the $\left(1 - \frac{\alpha}{2}\right)$ quantile of the t_{n-1} distribution. To get the 95% CI ($\alpha = 5\%$), we thus need $c_{0.025}$ which is the 0.975 quantile or 97.5^{th} percentile.

We already know how to calculate all these ingredients. If our sample is stored as a vector y, the following code will calculate them and the confidence interval:

```
ybar<- mean(y)
n    <- length(y)
s    <- sd(y)
se   <- s/sqrt(n)
c    <- qt(.975, n-1)
CI   <- c( ybar - c*se, ybar + c*se )
```

This "manual" way of calculating the CI is used in the solution to Example C.2. We will see a more convenient way to calculate the confidence interval together with corresponding t test in Section 1.7.4. In Section 1.9.3, we will calculate confidence intervals in a simulation experiment to help us understand the meaning of confidence intervals.

---

[18]The stripped-down textbook for Europe and Africa Wooldridge (2014) does not include the discussion of this material.

Wooldridge, Example C.2: Effect of Job Training Grants on Worker Productivity

We are analyzing scrap rates for firms that receive a job training grant in 1988. The scrap rates for 1987 and 1988 are printed in Wooldridge (2016, Table C.3) and are entered manually in the beginning of Script 1.28 (Example-C-2.R). We are interested in the change between the years. The calculation of its average as well as the confidence interval are performed precisely as shown above. The resulting CI is the same as the one presented in Wooldridge (2016) except for rounding errors we avoid by working with the exact numbers.

Output of Script 1.28: `Example-C-2.R`

```
> # Manually enter raw data from Wooldridge, Table C.3:
> SR87<-c(10,1,6,.45,1.25,1.3,1.06,3,8.18,1.67,.98,1,.45,
>                                 5.03,8,9,18,.28,7,3.97)

> SR88<-c(3,1,5,.5,1.54,1.5,.8,2,.67,1.17,.51,.5,.61,6.7,
>                                 4,7,19,.2,5,3.83)

> # Calculate Change (the parentheses just display the results):
> (Change <- SR88 - SR87)
 [1] -7.00  0.00 -1.00  0.05  0.29  0.20 -0.26 -1.00 -7.51 -0.50 -0.47
[12] -0.50  0.16  1.67 -4.00 -2.00  1.00 -0.08 -2.00 -0.14

> # Ingredients to CI formula
> (avgCh<- mean(Change))
[1] -1.1545

> (n      <- length(Change))
[1] 20

> (sdCh <- sd(Change))
[1] 2.400639

> (se     <- sdCh/sqrt(n))
[1] 0.5367992

> (c      <- qt(.975, n-1))
[1] 2.093024

> # Confidence intervall:
> c( avgCh - c*se, avgCh + c*se )
[1] -2.27803369 -0.03096631
```

Wooldridge, Example C.3: Race Discrimination in Hiring

We are looking into race discrimination using the data set `AUDIT.dta`. The variable `y` represents the difference in hiring rates between black and white applicants with the identical CV. After calculating the average, sample size, standard deviation and the standard error of the sample average, Script 1.29 (`Example-C-3.R`) calculates the value for the factor c as the 97.5 percentile of the standard normal distribution which is (very close to) 1.96. Finally, the 95% and 99% CI are reported.[19]

─────────── Output of Script 1.29: `Example-C-3.R` ───────────

```
> library(foreign)

> audit <- read.dta("http://fmwww.bc.edu/ec-p/data/wooldridge/audit.dta")

> # Ingredients to CI formula
> (avgy<- mean(audit$y))
[1] -0.1327801

> (n    <- length(audit$y))
[1] 241

> (sdy <- sd(audit$y))
[1] 0.4819709

> (se  <- sdy/sqrt(n))
[1] 0.03104648

> (c    <- qnorm(.975))
[1] 1.959964

> # 95% Confidence intervall:
> avgy + c * c(-se,+se)
[1] -0.19363006 -0.07193011

> # 99% Confidence intervall:
> avgy + qnorm(.995) * c(-se,+se)
[1] -0.21275051 -0.05280966
```

───────────

[19]Note that Wooldridge (2016) has a typo in the discussion of this example, therefore the numbers don't quite match for the 95% CI.

1.7.2. t Tests

Hypothesis tests are covered in Wooldridge (2016, Appendix C.6). The t test statistic for testing a hypothesis about the mean μ of a normally distributed random variable Y is shown in Equation C.35. Given the null hypothesis $H_0 : \mu = \mu_0$,

$$t = \frac{\bar{y} - \mu_0}{se(\bar{y})}. \tag{1.3}$$

We already know how to calculate the ingredients from Section 1.7.1. Given the calculations shown there, t for the null hypothesis $H_0 : \mu = 1$ would simply be

```
t <- (ybar-1) / se
```

The critical value for this test statistic depends on whether the test is one-sided or two-sided. The value needed for a two-sided test $c_{\frac{\alpha}{2}}$ was already calculated for the CI, the other values can be generated accordingly. The values for different degrees of freedom $n - 1$ and significance levels α are listed in Wooldridge (2016, Table G.2). Script 1.30 (`Critical-Values-t.R`) demonstrates how we can calculate our own table of critical values for the example of 19 degrees of freedom.

_____ **Output of Script 1.30: `Critical-Values-t.R`** _____

```
> # degrees of freedom = n-1:
> df <- 19

> # significance levels:
> alpha.one.tailed = c(0.1, 0.05, 0.025, 0.01, 0.005, .001)

> alpha.two.tailed = alpha.one.tailed * 2

> # critical values & table:
> CV <- qt(1 - alpha.one.tailed, df)

> cbind(alpha.one.tailed, alpha.two.tailed, CV)
     alpha.one.tailed alpha.two.tailed       CV
[1,]            0.100            0.200 1.327728
[2,]            0.050            0.100 1.729133
[3,]            0.025            0.050 2.093024
[4,]            0.010            0.020 2.539483
[5,]            0.005            0.010 2.860935
[6,]            0.001            0.002 3.579400
```

Wooldridge, Example C.5: Race Discrimination in Hiring

We continue Example C.3 and perform a one-sided t test of the null hypothesis $H_0 : \mu = 0$ against $H_1 : \mu < 0$ for the same sample. Before we can execute Script 1.31 (`Example-C-5.R`), we therefore have to run script `Example-C-3.R` to reuse the variables `avgy`, `se`, and `n`. As the output shows, the t test statistic is equal to -4.27. This is much smaller than the negative of the critical value for any sensible significance level. Therefore, we reject $H_0 : \mu = 0$ for this one-sided test, see Wooldridge (2016, Equation C.38).

—————— **Output of Script 1.31: `Example-C-5.R`** ——————

```
> # Note: we reuse variables from Example-C-3.R. It has to be run first!
> # t statistic for H0: mu=0:
> (t <- avgy/se)
[1] -4.276816

> # Critical values for t distribution with n-1=240 d.f.:
> alpha.one.tailed = c(0.1, 0.05, 0.025, 0.01, 0.005, .001)

> CV <- qt(1 - alpha.one.tailed, n-1)

> cbind(alpha.one.tailed, CV)
     alpha.one.tailed       CV
[1,]            0.100 1.285089
[2,]            0.050 1.651227
[3,]            0.025 1.969898
[4,]            0.010 2.341985
[5,]            0.005 2.596469
[6,]            0.001 3.124536
```

1.7.3. p Values

The advantage of using p values for statistical testing is that they are convenient to interpret. Instead of having to compare the test statistic with critical values which are implied by the significance level α, we directly compare p with α. For two-sided t tests, the formula for the p value is given in Wooldridge (2016, Equation C.42):

$$p = 2 \cdot \mathrm{P}(T_{n-1} > |t|) = 2\left(1 - F_{t_{n-1}}(|t|)\right) \tag{1.4}$$

where $F_{t_{n-1}}(\cdot)$ is the cdf of the t_{n-1} distribution which we know how to calculate from Table 1.5. Because we are working on a computer program that knows the cdf of the t distribution as **pt**, calculating p values is straightforward: Given we have already calculated the t statistic above, the p value would simply be

```
p <- 2 * (1 - pt( abs(t), n-1 ))
```

Wooldridge, Example C.6: Effect of Job Training Grants on Worker Productivity

We continue from Example C.2. Before we can execute Script 1.28 (`Example-C-2.R`), we have to run `Example-C-2.R` so we can reuse the variables `avgCh` and `se`. We test $H_0 : \mu = 0$ against $H_1 : \mu < 0$. The t statistic is -2.15. The formula for the p value for this one-sided test is given in Wooldridge (2016, Equation C.41). As can be seen in the output of Script 1.32 (`Example-C-6.R`), its value (using exact values of t) is around 0.022.

───────── **Output of Script 1.32:** `Example-C-6.R` ─────────

```
> # Note: we reuse variables from Example-C-3.R. It has to be run first!
> # t statistic for H0: mu=0:
> (t <- avgCh/se)
[1] -2.150711

> # p value
> (p <- pt(t,n-1))
[1] 0.02229063
```

Wooldridge, Example C.7: Race Discrimination in Hiring

In Example C.5, we found the t statistic for $H_0 : \mu = 0$ against $H_1 : \mu < 0$ to be $t = -4.276816$. The corresponding p value is calculated in Script 1.33 (`Example-C-7.R`). The number `1.369271e-05` is the scientific notation for $1.369271 \cdot 10^{-5} = .00001369271$. So the p value is around 0.0014% which is much smaller than any reasonable significance level. By construction, we draw the same conclusion as when we compare the t statistic with the critical value in Example C.5. We reject the null hypothesis that there is no discrimination.

───────── **Output of Script 1.33:** `Example-C-7.R` ─────────

```
> # t statistic for H0: mu=0:
> t <-  -4.276816

> # p value
> (p <- pt(t,240))
[1] 1.369273e-05
```

1.7.4. Automatic calculations

In Sections 1.7.1 through 1.7.3, we used R as an advanced calculator that can easily calculate statistics from data and knows the distribution tables. Real life is even more convenient. R has a huge number of commands that perform all these sorts of calculations automatically for various kinds of estimation and testing problems.

For our problem of testing a hypothesis about a population parameter, the command `t.test` is handy. For different hypotheses, it automatically provides

- the sample average $\bar{Y}$
- the sample size n
- the confidence interval (95% by default)
- the t statistic
- the p value

So we get all the information we previously calculated in several steps with one call of this command. With the vector `y` including the sample data, we can simply call

```
t.test(y)
```

This would implicitly calculate the relevant results for the two-sided test of the null $H_0 : \mu_y = \mu_0, H_1 : \mu_y \neq \mu_0$, where $\mu_0 = 0$ by default. The 95% CI is reported. We can choose different tests using the options

- **alternative="greater"** for $H_0 : \mu_y = \mu_0, H_1 : \mu_y > \mu_0$
- **alternative="less"** for $H_0 : \mu_y = \mu_0, H_1 : \mu_y < \mu_0$
- **mu=value** to set μ_0 =value instead of $\mu_0 = 0$
- **conf.level=value** to set the confidence level to value·100% instead of **conf.level=0.95**

To give a comprehensive example: Suppose you want to test $H_0 : \mu_y = 5$ against the one-sided alternative $H_1 : \mu_y > 5$ and obtain a 99% CI. The command would be

```
t.test(y, mu=5, alternative="greater", conf.level=0.99)
```

Examples C.2 – C.7 revisited:

Script 1.34 (Examples-C2-C6.R) replicates the same results as already shown in Examples C.2 and C.6 using the simple call of **t.test**. Reassuringly, it produces the same values we manually calculated above plus some other results. Script 1.35 (Examples-C3-C5-C7.R) does the same for the results in Examples C.3, C.5, and C.7.

—————— **Output of Script 1.34: Examples-C2-C6.R** ——————

```
> # data for the scrap rates examples:
> SR87<-c(10,1,6,.45,1.25,1.3,1.06,3,8.18,1.67,.98,1,.45,5.03,8,9,18,.28,
>                                                           7,3.97)

> SR88<-c(3,1,5,.5,1.54,1.5,.8,2,.67,1.17,.51,.5,.61,6.7,4,7,19,.2,5,3.83)

> Change <- SR88 - SR87

> # Example C.2: two-sided CI
> t.test(Change)

        One Sample t-test

data:  Change
t = -2.1507, df = 19, p-value = 0.04458
alternative hypothesis: true mean is not equal to 0
95 percent confidence interval:
 -2.27803369 -0.03096631
sample estimates:
mean of x
  -1.1545


> # Example C.6: 1-sided test:
> t.test(Change, alternative="less")

        One Sample t-test

data:  Change
t = -2.1507, df = 19, p-value = 0.02229
alternative hypothesis: true mean is less than 0
95 percent confidence interval:
      -Inf -0.2263028
sample estimates:
mean of x
  -1.1545
```

Output of Script 1.35: `Examples-C3-C5-C7.R`

```
> library(foreign)

> audit <- read.dta("http://fmwww.bc.edu/ec-p/data/wooldridge/audit.dta")

> # Example C.3: two-sided CI
> t.test(audit$y)

        One Sample t-test

data:  audit$y
t = -4.2768, df = 240, p-value = 2.739e-05
alternative hypothesis: true mean is not equal to 0
95 percent confidence interval:
 -0.1939385 -0.0716217
sample estimates:
 mean of x
-0.1327801


> # Examples C.5 & C.7: 1-sided test:
> t.test(audit$y, alternative="less")

        One Sample t-test

data:  audit$y
t = -4.2768, df = 240, p-value = 1.369e-05
alternative hypothesis: true mean is less than 0
95 percent confidence interval:
      -Inf -0.08151529
sample estimates:
 mean of x
-0.1327801
```

The command **t.test** is our first example of a function that returns a **list**. Instead of just displaying the results as we have done so far, we can store them as an object for further use. Section 1.2.6 described the general workings of these sorts of objects.

If we store the results for example as **testres <- t.test(...)**, the object **testres** contains all relevant information about the test results. Like a basic list, the names of all components can be displayed with **names(testres)**. They include

- **statistic** = value of the test statistic
- **p.value** = value of the p value of the test
- **conf.int** = confidence interval

A single component, for example **p.value** is accessed as **testres$p.value**. Script 1.36 (Test-Results-List.R) demonstrates this for the test in Example C.3.

──────── **Output of Script 1.36: Test-Results-List.R** ────────

```
> library(foreign)

> audit <- read.dta("http://fmwww.bc.edu/ec-p/data/wooldridge/audit.dta")

> # store test results as a list "testres"
> testres <- t.test(audit$y)

> # print results:
> testres

        One Sample t-test

data:  audit$y
t = -4.2768, df = 240, p-value = 2.739e-05
alternative hypothesis: true mean is not equal to 0
95 percent confidence interval:
 -0.1939385 -0.0716217
sample estimates:
 mean of x
-0.1327801


> # component names: which results can be accessed?
> names(testres)
[1] "statistic"   "parameter"   "p.value"     "conf.int"
[5] "estimate"    "null.value"  "alternative" "method"
[9] "data.name"

> # p-value
> testres$p.value
[1] 2.738542e-05
```

1.8. Advanced *R*

The material covered in this section is not necessary for most of what we will do in the remainder of this book, so it can be skipped. However, it is important enough to justify an own section in this chapter. We will only scratch the surface, though. For more details, you will have to look somewhere else, for example Matloff (2011), Teetor (2011) and Wickham (2014).

1.8.1. Conditional Execution

We might want some parts of our code to be executed only under certain conditions. Like most other programming languages, this can be achieved with an **if** statement. The structure is:

```
if (condition) expression1 else expression2
```

The **condition** has to be a single logical value (**TRUE** or **FALSE**). If it is **TRUE**, then **expression1** is executed, otherwise **expression2** which can also be omitted. A simple example would be

```
if (p<=0.05) decision<-"reject H0!" else decision<-"don't reject H0!"
```

The character object **decision** will take the respective value depending on the value of the numeric scalar **p**. Often, we want to conditionally execute several lines of code. This can easily be achieved by grouping the expressions in curly braces **{...}**. Note that the **else** statement (if it is used) needs to go on the same line as the closing brace of the **for** statement. So the structure will look like

```
if (condition) {
    [several...
    ...lines...
    ... of code]
} else {
    [different...
    ...lines...
    ... of code]
}
```

1.8.2. Loops

For repeatedly executing an expression (which can again be grouped by braces **{...}**), different kinds of loops are available. In this book, we will use them for Monte Carlo analyses introduced in Section 1.9. For our purposes, the **for** loop is well suited. Its typical structure is as follows:

```
for (loopvar in vector) {
    [some commands]
}
```

The loop variable **loopvar** will take the value of each element of **vector**, one after another. For each of these elements, **[some commands]** are executed. Often, **vector** will be a sequence like **1:100**.

A nonsense example which combines **for** loops with an **if** statement is the following:

```
for (i in 1:6) {
  if (i<4) {
    print(i^3)
  } else {
    print(i^2)
  }
}
```

Note that the **print** commands are necessary to print any results within expressions grouped by braces. The reader is encouraged to first form expectations about the output this will generate and then compare them with the actual results:

```
[1] 1
[1] 8
[1] 27
[1] 16
[1] 25
[1] 36
```

R offers more ways to repeat expressions, but we will not present them here. Interested readers can look up commands like **repeat**, **while**, **replicate**, **apply** or **lapply**.

1.8.3. Functions

Functions are special kinds of objects in *R*. There are many pre-defined functions – the first one we used was **sqrt**. Packages provide more functions to expand the capabilities of *R*. And now, we're ready to define our own little function. The command **function(arg1, arg2,...)** defines a new function which accepts the arguments **arg1, arg2**,... The function definition follows in arbitrarily many lines of code enclosed in curly braces. Within the function, the command **return(stuff)** means that **stuff** is to be returned as a result of the function call. For example, we can define the function **mysqrt** that expects one argument internally named **x** as

```
mysqrt <- function(x) {
  if(x>=0){
    return(sqrt(x))
  } else {
    return("You fool!")
  }
}
```

Once we have executed this function definition, **mysqrt** is known to the system and we can use it just like any other function:

```
> mysqrt(4)
[1] 2
> mysqrt(-1)
[1] "You fool!"
```

1.8.4. Outlook

While this section is called "Advanced *R*", we have admittedly only scratched the surface of semi-advanced topics. One topic we defer to Chapter 19 is how *R* can automatically create of formatted reports and publication-ready documents.

Another advanced topic is the optimization of computational speed. Like most other software packages used for econometrics, *R* is an interpreted language. A disadvantage compared to compiled languages like C++ or Fortran is that the execution speed for computationally intensive tasks is lower. So an example of seriously advanced topics for the real *R* geek is how to speed up computations. Possibilities include compiling *R* code, integrating C++ or Fortran code, and parallel computing.

Since real *R* geeks are not the target audience of this book, we will stop to even mention more intimidating possibilities and focus on implementing the most important econometric methods in the most straightforward and pragmatic way.

1.9. Monte Carlo Simulation

Appendix C.2 of Wooldridge (2016) contains a brief introduction to estimators and their properties.[20] In real-world applications, we typically have a data set corresponding to a random sample from a well-defined population. We don't know the population parameters and use the sample to estimate them.

When we generate a sample using a computer program as we have introduced in Section 1.6.4, we know the population parameters since we had to chose them when making the random draws. We could apply the same estimators to this artificial sample to estimate the population parameters. The tasks would be: (1) Select a population distribution and its parameters. (2) Generate a sample from this distribution. (3) Use the sample to estimate the population parameters.

If this sounds a little insane to you: Don't worry, that would be a healthy first reaction. We obtain a noisy estimate of something we know precisely. But this sort of analysis does in fact make sense. Because we estimate something we actually know, we are able to study the behavior of our estimator very well.

In this book, we mainly use this approach for illustrative and didactic reasons. In state-of-the-art research, it is widely used since it often provides the only way to learn about important features of estimators and statistical tests. A name frequently given to these sorts of analyses is Monte Carlo simulation in reference to the "gambling" involved in generating random samples.

1.9.1. Finite Sample Properties of Estimators

Let's look at a simple example and simulate a situation in which we want to estimate the mean μ of a normally distributed random variable

$$Y \sim \text{Normal}(\mu, \sigma^2) \tag{1.5}$$

using a sample of a given size n. The obvious estimator for the population mean would be the sample average $\bar{Y}$. But what properties does this estimator have? The informed reader immediately knows that the sampling distribution of $\bar{Y}$ is

$$\bar{Y} \sim \text{Normal}\left(\mu, \frac{\sigma^2}{n}\right) \tag{1.6}$$

Simulation provides a way to verify this claim.

Script 1.37 (`Simulate-Estimate.R`) shows a simulation experiment in action: We set the seed to ensure reproducibility and draw a sample of size $n = 100$ from the population distribution (with the population parameters $\mu = 10$ and $\sigma = 2$).[21] Then, we calculate the sample average as an estimate of μ. We see results for three different samples.

---

[20]The stripped-down textbook for Europe and Africa Wooldridge (2014) does not include this either.
[21]See Section 1.6.4 for the basics of random number generation.

───────── **Output of Script 1.37:** `Simulate-Estimate.R` ─────────

```
> # Set the random seed
> set.seed(123456)

> # Draw a sample given the population parameters
> sample <- rnorm(100,10,2)

> # Estimate the population mean with the sample average
> mean(sample)
[1] 10.03364

> # Draw a different sample and estimate again:
> sample <- rnorm(100,10,2)

> mean(sample)
[1] 9.913197

> # Draw a third sample and estimate again:
> sample <- rnorm(100,10,2)

> mean(sample)
[1] 10.21746
```

All sample means $\bar{Y}$ are around the true mean $\mu = 10$ which is consistent with our presumption formulated in Equation 1.6. It is also not surprising that we don't get the exact population parameter – that's the nature of the sampling noise. According to Equation 1.6, the results are expected to have a variance of $\frac{\sigma^2}{n} = 0.04$. Three samples of this kind are insufficient to draw strong conclusions regarding the validity of Equation 1.6. Good Monte Carlo simulation studies should use as many samples as possible.

In Section1.8.2, we introduced **for** loops. While they are not the most powerful technique available in R to implement a Monte Carlo study, we will stick to them since they are quite transparent and straightforward. The code shown in Script 1.38 (`Simulation-Repeated.R`) uses a **for** loop to draw 10 000 samples of size $n = 100$ and calculate the sample average for all of them. After setting the random seed, a vector `ybar` is initialized to 10 000 zeros using the **numeric** command. We will replace these zeros with the estimates one after another in the loop. In each of these replications $j = 1, 2, \ldots, 10\,000$, a sample is drawn, its average calculated and stored in position number `j` of `ybar`. In this way, we end up with a vector of 10 000 estimates from different samples. The script `Simulation-Repeated.R` does not generate any output.

───────── **Script 1.38:** `Simulation-Repeated.R` ─────────

```
# Set the random seed
set.seed(123456)

# initialize ybar to a vector of length r=10000 to later store results:
ybar <- numeric(10000)

# repeat 10000 times:
for(j in 1:10000) {
  # Draw a sample and store the sample mean in pos. j=1,2,... of ybar:
  sample <- rnorm(100,10,2)
  ybar[j] <- mean(sample)
}
```

Script 1.39 (`Simulation-Repeated-Results.R`) analyses these 10 000 estimates. Their average is very close to the presumption $\mu = 10$ from Equation 1.6. Also the simulated sampling variance is close to the theoretical result $\frac{\sigma^2}{n} = 0.04$. Finally, the estimated density (using a kernel density estimate) is compared to the theoretical normal distribution. The option **add=TRUE** of the **curve** command requests the normal curve to be drawn on top of the previous graph instead of creating a new one and **lty=2** changes the line type to a dashed curve. The result is shown in Figure 1.18. The two lines are almost indistinguishable except for the area close to the mode (where the kernel density estimator is known to have problems).

─────── **Output of Script 1.39:** `Simulation-Repeated-Results.R` ───────

```
> # The first 20 of 10000 estimates:
> ybar[1:20]
 [1] 10.033640  9.913197 10.217455 10.121745  9.837282 10.375066
 [7] 10.026097  9.777042  9.903131 10.012415  9.930439 10.394639
[13]  9.642143 10.196132  9.804443 10.203723  9.962646  9.620169
[19]  9.757859 10.328590

> # Simulated mean:
> mean(ybar)
[1] 9.998861

> # Simulated variance:
> var(ybar)
[1] 0.04034146

> # Simulated density:
> plot(density(ybar))

> curve( dnorm(x,10,sqrt(.04)), add=TRUE,lty=2)
```

Figure 1.18. Simulated and theoretical density of $\bar{Y}$

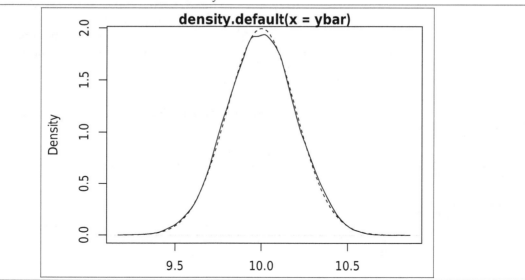

To summarize, the simulation results confirm the theoretical results in Equation 1.6. Mean, variance and density are very close and it seems likely that the remaining tiny differences are due to the fact that we "only" used 10 000 samples.

Remember: for most advanced estimators, such simulations are the only way to study some of their features since it is impossible to derive theoretical results of interest. For us, the simple example hopefully clarified the approach of Monte Carlo simulations and the meaning of the sampling distribution and prepared us for other interesting simulation exercises.

1.9.2. Asymptotic Properties of Estimators

Asymptotic analyses are concerned with large samples and with the behavior of estimators and other statistics as the sample size n increases without bound. For a discussion of these topics, see Wooldridge (2016, Appendix C.3). According to the **law of large numbers**, the sample average $\bar{Y}$ in the above example converges in probability to the population mean μ as $n \to \infty$. In (infinitely) large samples, this implies that $E(\bar{Y}) \to \mu$ and $\text{Var}(\bar{Y}) \to 0$.

With Monte Carlo simulation, we have a tool to see how this works out in our example. We just have to change the sample size in the code line **sample <- rnorm(100,10,2)** in Script 1.38 (`Simulation-Repeated.R`) from 100 to a different number and rerun the simulation code. Results for $n = 10, 50, 100$, and 1000 are presented in Figure 1.19.[22] Apparently, the variance of $\bar{Y}$ does in fact decrease. The graph of the density for $n = 1000$ is already very narrow and high indicating a small variance. Of course, we cannot actually increase n to infinity without crashing our computer, but it appears plausible that the density will eventually collapse into one vertical line corresponding to $\text{Var}(\bar{Y}) \to 0$ as $n \to \infty$.

In our example for the simulations, the random variable Y was normally distributed, therefore the sample average $\bar{Y}$ was also normal for any sample size. This can also be confirmed in Figure 1.19 where the respective normal densities were added to the graphs as dashed lines. The **central limit theorem** (CLT) claims that as $n \to \infty$, the sample mean $\bar{Y}$ of a random sample will eventually *always* be normally distributed, no matter what the distribution of Y is (unless it is very weird with an infinite variance). This is called convergence in distribution.

Let's check this with a very non-normal distribution, the χ^2 distribution with one degree of freedom. Its density is depicted in Figure 1.20.[23] It looks very different from our familiar bell-shaped normal density. The only line we have to change in the simulation code in Script 1.38 (`Simulation-Repeated.R`) is **sample <- rnorm(n,10,2)** which we have to replace with **sample <- rchisq(n,1)** according to Table 1.5. Figure 1.21 shows the simulated densities for different sample sizes and compares them to the normal distribution with the same mean $\mu = 1$ and standard deviation $\frac{s}{\sqrt{n}} = \sqrt{\frac{2}{n}}$. Note that the scales of the axes now differ between the sub-figures in order to provide a better impression of the shape of the densities. The effect of a decreasing variance works here in exactly the same way as with the normal population.

Not surprisingly, the distribution of $\bar{Y}$ is very different from a normal one in small samples like $n = 2$. With increasing sample size, the CLT works its magic and the distribution gets closer to the normal bell-shape. For $n = 10000$, the densities hardly differ at all so it's easy to imagine that they will eventually be the same as $n \to \infty$.

---

[22] In order to ensure the same scale in each graph, the axis limits were manually set instead of being chosen by R. This was done using the options **xlim=c(8.5,11.5),ylim=c(0,2)** in the **plot** command producing the estimated density.

[23] A motivated reader will already have figured out that this graph was generated by **curve(dchisq(x,1) ,0,3)**.

Figure 1.19. Density of $\bar{Y}$ with different sample sizes

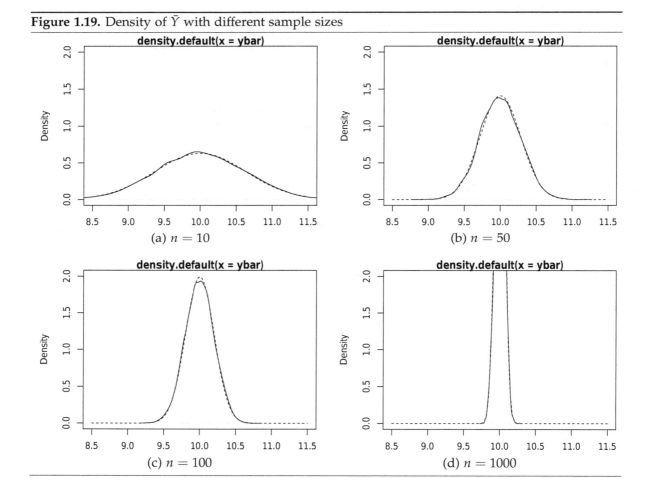

Figure 1.20. Density of the χ^2 distribution with 1 d.f.

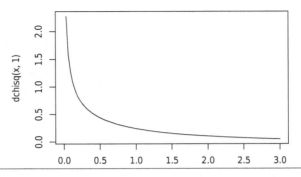

Figure 1.21. Density of $\bar{Y}$ with different sample sizes: χ^2 distribution

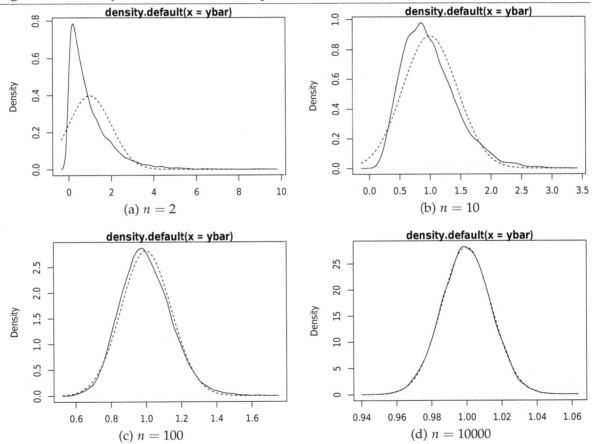

1.9.3. Simulation of Confidence Intervals and t Tests

In addition to repeatedly estimating population parameters, we can also calculate confidence intervals and conduct tests on the simulated samples. Here, we present a somewhat advanced simulation routine. The payoff of going through this material is that it might substantially improve our understanding of the workings of statistical inference.

We start from the same example as in Section 1.9.1: In the population, $Y \sim \text{Normal}(10, 4)$. We draw 10 000 samples of size $n = 100$ from this population. For each of the samples we calculate

- The 95% confidence interval and store the limits in the vectors `CIlower` and `CIupper`.
- The p value for the two-sided test of the correct null hypothesis $H_0 : \mu = 10 \Rightarrow$ vector `pvalue1`
- The p value for the two-sided test of the *incorrect* null hypothesis $H_0 : \mu = 9.5 \Rightarrow$ vector `pvalue2`

Finally, we calculate the logical vectors `reject1` and `reject2` that are **TRUE** if we reject the respective null hypothesis at $\alpha = 5\%$, i.e. if `pvalue1` or `pvalue2` are smaller than 0.05, respectively. Script 1.40 (`Simulation-Inference.R`) shows the R code for these simulations and a frequency table for the results `reject1` and `reject2`.

If theory and the implementation in R are accurate, the probability to reject a correct null hypothesis (i.e. to make a Type I error) should be equal to the chosen significance level α. In our simulation, we reject the correct hypothesis in 508=5.08% of the 10 000 samples.

The probability to reject a false hypothesis is called the power of a test. It depends on many things like the sample size and "how bad" the error of H_0 is, i.e. how far away μ_0 is from the true μ. Theory just tells us that the power is larger than α. In our simulation, the wrong null $H_0 : \mu = 9.5$ is rejected in 69.57% of the samples. The reader is strongly encouraged to tinker with the simulation code to verify the theoretical results that this power increases if μ_0 moves away from 10 and if the sample size n increases.

Figure 1.22 graphically presents the 95% CI for the first 100 simulated samples.[24] Each horizontal line represents one CI. In these first 100 samples, the true null was rejected in 3 cases. This fact means that for those three samples the CI does not cover $\mu_0 = 10$, see Wooldridge (2016, Appendix C.6) on the relationship between CI and tests. These three cases are drawn in black in the left part of the figure, whereas the others are gray.

The t-test rejects the false null hypothesis $H_0 : \mu = 9.5$ in 72 of the first 100 samples. Their CIs do not cover 9.5 and are drawn in black in the right part of Figure 1.22.

Output of Script 1.40: `Simulation-Inference.R` ──────

```
> # Set the random seed
> set.seed(123456)

> # initialize vectors to later store results:
> CIlower <- numeric(10000); CIupper <- numeric(10000)

> pvalue1 <- numeric(10000); pvalue2 <- numeric(10000)

> # repeat 10000 times:
> for(j in 1:10000) {
>    # Draw a sample
>    sample <- rnorm(100,10,2)
>    # test the (correct) null hypothesis mu=10:
>    testres1 <- t.test(sample,mu=10)
```

---

[24]For the sake of completeness, the code for generating these graphs is shown in Appendix IV, Script 1.41 (`Simulation-Inference-Figure.R`), but most readers will probably not find it important to look at it at this point.

```
>    # store CI & p value:
>    CIlower[j] <- testres1$conf.int[1]
>    CIupper[j] <- testres1$conf.int[2]
>    pvalue1[j] <- testres1$p.value
>    # test the (incorrect) null hypothesis mu=9.5 & store the p value:
>    pvalue2[j] <- t.test(sample,mu=9.5)$p.value
> }

> # Test results as logical value
> reject1<-pvalue1<=0.05;  reject2<-pvalue2<=0.05

> table(reject1)
reject1
FALSE   TRUE
 9492    508

> table(reject2)
reject2
FALSE   TRUE
 3043   6957
```

Figure 1.22. Simulation results: First 100 confidence intervals

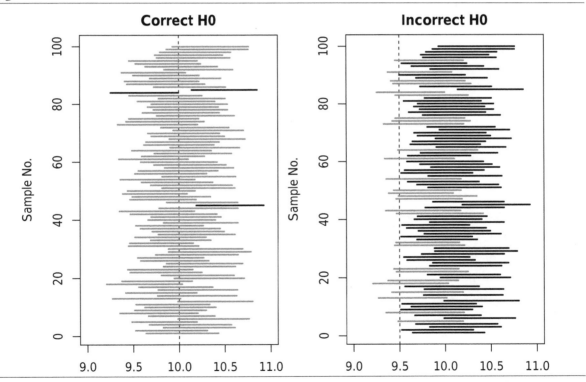

Part I.

Regression Analysis with Cross-Sectional Data

2. The Simple Regression Model

2.1. Simple OLS Regression

We are concerned with estimating the population parameters β_0 and β_1 of the simple linear regression model

$$y = \beta_0 + \beta_1 x + u \tag{2.1}$$

from a random sample of y and x. According to Wooldridge (2016, Section 2.2), the ordinary least squares (OLS) estimators are

$$\hat{\beta}_0 = \bar{y} - \hat{\beta}_1 \bar{x} \tag{2.2}$$

$$\hat{\beta}_1 = \frac{\text{Cov}(x, y)}{\text{Var}(x)}. \tag{2.3}$$

Based on these estimated parameters, the OLS regression line is

$$\hat{y} = \hat{\beta}_0 + \hat{\beta}_1 x. \tag{2.4}$$

For a given sample, we just need to calculate the four statistics $\bar{y}$, $\bar{x}$, $\text{Cov}(x, y)$, and $\text{Var}(x)$ and plug them into these equations. We already know how to make these calculations in R, see Section 1.5. Let's do it!

Wooldridge, Example 2.3: CEO Salary and Return on Equity

We are using the data set `CEOSAL1.dta` we already analyzed in Section 1.5. We consider the simple regression model

$$\text{salary} = \beta_0 + \beta_1 \text{roe} + u$$

where `salary` is the salary of a CEO in thousand dollars and `roe` is the return on investment in percent. In Script 2.1 (`Example-2-3.R`), we first load and "attach" the data set. We also calculate the four statistics we need for Equations 2.2 and 2.3 so we can reproduce the OLS formulas by hand. Finally, the parameter estimates are calculated.

So the OLS regression line is

$$\widehat{\text{salary}} = 963.1913 + 18.50119 \cdot \text{roe}$$

Output of Script 2.1: `Example-2-3.R`

```
> require(foreign)

> ceosal1<-read.dta("http://fmwww.bc.edu/ec-p/data/wooldridge/ceosal1.dta")

> attach(ceosal1)

> # ingredients to the OLS formulas
> cov(roe,salary)
[1] 1342.538

> var(roe)
[1] 72.56499

> mean(salary)
[1] 1281.12

> mean(roe)
[1] 17.18421

> # manual calculation of OLS coefficients
> ( b1hat <- cov(roe,salary)/var(roe) )
[1] 18.50119

> ( b0hat <- mean(salary) - b1hat*mean(roe) )
[1] 963.1913

> # "detach" the data frame
> detach(ceosal1)
```

While calculating OLS coefficients using this pedestrian approach is straightforward, there is a more convenient way to do it. Given the importance of OLS regression, it is not surprising that *R* has a specialized command to do the calculations automatically.

If the values of the dependent variable are stored in the vector y and those of the regressor are in the vector x, we can calculate the OLS coefficients as

```
lm( y ~ x )
```

The name of the command **lm** comes from the abbreviation of *linear model*. Its argument **y ~ x** is called a **formula** in *R* lingo. Essentially, it means that we want to model a left-hand-side variable **y** to be explained by a right-hand-side variable **x** in a linear fashion. We will discuss more general model formulae in Section 6.1.

If we have a data frame `df` with the variables `y` and `x`, instead of calling **lm(df$y ~ df$x)**, we can use the more elegant version

```
lm( y ~ x, data=df )
```

Wooldridge, Example 2.3: CEO Salary and Return on Equity (*cont'ed*)

In Script 2.2 (`Example-2-3-2.R`), we repeat the analysis we have already done manually. Besides the import of the data, there is only one line of code. The output of **lm** shows both estimated parameters: $\hat{\beta}_0$ under `(Intercept)` and $\hat{\beta}_1$ under the name of the explanatory variable `roe`. The values are the same we already calculated except for different rounding in the output.

```
────────────────── Output of Script 2.2: Example-2-3-2.R ──────────────────
> require(foreign)

> ceosal1<-read.dta("http://fmwww.bc.edu/ec-p/data/wooldridge/ceosal1.dta")

> # OLS regression
> lm( salary ~ roe, data=ceosal1 )

Call:
lm(formula = salary ~ roe, data = ceosal1)

Coefficients:
(Intercept)          roe
      963.2         18.5
```

From now on, we will rely on the built-in routine **lm** instead of doing the calculations manually. It is not only more convenient for calculating the coefficients, but also for further analyses as we will see soon.

lm returns its results in a special version of a **list**.[1] We can store these results in an object using code like

```
myolsres <- lm( y ~ x )
```

This will create an object with the name myolsres or overwrite it if it already existed. The name could of course be anything, for example yummy.chocolate.chip.cookies, but choosing telling variable names makes our life easier. This object does not only include the vector of OLS coefficients, but also information on the data source and much more we will get to know and use later on.

Given the results from a regression, plotting the regression line is straightforward. As we have already seen in Section 1.4.3, the command **abline(...)** can add a line to a graph. It is clever enough to understand our objective if we simply supply the regression result object as an argument.

Wooldridge, Example 2.3: CEO Salary and Return on Equity (*cont'ed*)

Script 2.3 (Example-2-3-3.R) demonstrates how to store the regression results in a variable CEOregres and then use it as an argument to **abline** to add the regression line to the scatter plot. It generates Figure 2.1.

```
────────────────── Script 2.3: Example-2-3-3.R ──────────────────
library(foreign)
ceosal1<-read.dta("http://fmwww.bc.edu/ec-p/data/wooldridge/ceosal1.dta")

# OLS regression
CEOregres <- lm( salary ~ roe, data=ceosal1 )

# Scatter plot (restrict y axis limits)
plot(ceosal1$roe, ceosal1$salary, ylim=c(0,4000))

# Add OLS regression line
abline(CEOregres)
```

---

[1]Remember a similar object returned by **t.test** (Section 1.7.4). General **list**s were introduced in Section 1.2.6

Figure 2.1. OLS regression line for Example 2-3

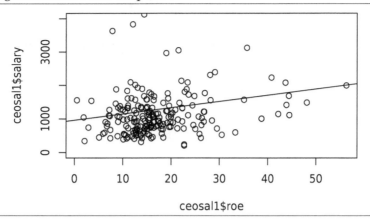

Wooldridge, Example 2.4: Wage and Education

We are using the data set `WAGE1.dta`. We are interested in studying the relation between education and wage, and our regression model is

$$\text{wage} = \beta_0 + \beta_1 \text{education} + u.$$

In Script 2.4 (`Example-2-4.R`), we analyze the data and find that the OLS regression line is

$$\widehat{\text{wage}} = -0.90 + 0.54 \cdot \text{education}$$

One additional year of education is associated with an increase of the typical wage by about 54 cents an hour.

──────── **Output of Script 2.4:** `Example-2-4.R` ────────

```
> library(foreign)

> wage1<-read.dta("http://fmwww.bc.edu/ec-p/data/wooldridge/wage1.dta")

> # OLS regression:
> lm(wage ~ educ, data=wage1)

Call:
lm(formula = wage ~ educ, data = wage1)

Coefficients:
(Intercept)          educ
    -0.9049        0.5414
```

Wooldridge, Example 2.5: Voting Outcomes and Campaign Expenditures

The data set VOTE1.dta contains information on campaign expenditures (shareA = share of campaign spending in %) and election outcomes (voteA = share of vote in %). The regression model

$$voteA = \beta_0 + \beta_1 shareA + u.$$

is estimated in Script 2.5 (Example-2-5.R). The OLS regression line turns out to be

$$\widehat{voteA} = 26.81 + 0.464 \cdot shareA.$$

The scatter plot with the regression line generated in the code is shown in Figure 2.2

─────────── **Output of Script 2.5: Example-2-5.R** ───────────

```
> require(foreign)

> vote1<-read.dta("http://fmwww.bc.edu/ec-p/data/wooldridge/vote1.dta")

> # OLS regression (parentheses for immediate output):
> ( VOTEres <- lm(voteA ~ shareA, data=vote1) )

Call:
lm(formula = voteA ~ shareA, data = vote1)

Coefficients:
(Intercept)        shareA
    26.8125        0.4638


> # scatter plot with regression line:
> plot(vote1$shareA, vote1$voteA)

> abline(VOTEres)
```

Figure 2.2. OLS regression line for Example 2-5

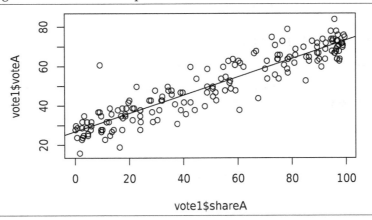

2.2. Coefficients, Fitted Values, and Residuals

The object returned by **lm** contains all relevant information on the regression. Since the object is a special kind of list, we can access the list elements just as those of a general list, see Section 1.2.6. After defining the regression results object **CEOregres** in Script 2.3 (Example-2-3-3.R), we can see the names of its components and access the first component **coefficients** with

```
> names(CEOregres)
 [1] "coefficients"  "residuals"     "effects"     "rank"
 [5] "fitted.values" "assign"        "qr"          "df.residual"
 [9] "xlevels"       "call"          "terms"       "model"
> CEOregres$coefficients
(Intercept)          roe
  963.19134     18.50119
```

Another way to interact with objects like this is through generic functions. They accept different types of arguments and, depending on the type, give appropriate results. As an example, the number of observations n is returned with **nobs(myolsres)** if the regression results are stored in the object myolsres.

Obviously, we are interested in the OLS coefficients. As seen above, they can be obtained as **myolsres$coefficients**. An alternative is the generic function **coef(myolsres)**. The coefficient vector has names attached to its elements. The name of the intercept parameter $\hat{\beta}_0$ is **"(Intercept)"** and the name of the slope parameter $\hat{\beta}_1$ is the variable name of the regressor x. In this way, we can access the parameters separately by using either the position (1 or 2) or the name as an index to the coefficients vector, review Section 1.2.4 for a general discussion of working with vectors.

Given these parameter estimates, calculating the predicted values $\hat{y}_i$ and residuals $\hat{u}_i$ for each observation $i = 1, ..., n$ is easy:

$$\hat{y}_i = \hat{\beta}_0 + \hat{\beta}_1 \cdot x_i \tag{2.5}$$

$$\hat{u}_i = y_i - \hat{y}_i \tag{2.6}$$

If the values of the dependent and independent variables are stored in the vectors y and x, respectively, we can estimate the model and do the calculations of these equations for all observations jointly using the code

```
myolsres <- lm( y ~ x )
bhat <- coef(myolsres)
yhat <- bhat["(Intercept)"] + bhat["x"] * x
uhat <- y - yhat
```

We can also use a more black-box approach which will give exactly the same results using the generic functions **fitted** and **resid** on the regression results object:

```
myolsres <- lm( y ~ x )
bhat <- coef(myolsres)
yhat <- fitted(myolsres)
uhat <- resid(myolsres)
```

Wooldridge, Example 2.6: CEO Salary and Return on Equity

We extend the regression example on the return on equity of a firm and the salary of its CEO in Script 2.6 (Example-2-6.R). After the OLS regression, we calculate fitted values and residuals. A table similar to Wooldridge (2016, Table 2.2) is generated displaying the values for the first 15 observations.

```
─────────── Output of Script 2.6: Example-2-6.R ───────────

> require(foreign)

> ceosal1<-read.dta("http://fmwww.bc.edu/ec-p/data/wooldridge/ceosal1.dta")

> # extract variables as vectors:
> sal <- ceosal1$salary

> roe <- ceosal1$roe

> # regression with vectors:
> CEOregres <- lm( sal ~ roe  )

> # obtain predicted values and residuals
> sal.hat <- fitted(CEOregres)

> u.hat <- resid(CEOregres)

> # Wooldridge, Table 2.2:
> cbind(roe, sal, sal.hat, u.hat)[1:15,]
    roe  sal  sal.hat        u.hat
1   14.1 1095 1224.058 -129.058071
2   10.9 1001 1164.854 -163.854261
3   23.5 1122 1397.969 -275.969216
4    5.9  578 1072.348 -494.348338
5   13.8 1368 1218.508  149.492288
6   20.0 1145 1333.215 -188.215063
7   16.4 1078 1266.611 -188.610785
8   16.3 1094 1264.761 -170.760660
9   10.5 1237 1157.454   79.546207
10  26.3  833 1449.773 -616.772523
11  25.9  567 1442.372 -875.372056
12  26.8  933 1459.023 -526.023116
13  14.8 1339 1237.009  101.991102
14  22.3  937 1375.768 -438.767778
15  56.3 2011 2004.808    6.191886
```

Wooldridge (2016, Section 2.3) presents and discusses three properties of OLS statistics which we will confirm for an example.

$$\sum_{i=1}^{n} \hat{u}_i = 0 \quad \Rightarrow \quad \bar{\hat{u}}_i = 0 \tag{2.7}$$

$$\sum_{i=1}^{n} x_i \hat{u}_i = 0 \quad \Rightarrow \quad \text{Cov}(x_i, \hat{u}_i) = 0 \tag{2.8}$$

$$\bar{y} = \hat{\beta}_0 + \hat{\beta}_1 \cdot \bar{x} \tag{2.9}$$

Wooldridge, Example 2.7: Wage and Education

We already know the regression results when we regress wage on education from Example 2.4. In Script 2.7 (Example-2-7.R), we calculate fitted values and residuals to confirm the three properties from Equations 2.7 through 2.9. Note that *R* as many statistics programs does all calculations in "double precision" implying that it is accurate for at least 15 significant digits. The output that checks the first property shows that the average residual is -2.334967e-16 which in scientific notation means $-2.334967 \cdot 10^{-16} = -0.0000000000000002334967$. The reason it is not exactly equal to 0 is a rounding error in the 16th digit. The same holds for the second property: The correlation between the regressor and the residual is zero except for minimal rounding error. The third property is also confirmed: If we plug the average value of the regressor into the regression line formula, we get the average value of the dependent variable.

─────────── **Output of Script 2.7:** `Example-2-7.R` ───────────

```
> library(foreign)

> wage1 <- read.dta("http://fmwww.bc.edu/ec-p/data/wooldridge/wage1.dta")

> WAGEregres <- lm(wage ~ educ, data=wage1)

> # obtain coefficients, predicted values and residuals
> b.hat <- coef(WAGEregres)

> wage.hat <- fitted(WAGEregres)

> u.hat <- resid(WAGEregres)

> # Confirm property (1):
> mean(u.hat)
[1] -1.19498e-16

> # Confirm property (2):
> cor(wage1$educ , u.hat)
[1] 4.349557e-16

> # Confirm property (3):
> mean(wage1$wage)
[1] 5.896103

> b.hat[1] + b.hat[2] * mean(wage1$educ)
(Intercept)
   5.896103
```

2.3. Goodness of Fit

The total sum of squares (SST), explained sum of squares (SSE) and residual sum of squares (SSR) can be written as

$$\text{SST} = \sum_{i=1}^{n}(y_i - \overline{y})^2 = (n-1)\cdot\text{Var}(y) \tag{2.10}$$

$$\text{SSE} = \sum_{i=1}^{n}(\hat{y}_i - \overline{y})^2 = (n-1)\cdot\text{Var}(\hat{y}) \tag{2.11}$$

$$\text{SSR} = \sum_{i=1}^{n}(\hat{u}_i - 0)^2 = (n-1)\cdot\text{Var}(\hat{u}) \tag{2.12}$$

where $\text{Var}(x)$ is the sample variance $\frac{1}{n-1}\sum_{i=1}^{n}(x_i - \overline{x})^2$

Wooldridge (2016, Equation 2.38) defines the coefficient of determination in terms of these terms. Because $(n-1)$ cancels out, it can be equivalently written as

$$R^2 = \frac{\text{Var}(\hat{y})}{\text{Var}(y)} = 1 - \frac{\text{Var}(\hat{u})}{\text{Var}(y)} \tag{2.13}$$

Wooldridge, Example 2.8: CEO Salary and Return on Equity

In the regression already studied in Example 2.6, the coefficient of determination is 0.0132. This is calculated in the two ways of Equation 2.13 in Script 2.8 (Example-2-8.R). In addition, it is calculated as the squared correlation coefficient of y and $\hat{y}$. Not surprisingly, all versions to do these calculations produce to the same result.

──────── Output of Script 2.8: `Example-2-8.R` ────────

```
> library(foreign)

> ceosal1<-read.dta("http://fmwww.bc.edu/ec-p/data/wooldridge/ceosal1.dta")

> CEOregres <- lm( salary ~ roe, data=ceosal1 )

> # Calculate predicted values & residuals:
> sal.hat <- fitted(CEOregres)

> u.hat <- resid(CEOregres)

> # Calculate R^2 in three different ways:
> sal <- ceosal1$salary

> var(sal.hat) / var(sal)
[1] 0.01318862

> 1 - var(u.hat) / var(sal)
[1] 0.01318862

> cor(sal, sal.hat)^2
[1] 0.01318862
```

We have already come across the command **summary** as a generic function that produces appropriate summaries for very different types of objects. We can also use it to get many interesting results for a regression. They are introduced one by one in the next sections. If the variable rres contains a result from a regression, **summary(rres)** will display

- Some statistics for the residual like the extreme values and the median
- A coefficient table. So far, we only discussed the OLS coefficients shown in the first column. The next columns will be introduced below.
- Some more information of which only R^2 is of interest to us so far. It is reported as `Multiple R-squared`.

Wooldridge, Example 2.9: Voting Outcomes and Campaign Expenditures

We already know the OLS coefficients to be $\hat{\beta}_0 = 26.8125$ and $\hat{\beta}_1 = 0.4638$ in the voting example (Script 2.5 (`Example-2-5.R`)). These values are again found in the output of the regression summary in Script 2.9 (`Example-2-9.R`). The coefficient of determination is reported as `Multiple R-squared` to be $R^2 = 0.8561$. Reassuringly, we get the same numbers as with the pedestrian calculations.

─────────────── Output of Script 2.9: `Example-2-9.R` ───────────────

```
> library(foreign)

> vote1 <- read.dta("http://fmwww.bc.edu/ec-p/data/wooldridge/vote1.dta")

> VOTEres <- lm(voteA ~ shareA, data=vote1)

> # Summary of the regression results
> summary(VOTEres)

Call:
lm(formula = voteA ~ shareA, data = vote1)

Residuals:
     Min       1Q   Median       3Q      Max
-16.8924  -4.0649  -0.1697   3.4972  29.9759

Coefficients:
            Estimate Std. Error t value Pr(>|t|)
(Intercept) 26.81254    0.88719   30.22   <2e-16 ***
shareA       0.46382    0.01454   31.90   <2e-16 ***
---
Signif. codes:  0 '***' 0.001 '**' 0.01 '*' 0.05 '.' 0.1 ' ' 1

Residual standard error: 6.385 on 171 degrees of freedom
Multiple R-squared:  0.8561,        Adjusted R-squared:  0.8553
F-statistic:  1018 on 1 and 171 DF,  p-value: < 2.2e-16


> # Calculate R^2 manually:
> var( fitted(VOTEres) ) / var( vote1$voteA )
[1] 0.8561459
```

2.4. Nonlinearities

For the estimation of logarithmic or semi-logarithmic models, the respective formula can be directly entered into the specification of `lm(...)` as demonstrated in Examples 2.10 and 2.11. For the interpretation as percentage effects and elasticities, see Wooldridge (2016, Section 2.4).

Wooldridge, Example 2.10: Wage and Education

Compared to Example 2.7, we simply change the command for the estimation to account for a logarithmic specification as shown in Script 2.10 (`Example-2-10.R`). The semi-logarithmic specification implies that wages are higher by about 8.3% for individuals with an additional year of education.

―――――――――― Output of Script 2.10: `Example-2-10.R` ――――――――――

```
> require(foreign)

> wage1 <- read.dta("http://fmwww.bc.edu/ec-p/data/wooldridge/wage1.dta")

> # Estimate log-level model
> lm( log(wage) ~ educ, data=wage1 )

Call:
lm(formula = log(wage) ~ educ, data = wage1)

Coefficients:
(Intercept)          educ
    0.58377       0.08274
```

Wooldridge, Example 2.11: CEO Salary and Firm Sales

We study the relationship between the sales of a firm and the salary of its CEO using a log-log specification. The results are shown in Script 2.11 (`Example-2-11.R`). If the sales increase by 1%, the salary of the CEO tends to increase by 0.257%.

―――――――――― Output of Script 2.11: `Example-2-11.R` ――――――――――

```
> require(foreign)

> ceosal1<-read.dta("http://fmwww.bc.edu/ec-p/data/wooldridge/ceosal1.dta")

> # Estimate log-log model
> lm( log(salary) ~ log(sales), data=ceosal1 )

Call:
lm(formula = log(salary) ~ log(sales), data = ceosal1)

Coefficients:
(Intercept)    log(sales)
     4.8220        0.2567
```

2.5. Regression through the Origin and Regression on a Constant

Wooldridge (2016, Section 2.6) discusses models without an intercept. This implies that the regression line is forced to go through the origin. In *R*, we can suppress the constant which is otherwise implicitly added to a formula by specifying

```
lm(y ~ 0 + x)
```

instead of `lm(y ~ x)`. The result is a model which only has a slope parameter.

Another topic discussed in this section is a linear regression model without a slope parameter, i.e. with a constant only. In this case, the estimated constant will be the sample average of the dependent variable. This can be implemented in *R* using the code

```
lm(y ~ 1)
```

Both special kinds of regressions are implemented in Script 2.12 (SLR-Origin-Const.R) for the example of the CEO salary and ROE we already analyzed in Example 2.8 and others. The resulting regression lines are plotted in Figure 2.3 which was generated using the last lines of code shown in the output.

─────────── **Output of Script 2.12:** SLR-Origin-Const.R ───────────

```
> library(foreign)

> ceosal1<-read.dta("http://fmwww.bc.edu/ec-p/data/wooldridge/ceosal1.dta")

> # Usual OLS regression:
> (reg1 <- lm( salary ~ roe, data=ceosal1))

Call:
lm(formula = salary ~ roe, data = ceosal1)

Coefficients:
(Intercept)           roe
      963.2          18.5


> # Regression without intercept (through origin):
> (reg2 <- lm( salary ~ 0 + roe, data=ceosal1))

Call:
lm(formula = salary ~ 0 + roe, data = ceosal1)

Coefficients:
  roe
63.54
```

```
> # Regression without slope (on a constant):
> (reg3 <- lm( salary ~ 1 , data=ceosal1))

Call:
lm(formula = salary ~ 1, data = ceosal1)

Coefficients:
(Intercept)
       1281


> # average y:
> mean(ceosal1$salary)
[1] 1281.12

> # Scatter Plot with all 3 regression lines
> plot(ceosal1$roe, ceosal1$salary, ylim=c(0,4000))

> abline(reg1, lwd=2, lty=1)

> abline(reg2, lwd=2, lty=2)

> abline(reg3, lwd=2, lty=3)

> legend("topleft",c("full","through origin","const only"),lwd=2,lty=1:3)
```

Figure 2.3. Regression through the Origin and on a Constant

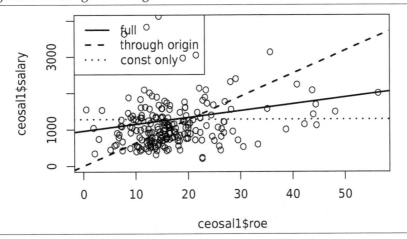

2.6. Expected Values, Variances, and Standard Errors

Wooldridge (2016) discusses the role of four assumptions under which the OLS parameter estimators have desirable properties. In short form they are

- **SLR.1**: Linear population regression function: $y = \beta_0 + \beta_1 x + u$
- **SLR.2**: Random sampling of x and y from the population
- **SLR.3**: Variation in the sample values $x_1, ..., x_n$
- **SLR.4**: Zero conditional mean: $\mathrm{E}(u|x) = 0$
- **SLR.5**: Homoscedasticity: $\mathrm{Var}(u|x) = \sigma^2$

Based on those, Wooldridge (2016) shows in Section 2.5:

- **Theorem 2.1**: Under **SLR.1** – **SLR.4**, OLS parameter estimators are unbiased.
- **Theorem 2.2**: Under **SLR.1** – **SLR.5**, OLS parameter estimators have a specific sampling variance.

Because the formulas for the sampling variance involve the variance of the error term, we also have to estimate it using the unbiased estimator

$$\hat{\sigma}^2 = \frac{1}{n-2} \cdot \sum_{i=1}^{n} \hat{u}_i^2 = \frac{n-1}{n-2} \cdot \mathrm{Var}(\hat{u}_i), \tag{2.14}$$

where $Var(\hat{u}_i) = \frac{1}{n-1} \cdot \sum_{i=1}^{n} \hat{u}_i^2$ is the usual sample variance. We have to use the degrees-of-freedom adjustment to account for the fact that we estimated the two parameters $\hat{\beta}_0$ and $\hat{\beta}_1$ for constructing the residuals. Its square root $\hat{\sigma} = \sqrt{\hat{\sigma}^2}$ is called **standard error of the regression (SER)** by Wooldridge (2016) and **residual standard error** by R.

The **standard errors (SE) of the estimators** are

$$\mathrm{se}(\hat{\beta}_0) = \sqrt{\frac{\hat{\sigma}^2 \overline{x^2}}{\sum_{i=1}^{n}(x - \overline{x})^2}} = \frac{1}{\sqrt{n-1}} \cdot \frac{\hat{\sigma}}{\mathrm{sd}(x)} \cdot \sqrt{\overline{x^2}} \tag{2.15}$$

$$\mathrm{se}(\hat{\beta}_1) = \sqrt{\frac{\sigma^2}{\sum_{i=1}^{n}(x - \overline{x})^2}} = \frac{1}{\sqrt{n-1}} \cdot \frac{\hat{\sigma}}{\mathrm{sd}(x)} \tag{2.16}$$

where $\mathrm{sd}(x)$ is the sample standard deviation $\sqrt{\frac{1}{n-1} \cdot \sum_{i=1}^{n}(x_i - \overline{x})^2}$.

In R, we can obviously do the calculations of Equations 2.14 through 2.16 explicitly. But the output of the **summary** command for linear regression results which we already discovered in Section 2.3 already contains the results. We use the following example to calculate the results in both ways to open the black box of the canned routine and convince ourselves that from now on we can rely on it.

Wooldridge, Example 2.12: Student Math Performance and the School Lunch Program

Using the data set `MEAP93.dta`, we regress a math performance score of schools on the share of students eligible for a federally funded lunch program. Wooldridge (2016) uses this example to demonstrate the importance of assumption SLR.4 and warns us against interpreting the regression results in a causal way. Here, we merely use the example to demonstrate the calculation of standard errors.

Script 2.13 (`Example-2-12.R`) first calculates the SER manually using the fact that the residuals $\hat{u}$ are available as **resid(results)**, see Section 2.2. Then, the SE of the parameters are calculated according to Equations 2.15 and 2.16, where the regressor is addressed as the variable in the data frame `df$lnchprg`.

Finally, we see the output of the **summary** command. The SE of the parameters are reported in the second column of the regression table, next to the parameter estimates. We will look at the other columns in chapter 4. The SER is reported as `Residual standard error` below the table. All three values are exactly the same as the manual results.

──────── **Output of Script 2.13: `Example-2-12.R`** ────────

```
> library(foreign)

> meap93<-read.dta("http://fmwww.bc.edu/ec-p/data/wooldridge/meap93.dta")

> # Estimate the model and save the results as "results"
> results <- lm(math10 ~ lnchprg, data=meap93)

> # Number of obs.
> ( n <- nobs(results) )
[1] 408

> # SER:
> (SER <- sd(resid(results)) * sqrt((n-1)/(n-2)) )
[1] 9.565938

> # SE of b0hat & b1hat, respectively:
> SER / sd(meap93$lnchprg) / sqrt(n-1) * sqrt(mean(meap93$lnchprg^2))
[1] 0.9975824

> SER / sd(meap93$lnchprg) / sqrt(n-1)
[1] 0.03483933

> # Automatic calculations:
> summary(results)

Call:
lm(formula = math10 ~ lnchprg, data = meap93)

Residuals:
    Min      1Q  Median      3Q     Max
-24.386  -5.979  -1.207   4.865  45.845

Coefficients:
            Estimate Std. Error t value Pr(>|t|)
(Intercept) 32.14271    0.99758  32.221   <2e-16 ***
lnchprg     -0.31886    0.03484  -9.152   <2e-16 ***
---
Signif. codes:  0 '***' 0.001 '**' 0.01 '*' 0.05 '.' 0.1 ' ' 1

Residual standard error: 9.566 on 406 degrees of freedom
Multiple R-squared:  0.171,      Adjusted R-squared:  0.169
F-statistic: 83.77 on 1 and 406 DF,  p-value: < 2.2e-16
```

2.7. Monte Carlo Simulations

In this section, we use Monte Carlo simulation experiments to revisit many of the topics covered in this chapter. It can be skipped but can help quite a bit to grasp the concepts of estimators, estimates, unbiasedness, the sampling variance of the estimators, and the consequences of violated assumptions. Remember that the concept of Monte Carlo simulations was introduced in Section 1.9.

2.7.1. One sample

In Section 1.9, we used simulation experiments to analyze the features of a simple mean estimator. We also discussed the sampling from a given distribution, the random seed and simple examples. We can use exactly the same strategy to analyze OLS parameter estimators.

Script 2.14 (`SLR-Sim-Sample.R`) shows how to draw a sample which is consistent with Assumptions SLR.1 through SLR.5. We simulate a sample of size $n = 1000$ with population parameters $\beta_0 = 1$ and $\beta_1 = 0.5$. We set the standard deviation of the error term u to $\sigma = 2$. Obviously, these parameters can be freely chosen and every reader is strongly encouraged to play around.

─────────── **Output of Script 2.14:** `SLR-Sim-Sample.R` ───────────

```
> # Set the random seed
> set.seed(1234567)

> # set sample size
> n<-1000

> # set true parameters: betas and sd of u
> b0<-1; b1<-0.5; su<-2

> # Draw a sample of size n:
> x <- rnorm(n,4,1)

> u <- rnorm(n,0,su)

> y <- b0 + b1*x + u

> # estimate parameters by OLS
> (olsres <- lm(y~x))

Call:
lm(formula = y ~ x)

Coefficients:
(Intercept)            x
     1.2092        0.4384


> # features of the sample for the variance formula:
> mean(x^2)
[1] 16.96644

> sum((x-mean(x))^2)
[1] 990.4104

> # Graph
> plot(x, y, col="gray", xlim=c(0,8) )
```

```
> abline(b0,b1,lwd=2)

> abline(olsres,col="gray",lwd=2)

> legend("topleft",c("pop. regr. fct.","OLS regr. fct."),
>                                    lwd=2,col=c("black","gray"))
```

Then a random sample of x and y is drawn in three steps:
- A sample of regressors x is drawn from an arbitrary distribution. The only thing we have to make sure to stay consistent with Assumption SLR.3 is that its variance is strictly positive. We choose a normal distribution with mean 4 and a standard deviation of 1.
- A sample of error terms u is drawn according to Assumptions SLR.4 and SLR.5: It has a mean of zero, and both the mean and the variance are unrelated to x. We simply choose a normal distribution with mean 0 and standard deviation $\sigma = 2$ for all 1000 observations independent of x. In Sections 2.7.3 and 2.7.4 we will adjust this to simulate the effects of a violation of these assumptions.
- Finally, we generate the dependent variable y according to the population regression function specified in Assumption SLR.1.

In an empirical project, we only observe x and y and not the realizations of the error term u. In the simulation, we "forget" them and the fact that we know the population parameters and estimate them from our sample using OLS. As motivated in Section 1.9, this will help us to study the behavior of the estimator in a sample like ours.

For our particular sample, the OLS parameter estimates are $\hat{\beta}_0 = 1.2092$ and $\hat{\beta}_1 = 0.4384$. The result of the graph generated in the last four lines of Script 2.14 (SLR-Sim-Sample.R) is shown in Figure 2.4. It shows the population regression function with intercept $\beta_0 = 1$ and slope $\beta_1 = 0.5$. It also shows the scatter plot of the sample drawn from this population. This sample led to our OLS regression line with intercept $\hat{\beta}_0 = 1.2092$ and slope $\hat{\beta}_1 = 0.4384$ shown in gray.

Figure 2.4. Simulated Sample and OLS Regression Line

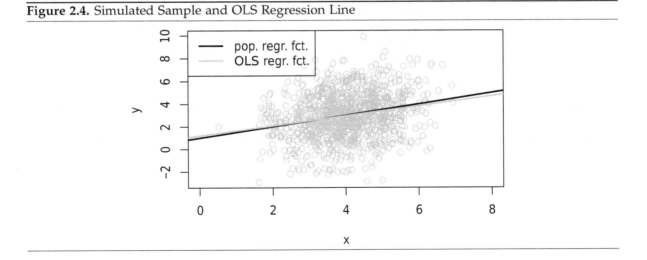

Since the SLR assumptions hold in our exercise, Theorems 2.1 and 2.2 of Wooldridge (2016) should apply. Theorem 2.1 implies for our model that the estimators are unbiased, i.e.

$$E(\hat{\beta}_0) = \beta_0 = 1 \qquad\qquad\qquad E(\hat{\beta}_1) = \beta_1 = 0.5$$

The estimates obtained from our sample are relatively close to their population values. Obviously, we can never expect to hit the population parameter exactly. If we change the random seed by specifying a different number in the first line of code of Script 2.14 (`SLR-Sim-Sample.R`), we get a different sample and different parameter estimates.

Theorem 2.2 of Wooldridge (2016) states the sampling variance of the estimators conditional on the sample values $\{x_1, \ldots, x_n\}$. It involves the the average squared value $\overline{x^2} = 16.966$ and the sum of squares $\sum_{i-1}^{n}(x - \overline{x})^2 = 990.41$ which we also know from the R output:

$$\text{Var}(\hat{\beta}_0) = \frac{\sigma^2 \overline{x^2}}{\sum_{i=1}^{n}(x - \overline{x})^2} = \frac{4 \cdot 16.966}{990.41} = 0.0685$$

$$\text{Var}(\hat{\beta}_1) = \frac{\sigma^2}{\sum_{i=1}^{n}(x - \overline{x})^2} = \frac{4}{990.41} = 0.0040$$

If Wooldridge (2016) is right, the standard error of $\hat{\beta}_1$ is $\sqrt{0.004} = 0.063$. So getting an estimate of $\hat{\beta}_1 = 0.438$ for one sample doesn't seem unreasonable given $\beta_1 = 0.5$.

2.7.2. Many Samples

Since the expected values and variances of our estimators are defined over separate random samples from the same population, it makes sense for us to repeat our simulation exercise over many simulated samples. Just as motivated in Section 1.9, the distribution of OLS parameter estimates across these samples will correspond to the sampling distribution of the estimators.

Script 2.16 (`SLR-Sim-Model-Condx.R`) implements this with the same **for** loop we introduced in Section 1.8.2 and already used for basic Monte Carlo simulations in Section 1.9.1. Remember that R enthusiasts might choose a different technique but for us, this implementation has the big advantage that it is very transparent. We analyze $r = 10\,000$ samples.

Note that we use the same values for x in all samples since we draw them outside of the loop. We do this to simulate the exact setup of Theorem 2.2 which reports the sampling variances *conditional* on x. In a more realistic setup, we would sample x along with y. The conceptual difference is subtle and the results hardly differ in reasonably large samples. We will come back to these issues in Chapter 5.[2]

For each sample, we estimate our parameters and store them in the respective position $j = 1, \ldots, r$ of the vectors `b0hat` and `b1hat`.

---

[2]In Script 2.15 (`SLR-Sim-Model.R`) shown on page 297, we implement the joint sampling from x and y. The results are essentially the same.

Script 2.16: `SLR-Sim-Model-Condx.R`

```
# Set the random seed
set.seed(1234567)

# set sample size and number of simulations
n<-1000; r<-10000

# set true parameters: betas and sd of u
b0<-1; b1<-0.5; su<-2

# initialize b0hat and b1hat to store results later:
b0hat <- numeric(r)
b1hat <- numeric(r)

# Draw a sample of x, fixed over replications:
x <- rnorm(n,4,1)

# repeat r times:
for(j in 1:r) {
  # Draw a sample of y:
  u <- rnorm(n,0,su)
  y <- b0 + b1*x + u

  # estimate parameters by OLS and store them in the vectors
  bhat <- coefficients( lm(y~x) )
  b0hat[j] <- bhat["(Intercept)"]
  b1hat[j] <- bhat["x"]
}
```

Script 2.17 (`SLR-Sim-Results.R`) gives descriptive statistics of the $r = 10,000$ estimates we got from our simulation exercise. Wooldridge (2016, Theorem 2.1) claims that the OLS estimators are unbiased, so we should expect to get estimates which are very close to the respective population parameters. This is clearly confirmed. The average value of $\hat{\beta}_0$ is very close to $\beta_0 = 1$ and the average value of $\hat{\beta}_1$ is very close to $\beta_1 = 0.5$.

The simulated sampling variances are $\widetilde{\text{Var}}(\hat{\beta}_0) = 0.069$ and $\widetilde{\text{Var}}(\hat{\beta}_1) = 0.004$. Also these values are very close to the ones we expected from Theorem 2.2. The last lines of code produce Figure 2.5. It shows the OLS regression lines for the first 20 simulated samples together with the population regression function.

Output of Script 2.17: `SLR-Sim-Results.R`

```
> # MC estimate of the expected values:
> mean(b0hat)
[1] 0.9985388

> mean(b1hat)
[1] 0.5000466

> # MC estimate of the variances:
> var(b0hat)
[1] 0.0690833

> var(b1hat)
[1] 0.004069063

> # Initialize empty plot
> plot( NULL, xlim=c(0,8), ylim=c(0,6), xlab="x", ylab="y")

> # add OLS regression lines
> for (j in 1:10) abline(b0hat[j],b1hat[j],col="gray")

> # add population regression line
> abline(b0,b1,lwd=2)

> # add legend
> legend("topleft",c("Population","OLS regressions"),
>                          lwd=c(2,1),col=c("black","gray"))
```

Figure 2.5. Population and Simulated OLS Regression Lines

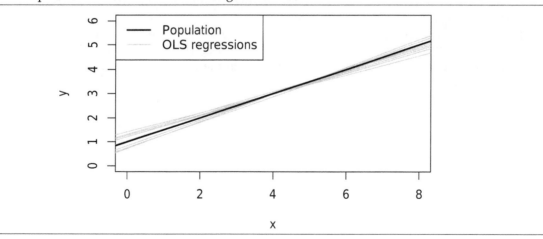

2.7.3. Violation of SLR.4

We will come back to a more systematic discussion of the consequences of violating the SLR assumptions below. At this point, we can already simulate the effects. In order to implement a violation of SLR.4 (zero conditional mean), consider a case where in the population u is not mean independent of x. A simple example is

$$\mathrm{E}(u|x) = \frac{x-4}{5}$$

What happens to our OLS estimator? Script 2.18 (`SLR-Sim-ViolSLR4.R`) implements a simulation of this model and is listed in the appendix (p. 298). The only line of code we changed compared to Script 2.16 (`SLR-Sim-Model-Condx.R`) is the sampling of u which now reads

```
u <- rnorm(n, (x-4)/5, su)
```

The simulation results are presented in the output of Script 2.19 (`SLR-Sim-Results-ViolSLR4.R`). Obviously, the OLS coefficients are now biased: The average estimates are far from the population parameters $\beta_0 = 1$ and $\beta_1 = 0.5$. This confirms that Assumption SLR.4 is required to hold for the unbiasedness shown in Theorem 2.1.

```
────────── Output of Script 2.19: SLR-Sim-Results-ViolSLR4.R ──────────

> # MC estimate of the expected values:
> mean(b0hat)
[1] 0.1985388

> mean(b1hat)
[1] 0.7000466

> # MC estimate of the variances:
> var(b0hat)
[1] 0.0690833

> var(b1hat)
[1] 0.004069063
```

2.7.4. Violation of SLR.5

Theorem 2.1 (unbiasdness) does not require Assumption SLR.5 (homoscedasticity), but Theorem 2.2 (sampling variance) does. As an example for a violation consider the population specification

$$\mathrm{Var}(u_i|x_i) = \frac{4}{e^{4.5}} \cdot e^{x_i},$$

so SLR.5 is clearly violated since the variance depends on x. Assumption SLR.4 holds. The factor in front ensures that the unconditional variance of $\mathrm{Var}(u) = 4$. Based on this unconditional variance only, the sampling variance should not change compared to the results above and we would still expect $\mathrm{Var}(\hat{\beta}_0) = 0.0685$ and $\mathrm{Var}(\hat{\beta}_1) = 0.0040$. But since Assumption SLR.5 is violated, Theorem 2.2 is not applicable.

Script 2.20 (`SLR-Sim-ViolSLR5.R`) implements a simulation of this model and is listed in the appendix (p. 298). Here, we only had to change the line of code for the sampling of u to

```
varu <- 4/exp(4.5) * exp(x)
u <- rnorm(n, 0, sqrt(varu) )
```

Script 2.21 (`SLR-Sim-Results-ViolSLR5.R`) demonstrates two effects: The unbiasedness provided by Theorem 2.1 is unaffected, but the formula for sampling variance provided by Theorem 2.2 is incorrect.

————— Output of Script 2.21: `SLR-Sim-Results-ViolSLR5.R` —————

```
> # MC estimate of the expected values:
> mean(b0hat)
[1] 1.0019

> mean(b1hat)
[1] 0.4992376

> # MC estimate of the variances:
> var(b0hat)
[1] 0.08967037

> var(b1hat)
[1] 0.007264373
```

3. Multiple Regression Analysis: Estimation

Running a multiple regression in R is as straightforward as running a simple regression using the **lm** command. Section 3.1 shows how it is done. Section 3.2 opens the black box and replicates the main calculations using matrix algebra. This is not required for the remaining chapters, so it can be skipped by readers who prefer to keep black boxes closed.

Section 3.3 should not be skipped since it dicusses the interpretation of regressions results and the prevalent omitted variables problems. Finally, Section 3.4 covers standard errors and multicollinearity for multiple regression.

3.1. Multiple Regression in Practice

Consider the population regression model

$$y = \beta_0 + \beta_1 x_1 + \beta_2 x_2 + \beta_3 x_3 + \cdots + \beta_k x_k + u \tag{3.1}$$

and suppose the variables y, x1, x2, x3, ... contain the respective data of our sample. We estimate the model parameters by OLS using the command

```
lm(y ~ x1+x2+x3+...)
```

The tilde ~ again separates the dependent variable from the regressors which are now separated using a + sign. We can add options as before. For example if the data are contained in a data frame df, we should add the option "data=df". The constant is again automatically added unless it is explicitly suppressed using **lm(y ~ 0+x1+x2+x3+...)**.

We are already familiar with the workings of **lm**: The command creates an object which contains all relevant information. A simple call like the one shown above will only display the parameter estimates. We can store the estimation results in a variable myres using the code **myres <- lm(...)** and then use this variable for further analyses. For a typical regression output including a coefficient table, call **summary(myres)**. Of course if this is all we want, we can leave out storing the result and simply call **summary(lm(...))** in one step. Further analyses involving residuals, fitted values and the like can be used exactly as presented in Chapter 2.

The output of **summary** includes parameter estimates, standard errors according to Theorem 3.2 of Wooldridge (2016), the coefficient of determination R^2, and many more useful results we cannot interpret yet before we have worked through Chapter 4.

Wooldridge, Example 3.1: Determinants of College GPA

This example from Wooldridge (2016) relates the college GPA (colGPA) to the high school GPA (hsGPA) and achievement test score (ACT) for a sample of 141 students. The commands and results can be found in Script 3.1 (Example-3-1.R). The OLS regression function is

$$\widehat{\text{colGPA}} = 1.286 + 0.453 \cdot \text{hsGPA} + 0.0094 \cdot \text{ACT}.$$

―――――――――― **Output of Script 3.1: `Example-3-1.R`** ――――――――――

```
> library(foreign)

> gpa1 <- read.dta("http://fmwww.bc.edu/ec-p/data/wooldridge/gpa1.dta")

> # Just obtain parameter estimates:
> lm(colGPA ~ hsGPA+ACT, data=gpa1)

Call:
lm(formula = colGPA ~ hsGPA + ACT, data = gpa1)

Coefficients:
(Intercept)          hsGPA            ACT
   1.286328       0.453456       0.009426


> # Store results under "GPAres" and display full table:
> GPAres <- lm(colGPA ~ hsGPA+ACT, data=gpa1)

> summary(GPAres)

Call:
lm(formula = colGPA ~ hsGPA + ACT, data = gpa1)

Residuals:
     Min        1Q    Median        3Q       Max
-0.85442  -0.24666  -0.02614   0.28127   0.85357

Coefficients:
            Estimate Std. Error t value Pr(>|t|)
(Intercept) 1.286328   0.340822   3.774 0.000238 ***
hsGPA       0.453456   0.095813   4.733 5.42e-06 ***
ACT         0.009426   0.010777   0.875 0.383297
---
Signif. codes:  0 '***' 0.001 '**' 0.01 '*' 0.05 '.' 0.1 ' ' 1

Residual standard error: 0.3403 on 138 degrees of freedom
Multiple R-squared:  0.1764,       Adjusted R-squared:  0.1645
F-statistic: 14.78 on 2 and 138 DF,  p-value: 1.526e-06
```

Wooldridge, Example 3.4: Determinants of College GPA

For the regression run in Example 3.1, the output of Script 3.1 (`Example-3-1.R`) reports $R^2 = 0.1764$, so about 17.6% of the variance in college GPA are explained by the two regressors.

Examples 3.2, 3.3, 3.5, 3.6: Further multiple regression examples

In order to get a feeling of the methods and results, we present the analyses including the full regression tables of the mentioned Examples from Wooldridge (2016) in Scripts 3.2 (`Example-3-2.R`) through 3.5 (`Example-3-6.R`). See Wooldridge (2016) for descriptions of the data sets and variables and for comments on the results.

—————— **Output of Script 3.2: `Example-3-2.R`** ——————

```
> library(foreign)

> wage1 <- read.dta("http://fmwww.bc.edu/ec-p/data/wooldridge/wage1.dta")

> # OLS regression:
> summary( lm(log(wage) ~ educ+exper+tenure, data=wage1) )

Call:
lm(formula = log(wage) ~ educ + exper + tenure, data = wage1)

Residuals:
     Min       1Q   Median       3Q      Max
-2.05802 -0.29645 -0.03265  0.28788  1.42809

Coefficients:
             Estimate Std. Error t value Pr(>|t|)
(Intercept) 0.284360   0.104190    2.729  0.00656 **
educ        0.092029   0.007330   12.555  < 2e-16 ***
exper       0.004121   0.001723    2.391  0.01714 *
tenure      0.022067   0.003094    7.133 3.29e-12 ***
---
Signif. codes:  0 '***' 0.001 '**' 0.01 '*' 0.05 '.' 0.1 ' ' 1

Residual standard error: 0.4409 on 522 degrees of freedom
Multiple R-squared:  0.316,      Adjusted R-squared:  0.3121
F-statistic: 80.39 on 3 and 522 DF,  p-value: < 2.2e-16
```

—————— **Output of Script 3.3: `Example-3-3.R`** ——————

```
> library(foreign)

> d401k <- read.dta("http://fmwww.bc.edu/ec-p/data/wooldridge/401k.dta")

> # OLS regression:
> summary( lm(prate ~ mrate+age, data=d401k) )

Call:
lm(formula = prate ~ mrate + age, data = d401k)

Residuals:
    Min      1Q  Median      3Q     Max
-81.162  -8.067   4.787  12.474  18.256

Coefficients:
            Estimate Std. Error t value Pr(>|t|)
(Intercept)  80.1191     0.7790  102.85  < 2e-16 ***
mrate         5.5213     0.5259   10.50  < 2e-16 ***
age           0.2432     0.0447    5.44 6.21e-08 ***
---
Signif. codes:  0 '***' 0.001 '**' 0.01 '*' 0.05 '.' 0.1 ' ' 1

Residual standard error: 15.94 on 1531 degrees of freedom
Multiple R-squared:  0.09225,    Adjusted R-squared:  0.09106
F-statistic: 77.79 on 2 and 1531 DF,  p-value: < 2.2e-16
```

────────── **Output of Script 3.4:** `Example-3-5.R` ──────────

```
> library(foreign)

> crime1<-read.dta("http://fmwww.bc.edu/ec-p/data/wooldridge/crime1.dta")

> # Model without avgsen:
> summary( lm(narr86 ~ pcnv+ptime86+qemp86, data=crime1) )

Call:
lm(formula = narr86 ~ pcnv + ptime86 + qemp86, data = crime1)

Residuals:
    Min      1Q  Median      3Q     Max
-0.7118 -0.4031 -0.2953  0.3452 11.4358

Coefficients:
             Estimate Std. Error t value Pr(>|t|)
(Intercept)  0.711772   0.033007  21.565  < 2e-16 ***
pcnv        -0.149927   0.040865  -3.669 0.000248 ***
ptime86     -0.034420   0.008591  -4.007 6.33e-05 ***
qemp86      -0.104113   0.010388 -10.023  < 2e-16 ***
---
Signif. codes:  0 '***' 0.001 '**' 0.01 '*' 0.05 '.' 0.1 ' ' 1

Residual standard error: 0.8416 on 2721 degrees of freedom
Multiple R-squared:  0.04132,    Adjusted R-squared:  0.04027
F-statistic:  39.1 on 3 and 2721 DF,  p-value: < 2.2e-16


> # Model with avgsen:
> summary( lm(narr86 ~ pcnv+avgsen+ptime86+qemp86, data=crime1) )

Call:
lm(formula = narr86 ~ pcnv + avgsen + ptime86 + qemp86, data = crime1)

Residuals:
    Min      1Q  Median      3Q     Max
-0.9330 -0.4247 -0.2934  0.3506 11.4403

Coefficients:
             Estimate Std. Error t value Pr(>|t|)
(Intercept)  0.706756   0.033151  21.319  < 2e-16 ***
pcnv        -0.150832   0.040858  -3.692 0.000227 ***
avgsen       0.007443   0.004734   1.572 0.115993
ptime86     -0.037391   0.008794  -4.252 2.19e-05 ***
qemp86      -0.103341   0.010396  -9.940  < 2e-16 ***
---
Signif. codes:  0 '***' 0.001 '**' 0.01 '*' 0.05 '.' 0.1 ' ' 1

Residual standard error: 0.8414 on 2720 degrees of freedom
Multiple R-squared:  0.04219,    Adjusted R-squared:  0.04079
F-statistic: 29.96 on 4 and 2720 DF,  p-value: < 2.2e-16
```

```
―――――――― Output of Script 3.5: Example-3-6.R ――――――――

> library(foreign)

> wage1 <- read.dta("http://fmwww.bc.edu/ec-p/data/wooldridge/wage1.dta")

> # OLS regression:
> summary( lm(log(wage) ~ educ, data=wage1) )

Call:
lm(formula = log(wage) ~ educ, data = wage1)

Residuals:
     Min       1Q   Median       3Q      Max
-2.21158 -0.36393 -0.07263  0.29712  1.52339

Coefficients:
            Estimate Std. Error t value Pr(>|t|)
(Intercept) 0.583773   0.097336   5.998 3.74e-09 ***
educ        0.082744   0.007567  10.935  < 2e-16 ***
---
Signif. codes:  0 '***' 0.001 '**' 0.01 '*' 0.05 '.' 0.1 ' ' 1

Residual standard error: 0.4801 on 524 degrees of freedom
Multiple R-squared:  0.1858,     Adjusted R-squared:  0.1843
F-statistic: 119.6 on 1 and 524 DF,  p-value: < 2.2e-16
```

3.2. OLS in Matrix Form

For applying regression methods to empirical problems, we do not actually need to know the formulas our software uses. In multiple regression, we need to resort to matrix algebra in order to find an explicit expression for the OLS parameter estimates. Wooldridge (2016) defers this discussion to Appendix E and we follow the notation used there. Going through this material is not required for applying multiple regression to real-world problems but is useful for a deeper understanding of the methods and their black-box implementations in software packages. In the following chapters, we will rely on the comfort of the canned routine **lm**, so this section may be skipped.

In matrix form, we store the regressors in a $n \times (k+1)$ matrix $\mathbf{X}$ which has a column for each regressor plus a column of ones for the constant. The sample values of the dependent variable are stored in a $n \times 1$ column vector $\mathbf{y}$. Wooldridge (2016) derives the OLS estimator $\hat{\beta} = (\hat{\beta}_0, \hat{\beta}_1, \hat{\beta}_2, \ldots, \hat{\beta}_k)'$ to be

$$\hat{\beta} = (\mathbf{X}'\mathbf{X})^{-1}\mathbf{X}'\mathbf{y}. \tag{3.2}$$

This equation involves three matrix operations which we know how to implement in R from Section 1.2.5:

- Transpose: The expression $\mathbf{X}'$ is **t(X)** in R
- Matrix multiplication: The expression $\mathbf{X}'\mathbf{X}$ is translated as **t(X)%*%X**
- Inverse: $(\mathbf{X}'\mathbf{X})^{-1}$ is written as **solve(t(X)%*%X)**

So we can collect everything and translate Equation 3.2 into the somewhat unsightly expression

```
bhat <- solve( t(X)%*%X ) %*% t(X)%*%y
```

The vector of residuals can be manually calculated as

$$\hat{\mathbf{u}} = \mathbf{y} - \mathbf{X}\hat{\boldsymbol{\beta}} \tag{3.3}$$

or translated into the R matrix language

```
uhat <- y - X %*% bhat
```

The formula for the estimated variance of the error term is

$$\hat{\sigma}^2 = \frac{1}{n-k-1}\hat{\mathbf{u}}'\hat{\mathbf{u}} \tag{3.4}$$

which is equivalent to `sigsqhat <- t(uhat) %*% uhat / (n-k-1)`. For technical reasons, it will be convenient to have this variable as a scalar instead of a 1×1 matrix, so we put this expression into the `as.numeric` function in our actual implementation:

```
sigsqhat <- as.numeric( t(uhat) %*% uhat / (n-k-1) )
```

The standard error of the regression (SER) is its the square root $\hat{\sigma} = \sqrt{\hat{\sigma}^2}$. The estimated OLS variance-covariance matrix according to Wooldridge (2016, Theorem E.2) is then

$$\widehat{\text{Var}(\hat{\boldsymbol{\beta}})} = \hat{\sigma}^2 (\mathbf{X}'\mathbf{X})^{-1} \tag{3.5}$$

```
Vbetahat <- sigsqhat * solve( t(X)%*%X )
```

Finally, the standard errors of the parameter estimates are the square roots of the main diagonal of $\text{Var}(\hat{\boldsymbol{\beta}})$ which can be expressed in R as

```
se <- sqrt( diag(Vbetahat) )
```

Script 3.6 (`OLS-Matrices.R`) implements this for the GPA regression from Example 3.1. Comparing the results to the built-in function (see Script 3.1 (`Example-3-1.R`)), it is reassuring that we get exactly the same numbers for the parameter estimates, SER ("`Residual standard error`"), and standard errors of the coefficients.

―――――――― **Output of Script 3.6: `OLS-Matrices.R`** ――――――――

```
> library(foreign)

> gpa1 <- read.dta("http://fmwww.bc.edu/ec-p/data/wooldridge/gpa1.dta")

> # Determine sample size & no. of regressors:
> n <- nrow(gpa1); k<-2

> # extract y
> y <- gpa1$colGPA

> # extract X & add a column of ones
> X <- cbind(1, gpa1$hsGPA, gpa1$ACT)

> # Display first rows of X:
> head(X)
     [,1] [,2] [,3]
[1,]    1  3.0   21
```

```
[2,]    1   3.2   24
[3,]    1   3.6   26
[4,]    1   3.5   27
[5,]    1   3.9   28
[6,]    1   3.4   25

> # Parameter estimates:
> ( bhat <- solve( t(X)%*%X ) %*% t(X)%*%y )
            [,1]
[1,] 1.286327767
[2,] 0.453455885
[3,] 0.009426012

> # Residuals, estimated variance of u and SER:
> uhat <- y - X %*% bhat

> sigsqhat <- as.numeric( t(uhat) %*% uhat / (n-k-1) )

> ( SER <- sqrt(sigsqhat) )
[1] 0.3403158

> # Estimated variance of the parameter estimators and SE:
> Vbetahat <- sigsqhat * solve( t(X)%*%X )

> ( se <- sqrt( diag(Vbetahat) ) )
[1] 0.34082212 0.09581292 0.01077719
```

3.3. Ceteris Paribus Interpretation and Omitted Variable Bias

The parameters in a multiple regression can be interpreted as partial effects. In a general model with k regressors, the estimated slope parameter β_j associated with variable x_j is the change of $\hat{y}$ as x_j increases by one unit *and the other variables are held fixed*.

Wooldridge (2016) discusses this interpretation in Section 3.2 and offers a useful formula for interpreting the difference between simple regression results and this *ceteris paribus* interpretation of multiple regression: Consider a regression with two explanatory variables:

$$\hat{y} = \hat{\beta}_0 + \hat{\beta}_1 x_1 + \hat{\beta}_2 x_2 \tag{3.6}$$

The parameter $\hat{\beta}_1$ is the estimated effect of increasing x_1 by one unit while keeping x_2 fixed. In contrast, consider the simple regression including only x_1 as a regressor:

$$\tilde{y} = \tilde{\beta}_0 + \tilde{\beta}_1 x_1. \tag{3.7}$$

The parameter $\tilde{\beta}_1$ is the estimated effect of increasing x_1 by one unit (and NOT keeping x_2 fixed). It can be related to $\hat{\beta}_1$ using the formula

$$\tilde{\beta}_1 = \hat{\beta}_1 + \hat{\beta}_2 \tilde{\delta}_1 \tag{3.8}$$

where $\tilde{\delta}_1$ is the slope parameter of the linear regression of x_2 on x_1

$$\tilde{x}_2 = \tilde{\delta}_0 + \tilde{\delta}_1 x_1. \tag{3.9}$$

This equation is actually quite intuitive: As x_1 increases by one unit,

- Predicted y directly increases by $\hat{\beta}_1$ units (*ceteris paribus* effect, Equ. 3.6).

- Predicted x_2 increases by $\tilde{\delta}_1$ units (see Equ. 3.9).
- Each of these $\tilde{\delta}_1$ units leads to an increase of predicted y by $\hat{\beta}_2$ units, giving a total indirect effect of $\tilde{\delta}_1 \hat{\beta}_2$ (see again Equ. 3.6)
- The overall effect $\tilde{\beta}_1$ is the sum of the direct and indirect effects (see Equ. 3.8).

We revisit Example 3.1 to see whether we can demonstrate equation 3.8 in *R*. Script 3.7 (Omitted-Vars.R) repeats the regression of the college GPA (colGPA) on the achievement test score (ACT) and the high school GPA (hsGPA). We study the *ceteris paribus* effect of ACT on colGPA which has an estimated value of $\hat{\beta}_1 = 0.0094$. The estimated effect of hsGPA is $\hat{\beta}_2 = 0.453$. The slope parameter of the regression corresponding to Eq. 3.9 is $\tilde{\delta}_1 = 0.0389$. Plugging these values into Equ. 3.8 gives a total effect of $\tilde{\beta}_1 = 0.0271$ which is exactly what the simple regression at the end of the output delivers.

─────────────── **Output of Script 3.7: Omitted-Vars.R** ───────────────

```
> library(foreign)

> gpa1 <- read.dta("http://fmwww.bc.edu/ec-p/data/wooldridge/gpa1.dta")

> # Parameter estimates for full and simple model:
> beta.hat <- coef( lm(colGPA ~ ACT+hsGPA, data=gpa1) )

> beta.hat
(Intercept)          ACT        hsGPA
1.286327767 0.009426012 0.453455885

> # Relation between regressors:
> delta.tilde <- coef( lm(hsGPA ~ ACT, data=gpa1) )

> delta.tilde
(Intercept)          ACT
 2.46253658   0.03889675

> # Omitted variables formula for beta1.tilde:
> beta.hat["ACT"] + beta.hat["hsGPA"]*delta.tilde["ACT"]
       ACT
0.02706397

> # Actual regression with hsGPA omitted:
> lm(colGPA ~ ACT, data=gpa1)

Call:
lm(formula = colGPA ~ ACT, data = gpa1)

Coefficients:
(Intercept)          ACT
    2.40298      0.02706
```

In this example, the indirect effect is is actually stronger than the direct effect. ACT predicts colGPA mainly because it is related to hsGPA which in turn is strongly related to colGPA.

These relations hold for the estimates from a given sample. In Section 3.3, Wooldridge (2016) discusses how to apply the same sort of arguments to the OLS estimators which are random variables varying over different samples. Omitting relevant regressors causes bias if we are interested in estimating partial effects. In practice, it is difficult to include *all* relevant regressors making of omitted variables a prevalent problem. It is important enough to have motivated an vast amount of methodological and applied research. More advanced techniques like instrumental variables or panel data methods try to solve the problem in cases where we cannot add all relevant regressors, for example because they are unobservable. We will come back to this in Part 3.

3.4. Standard Errors, Multicollinearity, and VIF

We have already seen the matrix formula for the conditional variance-covariance matrix under the usual assumptions including homoscedasticity (MLR.5) in Equation 3.5. Theorem 3.2 provides another useful formula for the variance of a single parameter β_j, i.e. for a single element on the main diagonal of the variance-covariance matrix:

$$\text{Var}(\beta_j) = \frac{\sigma^2}{SST_j(1 - R_j^2)} = \frac{1}{n-1} \cdot \frac{\hat{\sigma}^2}{\text{Var}(x_j)} \cdot \frac{1}{1 - R_j^2}, \tag{3.10}$$

where $SST_j = \sum_{i=1}^{n}(x_{ji} - \overline{x}_j)^2 = (n-1) \cdot Var(x_j)$ is the total sum of squares and R_j^2 is the usual coefficient of determination from a regression of x_j on all of the other regressors.[1]

The variance of $\hat{\beta}_j$ consists of three parts:

- $\frac{1}{n-1}$: The variance is smaller for larger samples.

- $\frac{\hat{\sigma}^2}{\text{Var}(x_j)}$: The variance is smaller if the regressor x_j varies a lot relative to the error term.

- $\frac{1}{1-R_j^2}$: This variance inflation factor (VIF) accounts for (imperfect) multicollinearity. If x_j is highly related to the other regressors, R_j^2 and therefore also VIF_j and the variance of $\hat{\beta}_j$ are large.

We have to estimate the error variance σ^2 to get an estimated variance (conditional on the regressors). Its square root is the standard error

$$\text{se}(\hat{\beta}_j) = \frac{1}{\sqrt{n-1}} \cdot \frac{\hat{\sigma}}{\text{sd}(x_j)} \cdot \frac{1}{\sqrt{1 - R_j^2}}. \tag{3.11}$$

It is not directly obvious that this formula leads to the same results as the matrix formula in Equation 3.5. We will validate this formula by replicating Example 3.1 which we also used for manually calculating the SE using the matrix formula above. The calculations are shown in Script 3.8 (MLR-SE.R).

We also use this example to demonstrate how to extract results which are reported by the **summary** of the **lm** results. Given its results are stored in variable sures using the results of **sures <- summary(lm(...))**, we can easily access the results using **sures\$resultname** where the resultname can be any of the following:

- **coefficients** for a matrix of the regression table (including coefficients, SE, ...)

- **residuals** for a vector of residuals

- **sigma** for the SER

- **r.squared** for R^2

- and more.[2]

---

[1] Note that here, we use the usual sample variance formula $Var(x_j) = \frac{1}{n-1} \sum_{i=1}^{n}(x_{ji} - \overline{x}_j)^2$

[2] As with any other list, a full listing of result names can again be obtained by **names(sures)** if sures stores the results.

─────────────── **Output of Script 3.8:** `MLR-SE.R` ───────────────

```
> library(foreign)

> gpa1 <- read.dta("http://fmwww.bc.edu/ec-p/data/wooldridge/gpa1.dta")

> # Full estimation results including automatic SE :
> res <- lm(colGPA ~ hsGPA+ACT, data=gpa1)

> summary(res)

Call:
lm(formula = colGPA ~ hsGPA + ACT, data = gpa1)

Residuals:
     Min       1Q   Median       3Q      Max
-0.85442 -0.24666 -0.02614  0.28127  0.85357

Coefficients:
            Estimate Std. Error t value Pr(>|t|)
(Intercept) 1.286328   0.340822   3.774 0.000238 ***
hsGPA       0.453456   0.095813   4.733 5.42e-06 ***
ACT         0.009426   0.010777   0.875 0.383297
---
Signif. codes:  0 '***' 0.001 '**' 0.01 '*' 0.05 '.' 0.1 ' ' 1

Residual standard error: 0.3403 on 138 degrees of freedom
Multiple R-squared:  0.1764,     Adjusted R-squared:  0.1645
F-statistic: 14.78 on 2 and 138 DF,  p-value: 1.526e-06


> # Extract SER (instead of calculation via residuals)
> ( SER <- summary(res)$sigma )
[1] 0.3403158

> # regressing hsGPA on ACT for calculation of R2 & VIF
> ( R2.hsGPA  <- summary( lm(hsGPA~ACT, data=gpa1) )$r.squared )
[1] 0.1195815

> ( VIF.hsGPA <- 1/(1-R2.hsGPA) )
[1] 1.135823

> # manual calculation of SE of hsGPA coefficient:
> n <- nobs(res)

> ( SE.hsGPA <- 1/sqrt(n-1) * SER/sd(gpa1$hsGPA)  * sqrt(VIF.hsGPA) )
[1] 0.09581292
```

This is used in Script 3.8 (`MLR-SE.R`) to extract the SER of the main regression and the R_j^2 from the regression of `hsGPA` on `ACT` which is needed for calculating the VIF for the coefficient of `hsGPA`.[3] The other ingredients of formula 3.11 are straightforward. The standard error calculated this way is exactly the same as the one of the built-in command and the matrix formula used in Script 3.6 (`OLS-Matrices.R`).

───────────────

[3]We could have calculated these values manually like in Scripts 2.8 (`Example-2-8.R`), 2.13 (`Example-2-12.R`) or 3.6 (`OLS-Matrices.R`).

A convenient way to automatically calculate variance inflation factors (VIF) is provided by the package **car**. Remember from Section 1.1.3 that in order to use this package, we have to install it once per computer using **install.packages("car")**. Then we can load it with the command **library(car)**. Among other useful tools, this package implements the command **vif(lmres)** where lmres is a regression result from **lm**. It delivers a list of VIF for each of the regressors as demonstrated in Script 3.9 (MLR-VIF.R).

We extend Example 3.6. and regress individual log wage on education (educ), potential overall work experience (exper), and the number of years with current employer (tenure). We could imagine that these three variables are correlated with each other, but the results show no big VIF. The largest one is for the coefficient of exper. Its variance is higher by a factor of (only) 1.478 than in a world in which it were uncorrelated with the other regressors. So we don't have to worry about multicollinearity here.

———— Output of Script 3.9: `MLR-VIF.R` ————

```
> library(foreign)

> wage1 <- read.dta("http://fmwww.bc.edu/ec-p/data/wooldridge/wage1.dta")

> # OLS regression:
> lmres <- lm(log(wage) ~ educ+exper+tenure, data=wage1)

> # Regression output:
> summary(lmres)

Call:
lm(formula = log(wage) ~ educ + exper + tenure, data = wage1)

Residuals:
     Min       1Q   Median       3Q      Max
-2.05802 -0.29645 -0.03265  0.28788  1.42809

Coefficients:
             Estimate Std. Error t value Pr(>|t|)
(Intercept) 0.284360   0.104190    2.729  0.00656 **
educ        0.092029   0.007330   12.555  < 2e-16 ***
exper       0.004121   0.001723    2.391  0.01714 *
tenure      0.022067   0.003094    7.133 3.29e-12 ***
---
Signif. codes:  0 '***' 0.001 '**' 0.01 '*' 0.05 '.' 0.1 ' ' 1

Residual standard error: 0.4409 on 522 degrees of freedom
Multiple R-squared:  0.316,       Adjusted R-squared:  0.3121
F-statistic: 80.39 on 3 and 522 DF,  p-value: < 2.2e-16


> # Load package "car" (has to be installed):
> library(car)

> # Automatically calculate VIF :
> vif(lmres)
    educ    exper   tenure
1.112771 1.477618 1.349296
```

4. Multiple Regression Analysis: Inference

Section 4.1 of Wooldridge (2016) adds assumption MLR.6 (normal distribution of the error term) to the previous assumptions MLR.1 through MLR.5. Together, these assumptions constitute the classical linear model (CLM).

The main additional result we get from this assumption is stated in Theorem 4.1: The OLS parameter estimators are normally distributed (conditional on the regressors $x_1, ..., x_k$). The benefit of this result is that it allows us to do statistical inference similar to the approaches discussed in section 1.7 for the simple estimator of the mean of a normally distributed random variable.

4.1. The t Test

After the sign and magnitude of the estimated parameters, empirical research typically pays most attention to the results of t tests discussed in this section.

4.1.1. General Setup

An important type of hypotheses we are often interested in is of the form

$$H_0 : \beta_j = a_j, \tag{4.1}$$

where a_j is some given number, very often $a_j = 0$. For the most common case of two-tailed tests, the alternative hypothesis is

$$H_1 : \beta_j \neq a_j, \tag{4.2}$$

and for one-tailed tests it is either one of

$$H_1 : \beta_j < a_j \qquad \text{or} \qquad H_1 : \beta_j > a_j. \tag{4.3}$$

These hypotheses can be conveniently tested using a t test which is based on the test statistic

$$t = \frac{\hat{\beta}_j - a_j}{\text{se}(\hat{\beta}_j)}. \tag{4.4}$$

If H_0 is in fact true and the CLM assumptions hold, then this statistic has a t distribution with $n - k - 1$ degrees of freedom.

4.1.2. Standard case

Very often, we want to test whether there is any relation at all between the dependent variable y and a regressor x_j and do not want to impose a sign on the partial effect *a priori*. This is a mission for the standard two-sided t test with the hypothetical value $a_j = 0$, so

$$H_0 : \beta_j = 0, \qquad H_1 : \beta_j \neq 0, \tag{4.5}$$

$$t_{\hat{\beta}_j} = \frac{\hat{\beta}_j}{\text{se}(\hat{\beta}_j)} \tag{4.6}$$

The subscript on the t statistic indicates that this is "the" t value for $\hat{\beta}_j$ for this frequent version of the test. Under H_0, it has the t distribution with $n - k - 1$ degrees of freedom implying that the probability that $|t_{\hat{\beta}_j}| > c$ is equal to α if c is the $1 - \frac{\alpha}{2}$ quantile of this distribution. If α is our significance level (e.g. $\alpha = 5\%$), then we

$$\text{reject } H_0 \text{ if } |t_{\hat{\beta}_j}| > c$$

in our sample. For the typical significance level $\alpha = 5\%$, the critical value c will be around 2 for reasonably large degrees of freedom and approach the counterpart of 1.96 from the standard normal distribution in very large samples.

The p value indicates the smallest value of the significance level α for which we would still reject H_0 using our sample. So it is the probability for a random variable T with the respective t distribution that $|T| > |t_{\hat{\beta}_j}|$ where $t_{\hat{\beta}_j}$ is the value of the t statistic in our particular sample. In our two-tailed test, it can be calculated as

$$p_{\hat{\beta}_j} = 2 \cdot F_{t_{n-k-1}}(-|t_{\hat{\beta}_j}|), \tag{4.7}$$

where $F_{t_{n-k-1}}(\cdot)$ is the cdf of the t distribution with $n - k - 1$ degrees of freedom. If our software provides us with the relevant p values, they are easy to use: We

$$\text{reject } H_0 \text{ if } p_{\hat{\beta}_j} \leq \alpha.$$

Since this standard case of a t test is so common, R provides us with the relevant t and p values directly in the **summary** of the estimation results we already saw in the previous chapter. The regression table includes for all regressors and the intercept

- Parameter estimates and standard errors, see Section 3.1.
- The test statistics $t_{\hat{\beta}_j}$ from Equation 4.6 in the column `t value`
- The respective p values $p_{\hat{\beta}_j}$ from Equation 4.7 in the column `Pr(>|t|)`
- Symbols to quickly see the range of the p value where for example "$\star\star\star$" implies $0 < p_{\hat{\beta}_j} \leq 0.001$ and "$\star$" implies $0.01 < p_{\hat{\beta}_j} \leq 0.05$. The meaning of all symbols can be seen in the legend below the table.

Wooldridge, Example 4.3: Determinants of College GPA

We have repeatedly used the data set `GPA1.dta` in Chapter 3. This example uses three regressors and estimates a regression model of the form

$$\text{colGPA} = \beta_0 + \beta_1 \cdot \text{hsGPA} + \beta_2 \cdot \text{ACT} + \beta_3 \cdot \text{skipped} + u$$

For the critical values of the t tests, using the normal approximation instead of the exact t distribution with $n - k - 1 = 137$ d.f. doesn't make much of a difference:

```
> # CV for alpha=5% and 1% using the t distribution with 137 d.f.:
> alpha <- c(0.05, 0.01)

> qt(1-alpha/2, 137)
[1] 1.977431 2.612192

> # Critical values for alpha=5% and 1% using the normal approximation:
> qnorm(1-alpha/2)
[1] 1.959964 2.575829
```

Script 4.1 (`Example-4-3.R`) presents the standard **summary** which directly contains all the information to test the hypotheses in Equation 4.5 for all parameters. The t statistics for all coefficients except β_2 are larger in absolute value than the critical value $c = 2.61$ (or $c = 2.58$ using the normal approximation) for $\alpha = 1\%$. So we would reject H_0 for all usual significance levels. By construction, we draw the same conclusions from the p values (or the symbols next to it).

In order to confirm that R is exactly using the formulas of Wooldridge (2016), we next reconstruct the t and p values manually. The whole regression table is stored as **sumres$coefficients**, where `sumres` contains the summary results, see Section 3.4. We extract the first two columns of it as the coefficients and standard errors, respectively. Then we simply apply Equations 4.6 and 4.7.

───────── Output of Script 4.1: `Example-4-3.R` ─────────

```
> library(foreign)

> gpa1 <- read.dta("http://fmwww.bc.edu/ec-p/data/wooldridge/gpa1.dta")

> # Store results under "sumres" and display full table:
> ( sumres <- summary( lm(colGPA ~ hsGPA+ACT+skipped, data=gpa1) ) )

Call:
lm(formula = colGPA ~ hsGPA + ACT + skipped, data = gpa1)

Residuals:
     Min       1Q   Median       3Q      Max
-0.85698 -0.23200 -0.03935  0.24816  0.81657

Coefficients:
            Estimate Std. Error t value Pr(>|t|)
(Intercept)  1.38955    0.33155   4.191 4.95e-05 ***
hsGPA        0.41182    0.09367   4.396 2.19e-05 ***
ACT          0.01472    0.01056   1.393  0.16578
```

```
skipped     -0.08311    0.02600   -3.197   0.00173 **
---
Signif. codes:  0 '***' 0.001 '**' 0.01 '*' 0.05 '.' 0.1 ' ' 1

Residual standard error: 0.3295 on 137 degrees of freedom
Multiple R-squared:  0.2336,      Adjusted R-squared:  0.2168
F-statistic: 13.92 on 3 and 137 DF,  p-value: 5.653e-08


> # Manually confirm the formulas: Extract coefficients and SE
> regtable <- sumres$coefficients

> bhat <- regtable[,1]

> se   <- regtable[,2]

> # Reproduce t statistic
> ( tstat <- bhat / se )
(Intercept)       hsGPA        ACT      skipped
   4.191039    4.396260   1.393319   -3.196840

> # Reproduce p value
> ( pval   <- 2*pt(-abs(tstat),137) )
 (Intercept)        hsGPA         ACT       skipped
4.950269e-05 2.192050e-05 1.657799e-01 1.725431e-03
```

4.1.3. Other hypotheses

For a one-tailed test, the critical value c of the t test and the p values have to be adjusted appropriately. Wooldridge (2016) provides a general discussion in Section 4.2. For testing the null hypothesis $H_0 : \beta_j = a_j$, the tests for the three common alternative hypotheses are summarized in Table 4.1:

Table 4.1. One- and two-tailed t Tests for $H_0 : \beta_j = a_j$

$H_1:$	$\beta_j \neq a_j$	$\beta_j > a_j$	$\beta_j < a_j$
c=quantile	$1 - \frac{\alpha}{2}$	$1 - \alpha$	$1 - \alpha$
reject H_0 if	$|t_{\hat{\beta}_j}| > c$	$t_{\hat{\beta}_j} > c$	$t_{\hat{\beta}_j} < -c$
p value	$2 \cdot F_{t_{n-k-1}}(-|t_{\hat{\beta}_j}|)$	$F_{t_{n-k-1}}(-t_{\hat{\beta}_j})$	$F_{t_{n-k-1}}(t_{\hat{\beta}_j})$

Given the standard regression output like the one in Script 4.1 (Example-4-3.R) including the p value for two-sided tests $p_{\hat{\beta}_j}$, we can easily do one-sided t tests for the null hypothesis $H_0 : \beta_j = 0$ in two steps:

- Is $\hat{\beta}_j$ positive (if $H_1 : \beta_j > 0$) or negative (if $H_1 : \beta_j < 0$)?
    - No → do not reject H_0 since this cannot be evidence against H_0.
    - Yes → The relevant p value is half of the reported $p_{\hat{\beta}_j}$.
        $\Rightarrow$ Reject H_0 if $p = \frac{1}{2}p_{\hat{\beta}_j} < \alpha$.

Wooldridge, Example 4.1: Hourly Wage Equation

We have already estimated the wage equation

$$\log(\text{wage}) = \beta_0 + \beta_1 \cdot \text{educ} + \beta_2 \cdot \text{exper} + \beta_3 \cdot \text{tenure} + u$$

in Example 3.2. Now we are ready to test $H_0 : \beta_2 = 0$ against $H_1 : \beta_2 > 0$. For the critical values of the t tests, using the normal approximation instead of the exact t distribution with $n - k - 1 = 522$ d.f. doesn't make any relevant difference:

```
> # CV for alpha=5% and 1% using the t distribution with 522 d.f.:
> alpha <- c(0.05, 0.01)

> qt(1-alpha, 522)
[1] 1.647778 2.333513

> # Critical values for alpha=5% and 1% using the normal approximation:
> qnorm(1-alpha)
[1] 1.644854 2.326348
```

Script 4.2 (`Example-4-1.R`) shows the standard regression output. The reported t statistic for the parameter of `exper` is $t_{\hat{\beta}_2} = 2.391$ which is larger than the critical value $c = 2.33$ for the significance level $\alpha = 1\%$, so we reject H_0. By construction, we get the same answer from looking at the p value. Like always, the reported $p_{\hat{\beta}_j}$ value is for a two-sided test, so we have to divide it by 2. The resulting value $p = \frac{0.01714}{2} = 0.00857 < 0.01$, so we reject H_0 using an $\alpha = 1\%$ significance level.

─────────── **Output of Script 4.2: `Example-4-1.R`** ───────────

```
> library(foreign)

> wage1 <- read.dta("http://fmwww.bc.edu/ec-p/data/wooldridge/wage1.dta")

> # OLS regression:
> summary( lm(log(wage) ~ educ+exper+tenure, data=wage1) )

Call:
lm(formula = log(wage) ~ educ + exper + tenure, data = wage1)

Residuals:
     Min       1Q   Median       3Q      Max
-2.05802 -0.29645 -0.03265  0.28788  1.42809

Coefficients:
             Estimate Std. Error t value Pr(>|t|)
(Intercept) 0.284360   0.104190    2.729  0.00656 **
educ        0.092029   0.007330   12.555  < 2e-16 ***
exper       0.004121   0.001723    2.391  0.01714 *
tenure      0.022067   0.003094    7.133 3.29e-12 ***
---
Signif. codes:  0 '***' 0.001 '**' 0.01 '*' 0.05 '.' 0.1 ' ' 1

Residual standard error: 0.4409 on 522 degrees of freedom
Multiple R-squared:  0.316,        Adjusted R-squared:  0.3121
F-statistic: 80.39 on 3 and 522 DF,  p-value: < 2.2e-16
```

4.2. Confidence Intervals

We have already looked at Confidence intervals (CI) for the mean of a normally distributed random variable in Sections 1.7 and 1.9.3. CI for the regression parameters are equally easy to construct and closely related to t tests. Wooldridge (2016, Section 4.3) provides a succinct discussion. The 95% confidence interval for parameter β_j is simply

$$\hat{\beta}_j \pm c \cdot \text{se}(\hat{\beta}_j), \tag{4.8}$$

where c is the same critical value for the two-sided t test using a significance level $\alpha = 5\%$. Wooldridge (2016) shows examples of how to manually construct these CI.

  R provides a convenient way to calculate the CI for all parameters: If the regression results are stored in a variable `myres`, the command **confint(myres)** gives a table of 95% confidence intervals. Other levels can be chosen using the option **level = *value***. The 99% CI are for example obtained as **confint(myres,level=0.99)**.

Wooldridge, Example 4.8: Model of R& D Expenditures

We study the relationship between the R&D expenditures of a firm, its size, and the profit margin for a sample of 32 firms in the chemical industry. The regression equation is

$$\log(\text{rd}) = \beta_0 + \beta_1 \cdot \log(\text{educ}) + \beta_2 \cdot \text{profmarg} + u$$

Script 4.3 (`Example-4-8.R`) presents the regression results as well as the 95% and 99% CI. See Wooldridge (2016) for the manual calculation of the CI and comments on the results.

─────────────── **Output of Script 4.3: `Example-4-8.R`** ───────────────

```
> library(foreign)

> rdchem<-read.dta("http://fmwww.bc.edu/ec-p/data/wooldridge/rdchem.dta")

> # OLS regression:
> myres <- lm(log(rd) ~ log(sales)+profmarg, data=rdchem)

> # Regression output:
> summary(myres)

Call:
lm(formula = log(rd) ~ log(sales) + profmarg, data = rdchem)

Residuals:
     Min       1Q   Median       3Q      Max
-0.97675 -0.31501 -0.05835  0.39015  1.21781

Coefficients:
            Estimate Std. Error t value Pr(>|t|)
(Intercept) -4.37835    0.46801  -9.355 2.93e-10 ***
log(sales)   1.08423    0.06019  18.012  < 2e-16 ***
profmarg     0.02166    0.01278   1.695    0.101
---
Signif. codes:  0 '***' 0.001 '**' 0.01 '*' 0.05 '.' 0.1 ' ' 1

Residual standard error: 0.5136 on 29 degrees of freedom
Multiple R-squared:  0.918,          Adjusted R-squared:  0.9123
```

```
F-statistic: 162.2 on 2 and 29 DF,  p-value: < 2.2e-16


> # 95% CI:
> confint(myres)
                    2.5 %        97.5 %
(Intercept) -5.335542567  -3.42115403
log(sales)   0.961117144   1.20733872
profmarg    -0.004482681   0.04780146

> # 99% CI:
> confint(myres, level=0.99)
                   0.5 %        99.5 %
(Intercept) -5.66837301  -3.08832358
log(sales)   0.91830972   1.25014614
profmarg    -0.01357266   0.05689144
```

4.3. Linear Restrictions: F Tests

Wooldridge (2016, Sections 4.4 and 4.5) discusses more general tests than those for the null hypotheses in Equation 4.1. They can involve one or more hypotheses involving one or more population parameters in a linear fashion.

We follow the illustrative example of Wooldridge (2016, Section 4.5) and analyze major league baseball players' salaries using the data set MLB1.dta and the regression model

$$\log(\texttt{salary}) = \beta_0 + \beta_1 \cdot \texttt{years} + \beta_2 \cdot \texttt{gamesyr} + \beta_3 \cdot \texttt{bavg} + \beta_4 \cdot \texttt{hrunsyr} + \beta_5 \cdot \texttt{rbisyr} + u \quad (4.9)$$

We want to test whether the performance measures batting average (bavg), home runs per year (hrunsyr), and runs batted in per year (rbisyr) have an impact on the salary once we control for the number of years as an active player (years) and the number of games played per year (gamesyr). So we state our null hypothesis as $H_0 : \beta_3 = 0, \beta_4 = 0, \beta_5 = 0$ versus $H_1 : H_0$ is false, i.e. at least one of the performance measures matters.

The test statistic of the F test is based on the relative difference between the sum of squared residuals in the general (unrestricted) model and a restricted model in which the hypotheses are imposed SSR_{ur} and SSR_r, respectively. In our example, the restricted model is one in which bavg, hrunsyr, and rbisyr are excluded as regressors. If both models involve the same dependent variable, it can also be written in terms of the coefficient of determination in the unrestricted and the restricted model R^2_{ur} and R^2_r, respectively:

$$F = \frac{\text{SSR}_r - \text{SSR}_{ur}}{\text{SSR}_{ur}} \cdot \frac{n - k - 1}{q} = \frac{R^2_{ur} - R^2_r}{1 - R^2_{ur}} \cdot \frac{n - k - 1}{q}, \quad (4.10)$$

where q is the number of restrictions (in our example, $q = 3$). Intuitively, if the null hypothesis is correct, then imposing it as a restriction will not lead to a significant drop in the model fit and the F test statistic should be relatively small. It can be shown that under the CLM assumptions and the null hypothesis, the statistic has an F distribution with the numerator degrees of freedom equal to q and the denominator degrees of freedom of $n - k - 1$. Given a significance level α, we will reject H_0 if $F > c$, where the critical value c is the $1 - \alpha$ quantile of the relevant $F_{q,n-k-1}$ distribution. In our example, $n = 353, k = 5, q = 3$. So with $\alpha = 1\%$, the critical value is 3.84 and can be calculated using the **qf** function as

```
> # CV for alpha=1% using the F distribution with 3 and 347 d.f.:
> qf(1-0.01, 3,347)
[1] 3.83852
```

Script 4.4 (`F-Test-MLB.R`) shows the calculations for this example. The result is F = 9.55 > 3.84, so we clearly reject H_0. We also calculate the p value for this test. It is $p = 4.47 \cdot 10^{-06} = 0.00000447$, so we reject H_0 for any reasonable significance level.

──────────────── **Output of Script 4.4:** `F-Test-MLB.R` ────────────────

```
> library(foreign)

> mlb1 <- read.dta("http://fmwww.bc.edu/ec-p/data/wooldridge/mlb1.dta")

> # Unrestricted OLS regression:
> res.ur <- lm(log(salary) ~ years+gamesyr+bavg+hrunsyr+rbisyr, data=mlb1)

> # Restricted OLS regression:
> res.r <- lm(log(salary) ~ years+gamesyr, data=mlb1)

> # R2:
> ( r2.ur <- summary(res.ur)$r.squared )
[1] 0.6278028

> ( r2.r <- summary(res.r)$r.squared )
[1] 0.5970716

> # F statistic:
> ( F <- (r2.ur-r2.r) / (1-r2.ur) * 347/3 )
[1] 9.550257

> # p value = 1-cdf of the appropriate F distribution:
> 1-pf(F, 3,347)
[1] 4.47369e-06
```

It should not be surprising that there is a more convenient way to do this in *R*. The package **car** provides a command **linearHypothesis** which is well suited for these kinds of tests.[1] Given the unrestricted estimation results are stored in a variable `res`, an *F* test is conducted with

```
linearHypothesis(res, myH0)
```

where `myH0` describes the null hypothesis to be tested. It is a vector of length q where each restriction is described as a text in which the variable name takes the place of its parameter. In our example, H_0 is that the three parameters of `bavg`, `hrunsyr`, and `rbisyr` are all equal to zero, which translates as **myH0 <- c("bavg=0","hrunsyr=0","rbisyr=0")**. The "=0" can also be omitted since this is the default hypothesis. Script 4.5 (`F-Test-MLB-auto.R`) implements this for the same test as the manual calculations done in Script 4.4 (`F-Test-MLB.R`) and results in exactly the same *F* statistic and *p* value.

───────────────────────

[1] See Section 1.1.3 for how to use packages.

─────── **Output of Script 4.5: F-Test-MLB-auto.R** ───────

```
> library(foreign)

> mlb1 <- read.dta("http://fmwww.bc.edu/ec-p/data/wooldridge/mlb1.dta")

> # Unrestricted OLS regression:
> res.ur <- lm(log(salary) ~ years+gamesyr+bavg+hrunsyr+rbisyr, data=mlb1)

> # Load package "car" (which has to be installed on the computer)
> library(car)

> # F test
> myH0 <- c("bavg","hrunsyr","rbisyr")

> linearHypothesis(res.ur, myH0)
Linear hypothesis test

Hypothesis:
bavg = 0
hrunsyr = 0
rbisyr = 0

Model 1: restricted model
Model 2: log(salary) ~ years + gamesyr + bavg + hrunsyr + rbisyr

  Res.Df    RSS Df Sum of Sq      F    Pr(>F)
1    350 198.31
2    347 183.19  3    15.125 9.5503 4.474e-06 ***
---
Signif. codes:  0 '***' 0.001 '**' 0.01 '*' 0.05 '.' 0.1 ' ' 1
```

This function can also be used to test more complicated null hypotheses. For example, suppose a sports reporter claims that the batting average plays no role and that the number of home runs has twice the impact as the number of runs batted in. This translates (using variable names instead of numbers as subscripts) as $H_0 : \beta_{bavg} = 0, \beta_{hrunsyr} = 2 \cdot \beta_{rbisyr}$. For R, we translate it as **myH0 <- c("bavg=0", "hrunsyr=2*rbisyr")**. The output of Script 4.6 (F-Test-MLB-auto2.R) shows the results of this test. The p value is $p = 0.6$, so we cannot reject H_0.

─────── **Output of Script 4.6: F-Test-MLB-auto2.R** ───────

```
> # F test (F-Test-MLB-auto.R has to be run first!)
> myH0 <- c("bavg", "hrunsyr=2*rbisyr")

> linearHypothesis(res.ur, myH0)
Linear hypothesis test

Hypothesis:
bavg = 0
hrunsyr - 2 rbisyr = 0

Model 1: restricted model
Model 2: log(salary) ~ years + gamesyr + bavg + hrunsyr + rbisyr

  Res.Df    RSS Df Sum of Sq      F Pr(>F)
1    349 183.73
2    347 183.19  2   0.54035 0.5118 0.5999
```

If we are interested in testing the null hypothesis that a set of coefficients with similar names are equal to zero, the function **matchCoefs(res,expr)** can be handy. It provides the names of all coefficients in result res which contain the expression expr. Script 4.7 (F-Test-MLB-auto3.R) presents an example how this works. A more realistic example is given in Section 7.5 where we can automatically select all interaction coefficients.

─────────────────── **Output of Script 4.7: F-Test-MLB-auto3.R** ───────────────────

```
> # Note: Script "F-Test-MLB-auto.R" has to be run first to create res.ur.
> # Which variables used in res.ur contain "yr" in their names?
> myH0 <- matchCoefs(res.ur,"yr")

> myH0
[1] "gamesyr" "hrunsyr" "rbisyr"

> # F test (F-Test-MLB-auto.R has to be run first!)
> linearHypothesis(res.ur, myH0)
Linear hypothesis test

Hypothesis:
gamesyr = 0
hrunsyr = 0
rbisyr = 0

Model 1: restricted model
Model 2: log(salary) ~ years + gamesyr + bavg + hrunsyr + rbisyr

  Res.Df     RSS Df Sum of Sq      F    Pr(>F)
1    350  311.67
2    347  183.19  3    128.48 81.125 < 2.2e-16 ***
---
Signif. codes:  0 '***' 0.001 '**' 0.01 '*' 0.05 '.' 0.1 ' ' 1
```

Both the most important and the most straightforward F test is the one for **overall significance**. The null hypothesis is that all parameters except for the constant are equal to zero. If this null hypothesis holds, the regressors do not have any joint explanatory power for y. The results of such a test are automatically included in the last line of **summary(lm(...))**. As an example, see Script 4.3 (Example-4-8.R). The null hypothesis that neither the sales nor the margin have any relation to R&D spending is clearly rejected with an F statistic of 162.2 and a p value smaller than 10^{-15}.

4.4. Reporting Regression Results

Now we know most of the statistics shown in a typical regression output. Wooldridge (2016) provides a discussion of how to report them in Section 4.6. We will come back to these issues in more detail in Chapter 19. Here is already a preview of how to conveniently generate tables of different regression results very much like suggested in Wooldridge (2016, Example 4.10).

There are numerous *R* packages that deal with automatically generating useful regression tables. A notable example is the package ***stargazer*** which implements a command with the same name.[2] Given a list of regression results, it generates a table including all of them. It is quite useful with the default settings and can be adjusted using various options. It generates a table either as text or as a LaTeX code (for those who know what that means). We demonstrate this using the following example.

Wooldridge, Example 4.10: Salary-Pension Tradeoff for Teachers

Wooldridge (2016) discusses a model of the tradeoff between salary and pensions for teachers. It boils down to the regression specification

$$\log(\texttt{salary}) = \beta_0 + \beta_1 \cdot (\texttt{benefits/salary}) + \texttt{other factors} + u$$

Script 4.8 (`Example-4-10.R`) loads the data, generates the new variable `b_s = (benefits/salary)` and runs three regressions with different sets of `other factors`. The **stargazer** command is then used to display the results in a clearly arranged table of all relevant results. We choose the options **type="text"** to request a text output (instead of a LaTeX table) and **keep.stat=c("n","rsq")** to have n and R^2 reported in the table.

_____ Output of Script 4.8: `Example-4-10.R` _____

```
> library(foreign)

> meap93<-read.dta("http://fmwww.bc.edu/ec-p/data/wooldridge/meap93.dta")

> # define new variable within data frame
> meap93$b_s <- meap93$benefits / meap93$salary

> # Estimate three different models
> model1<- lm(log(salary) ~ b_s                              , data=meap93)

> model2<- lm(log(salary) ~ b_s+log(enroll)+log(staff), data=meap93)

> model3<- lm(log(salary) ~ b_s+log(enroll)+log(staff)+droprate+gradrate
>                                                       , data=meap93)

> # Load package and display table of results
> library(stargazer)
```

---

[2]See Section 1.1.3 for how to use packages.

```
> stargazer(list(model1,model2,model3),type="text",keep.stat=c("n","rsq"))
```

```
=========================================
                    Dependent variable:
                -------------------------------
                        log(salary)
                   (1)        (2)        (3)
-----------------------------------------
b_s            -0.825***  -0.605***  -0.589***
                (0.200)    (0.165)    (0.165)

log(enroll)                0.087***   0.088***
                           (0.007)    (0.007)

log(staff)                -0.222***  -0.218***
                           (0.050)    (0.050)

droprate                             -0.0003
                                      (0.002)

gradrate                              0.001
                                      (0.001)

Constant       10.523***  10.844***  10.738***
                (0.042)    (0.252)    (0.258)

-----------------------------------------
Observations     408        408        408
R2              0.040      0.353      0.361
=========================================
Note:           *p<0.1; **p<0.05; ***p<0.01
```

5. Multiple Regression Analysis: OLS Asymptotics

Asymptotic theory allow us to relax some assumptions needed to derive the sampling distribution of estimators if the sample size is large enough. For running a regression in a software package, it does not matter whether we rely on stronger assumptions or on asymptotic arguments. So we don't have to learn anything new regarding the implementation.

Instead, this chapter aims to improve on our intuition regarding the workings of asymptotics by looking at some simulation exercises in Section 5.1. Section 5.2 briefly discusses the implementation of the regression-based LM test presented by Wooldridge (2016, Section 5.2).

5.1. Simulation Exercises

In Section 2.7, we already used Monte Carlo Simulation methods to study the mean and variance of OLS estimators under the assumptions SLR.1–SLR.5. Here, we will conduct similar experiments but will look at the whole sampling distribution of OLS estimators similar to Section 1.9.2 where we demonstrated the central limit theorem for the sample mean. Remember that the sampling distribution is important since confidence intervals, t and F tests and other tools of inference rely on it.

Theorem 4.1 of Wooldridge (2016) gives the normal distribution of the OLS estimators (conditional on the regressors) based on assumptions MLR.1 through MLR.6. In contrast, Theorem 5.2 states that *asymptotically*, the distribution is normal by assumptions MLR.1 through MLR.5 only. Assumption MLR.6 – the normal distribution of the error terms – is not required if the sample is large enough to justify asymptotic arguments.

In other words: In small samples, the parameter estimates have a normal sampling distribution only if

- the error terms are normally distributed and
- we condition on the regressors.

To see how this works out in practice, we set up a series of simulation experiments. Section 5.1.1 simulates a model consistent with MLR.1 through MLR.6 and keeps the regressors fixed. Theory suggests that the sampling distribution of $\hat{\beta}$ is normal, independent of the sample size. Section 5.1.2 simulates a violation of assumption MLR.6. Normality of $\hat{\beta}$ only holds asymptotically, so for small sample sizes we suspect a violation. Finally, we will look closer into what "conditional on the regressors" means and simulate a (very plausible) violation of this in Section 5.1.3.

5.1.1. Normally Distributed Error Terms

Script 5.1 (Sim-Asy-OLS-norm.R) draws 10 000 samples of a given size (which has to be stored in variable n before) from a population that is consistent with assumptions MLR.1 through MLR.6. The error terms are specified to be standard normal. The slope estimate $\hat{\beta}_1$ is stored for each of the samples. For a more detailed discussion of the implementation, see Section 2.7.2 where a very similar simulation exercise is introduced.

_____ Script 5.1: Sim-Asy-OLS-norm.R _____

```
# Set the random seed
set.seed(1234567)
# set true parameters: intercept & slope
b0<-1; b1<-0.5
# initialize b1hat to store 10000 results:
b1hat <- numeric(10000)

# Draw a sample of x, fixed over replications:
x <- rnorm(n,4,1)
# repeat r times:
for(j in 1:10000) {
  # Draw a sample of u (std. normal):
  u <- rnorm(n)
  # Draw a sample of y:
  y <- b0 + b1*x + u
  # regress y on x and store slope estimate at position j
  bhat <- coef( lm(y~x) )
  b1hat[j] <- bhat["x"]
}
```

This code was run for different sample sizes. The density estimate together with the corresponding normal density are shown in Figure 5.1. Not surprisingly, all distributions look very similar to the normal distribution – this is what Theorem 4.1 predicted. Note that the fact that the sampling variance decreases as n rises is only obvious if we pay attention to the different scales of the axes.

5.1.2. Non-Normal Error Terms

The next step is to simulate a violation of assumption MLR.6. In order to implement a rather drastic violation of the normality assumption similar to Section 1.9.2, we implement a "standardized" χ^2 distribution with one degree of freedom. More specifically, let v be distributed as $\chi^2_{[1]}$. Because this distribution has a mean of 1 and a variance of 2, the error term $u = \frac{v-1}{\sqrt{2}}$ has a mean of 0 and a variance of 1. This simplifies the comparison to the exercise with the standard normal errors above. Figure 5.2 plots the density functions of the standard normal distribution used above and the "standardized" χ^2 distribution. Both have a mean of 0 and a variance of 1 but very different shapes.

Script 5.2 (Sim-Asy-OLS-chisq.R) implements a simulation of this model and is listed in the appendix (p. 304). The only line of code we changed compared to the previous Script 5.1 (Sim-Asy-OLS-norm.R) is the sampling of u where we replace drawing from a standard normal distribution using **u <- rnorm(n)** with sampling from the standardized $\chi^2_{[1]}$ distribution with

```
u <- ( rchisq(n,1)-1 ) / sqrt(2)
```

For each of the same sample sizes used above, we again estimate the slope parameter for 10 000 samples. The densities of $\hat{\beta}_1$ are plotted in Figure 5.3 together with the respective normal distributions with the corresponding variances. For the small sample sizes, the deviation from the normal distribution is strong. Note that the dashed normal distributions have the same mean and variance. The main difference is the kurtosis which is larger than 8 in the simulations for $n = 5$ compared to the normal distribution for which the kurtosis is equal to 3.

For larger sample sizes, the sampling distribution of $\hat{\beta}_1$ converges to the normal distribution. For $n = 100$, the difference is much smaller but still discernible. For $n = 1\,000$, it cannot be detected

Figure 5.1. Density of $\hat{\beta}_1$ with different sample sizes: normal error terms

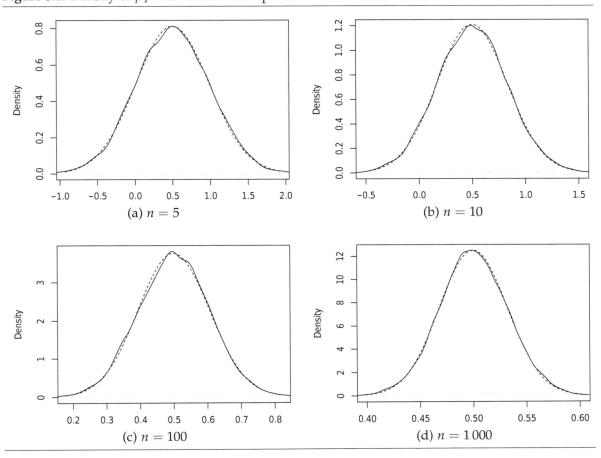

      (a) $n = 5$ (b) $n = 10$

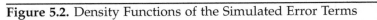

      (c) $n = 100$ (d) $n = 1\,000$

Figure 5.2. Density Functions of the Simulated Error Terms

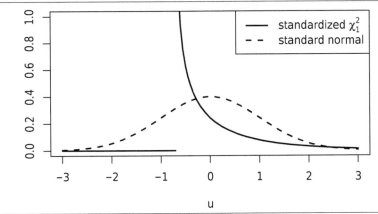

Figure 5.3. Density of $\hat{\beta}_1$ with different sample sizes: non-normal error terms

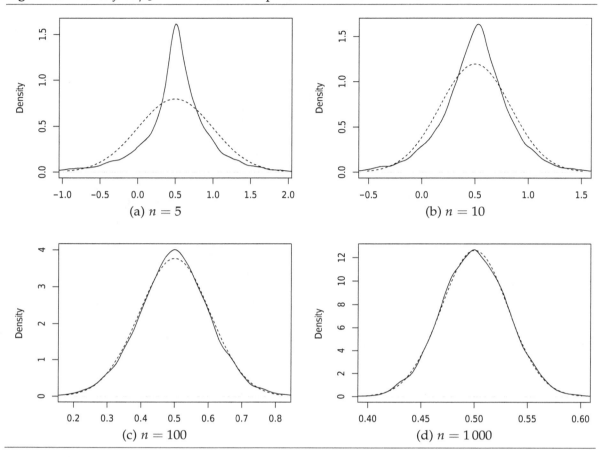

anymore in our simulation exercise. How large the sample needs be depends among other things on the severity of the violations of MLR.6. If the distribution of the error terms is not as extremely non-normal as in our simulations, smaller sample sizes like the rule of thumb $n = 30$ might suffice for valid asymptotics.

5.1.3. (Not) Conditioning on the Regressors

There is a more subtle difference between the finite-sample results regarding the variance (Theorem 3.2) and distribution (Theorem 4.1) on one hand and the corresponding asymptotic results (Theorem 5.2). The former results describe the sampling distribution "conditional on the sample values of the independent variables". This implies that as we draw different samples, the values of the regressors $x_1, \ldots, x_k$ remain the same and only the error terms and dependent variables change.

In our previous simulation exercises in Scripts like 2.16 (SLR-Sim-Model-Condx.R), 5.1 (Sim-Asy-OLS-norm.R), and 5.2 (Sim-Asy-OLS-chisq.R), this is implemented by making random draws of x outside of the simulation loop. This is a realistic description of how data is generated only in some simple experiments: The experimenter chooses the regressors for the sample, conducts the experiment and measures the dependent variable.

In most applications we are concerned with, this is an unrealistic description of how we obtain our data. If we draw a sample of individuals, both their dependent and independent variables differ across samples. In these cases, the distribution "conditional on the sample values of the independent variables" can only serve as an approximation of the actual distribution with varying regressors. For large samples, this distinction is irrelevant and the asymptotic distribution is the same.

Let's see how this plays out in an example. Script 5.3 (Sim-Asy-OLS-uncond.R) differs from Script 5.1 (Sim-Asy-OLS-norm.R) only by moving the generation of the regressors into the loop in which the 10 000 samples are generated. This is inconsistent with Theorem 4.1, so for small samples, we don't know the distribution of $\hat{\beta}_1$. Theorem 5.2 is applicable, so for (very) large samples, we know that the estimator is normally distributed.

<hr/>
Script 5.3: Sim-Asy-OLS-uncond.R

```
# Set the random seed
set.seed(1234567)
# set true parameters: intercept & slope
b0<-1; b1<-0.5
# initialize b1hat to store 10000 results:
b1hat <- numeric(10000)

# repeat r times:
for(j in 1:10000) {
  # Draw a sample of x, varying over replications:
  x <- rnorm(n,4,1)
  # Draw a sample of u (std. normal):
  u <- rnorm(n)
  # Draw a sample of y:
  y <- b0 + b1*x + u
  # regress y on x and store slope estimate at position j
  bhat <- coef( lm(y~x) )
  b1hat[j] <- bhat["x"]
}
```

Figure 5.4 shows the distribution of the 10 000 estimates generated by Script 5.3 (Sim-Asy-OLS-uncond.R) for $n = 5, 10, 100$, and 1 000. As we expected from theory, the distribution is (close to) normal for large samples. For small samples, it deviates quite a bit. The kurtosis is 8.7 for a sample size of $n = 5$ which is far away from the kurtosis of 3 of a normal distribution.

Figure 5.4. Density of $\hat{\beta}_1$ with different sample sizes: varying regressors

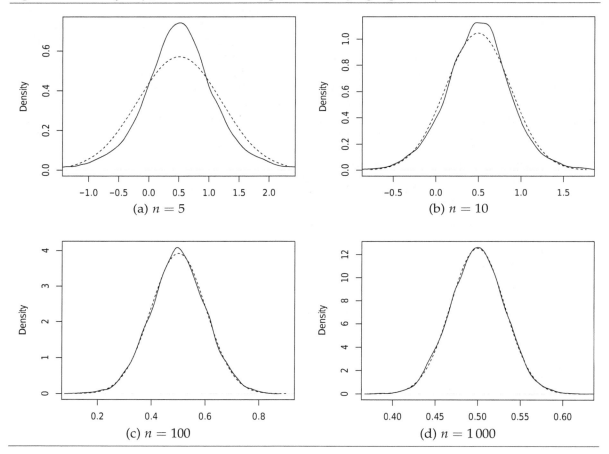

(a) $n = 5$

(b) $n = 10$

(c) $n = 100$

(d) $n = 1\,000$

5.2. LM Test

As an alternative to the *F* tests discussed in Section 4.3, *LM* tests for the same sort of hypotheses can be very useful with large samples. In the linear regression setup, the test statistic is

$$LM = n \cdot R_{\tilde{u}}^2,$$

where *n* is the sample size and $R_{\tilde{u}}^2$ is the usual R^2 statistic in a regression of the residual $\tilde{u}$ from the restricted model on the unrestricted set of regressors. Under the null hypothesis, it is asymptotically distributed a χ_q^2 with *q* denoting the number of restrictions. Details are given in Wooldridge (2016, Section 5.2).

The implementation in *R* is straightforward if we remember that the residuals can be obtained with the **resid** command.

Wooldridge, Example 5.3: Economic Model of Crime

We analyze the same data on the number of arrests as in Example 3.5. The unrestricted regression model equation is

$$\texttt{narr86} = \beta_0 + \beta_1\texttt{pcnv} + \beta_2\texttt{avgsen} + \beta_3\texttt{tottime} + \beta_4\texttt{ptime86} + \beta_5\texttt{qemp86} + u.$$

The dependent variable `narr86` reflects the number of times a man was arrested and is explained by the proportion of prior arrests (`pcnv`), previous average sentences (`avgsen`), the time spend in prison before 1986 (`tottime`), the number of months in prison in 1986 (`ptime86`), and the number of quarters unemployed in 1986 (`qemp86`).
The joint null hypothesis is

$$H_0 : \beta_2 = \beta_3 = 0,$$

so the restricted set of regressors excludes `avgsen` and `tottime`. Script 5.4 (`Example-5-3.R`) shows an implementation of this *LM* test. The restricted model is estimated and its residuals `utilde=`$\tilde{u}$ are calculated. They are regressed on the unrestricted set of regressors. The R^2 from this regression is 0.001494, so the *LM* test statistic is calculated to be around $LM = 0.001494 \cdot 2725 = 4.071$. This is smaller than the critical value for a significance level of $\alpha = 10\%$, so we do not reject the null hypothesis. We can also easily calculate the *p* value in *R* using the χ^2 cdf **qchisq**. It turns out to be 0.1306.
The same hypothesis can be tested using the *F* presented in Section 4.3 using the command **linearHypothesis**. In this example, it delivers the same *p* value up to three digits.

──────── **Output of Script 5.4:** `Example-5-3.R` ────────

```
> library(foreign)

> crime1<-read.dta("http://fmwww.bc.edu/ec-p/data/wooldridge/crime1.dta")

> # 1. Estimate restricted model:
> restr <- lm(narr86 ~ pcnv+ptime86+qemp86, data=crime1)

> # 2. Regression of residuals from restricted model:
> utilde <- resid(restr)

> LMreg <- lm(utilde ~ pcnv+ptime86+qemp86+avgsen+tottime, data=crime1)

> # R-squared:
> (r2 <- summary(LMreg)$r.squared )
[1] 0.001493846

> # 3. Calculation of LM test statistic:
> LM <- r2 * nobs(LMreg)

> LM
[1] 4.070729

> # 4. Critical value from chi-squared distribution, alpha=10%:
> qchisq(1-0.10, 2)
[1] 4.60517

> # Alternative to critical value: p value
> 1-pchisq(LM, 2)
[1] 0.1306328

> # Alternative: automatic F test (see above)
> library(car)

> unrestr <- lm(narr86 ~ pcnv+ptime86+qemp86+avgsen+tottime, data=crime1)

> linearHypothesis(unrestr, c("avgsen=0","tottime=0"))
Linear hypothesis test

Hypothesis:
avgsen = 0
tottime = 0

Model 1: restricted model
Model 2: narr86 ~ pcnv + ptime86 + qemp86 + avgsen + tottime

  Res.Df    RSS Df Sum of Sq      F Pr(>F)
1   2721 1927.3
2   2719 1924.4  2     2.879 2.0339  0.131
```

6. Multiple Regression Analysis: Further Issues

In this chapter, we cover some issues regarding the implementation of regression analyses. Section 6.1 discusses more flexible specification of regression equations such as variable scaling, standardization, polynomials and interactions. They can be conveniently included the the R **formula** and used in the **lm** command for OLS estimation. Section 6.2 is concerned with predictions and their confidence and prediction intervals.

6.1. Model Formulae

If we run a regression in R using a syntax like **lm(y~x1+x2+x3,...)**, the expression **y~x1+x2+x3** is referred to as a model **formula**. It is a compact symbolic way to describe our regression equation. The dependent variable is separated from the regressors by a "**~**" and the regressors are separated by a "**+**" indicating that they enter the equation in a linear fashion. A constant is added by default. Such formulae can be specified in more complex ways to indicate different kinds of regression equations. We will cover the most important ones in this section.

6.1.1. Data Scaling: Arithmetic Operations Within a Formula

Wooldridge (2016) discusses how different scaling of the variables in the model affects the parameter estimates and other statistics in Section 6.1. As an example, a model relating the birth weight to cigarette smoking of the mother during pregnancy and the family income. The basic model equationis

$$\text{bwght} = \beta_0 + \beta_1 \text{cigs} + \beta_2 \text{faminc} + u \tag{6.1}$$

which translates into R formula syntax as **bwght~cigs+faminc**.

If we want to measure the weight in pounds rather than ounces, there are two ways to implement different rescaling in R. We can

- Define a different variable like **bwghtlbs <- bwght/16** and use this variable in the formula: **bwghtlbs~cigs+faminc**
- Specify this rescaling directly in the formula: **I(bwght/16)~cigs+faminc**

The latter approach can be more convenient. Note that the **I(...)** brackets any parts of the formula in which we specify arithmetic transformations.[1]

If we want to measure the number of cigarettes smoked per day in packs, we could again define a new variable **packs <- cigs/20** and use it as a regressor or simply specify the formula **bwght~I(cigs/20)+faminc**. Here, the importance to use the **I** function is easy to see. If we specified the formula **bwght~I(cigs/20+faminc)** instead, we would have a (nonsense) model with only one regressor: the sum of the packs smoked and the income.

---

[1]The function **I()** could actually be left out in this example. But in other examples, this would create confusion so it is a good idea to use it whenever we specify arithmetic transformations.

Script 6.1 (Data-Scaling.R) demonstrates these features. As discussed in Wooldridge (2016, Section 6.1), dividing the dependent variable by 16 changes all coefficients by the same factor $\frac{1}{16}$ and dividing a regressor by 20 changes its coefficient by the factor 20. Other statistics like R^2 are unaffected.

─────────────────── **Output of Script 6.1: Data-Scaling.R** ───────────────────

```
> library(foreign)

> bwght <- read.dta("http://fmwww.bc.edu/ec-p/data/wooldridge/bwght.dta")

> # Basic model:
> lm( bwght ~ cigs+faminc, data=bwght)

Call:
lm(formula = bwght ~ cigs + faminc, data = bwght)

Coefficients:
(Intercept)          cigs        faminc
  116.97413      -0.46341       0.09276


> # Weight in pounds, manual way:
> bwght$bwghtlbs <- bwght$bwght/16

> lm( bwghtlbs ~ cigs+faminc, data=bwght)

Call:
lm(formula = bwghtlbs ~ cigs + faminc, data = bwght)

Coefficients:
(Intercept)          cigs        faminc
   7.310883     -0.028963      0.005798


> # Weight in pounds, direct way:
> lm( I(bwght/16) ~ cigs+faminc, data=bwght)

Call:
lm(formula = I(bwght/16) ~ cigs + faminc, data = bwght)

Coefficients:
(Intercept)          cigs        faminc
   7.310883     -0.028963      0.005798


> # Packs of cigarettes:
> lm( bwght ~ I(cigs/20) +faminc, data=bwght)

Call:
lm(formula = bwght ~ I(cigs/20) + faminc, data = bwght)

Coefficients:
(Intercept)    I(cigs/20)        faminc
  116.97413      -9.26815       0.09276
```

6.1.2. Standardization: Beta Coefficients

A specific arithmetic operation is the standardization. A variable is standardized by subtracting its mean and dividing by its standard deviation. For example, the standardized dependent variable y and regressor x_1 are

$$z_y = \frac{y - \bar{y}}{\text{sd}(y)} \qquad z_{x_1} = \frac{x_1 - \bar{x}_1}{\text{sd}(x_1)} \tag{6.2}$$

If regression model only contains standardized variables, the coefficients have a special interpretation. They measure by how many *standard deviations y* changes as the respective independent variable increases by *one standard deviation*. Inconsistent with the notation used here, they are sometimes referred to as beta coefficients.

In *R*, we can use the same type of arithmetic transformations as in section 6.1.1 to subtract the mean and divide by the standard deviation. But it can also be done more conveniently by using the function **scale** directly for all variables we want to standardize. The equation and the corresponding *R* formula in a model with two standardized regressors would be

$$z_y = b_1 z_{x1} + b_2 z_{x2} + u \tag{6.3}$$

which translates into R syntax as **scale(y)~0+scale(x1)+scale(x2)**. The model does not include a constant because all averages are removed in the standardization. The constant is explicitly suppressed in *R* using the **0+** in the formula, see Section 2.5.

Wooldridge, Example 6.1: Effects of Pollution on Housing Prices

We are interested in how air pollution (nox) and other neighborhood characteristics affect the value of a house. A model using standardization for all variables is expressed in an *R* formula as
    scale(price)~0+scale(nox)+scale(crime)+scale(rooms)+scale(dist)+scale(stratio)
The output of Script 6.2 (Example-6-1.R) shows the parameters estimates of this model. The house price drops by 0.34 standard deviations as the air pollution increases by one standard deviation.

Output of Script 6.2: `Example-6-1.R`

```
> library(foreign)

> hprice2<-read.dta("http://fmwww.bc.edu/ec-p/data/wooldridge/hprice2.dta")

> # Estimate model with standardized variables:
> lm(scale(price) ~ 0+scale(nox)+scale(crime)+scale(rooms)+
>                         scale(dist)+scale(stratio), data=hprice2)

Call:
lm(formula = scale(price) ~ 0 + scale(nox) + scale(crime) + scale(rooms) +
    scale(dist) + scale(stratio), data = hprice2)

Coefficients:
    scale(nox)     scale(crime)     scale(rooms)     scale(dist)
       -0.3404          -0.1433           0.5139         -0.2348
scale(stratio)
       -0.2703
```

6.1.3. Logarithms

We have already seen in Section 2.4 that we can include the function **log** directly in formulas to represent logarithmic and semi-logarithmic models. A simple example of a partially logarithmic model and its R formulary would be

$$\log(y) = \beta_0 + \beta_1 \log(x_1) + \beta_2 x_2 + u \tag{6.4}$$

which in the language of R can be expressed as **log(y)~log(x1)+x2**.

Script 6.3 (Formula-Logarithm.R) show this again for the house price example. As the air pollution nox increases by *one percent*, the house price drops by about 0.72 *percent*. As the number of rooms increases by *one*, the value of the house increases by roughly 30.6%. Wooldridge (2016, Section 6.2) discusses how the latter value is only an approximation and the actual estimated effect is $(\exp(0.306) - 1) = 0.358$ which is 35.8%.

––––––––––– **Output of Script 6.3: Formula-Logarithm.R** –––––––––––

```
> library(foreign)

> hprice2<-read.dta("http://fmwww.bc.edu/ec-p/data/wooldridge/hprice2.dta")

> # Estimate model with logs:
> lm(log(price)~log(nox)+rooms, data=hprice2)

Call:
lm(formula = log(price) ~ log(nox) + rooms, data = hprice2)

Coefficients:
(Intercept)        log(nox)            rooms
     9.2337         -0.7177           0.3059
```

6.1.4. Quadratics and Polynomials

Specifying quadratic terms or higher powers of regressors can be a useful way to make a model more flexible by allowing the partial effects or (semi-)elasticities to decrease or increase with the value of the regressor.

Instead of creating additional variables containing the squared value of a regressor, in R we can simply add **I(x^2)** to a formula. Higher order terms are specified accordingly. A simple cubic model and its corresponding R formula are

$$y = \beta_0 + \beta_1 x + \beta_2 x^2 + \beta_3 x^3 + u \tag{6.5}$$

which translates to **y~x+I(x^2)+I(x^3)** in R syntax.

For nonlinear models like this, it is often useful to get a graphical illustration of the effects. Section 6.2.3 shows how to conveniently generate these.

Wooldridge, Example 6.2: Effects of Pollution on Housing Prices

This example of Wooldridge (2016) demonstrates the combination of logarithmic and quadratic specifications. The model for house prices is

$$\log(\texttt{price}) = \beta_0 + \beta_1 \log(\texttt{nox}) + \beta_2 \log(\texttt{dist}) + \beta_3 \texttt{rooms} + \beta_4 \texttt{rooms}^2 + \beta_5 \texttt{stratio} + u.$$

Script 6.4 (`Example-6-2.R`) implements this model and presents detailed results including t statistics and their p values. The quadratic term of `rooms` has a significantly positive coefficient $\hat{\beta}_4$ implying that the semi-elasticity increases with more rooms. The negative coefficient for `rooms` and the positive coefficient for `rooms`^{2} imply that for "small" numbers of rooms, the price *decreases* with the number of rooms and for "large" values, it *increases*. The number of rooms implying the smallest price can be found as[2]

$$\texttt{rooms}^* = \frac{-\beta_3}{2\beta_4} \approx 4.4.$$

─── Output of Script 6.4: `Example-6-2.R` ───

```
> library(foreign)

> hprice2<-read.dta("http://fmwww.bc.edu/ec-p/data/wooldridge/hprice2.dta")

> res<- lm(log(price)~log(nox)+log(dist)+rooms+I(rooms^2)+
>              stratio,data=hprice2)

> summary(res)

Call:
lm(formula = log(price) ~ log(nox) + log(dist) + rooms + I(rooms^2) +
    stratio, data = hprice2)

Residuals:
     Min      1Q   Median      3Q      Max
-1.04285 -0.12774  0.02038  0.12650  1.25272

Coefficients:
             Estimate Std. Error t value Pr(>|t|)
(Intercept) 13.385477   0.566473  23.630  < 2e-16 ***
log(nox)    -0.901682   0.114687  -7.862 2.34e-14 ***
log(dist)   -0.086781   0.043281  -2.005  0.04549 *
rooms       -0.545113   0.165454  -3.295  0.00106 **
I(rooms^2)   0.062261   0.012805   4.862 1.56e-06 ***
stratio     -0.047590   0.005854  -8.129 3.42e-15 ***
---
Signif. codes:  0 `***' 0.001 `**' 0.01 `*' 0.05 `.' 0.1 ` ' 1

Residual standard error: 0.2592 on 500 degrees of freedom
Multiple R-squared:  0.6028,        Adjusted R-squared:  0.5988
F-statistic: 151.8 on 5 and 500 DF,  p-value: < 2.2e-16
```

---

[2] We need to find `rooms`* to minimize $\beta_3 \texttt{rooms} + \beta_4 \texttt{rooms}^2$. Setting the first derivative $\beta_3 + 2\beta_4 \texttt{rooms}$ equal to zero and solving for `rooms` delivers the result.

6.1.5. Interaction Terms

Models with interaction terms allow the effect of one variable x_1 to depend on the value of another variable x_2. A simple model including an interaction term would be

$$y = \beta_0 + \beta_1 x_1 + \beta_2 x_2 + \beta_3 x_1 x_2 + u. \tag{6.6}$$

Of course, we can implement this in *R* by defining a new variable containing the product of the two regressors. But again, a direct specification in the model formula is more convenient. The expression **x1:x2** within a formula adds the interaction term $x_1 x_2$. Even more conveniently, **x1*x2** adds not only the interaction but also both original variables allowing for a very concise syntax. So the model in equation 6.6 can be specified in *R* as either of the two formulas

$$\textbf{y ~ x1+x2+x1:x2} \qquad \Leftrightarrow \qquad \textbf{y ~ x1*x2}$$

If one variable x_1 is interacted with a set of other variables, they can be grouped by parentheses to allow for a compact syntax. For example, a model equation and its *R* formula could be

$$y = \beta_0 + \beta_1 x_1 + \beta_2 x_2 + \beta_3 x_3 + \beta_4 x_1 x_2 + \beta_5 x_1 x_3 + u. \tag{6.7}$$

The shortest way to express this in *R* syntax is **y ~ x1*(x2+x3)**.

Wooldridge, Example 6.3: Effects of Attendance on Final Exam Performance

This example analyzes a model including a standardized dependent variable, quadratic terms and an interaction. Standardized scores in the final exam are explained by class attendance, prior performance and an interaction term:

$$\texttt{stndfnl} = \beta_0 + \beta_1 \texttt{atndrte} + \beta_2 \texttt{priGPA} + \beta_3 \texttt{ACT} + \beta_4 \texttt{priGPA}^2 + \beta_5 \texttt{ACT}^2 + \beta_6 \texttt{priGPA} \cdot \texttt{atndrte} + u$$

Script 6.5 (Example-6-3.R) estimates this model. The effect of attending classes is

$$\frac{\partial \texttt{stndfnl}}{\partial \texttt{atndrte}} = \beta_1 + \beta_6 \texttt{priGPA}.$$

For the average $\overline{\texttt{priGPA}} = 2.59$, the script estimates this partial effect to be around 0.0078. It tests the null hypothesis that this effect is zero using a simple F test, see Section 4.3. With a p value of 0.0034, this hypothesis can be rejected at all common significance levels.

```
─────────── Output of Script 6.5: Example-6-3.R ───────────

> library(foreign)

> attend <- read.dta("http://fmwww.bc.edu/ec-p/data/wooldridge/attend.dta")

> # Estimate model with interaction effect:
> (myres<-lm(stndfnl~atndrte*priGPA+ACT+I(priGPA^2)+I(ACT^2), data=attend))

Call:
lm(formula = stndfnl ~ atndrte * priGPA + ACT + I(priGPA^2) +
    I(ACT^2), data = attend)

Coefficients:
   (Intercept)          atndrte            priGPA              ACT
      2.050293        -0.006713         -1.628540         -0.128039
    I(priGPA^2)         I(ACT^2)   atndrte:priGPA
      0.295905         0.004533         0.005586


> # Estimate for partial effect at priGPA=2.59:
> b <- coef(myres)

> b["atndrte"] + 2.59*b["atndrte:priGPA"]
    atndrte
0.007754572

> # Test partial effect for priGPA=2.59:
> library(car)

> linearHypothesis(myres,c("atndrte+2.59*atndrte:priGPA"))
Linear hypothesis test

Hypothesis:
atndrte  + 2.59 atndrte:priGPA = 0

Model 1: restricted model
Model 2: stndfnl ~ atndrte * priGPA + ACT + I(priGPA^2) + I(ACT^2)

  Res.Df    RSS Df Sum of Sq      F   Pr(>F)
1    674 519.34
2    673 512.76  1    6.5772 8.6326 0.003415 **
---
Signif. codes:  0 '***' 0.001 '**' 0.01 '*' 0.05 '.' 0.1 ' ' 1
```

6.2. Prediction

In this section, we are concerned with predicting the value of the dependent variable y given certain values of the regressors $x_1, \ldots, x_k$. If these are the regressor values in our estimation sample, we called these predictions "fitted values" and discussed their calculation in Section 2.2. Now, we generalize this to arbitrary values and add standard errors, confidence intervals, and prediction intervals.

6.2.1. Confidence Intervals for Predictions

Given a model

$$y = \beta_0 + \beta_1 x_1 + \beta_2 x_2 + \cdots + \beta_k x_k + u \tag{6.8}$$

we are interested in the expected value of y given the regressors take specific values $c_1, c_2, \ldots, c_k$:

$$\theta_0 = \mathrm{E}(y|x_1 = c_1, \ldots, x_k = c_k) = \beta_0 + \beta_1 c_1 + \beta_2 c_2 + \cdots + \beta_k c_k. \tag{6.9}$$

The natural point estimates are

$$\hat{\theta}_0 = \hat{\beta}_0 + \hat{\beta}_1 c_1 + \hat{\beta}_2 c_2 + \cdots + \hat{\beta}_k c_k \tag{6.10}$$

and can readily be obtained once the parameter estimates $\hat{\beta}_0, \ldots, \hat{\beta}_k$ are calculated.

Standard errors and confidence intervals are less straightforward to compute. Wooldridge (2016, Section 6.4) suggests a smart way to obtain these from a modified regression. *R* provides an even simpler and more convenient approach.

The command **predict** can not only automatically calculate $\hat{\theta}_0$ but also its standard error and confidence intervals. Its arguments are

- The regression results. If they are stored in a variable `reg` by a command like `reg <- lm(y~x1+x2+x3,...)`, we can just supply the name `reg`.
- A data frame containing the values of the regressors $c_1, \ldots c_k$ of the regressors $x_1, \ldots x_k$ with the same variable names as in the data frame used for estimation. If we don't have one yet, it can for example be specified as `data.frame(x1=c1, x2=c2,..., xk=ck)` where `x1` through `xk` are the variable names and `c1` through `ck` are the values which can also specified as vectors to get predictions at several values of the regressors. See Section 1.3.1 for more on data frames.
- `se.fit=TRUE` to also request standard errors of the predictions
- `interval="confidence"` to also request confidence intervals (or for prediction intervals `interval="prediction"`, see below)
- `level=0.99` to choose the 99% confidence interval instead of the default 95%. Of course, arbitrary other values are possible.
- and more.

If the model formula contains some of the advanced features such as rescaling, quadratic terms and interactions presented in Section 6.1, **predict** is clever enough to make the same sort of transformations for the predictions. Example 6.5 demonstrates some of the features.

Wooldridge, Example 6.5: Confidence Interval for Predicted College GPA

We try to predict the college GPA, for example to support the admission decisions for our college. Our regression model equation is

$$\text{colgpa} = \beta_0 + \beta_1\text{sat} + \beta_2\text{hsperc} + \beta_3\text{hsize} + \beta_4\text{hsize}^2 + u.$$

Script 6.6 (`Example-6-5.R`) shows the implementation of the estimation and prediction. The estimation results are stored as the variable `reg`. The values of the regressors for which we want to do the prediction are stored in the new data frame `cvalues`. Then command **predict** is called with these two arguments. For an SAT score of 1200, a high school percentile of 30 and a high school size of 5 (i.e. 500 students), the predicted college GPA is 2.7. Wooldridge (2016) obtains the same value using a general but more cumbersome regression approach. The 95% confidence interval is reported with the next command. With 95% confidence we can say that the expected college GPA for students with these features is between 2.66 and 2.74.

Finally, we define three types of students with different values of `sat`, `hsperc`, and `hsize`. The data frame `cvalues` is filled with these numbers and displayed as a table. For these three regressor variables, we obtain the 99% confidence intervals.

Output of Script 6.6: `Example-6-5.R`

```
> library(foreign)

> gpa2 <- read.dta("http://fmwww.bc.edu/ec-p/data/wooldridge/gpa2.dta")

> # Regress and report coefficients
> reg <- lm(colgpa~sat+hsperc+hsize+I(hsize^2),data=gpa2)

> reg

Call:
lm(formula = colgpa ~ sat + hsperc + hsize + I(hsize^2), data = gpa2)

Coefficients:
(Intercept)          sat       hsperc         hsize    I(hsize^2)
   1.492652     0.001492    -0.013856     -0.060881      0.005460


> # Generate data set containing the regressor values for predictions
> cvalues <- data.frame(sat=1200, hsperc=30, hsize=5)

> # Point estimate of prediction
> predict(reg, cvalues)
       1
2.700075

> # Point estimate and 95% confidence interval
> predict(reg, cvalues, interval = "confidence")
       fit      lwr      upr
1 2.700075 2.661104 2.739047

> # Define three sets of regressor variables
> cvalues <- data.frame(sat=c(1200,900,1400), hsperc=c(30,20,5),
>                                              hsize=c(5,3,1))
```

```
> cvalues
   sat hsperc hsize
1 1200     30     5
2  900     20     3
3 1400      5     1

> # Point estimates and 99% confidence intervals for these
> predict(reg, cvalues, interval = "confidence", level=0.99)
       fit      lwr      upr
1 2.700075 2.648850 2.751301
2 2.425282 2.388540 2.462025
3 3.457448 3.385572 3.529325
```

6.2.2. Prediction Intervals

Confidence intervals reflect the uncertainty about the *expected value* of the dependent variable given values of the regressors. If we are interested in predicting the college GPA of an *individual*, we have to account for the additional uncertainty regarding the unobserved characteristics reflected by the error term u.

Wooldridge (2016) explains how to calculate the prediction interval manually and gives an example. In practice, we can do these calculation automatically in R using the option **interval="prediction"** of **predict**. This is demonstrated in Example 6.6.

Wooldridge, Example 6.6: Prediction Interval for College GPA

We use the same model as in Example 6.5. to predict the college GPA. Script 6.7 (Example-6-6.R) calculates the 95% prediction interval for the same values of the regressors as in Example 6.5. The only difference is the option **interval="prediction"** instead of **interval="confidence"**. The results are the same as those manually calculated by Wooldridge (2016).

──────────────── Output of Script 6.7: Example-6-6.R ────────────────

```
> library(foreign)

> gpa2 <- read.dta("http://fmwww.bc.edu/ec-p/data/wooldridge/gpa2.dta")

> # Regress (as before)
> reg <- lm(colgpa~sat+hsperc+hsize+I(hsize^2),data=gpa2)

> # Define three sets of regressor variables (as before)
> cvalues <- data.frame(sat=c(1200,900,1400), hsperc=c(30,20,5),
>                                              hsize=c(5,3,1))

> # Point estimates and 95% prediction intervals for these
> predict(reg, cvalues, interval = "prediction")
       fit      lwr      upr
1 2.700075 1.601749 3.798402
2 2.425282 1.327292 3.523273
3 3.457448 2.358452 4.556444
```

6.2.3. Effect Plots for Nonlinear Specifications

In models with quadratic or other nonlinear terms, the coefficients themselves are often difficult to interpret directly. We have to do additional calculations to obtain the partial effect at different values of the regressors or derive the extreme points. In Example 6.2, we found the number of rooms implying the minimum predicted house price to be around 4.4.

For a better visual understanding of the implications of our model, it is often useful to calculate predictions for *different values of one regressor* of interest while keeping *the other regressors fixed* at certain values like their overall sample means. By plotting the results against the regressor value, we get a very intuitive graph showing the estimated *ceteris paribus* effects of the regressor.

We already know how to calculate predictions and their confidence intervals from Section 6.2.1. Script 6.8 (`Effects-Manual.R`) repeats the regression from Example 6.2 and creates an effects plot for the number of rooms manually. The number of rooms is varied between 4 and 8 and the other variables are set to their respective sample means for all predictions. The regressor values and the implied predictions are shown in a table and then plotted using **matplot** for automatically including the confidence bands. The resulting graph is shown in Figure 6.1(a).

The package ***effects*** provides the convenient command **effect**. It creates the same kind of plots we just generated, but it is more convenient to use and the result is nicely formatted. After storing the regression results in variable `res`, Figure 6.1(b) is produced with the simple command

```
plot( effect("rooms",res) )
```

The full Code including loading the data and running the regression is in Script 6.9 (`Effects-Automatic.R`). We see the minimum at a number of rooms of around 4.4. We also see the observed values of `rooms` as ticks on the axis. Obviously nearly all observations are in the area right of the minimum where the slope is positive.

—— **Output of Script 6.8: `Effects-Manual.R`** ——

```
> # Repeating the regression from Example 6.2:
> library(foreign)

> hprice2<-read.dta("http://fmwww.bc.edu/ec-p/data/wooldridge/hprice2.dta")

> res <- lm( log(price) ~ log(nox)+log(dist)+rooms+I(rooms^2)+stratio,
>                                               data=hprice2)

> # Predictions: Values of the regressors:
> # rooms = 4-8, all others at the sample mean:
> X <- data.frame(rooms=seq(4,8),nox=5.5498,dist=3.7958,stratio=18.4593)

> # Calculate predictions and confidence interval:
> pred <- predict(res, X, interval = "confidence")

> # Table of regressor values, predictions and CI:
> cbind(X,pred)
  rooms    nox   dist stratio       fit       lwr       upr
1     4 5.5498 3.7958 18.4593  9.661698  9.499807  9.823589
2     5 5.5498 3.7958 18.4593  9.676936  9.610210  9.743661
3     6 5.5498 3.7958 18.4593  9.816696  9.787050  9.846341
4     7 5.5498 3.7958 18.4593 10.080978 10.042404 10.119553
5     8 5.5498 3.7958 18.4593 10.469783 10.383355 10.556211

> # Plot
> matplot(X$rooms, pred, type="l", lty=c(1,2,2))
```

Figure 6.1. Nonlinear Effects in Example 6.2

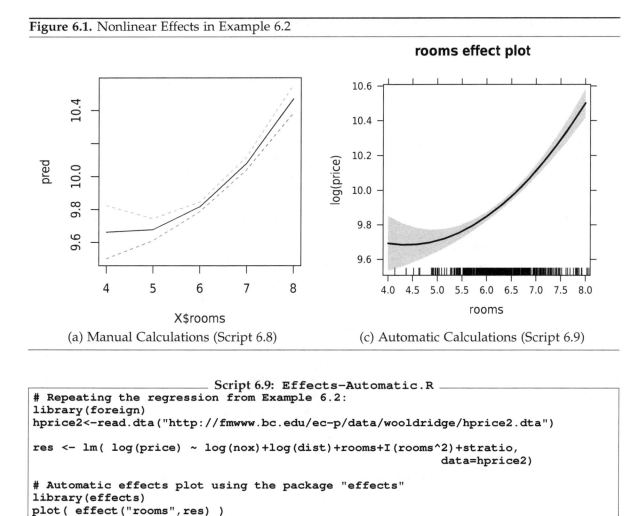

(a) Manual Calculations (Script 6.8)   (c) Automatic Calculations (Script 6.9)

Script 6.9: Effects-Automatic.R

```
# Repeating the regression from Example 6.2:
library(foreign)
hprice2<-read.dta("http://fmwww.bc.edu/ec-p/data/wooldridge/hprice2.dta")

res <- lm( log(price) ~ log(nox)+log(dist)+rooms+I(rooms^2)+stratio,
                                              data=hprice2)

# Automatic effects plot using the package "effects"
library(effects)
plot( effect("rooms",res) )
```

7. Multiple Regression Analysis with Qualitative Regressors

Many variables of interest are qualitative rather than quantitative. Examples include gender, race, labor market status, marital status, and brand choice. In this chapter, we discuss use use of qualitative variables as regressors. Wooldridge (2016, Section 7.5) also covers linear probability models with a binary dependent variable in a linear regression. Since this does not change the implementation, we will skip this topic here and cover binary dependent variables in Chapter 17.

Qualtitative information can be represented as binary or dummy variables which can only take the value zero or one. In Section 7.1, we see that dummy variables can be used as regressors just as any other variable. An even more natural way to store yes/no type of information in R is to use logical variables which can also be directly used as regressors, see Section 7.2.

While qualitative variables with more than two outcomes can be represented by a set of dummy variables, the more natural and convenient way to do this in R are factor variables as covered in Section 7.3. A special case in which we wish to break a numeric variable into categories is discussed in Section 7.4. Finally, Section 7.5 revisits interaction effects and shows how these can be used with factor variables to conveniently allow and test for difference in the regression equation.

7.1. Linear Regression with Dummy Variables as Regressors

If qualitative information are stored as dummy variables (i.e. variables taking the values zero or one), these can easily be used as regressors in linear regression. If a single dummy variable is used in a model, its coefficient represents the difference in the intercept between groups, see Wooldridge (2016, Section 7.2).

A qualitative variable can also take $g > 2$ values. A variable `MobileOS` could for example take one of the $g = 4$ values "Android", "iOS", "Windows", or "other". These information can be represented by $g - 1$ dummy variables, each taking the values zero or one, where one category is left out to serve as a reference category. They take the value one if the respective operating system is used and zero otherwise. Wooldridge (2016, Section 7.3) gives more information on these variables and their interpretation.

Here, we are concerned with implementing linear regressions with dummy variables as regressors. Everything works as before once we have generated the dummy variables. In the example data sets provided with Wooldridge (2016), this has usually already been done for us, so we don't have to learn anything new in terms of implementation. We show two examples.

Wooldridge, Example 7.1: Hourly Wage Equation

We are interested in the wage differences by gender and regress the hourly wage on a dummy variable which is equal to one for females and zero for males. We also include regressors for education, experience, and tenure. The implementation with `lm` is standard and the dummy variable `female` is used just as any other regressor as shown in Script 7.1 (`Example-7-1.R`). Its estimated coefficient of -1.81 indicates that on average, a woman makes \$1.81 per hour less than a man *with the same education, experience, and tenure.*

```
──────────── Output of Script 7.1: Example-7-1.R ────────────

> library(foreign)

> wage1 <- read.dta("http://fmwww.bc.edu/ec-p/data/wooldridge/wage1.dta")

> lm(wage ~ female+educ+exper+tenure, data=wage1)

Call:
lm(formula = wage ~ female + educ + exper + tenure, data = wage1)

Coefficients:
(Intercept)      female         educ         exper        tenure
    -1.5679     -1.8109       0.5715        0.0254        0.1410
```

Wooldridge, Example 7.6: Log Hourly Wage Equation

We used log wage as the dependent variable and distinguish gender and marital status using a qualitative variable with the four outcomes "single female", "single male", "married female", and "married male". We actually implement this regression using an interaction term between married and female in Script 7.2 (Example-7-6.R). *Relative to the reference group* of single males *with the same education, experience, and tenure*, married males make about 21.3% more (the coefficient of married), and single females make about 11.0% less (the coefficient of female). The coefficient of the interaction term implies that married females make around 30.1%-21.3%=8.7% less *than single females*, 30.1%+11.0%=41.1% less than married males, and 30.1%+11.0%-21.3%=19.8% less than single males. Note once again that the approximate interpretation as percent may be inaccurate, see Section 6.1.3.

```
──────────── Output of Script 7.2: Example-7-6.R ────────────

> library(foreign)

> wage1 <- read.dta("http://fmwww.bc.edu/ec-p/data/wooldridge/wage1.dta")

> lm(log(wage) ~married*female+educ+exper+I(exper^2)+tenure+I(tenure^2),
>                                                    data=wage1)

Call:
lm(formula = log(wage) ~ married * female + educ + exper + I(exper^2) +
    tenure + I(tenure^2), data = wage1)

Coefficients:
   (Intercept)         married          female            educ
     0.3213781       0.2126757      -0.1103502       0.0789103
         exper       I(exper^2)          tenure       I(tenure^2)
     0.0268006      -0.0005352       0.0290875      -0.0005331
 married:female
    -0.3005931
```

7.2. Logical Variables

A natural way for storing qualitative yes/no information in *R* is to use logical variables introduced in Section 1.2.3. They can take the values **TRUE** or **FALSE** and can be transformed into a 0/1 dummy variables with the function **as.numeric** where **TRUE=1** and **FALSE=0**. 0/1-coded dummies can *vice versa* be transformed into logical variables with **as.logical**.

Instead of transforming logical variables into dummies, they can be directly used as regressors. The coefficient is then named varnameTRUE. Script 7.3 (Example-7-1-logical.R) repeats the analysis of Example 7.1 with the regressor female being coded as a logical instead of a 0/1 dummy variable.

———— **Output of Script 7.3: Example-7-1-logical.R** ————

```
> library(foreign)

> wage1 <- read.dta("http://fmwww.bc.edu/ec-p/data/wooldridge/wage1.dta")

> # replace "female" with logical variable
> wage1$female <- as.logical(wage1$female)

> table(wage1$female)

FALSE   TRUE
  274    252

> # regression with logical variable
> lm(wage ~ female+educ+exper+tenure, data=wage1)

Call:
lm(formula = wage ~ female + educ + exper + tenure, data = wage1)

Coefficients:
(Intercept)    femaleTRUE         educ        exper       tenure
    -1.5679       -1.8109       0.5715       0.0254       0.1410
```

In real-world data sets, qualitative information is often not readily coded as logical or dummy variables, so we might want to create our own regressors. Suppose a qualitative variable OS takes one of the three string values "Android", "iOS", "Windows", or "other". We can manually define the three relevant logical variables with "Android" as the reference category with

```
iOS  <- OS=="iOS"
wind <- OS=="Windows"
oth  <- OS=="other"
```

The package *dummies* provides convenient functions to automatically generate dummy variables. But a even more convenient and elegant way to deal with qualitative variables in *R* are factor variables discussed in the next section.

7.3. Factor variables

We have introduced factor variables in Section 1.2.3. They take one of a given set of outcomes which can be labeled arbitrarily. This makes factors the natural variable type to store qualitative information. If a data set is imported from a text file, string columns are automatically converted into factor variables. We can transform any variable into a factor variable using **as.factor**.

One of the convenient features of factor variables is that they can be directly added to the list of regressors. R is clever enough to implicitly add $g - 1$ dummy variables if the factor has g outcomes. As a reference category, the first category is left out by default. The command **relevel(var,val)** chooses the outcome val as the reference for variable var.

Script 7.4 (Regr-Factors.R) shows how factor variables are used. It uses the data set **CPS1985** from the package **AER**.[1] This data set is similar to the one used in Examples 7.1 and 7.6 in that it contains wage and other data for 534 individuals. Many of the variables like gender and occupation are qualitative and readily defined as factors in this data set. The frequency tables for these two variables are shown in the output. The variable gender has two categories male and female. The variable occupation has six categories.

When we directly add these factors as regressors, R automatically chooses the first categories male and worker as the reference and implicitly enters dummy variables for the other categories. In the output, the coefficients are labeled with a combination of the variable and category name. As an example, the estimated coefficient of -0.224 for genderfemale implies that women make about 22.4% less than men who are the same in terms of the other regressors. Employees in management positions earn around 15.3% more than otherwise equal workers (who are the reference category).

We can choose different reference categories using the **relevel** command. In the example, we choose female and management. When we rerun the same regression command, we see the expected results: Variables like education and experience get the same coefficients. The dummy variable for males gets the negative of what the females got previously. Obviously, it is equivalent to say "female log wages are lower by 0.224" and "male log wages are hihger by 0.224".

The coefficients for the occupation are now relative to management. From the first regression we already knew that managers make 15.3% more than workers, so it is not surprising that in the second regression we find that workers make 15.3% less than managers. The other occupation coefficients are lower by 0.15254 implying the same relative comparisons as in the first results.

─────────── **Output of Script 7.4: Regr-Factors.R** ───────────

```
> data(CPS1985,package="AER")

> # Table of categories and frequencies for two factor variables:
> table(CPS1985$gender)

  male female
   289    245

> table(CPS1985$occupation)

    worker  technical   services     office      sales management
       156        105         83         97         38         55

> # Directly using factor variables in regression formula:
> lm(log(wage) ~ education+experience+gender+occupation, data=CPS1985)
```

---

[1]Remember that packages have to installed once before we can use them. With an active internet connection, the command to automatically do this is **install.packages("AER")**.

```
Call:
lm(formula = log(wage) ~ education + experience + gender + occupation,
    data = CPS1985)

Coefficients:
         (Intercept)               education              experience
             0.97629                 0.07586                 0.01188
        genderfemale    occupationtechnical     occupationservices
            -0.22385                 0.14246                -0.21004
      occupationoffice        occupationsales   occupationmanagement
            -0.05477                -0.20757                 0.15254


> # Manually redefine the  reference category:
> CPS1985$gender <- relevel(CPS1985$gender,"female")

> CPS1985$occupation <- relevel(CPS1985$occupation,"management")

> # Rerun regression:
> lm(log(wage) ~ education+experience+gender+occupation, data=CPS1985)
Call:
lm(formula = log(wage) ~ education + experience + gender + occupation,
    data = CPS1985)

Coefficients:
         (Intercept)               education              experience
             0.90498                 0.07586                 0.01188
          gendermale       occupationworker    occupationtechnical
             0.22385                -0.15254                -0.01009
  occupationservices       occupationoffice        occupationsales
            -0.36259                -0.20731                -0.36011
```

7.4. Breaking a Numeric Variable Into Categories

Sometimes, we do not use a numeric variable directly in a regression model because the implied linear relation seems implausible or inconvenient to interpret. As an alternative to working with transformations such as logs and quadratic terms, it sometimes makes sense to estimate different levels for different ranges of the variable. Wooldridge (2016, Example 7.8) gives the example of the ranking of a law school and how it relates to the starting salary of its graduates.

Given a numeric variable, we need to generate a categorical (factor) variable to represent the range into which the rank of a school falls. In *R*, the command **cut** is very convenient for this. It takes a numeric variable and a vector of cut points and returns a factor variable. By default, the upper cut points are included in the corresponding range.

Wooldridge, Example 7.8: Effects of Law School Rankings on Starting Salaries

The variable `rank` of the data set `LAWSCH85.dta` is the rank of the law school as a number between 1 and 175. We would like to compare schools in the top 10, ranks 11–25, 26–40, 41–60, and 61–100 to the reference group of ranks above 100. So in Script 7.5 (`Example-7-8.R`), we store the cut points 0,10,25,40,60,100, and 175 in a variable `cutpts`. In the data frame `data`, we create our new variable `rankcat` using the **cut** command.

To be consistent with Wooldridge (2016), we do not want the top 10 schools as a reference category but the last category. It is chosen using the **relevel** command. The regression results imply that graduates from the top 10 schools collect a starting salary which is around 70% higher than those of the schools below rank 100. In fact, this approximation is inaccurate with these large numbers and the coefficient of 0.7 actually implies a difference of exp(0.7-1)=1.013 or 101.3%.

Output of Script 7.5: `Example-7-8.R`

```
> library(foreign)

> lawsch85<-
>       read.dta("http://fmwww.bc.edu/ec-p/data/wooldridge/lawsch85.dta")

> # Define cut points for the rank
> cutpts <- c(0,10,25,40,60,100,175)

> # Create factor variable containing ranges for the rank
> lawsch85$rankcat <- cut(lawsch85$rank, cutpts)

> # Display frequencies
> table(lawsch85$rankcat)

    (0,10]    (10,25]    (25,40]    (40,60]   (60,100]  (100,175]
        10         16         13         18         37         62

> # Choose reference category
> lawsch85$rankcat <- relevel(lawsch85$rankcat,"(100,175]")

> # Run regression
> lm(log(salary)~rankcat+LSAT+GPA+log(libvol)+log(cost), data=lawsch85)

Call:
lm(formula = log(salary) ~ rankcat + LSAT + GPA + log(libvol) +
    log(cost), data = lawsch85)

Coefficients:
    (Intercept)     rankcat(0,10]    rankcat(10,25]    rankcat(25,40]
      9.1652952         0.6995659         0.5935434         0.3750763
  rankcat(40,60]    rankcat(60,100]              LSAT               GPA
      0.2628191         0.1315950         0.0056908         0.0137255
     log(libvol)         log(cost)
      0.0363619         0.0008412
```

7.5. Interactions and Differences in Regression Functions Across Groups

Dummy and factor variables can be interacted just like any other variable. Wooldridge (2016, Section 7.4) discusses the specification and interpretation in this setup. An important case is a model in which one or more dummy variables are interacted with all other regressors. This allows the whole regression model to differ by groups of observations identified by the dummy variable(s).

The example from Wooldridge (2016, Section 7.4) is replicated in Script 7.6 (Dummy-Interact.R). Note that the example only applies to the subset of data with spring==1. We use the **subset** option of **lm** directly to define the estimation sample. Other than that, the script does not introduce any new syntax but combines two tricks we have seen previously:

- The dummy variable female is interacted with all other regressors using the "*" formula syntax with the other variables contained in parentheses, see Section 6.1.5.
- The F test for all interaction effects is performed using the command **linearHypothesis** from the package **car**. The function **matchCoefs** is used to specify the null hypothesis that all coefficients with the expression female in their names are zero, see Section 4.3.

─────────── Output of Script 7.6: Dummy-Interact.R ───────────

```
> library(foreign)

> gpa3 <- read.dta("http://fmwww.bc.edu/ec-p/data/wooldridge/gpa3.dta")

> # Model with full interactions with female dummy (only for spring data)
> reg<-lm(cumgpa~female*(sat+hsperc+tothrs), data=gpa3, subset=(spring==1))

> summary(reg)

Call:
lm(formula = cumgpa ~ female * (sat + hsperc + tothrs), data = gpa3,
    subset = (spring == 1))

Residuals:
     Min       1Q   Median       3Q      Max
-1.51370 -0.28645 -0.02306  0.27555  1.24760

Coefficients:
                Estimate Std. Error t value Pr(>|t|)
(Intercept)    1.4808117  0.2073336   7.142 5.17e-12 ***
female        -0.3534862  0.4105293  -0.861  0.38979
sat            0.0010516  0.0001811   5.807 1.40e-08 ***
hsperc        -0.0084516  0.0013704  -6.167 1.88e-09 ***
tothrs         0.0023441  0.0008624   2.718  0.00688 **
female:sat     0.0007506  0.0003852   1.949  0.05211 .
female:hsperc -0.0005498  0.0031617  -0.174  0.86206
female:tothrs -0.0001158  0.0016277  -0.071  0.94331
---
Signif. codes:  0 '***' 0.001 '**' 0.01 '*' 0.05 '.' 0.1 ' ' 1

Residual standard error: 0.4678 on 358 degrees of freedom
Multiple R-squared:  0.4059,     Adjusted R-squared:  0.3943
F-statistic: 34.95 on 7 and 358 DF,  p-value: < 2.2e-16
```

```
> # F-Test from package "car". H0: the interaction coefficients are zero
> # matchCoefs(...) selects all coeffs with names containing "female"
> library(car)

> linearHypothesis(reg, matchCoefs(reg, "female"))
Linear hypothesis test

Hypothesis:
female = 0
female:sat = 0
female:hsperc = 0
female:tothrs = 0

Model 1: restricted model
Model 2: cumgpa ~ female * (sat + hsperc + tothrs)

  Res.Df    RSS Df Sum of Sq      F    Pr(>F)
1    362 85.515
2    358 78.355  4    7.1606 8.1791 2.545e-06 ***
---
Signif. codes:  0 '***' 0.001 '**' 0.01 '*' 0.05 '.' 0.1 ' ' 1
```

We can estimate the same model parameters by running two separate regressions, one for females and one for males, see Script 7.7 (Dummy-Interact-Sep.R). We see that in the joint model, the parameters without interactions ((Intercept), sat, hsperc, and tothrs) apply to the males and the interaction parameters reflect the *differences* to the males.

To reconstruct the parameters for females from the joint model, we need to add the two respective parameters. The intercept for females is $1.4808117 - 0.3534862 = 1.127325$ and the coefficient of sat for females is $0.0010516 + 0.0007506 = 0.0018022$.

─────────────── Output of Script 7.7: Dummy-Interact-Sep.R ───────────────

```
> library(foreign)

> gpa3 <- read.dta("http://fmwww.bc.edu/ec-p/data/wooldridge/gpa3.dta")

> # Estimate model for males (& spring data)
> lm(cumgpa~sat+hsperc+tothrs, data=gpa3, subset=(spring==1&female==0))

Call:
lm(formula = cumgpa ~ sat + hsperc + tothrs, data = gpa3, subset = (spring ==
    1 & female == 0))

Coefficients:
(Intercept)          sat        hsperc        tothrs
   1.480812     0.001052     -0.008452      0.002344


> # Estimate model for females (& spring data)
> lm(cumgpa~sat+hsperc+tothrs, data=gpa3, subset=(spring==1&female==1))

Call:
lm(formula = cumgpa ~ sat + hsperc + tothrs, data = gpa3, subset = (spring ==
    1 & female == 1))

Coefficients:
(Intercept)          sat        hsperc        tothrs
   1.127325     0.001802     -0.009001      0.002228
```

8. Heteroscedasticity

The homoscedasticity assumptions SLR.5 for the simple regression model and MLR.5 for the multiple regression model require that the variance of the error terms is unrelated to the regressors, i.e.

$$\text{Var}(u|x_1, \ldots, x_k) = \sigma^2. \tag{8.1}$$

Unbiasedness and consistency (Theorems 3.1, 5.1) do not depend on this assumption, but the sampling distribution (Theorems 3.2, 4.1, 5.2) does. If homoscedasticity is violated, the standard errors are invalid and all inferences from t, F and other tests based on them are unreliable. Also the (asymptotic) efficiency of OLS (Theorems 3.4, 5.3) depends on homoscedasticity. Generally, homoscedasticity is difficult to justify from theory. Different kinds of individuals might have different amounts of unobserved influences in ways that depend on regressors.

We cover three topics: Section 8.1 shows how the formula of the estimated variance-covariance can be adjusted so it does not require homoscedasticity. In this way, we can use OLS to get unbiased and consistent parameter estimates and draw inference from valid standard errors and tests. Section 8.2 presents tests for the existence of heteroscedasticity. Section 8.3 discusses weighted least squares (WLS) as an alternative to OLS. This estimator can be more efficient in the presence of heteroscedasticity.

8.1. Heteroscedasticity-Robust Inference

Wooldridge (2016, Section 8.2) presents formulas for heteroscedasticity-robust standard errors. In R, an easy way to do these calculations is to use the package *car* which we have used before. It provides the command **hccm** (for **h**eteroscedasticity-**c**orrected **c**ovariance **m**atrices) that can produce several refined versions of the White formula presented by Wooldridge (2016).[1]

If the estimation results obtained by **lm** are stored in the variable reg, the variance-covariance matrix can be calculated using

- **hccm(reg)** for the default refined version of White's robust variance-covariance matrix
- **hccm(reg,type="hc0")** for the classical version of White's robust variance-covariance matrix presented by Wooldridge (2016, Section 8.2). Also other versions can be chosen with the **type** option.

---

[1]The package *sandwich* provides the same functionality as **hccm** using the specification **vcovHC** and can be used more flexibly for advanced analyses.

For a convenient regression table with coefficients, standard errors, t statistics and their p values based on arbitrary variance-covariance matrices, the command **coeftest** from the package *lmtest* is useful. In addition to the regression results `reg`, it expects either a readily calculated variance-covariance matrix or the function (such as **hccm**) to calculate it. The syntax is

- **coeftest(reg)** for the default homoscedasticity-based standard errors
- **coeftest(reg, vcov=hccm)** for the refined version of White's robust SE
- **coeftest(reg, vcov=hccm(reg,type="hc0"))** for the classical version of White's robust SE. Other versions can be chosen accordingly.

For general F-tests, we have repeatedly used the command **linearHypothesis** from the package *car*. The good news is that it also accepts alternative variance-covariance specifications and is also compatible with **hccm**. To perform F tests of the joint hypothesis described in `myH0` for an estimated model `reg`, the syntax is[2]

- **linearHypothesis(reg, myH0)** for the default homoscedasticity-based covariance matrix
- **linearHypothesis(reg, myH0, vcov=hccm)** for the refined version of White's robust covariance matrix
- **linearHypothesis(reg, myH0, vcov=hccm(reg,type="hc0"))** for the classical version of White's robust covariance matrix. Again, other types can be chosen accordingly.

Wooldridge, Example 8.2: Heteroscedasticity-Robust Inference

Scripts 8.1 (`Example-8-2.R`) and 8.2 (`Example-8-2-cont.R`) demonstrate these commands. After the estimation, the regression table is displayed for the usual standard errors and the refined robust standard errors. The classical White version reported in Wooldridge (2016) can be obtained using the syntax printed above. For the F tests shown in Script 8.2 (`Example-8-2-cont.R`), three versions are calculated and displayed.

The results generally do not differ a lot between the different version. This is an indication that heteroscedasticity might not be a big issue in this example. To be sure, we would like to have a formal test as discussed in the next section.

---

[2]For a discussion how to formulate null hypotheses, see Section 4.3.

—————— **Output of Script 8.1:** `Example-8-2.R` ——————

```
> library(foreign)

> gpa3 <- read.dta("http://fmwww.bc.edu/ec-p/data/wooldridge/gpa3.dta")

> # load packages (which need to be installed!)
> library(lmtest); library(car)

> # Estimate model (only for spring data)
> reg <- lm(cumgpa~sat+hsperc+tothrs+female+black+white,
>                                    data=gpa3, subset=(spring==1))

> # Usual SE:
> coeftest(reg)

t test of coefficients:

              Estimate   Std. Error  t value   Pr(>|t|)
(Intercept)   1.47006477  0.22980308  6.3971  4.942e-10 ***
sat           0.00114073  0.00017856  6.3885  5.197e-10 ***
hsperc       -0.00856636  0.00124042 -6.9060  2.275e-11 ***
tothrs        0.00250400  0.00073099  3.4255  0.0006847 ***
female        0.30343329  0.05902033  5.1412  4.497e-07 ***
black        -0.12828369  0.14737012 -0.8705  0.3846163
white        -0.05872173  0.14098956 -0.4165  0.6772953
---
Signif. codes:  0 '***' 0.001 '**' 0.01 '*' 0.05 '.' 0.1 ' ' 1


> # Refined White heteroscedasticity-robust SE:
> coeftest(reg, vcov=hccm)

t test of coefficients:

              Estimate   Std. Error  t value   Pr(>|t|)
(Intercept)   1.47006477  0.22938036  6.4089  4.611e-10 ***
sat           0.00114073  0.00019532  5.8402  1.169e-08 ***
hsperc       -0.00856636  0.00144359 -5.9341  6.963e-09 ***
tothrs        0.00250400  0.00074930  3.3418  0.00092   ***
female        0.30343329  0.06003964  5.0539  6.911e-07 ***
black        -0.12828369  0.12818828 -1.0007  0.31762
white        -0.05872173  0.12043522 -0.4876  0.62615
---
Signif. codes:  0 '***' 0.001 '**' 0.01 '*' 0.05 '.' 0.1 ' ' 1
```

─────────── **Output of Script 8.2: `Example-8-2-cont.R`** ───────────

```
> # F-Tests using different variance-covariance formulas:
> myH0 <- c("black","white")

> # Ususal VCOV
> linearHypothesis(reg, myH0)
Linear hypothesis test

Hypothesis:
black = 0
white = 0

Model 1: restricted model
Model 2: cumgpa ~ sat + hsperc + tothrs + female + black + white

  Res.Df    RSS Df Sum of Sq      F Pr(>F)
1    361 79.362
2    359 79.062  2   0.29934 0.6796 0.5075

> # Refined White VCOV
> linearHypothesis(reg, myH0, vcov=hccm)
Linear hypothesis test

Hypothesis:
black = 0
white = 0

Model 1: restricted model
Model 2: cumgpa ~ sat + hsperc + tothrs + female + black + white

Note: Coefficient covariance matrix supplied.

  Res.Df Df      F Pr(>F)
1    361
2    359  2 0.6725 0.5111

> # Classical White VCOV
> linearHypothesis(reg, myH0, vcov=hccm(reg,type="hc0"))
Linear hypothesis test

Hypothesis:
black = 0
white = 0

Model 1: restricted model
Model 2: cumgpa ~ sat + hsperc + tothrs + female + black + white

Note: Coefficient covariance matrix supplied.

  Res.Df Df      F Pr(>F)
1    361
2    359  2 0.7478 0.4741
```

8.2. Heteroscedasticity Tests

The Breusch-Pagan (BP) test for heteroscedasticity is easy to implement with basic OLS routines. After a model

$$y = \beta_0 + \beta_1 x_1 + \cdots + \beta_k x_k + u \tag{8.2}$$

is estimated, we obtain the residuals $\hat{u}_i$ for all observations $i = 1, \ldots, n$. We regress their squared value on all independent variables from the original equation. We can either look at the standard F test of overall significance printed for example by the **summary** of **lm** results. Or we can use an LM test by multiplying the R^2 from the second regression with the number of observations.

In R, this is easily done. Remember that the residuals from a regression can be obtained by the **resid** function. Their squared value can be stored in a new variable to be used as a dependent variable in the second stage. Alternatively, the function call can be directly entered as the left-hand side of the regression formula as demonstrated in Script 8.3 (`Example-8-4.R`).

The LM version of the BP test is even more convenient to use with the **bptest** command provided by the **lmtest** package. There is no need to perform the second regression and we directly get the test statistic and corresponding p value.

Wooldridge, Example 8.4: Heteroscedasticity in a Housing Price Equation

Script 8.3 (`Example-8-4.R`) implements the F and LM versions of the BP test. The command **bptest** simply takes the regression results as an argument and delivers a test statistic of $LM = 14.09$. The corresponding p value is smaller than 0.003 so we reject homoscedasticity for all reasonable significance levels.

The output also shows the manual implementation of a second stage regression where we regress squared residuals on the independent variables. We can directly interpret the reported F statistic of 5.34 and its p value of 0.002 as the F version of the BP test. We can manually calculate the LM statistic by multiplying the reported $R^2 = 0.16$ with the number of observations $n = 88$.

We replicate the test for an alternative model with logarithms discussed by Wooldridge (2016) together with the White test in Example 8.5 and Script 8.4 (`Example-8-5.R`).

_____ Output of Script 8.3: `Example-8-4.R` _____

```
> library(foreign)

> hprice1<-read.dta("http://fmwww.bc.edu/ec-p/data/wooldridge/hprice1.dta")

> # Estimate model
> reg <- lm(price~lotsize+sqrft+bdrms, data=hprice1)

> reg

Call:
lm(formula = price ~ lotsize + sqrft + bdrms, data = hprice1)

Coefficients:
(Intercept)      lotsize         sqrft         bdrms
 -21.770308     0.002068      0.122778     13.852522


> # Automatic BP test
> library(lmtest)

> bptest(reg)
```

```
         studentized Breusch-Pagan test

data:  reg
BP = 14.092, df = 3, p-value = 0.002782


> # Manual regression of squared residuals
> summary(lm( resid(reg)^2 ~ lotsize+sqrft+bdrms, data=hprice1))

Call:
lm(formula = resid(reg)^2 ~ lotsize + sqrft + bdrms, data = hprice1)

Residuals:
   Min    1Q Median    3Q    Max
 -9044  -2212  -1256   -97  42582

Coefficients:
              Estimate Std. Error t value Pr(>|t|)
(Intercept) -5.523e+03  3.259e+03  -1.694  0.09390 .
lotsize      2.015e-01  7.101e-02   2.838  0.00569 **
sqrft        1.691e+00  1.464e+00   1.155  0.25128
bdrms        1.042e+03  9.964e+02   1.046  0.29877
---
Signif. codes:  0 '***' 0.001 '**' 0.01 '*' 0.05 '.' 0.1 ' ' 1

Residual standard error: 6617 on 84 degrees of freedom
Multiple R-squared:  0.1601,       Adjusted R-squared:  0.1301
F-statistic: 5.339 on 3 and 84 DF,  p-value: 0.002048
```

The White test is a variant of the BP test where in the second stage, we do not regress the squared first-stage residuals on the regressors only but either also on interactions and polynomials of them or on the fitted values $\hat{y}$ and $\hat{y}^2$. This can easily be done in a manual second-stage regression remembering that the fitted values can be obtained with the **fitted** function.

Conveniently, we can also use the **bptest** command to do the calculations of the *LM* version of the test including the p values automatically. All we have to do is to explain that in the second stage we want a different set of regressors. Given the original regression results are stored as reg, this is done by specifying

```
bptest(reg, ~ regressors)
```

In the "special form" of the White test, the regressors are fitted and their squared values, so the command can be compactly written as

```
bptest( reg, ~ fitted(reg) + I(fitted(reg)^2) )
```

Wooldridge, Example 8.5: BP and White test in the Log Housing Price Equation

Script 8.4 (Example-8-5.R) implements the BP and the White test for a model that now contains logarithms of the dependent variable and two independent variables. Both the BP and the White test do not reject the null hypothesis at conventional significance levels with p values of 0.238 and 0.178, respectively.

─────── **Output of Script 8.4:** `Example-8-5.R` ───────

```
> library(foreign)

> hprice1<-read.dta("http://fmwww.bc.edu/ec-p/data/wooldridge/hprice1.dta")

> # Estimate model
> reg <- lm(log(price)~log(lotsize)+log(sqrft)+bdrms, data=hprice1)

> reg

Call:
lm(formula = log(price) ~ log(lotsize) + log(sqrft) + bdrms,
    data = hprice1)

Coefficients:
 (Intercept)   log(lotsize)     log(sqrft)            bdrms
    -1.29704        0.16797        0.70023          0.03696


> # BP test
> library(lmtest)

> bptest(reg)

        studentized Breusch-Pagan test

data:  reg
BP = 4.2232, df = 3, p-value = 0.2383


> # White test
> bptest(reg, ~ fitted(reg) + I(fitted(reg)^2) )

        studentized Breusch-Pagan test

data:  reg
BP = 3.4473, df = 2, p-value = 0.1784
```

8.3. Weighted Least Squares

Weighted Least Squares (WLS) attempts to provide a more efficient alternative to OLS. It is a special version of a feasible generalized least squares (FGLS) estimator. Instead of the sum of squared residuals, their weighted sum is minimized. If the weights are inversely proportional to the variance, the estimator is efficient. Also the usual formula for the variance-covariance matrix of the parameter estimates and standard inference tools are valid.

We can obtain WLS parameter estimates by multiplying each variable in the model with the square root of the weight as shown by Wooldridge (2016, Section 8.4). In *R*, it is more convenient to use the option **weight=...** of the command **lm**. This provides a more concise syntax and takes care of correct residuals, fitted values, predictions, and the like in terms of the original variables.

Wooldridge, Example 8.6: Financial Wealth Equation

Script 8.5 (Example-8-6.R) implements both OLS and WLS estimation for a regression of financial wealth (nettfa) on income (inc), age (age), gender (male) and eligibility for a pension plan (e401k) using the data set 401ksubs.dta. Following Wooldridge (2016), we assume that the variance is proportional to the income variable inc. Therefore, the optimal weight is $\frac{1}{inc}$ which is given as the **weight** in the **lm** call.

─────────── Output of Script 8.5: `Example-8-6.R` ───────────

```
> library(foreign)

> d401k<-read.dta("http://fmwww.bc.edu/ec-p/data/wooldridge/401ksubs.dta")

> # OLS (only for singles: fsize==1)
> lm(nettfa ~ inc + I((age-25)^2) + male + e401k,
>                                    data=d401k, subset=(fsize==1))

Call:
lm(formula = nettfa ~ inc + I((age - 25)^2) + male + e401k, data = d401k,
    subset = (fsize == 1))

Coefficients:
    (Intercept)              inc   I((age - 25)^2)             male
      -20.98499          0.77058          0.02513          2.47793
          e401k
        6.88622


> # WLS
> lm(nettfa ~ inc + I((age-25)^2) + male + e401k, weight=1/inc,
>                                    data=d401k, subset=(fsize==1))

Call:
lm(formula = nettfa ~ inc + I((age - 25)^2) + male + e401k, data = d401k,
    subset = (fsize == 1), weights = 1/inc)

Coefficients:
    (Intercept)              inc   I((age - 25)^2)             male
      -16.70252          0.74038          0.01754          1.84053
          e401k
        5.18828
```

We can also use heteroscedasticity-robust statistics from Section 8.1 to account for the fact that our variance function might be misspecified. Script 8.6 (`WLS-Robust.R`) repeats the WLS estimation of Example 8.6 but reports non-robust and robust standard errors and t statistics. It replicates Wooldridge (2016, Table 8.2) with the only difference that we use a refined version of the robust SE formula. There is nothing special about the implementation. The fact that we used weights is correctly accounted for in the following calculations.

───────── **Output of Script 8.6: `WLS-Robust.R`** ─────────

```
> library(foreign)

> d401k<-read.dta("http://fmwww.bc.edu/ec-p/data/wooldridge/401ksubs.dta")

> # WLS
> wlsreg <- lm(nettfa ~ inc + I((age-25)^2) + male + e401k,
>                           weight=1/inc, data=d401k, subset=(fsize==1))

> # non-robust results
> library(lmtest); library(car)

> coeftest(wlsreg)

t test of coefficients:

                  Estimate  Std. Error t value  Pr(>|t|)
(Intercept)    -16.7025205   1.9579947 -8.5304  < 2.2e-16 ***
inc              0.7403843   0.0643029 11.5140  < 2.2e-16 ***
I((age - 25)^2)  0.0175373   0.0019315  9.0796  < 2.2e-16 ***
male             1.8405293   1.5635872  1.1771  0.239287
e401k            5.1882807   1.7034258  3.0458  0.002351 **
---
Signif. codes:  0 `***' 0.001 `**' 0.01 `*' 0.05 `.' 0.1 ` ' 1


> # robust results (Refined White SE:)
> coeftest(wlsreg,hccm)

t test of coefficients:

                  Estimate  Std. Error t value  Pr(>|t|)
(Intercept)    -16.7025205   2.2482355 -7.4292 1.606e-13 ***
inc              0.7403843   0.0752396  9.8403  < 2.2e-16 ***
I((age - 25)^2)  0.0175373   0.0025924  6.7650 1.742e-11 ***
male             1.8405293   1.3132477  1.4015 0.1612159
e401k            5.1882807   1.5743329  3.2955 0.0009994 ***
---
Signif. codes:  0 `***' 0.001 `**' 0.01 `*' 0.05 `.' 0.1 ` ' 1
```

The assumption made in Example 8.6 that the variance is proportional to a regressor is usually hard to justify. Typically, we don't not know the variance function and have to estimate it. This feasible GLS (FGLS) estimator replaces the (allegedly) known variance function with an estimated one.

We can estimate the relation between variance and regressors using a linear regression of the log of the squared residuals from an initial OLS regression $\log(\hat{u}^2)$ as the dependent variable. Wooldridge (2016, Section 8.4) suggests two versions for the selection of regressors:

- the regressors $x_1, \ldots, x_k$ from the original model similar to the BP test
- $\hat{y}$ and $\hat{y}^2$ from the original model similar to the White test

As the estimated error variance, we can use $\exp\left(\widehat{\log(\hat{u}^2)}\right)$. Its inverse can then be used as a weight in WLS estimation.

Wooldridge, Example 8.7: Demand for Cigarettes

Script 8.7 (Example-8-7.R) studies the relationship between daily cigarette consumption `cigs`, individual characteristics, and restaurant smoking restrictions `restaurn`. After the initial OLS regression, a BP test is performed which clearly rejects homoscedasticity (see previous section for the BP test). After the regression of log squared residuals on the regressors, the FGLS weights are calculated and used in the WLS regression. See Wooldridge (2016) for a discussion of the results.

————————— **Output of Script 8.7:** `Example-8-7.R` —————————

```
> library(foreign)

> smoke <- read.dta("http://fmwww.bc.edu/ec-p/data/wooldridge/smoke.dta")

> # OLS
> olsreg<-lm(cigs~log(income)+log(cigpric)+educ+age+I(age^2)+restaurn,
>                                                            data=smoke)

> olsreg

Call:
lm(formula = cigs ~ log(income) + log(cigpric) + educ + age +
    I(age^2) + restaurn, data = smoke)

Coefficients:
 (Intercept)    log(income)   log(cigpric)         educ          age
   -3.639826       0.880268      -0.750862    -0.501498     0.770694
     I(age^2)       restaurn
   -0.009023      -2.825085


> # BP test
> library(lmtest)

> bptest(olsreg)

        studentized Breusch-Pagan test

data:  olsreg
BP = 32.258, df = 6, p-value = 1.456e-05


> # FGLS: estimation of the variance function
> logu2 <- log(resid(olsreg)^2)

> varreg<-lm(logu2~log(income)+log(cigpric)+educ+age+I(age^2)+restaurn,
>                                                            data=smoke)

> # FGLS: WLS
> w <- 1/exp(fitted(varreg))

> lm(cigs~log(income)+log(cigpric)+educ+age+I(age^2)+restaurn,
>                                         weight=w ,data=smoke)

Call:
lm(formula = cigs ~ log(income) + log(cigpric) + educ + age +
    I(age^2) + restaurn, data = smoke, weights = w)

Coefficients:
 (Intercept)    log(income)   log(cigpric)         educ          age
    5.635463       1.295239      -2.940312    -0.463446     0.481948
     I(age^2)       restaurn
   -0.005627      -3.461064
```

9. More on Specification and Data Issues

This chapter covers different topics of model specification and data problems. Section 9.1 asks how statistical tests can help us specify the "correct" functional form given the numerous options we have seen in Chapters 6 and 7. Section 9.2 shows some simulation results regarding the effects of measurement errors in dependent and independent variables. Sections 9.3 covers missing values and how R deals with them. In Section 9.4, we briefly discuss outliers and Section 9.5, the LAD estimator is presented.

9.1. Functional Form Misspecification

We have seen many ways to flexibly specify the relation between the dependent variable and the regressors. An obvious question to ask is whether or not a given specification is the "correct" one. The Regression Equation Specification Error Test (RESET) is a convenient tool to test the null hypothesis that the functional form is adequate.

Wooldridge (2016, Section 9.1) shows how to implement it using a standard F test in a second regression that contains polynomials of fitted values from the original regression. We already know how to obtain fitted values and run an F test, so the implementation is straightforward. Even more convenient is the boxed routine **resettest** from the package **lmtest**. We just have to supply the regression we want to test and the rest is done automatically.

Wooldridge, Example 9.2: Housing Price Equation

Script 9.1 (Example-9-2-manual.R) implements the RESET test using the procedure described by Wooldridge (2016) for the housing price model. As previously, we get the fitted values from the original regression using **fitted**. Their polynomials are directly entered into the formula of the second regression using the **I()** function, see Section 6.1.4. The F test is easily done using **linearHypothesis** with **matchCoefs** as described in Section 4.3.

The same results are obtained more conveniently using the command **resettest** in Script 9.2 (Example-9-2-automatic.R). Both implementations deliver the same results: The test statistic is $F = 4.67$ with a p value of $p = 0.012$, so we reject the null hypothesis that this equation is correctly specified at a significance level of $\alpha = 5\%$.

―――――――――― Output of Script 9.1: `Example-9-2-manual.R` ――――――――――

```
> library(foreign)

> hprice1<-read.dta("http://fmwww.bc.edu/ec-p/data/wooldridge/hprice1.dta")

> # original linear regression
> orig <- lm(price ~ lotsize+sqrft+bdrms, data=hprice1)

> # regression for RESET test
> RESETreg <- lm(price ~ lotsize+sqrft+bdrms+I(fitted(orig)^2)+
>                                        I(fitted(orig)^3), data=hprice1)
```

```
> RESETreg

Call:
lm(formula = price ~ lotsize + sqrft + bdrms + I(fitted(orig)^2) +
    I(fitted(orig)^3), data = hprice1)

Coefficients:
      (Intercept)              lotsize                sqrft
        1.661e+02            1.537e-04            1.760e-02
            bdrms    I(fitted(orig)^2)    I(fitted(orig)^3)
        2.175e+00            3.534e-04            1.546e-06


> # RESET test. H0: all coeffs including "fitted" are=0
> library(car)

> linearHypothesis(RESETreg, matchCoefs(RESETreg,"fitted"))
Linear hypothesis test

Hypothesis:
I(fitted(orig)^2) = 0
I(fitted(orig)^3) = 0

Model 1: restricted model
Model 2: price ~ lotsize + sqrft + bdrms + I(fitted(orig)^2) + I(fitted(orig)^3)

  Res.Df     RSS Df Sum of Sq      F  Pr(>F)
1     84  300724
2     82  269984  2     30740 4.6682 0.01202 *
---
Signif. codes:  0 '***' 0.001 '**' 0.01 '*' 0.05 '.' 0.1 ' ' 1
```

──────────────── Output of Script 9.2: `Example-9-2-automatic.R` ────────────────

```
> library(foreign)

> hprice1<-read.dta("http://fmwww.bc.edu/ec-p/data/wooldridge/hprice1.dta")

> # original linear regression
> orig <- lm(price ~ lotsize+sqrft+bdrms, data=hprice1)

> # RESET test
> library(lmtest)

> resettest(orig)

        RESET test

data:  orig
RESET = 4.6682, df1 = 2, df2 = 82, p-value = 0.01202
```

Wooldridge (2016, Section 9.2) also discusses tests of non-nested models. As an example, a test of both models against a comprehensive model containing the all regressors is mentioned. Such a test can conveniently be implemented in R using the command **encomptest** from the package *lmtest*. Script 9.3 (Nonnested-Test.R) shows this test in action for the same application as Example 9.2.

The two alternative models for the housing price are

$$\text{price} = \beta_0 + \beta_1 \texttt{lotsize} + \beta_2 \texttt{sqrft} + \beta_3 \texttt{bdrms} + u \tag{9.1}$$

$$\text{price} = \beta_0 + \beta_1 \log(\texttt{lotsize}) + \beta_2 \log(\texttt{sqrft}) + \beta_3 \texttt{bdrms} + u \tag{9.2}$$

The output shows the "encompassing model" E with all variables. Both models are rejected against this comprehensive model.

—————— **Output of Script 9.3: Nonnested-Test.R** ——————

```
> library(foreign)

> hprice1<-read.dta("http://fmwww.bc.edu/ec-p/data/wooldridge/hprice1.dta")

> # two alternative models
> model1 <- lm(price ~      lotsize  +      sqrft  + bdrms, data=hprice1)

> model2 <- lm(price ~ log(lotsize) + log(sqrft) + bdrms, data=hprice1)

> # Test against comprehensive model
> library(lmtest)

> encomptest(model1,model2, data=hprice1)
Encompassing test

Model 1: price ~ lotsize + sqrft + bdrms
Model 2: price ~ log(lotsize) + log(sqrft) + bdrms
Model E: price ~ lotsize + sqrft + bdrms + log(lotsize) + log(sqrft)
          Res.Df Df       F     Pr(>F)
M1 vs. ME     82 -2  7.8613  0.0007526 ***
M2 vs. ME     82 -2  7.0508  0.0014943 **
---
Signif. codes:  0 '***' 0.001 '**' 0.01 '*' 0.05 '.' 0.1 ' ' 1
```

9.2. Measurement Error

If a variable is not measured accurately, the consequences depend on whether the measurement error affects the dependent or an explanatory variable. If the **dependent variable** is mismeasured, the consequences can be mild. If the measurement error is unrelated to the regressors, the parameter estimates get less precise, but they are still consistent and the usual inferences from the results is valid.

The simulation exercise in Script 9.4 (Sim-ME-Dep.R) draws 10 000 samples of size $n = 1 000$ according to the model with measurement error in the dependent variable

$$y^* = \beta_0 + \beta_1 x + u, \qquad y = y^* + e_0. \tag{9.3}$$

The assumption is that we do not observe the true values of the dependent variable y^* but our measure y is contaminated with a measurement error e_0.

_____ **Script 9.4: Sim-ME-Dep.R** _____

```
# Set the random seed
set.seed(1234567)
# set true parameters: intercept & slope
b0<-1; b1<-0.5
# initialize b1hat to store 10000 results:
b1hat <- numeric(10000)
b1hat.me <- numeric(10000)

# Draw a sample of x, fixed over replications:
x <- rnorm(1000,4,1)
# repeat r times:
for(j in 1:10000) {
  # Draw a sample of u
  u <- rnorm(1000)
  # Draw a sample of ystar:
  ystar <- b0 + b1*x + u
  # regress ystar on x and store slope estimate at position j
  bhat <- coef( lm(ystar~x) )
  b1hat[j] <- bhat["x"]
  # Measurement error and mismeasured y:
  e0 <- rnorm(1000)
  y <- ystar+e0
  # regress y on x and store slope estimate at position j
  bhat.me <- coef( lm(y~x) )
  b1hat.me[j] <- bhat.me["x"]
}

# Mean with and without ME
c( mean(b1hat), mean(b1hat.me) )
# Variance with and without ME
c( var(b1hat), var(b1hat.me) )
```

In the simulation, the parameter estimates using both the correct y^* and the mismeasured y are stored as the variables b1hat and b1hat.me, respectively. As expected, the simulated mean of both variables is close to the expected value of $\beta_1 = 0.5$. The variance of b1hat.me is around 0.002 which is twice as high as the variance of b1hat. This was expected since in our simulation, u and e_0 are both independent standard normal variables, so $\mathrm{Var}(u) = 1$ and $\mathrm{Var}(u + e_0) = 2$:

```
> # Mean with and without ME
> c( mean(b1hat), mean(b1hat.me) )
[1] 0.5003774 0.5001819

> # Variance with and without ME
> c( var(b1hat), var(b1hat.me) )
[1] 0.0009990556 0.0019991960
```

If an **explanatory variable** is mismeasured, the consequences are usually more dramatic. Even in the classical errors-in-variables case where the measurement error is unrelated to the regressors, the parameter estimates are biased and inconsistent. This model is

$$y = \beta_0 + \beta_1 x^* + u, \qquad x = x^* + e_1 \tag{9.4}$$

where the measurement error e_1 is independent of both x^* and u. Wooldridge (2016, Section 9.4) shows that if we regress y on x instead of x^*,

$$\text{plim}\hat{\beta}_1 = \beta_1 \cdot \frac{\text{Var}(x^*)}{\text{Var}(x^*) + \text{Var}(e_1)}. \tag{9.5}$$

The simulation in Script 9.5 (`Sim-ME-Explan.R`) draws 10 000 samples of size $n = 1\,000$ from this model.

——————————————— Script 9.5: **Sim-ME-Explan.R** ———————————————

```
# Set the random seed
set.seed(1234567)
# set true parameters: intercept & slope
b0<-1; b1<-0.5
# initialize b1hat to store 10000 results:
b1hat <- numeric(10000)
b1hat.me <- numeric(10000)

# Draw a sample of x, fixed over replications:
xstar <- rnorm(1000,4,1)
# repeat r times:
for(j in 1:10000) {
  # Draw a sample of u
  u <- rnorm(1000)
  # Draw a sample of ystar:
  y <- b0 + b1*xstar + u
  # regress y on xstar and store slope estimate at position j
  bhat <- coef( lm(y~xstar) )
  b1hat[j] <- bhat["xstar"]
  # Measurement error and mismeasured y:
  e1 <- rnorm(1000)
  x <- xstar+e1
  # regress y on x and store slope estimate at position j
  bhat.me <- coef( lm(y~x) )
  b1hat.me[j] <- bhat.me["x"]
}

# Mean with and without ME
c( mean(b1hat), mean(b1hat.me) )
# Variance with and without ME
c( var(b1hat), var(b1hat.me) )
```

Since in this simulation, $\text{Var}(x^*) = \text{Var}(e_1) = 1$, equation 9.5 implies that $\text{plim}\hat{\beta}_1 = \frac{1}{2}\beta_1 = 0.25$. This is confirmed by the simulation results. While the mean of the estimate `b1hat` using the correct regressor again is around 0.5, the mean parameter estimate using the mismeasured regressor is about 0.25:

```
> # Mean with and without ME
> c( mean(b1hat), mean(b1hat.me) )
[1] 0.5003774 0.2490821

> # Variance with and without ME
> c( var(b1hat), var(b1hat.me) )
[1] 0.0009990556 0.0005363206
```

9.3. Missing Data and Nonrandom Samples

In many data sets, we fail to observe all variables for each observational unit. An important case is survey data where the respondents refuse or fail to answer some questions. In *R*, missing data can be represented by different values of the variable:

- **NA** (not available) indicates that we do not have the information.
- **NaN** (not a number) indicates that the value is not defined. It is usually the result of operations like $\frac{0}{0}$ or the logarithm of a negative number.

The function **is.na(*value*)** returns TRUE if *value* is either **NA** or **NaN** and FALSE otherwise. Note that operations resulting in $\pm\infty$ like $\log(0)$ or $\frac{1}{0}$ are not coded as **NaN** but as **Inf** or **−Inf**. Unlike some other statistical software packages, *R* can do calculations with these numbers. Script 9.6 (NA-NaN-Inf.R) gives some examples.

```
─────────────── Output of Script 9.6: NA-NaN-Inf.R ───────────────

> x <- c(-1,0,1,NA,NaN,-Inf,Inf)

> logx <- log(x)

> invx <- 1/x

> ncdf <- pnorm(x)

> isna <- is.na(x)

> data.frame(x,logx,invx,ncdf,isna)
     x logx invx      ncdf  isna
1   -1  NaN   -1 0.1586553 FALSE
2    0 -Inf  Inf 0.5000000 FALSE
3    1    0    1 0.8413447 FALSE
4   NA   NA   NA        NA  TRUE
5  NaN  NaN  NaN       NaN  TRUE
6 -Inf  NaN    0 0.0000000 FALSE
7  Inf  Inf    0 1.0000000 FALSE
```

Depending on the data source, real-world data sets can have different rules for indicating missing information. Sometimes, impossible numeric values are used. For example, a survey including the number of years of education as a variable educ might have a value like "9999" to indicate missing information. For any software package, it is highly recommended to change these to proper missing-value codes early in the data-handling process. Otherwise, we take the risk that some statistical method interprets those values as "this person went to school for 9999 years" producing highly nonsensical results. For the education example, if the variable educ is in the data frame mydata this can be done with

```
mydata$educ[mydata$educ==9999] <- NA
```

We can also create logical variables indicating missing values using the function **is.na(*variable*)**. It will generate a new logical variable of the same length which is **TRUE** whenever *variable* is either **NA** or **NaN**. The function can also be used on data frames. The command **is.na(*mydata*)** will return another data frame with the same dimensions and variable names but full of logical indicators for missing observations. It is useful to count the missings for each variable in a data frame with

```
colSums(is.na(mydata))
```

The function **complete.cases(*mydata*)** generates one logical vector indicating the rows of the data frame that don't have any missing information.

Script 9.7 (`Missings.R`) demonstrates these commands for the data set `LAWSCH85.dta` which contains data on law schools. Of the 156 schools, 6 do not report median LSAT scores. Looking at all variables, the most missings are found for the `age` of the school – we don't know it for 45 schools. For only 90 of the 156 schools, we have the full set of variables, for the other 66, one or more variable is missing.

—————— **Output of Script 9.7: `Missings.R`** ——————

```
> library(foreign)

> lawsch<-read.dta("http://fmwww.bc.edu/ec-p/data/wooldridge/lawsch85.dta")

> # extract LSAT
> lsat <- lawsch$LSAT

> # Create logical indicator for missings
> missLSAT <- is.na(lawsch$LSAT)

> # LSAT and indicator for Schools No. 120-129:
> rbind(lsat,missLSAT)[,120:129]
         [,1] [,2] [,3] [,4] [,5] [,6] [,7] [,8] [,9] [,10]
lsat      156  159  157  167   NA  158  155  157   NA   163
missLSAT    0    0    0    0    1    0    0    0    1     0

> # Frequencies of indicator
> table(missLSAT)
missLSAT
FALSE  TRUE
  150     6

> # Missings for all variables in data frame (counts)
> colSums(is.na(lawsch))
   rank   salary     cost     LSAT      GPA   libvol  faculty      age
      0        8        6        6        7        1        4       45
 clsize    north    south     east     west  lsalary  studfac    top10
      3        0        0        0        0        8        6        0
  r11_25   r26_40   r41_60   llibvol    lcost
      0        0        0        1        6

> # Indicator for complete cases
> compl <- complete.cases(lawsch)

> table(compl)
compl
FALSE  TRUE
   66    90
```

The question how to deal with missing values is not trivial and depends on many things. *R* offers different strategies. The strictest approach is used by default for basic statistical functions such as **mean**. If we don't know all the numbers, we cannot calculate their average. So by default, **mean** and other commands return **NA** if at least one value is missing.

In many cases, this is overly pedantic. A widely used strategy is to simply remove the observations with missing values and do the calculations for the remaining ones. For commands like **mean**, this is requested with the option **na.rm=TRUE**. Regression commands like **lm** do this by default. If observations are excluded due to missing values, the **summary** of the results contain a line stating
`(XXX observations deleted due to missingness)`

Script 9.8 (`Missings-Analyses.R`) gives examples of these features. There are more advanced methods for dealing with missing data implemented in *R*, for example package *mi* provides multiple imputation algorithms. But these methods are beyond the scope of this book.

Output of Script 9.8: `Missings-Analyses.R`

```
> library(foreign)

> lawsch<-read.dta("http://fmwww.bc.edu/ec-p/data/wooldridge/lawsch85.dta")

> # Mean of a variable with missings:
> mean(lawsch$LSAT)
[1] NA

> mean(lawsch$LSAT,na.rm=TRUE)
[1] 158.2933

> # Regression with missings
> summary(lm(log(salary)~LSAT+cost+age, data=lawsch))

Call:
lm(formula = log(salary) ~ LSAT + cost + age, data = lawsch)

Residuals:
     Min       1Q   Median       3Q      Max
-0.40989 -0.09438  0.00317  0.10436  0.45483

Coefficients:
              Estimate Std. Error t value Pr(>|t|)
(Intercept) 4.384e+00  6.781e-01   6.465 4.94e-09 ***
LSAT        3.722e-02  4.501e-03   8.269 1.06e-12 ***
cost        1.114e-05  4.321e-06   2.577 0.011563 *
age         1.503e-03  4.354e-04   3.453 0.000843 ***
---
Signif. codes:  0 '***' 0.001 '**' 0.01 '*' 0.05 '.' 0.1 ' ' 1

Residual standard error: 0.1545 on 91 degrees of freedom
  (61 observations deleted due to missingness)
Multiple R-squared:  0.6708,      Adjusted R-squared:  0.6599
F-statistic: 61.81 on 3 and 91 DF,  p-value: < 2.2e-16
```

9.4. Outlying Observations

Wooldridge (2016, Section 9.5) offers a very useful discussion of outlying observations. One of the important messages from the discussion is that dealing with outliers is a tricky business. *R* offers a function **studres** to automatically calculate all studentized residuals discussed there. For the R&D example from Wooldridge (2016), Script 9.9 (Outliers.R) calculates them and reports the highest and the lowest number. It also generates the histogram with overlayed density plot in Figure 9.1. Especially the highest value of 4.55 appears to be an extremely outlying value.

R offers many more tools for analyzing outliers. Notable example include the function **influence.measures** which gives a table of different measures of leverage and influence for all observations. The package *car* offers other useful analyses and graphs.

─── **Output of Script 9.9: Outliers.R** ───

```
> library(foreign)

> rdchem <- read.dta("http://fmwww.bc.edu/ec-p/data/wooldridge/rdchem.dta")

> # Regression
> reg <- lm(rdintens~sales+profmarg, data=rdchem)

> # Studentized residuals for all observations:
> studres <- rstudent(reg)

> # Display extreme values:
> min(studres)
[1] -1.818638

> max(studres)
[1] 4.554043

> # Histogram (and overlayed density plot):
> hist(studres, freq=FALSE)

> lines(density(studres), lwd=2)
```

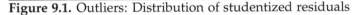

Figure 9.1. Outliers: Distribution of studentized residuals

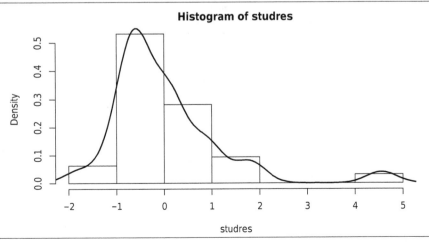

9.5. Least Absolute Deviations (LAD) Estimation

As an alternative to OLS, the least absolute deviations (LAD) estimator is less sensitive to outliers. Instead of minimizing the sum of *squared* residuals, it minimizes the sum of the *absolute values* of the residuals.

Wooldridge (2016, Section 9.6) explains that the LAD estimator attempts to estimate the parameters of the conditional median $\text{Med}(y|x_1, \ldots, x_k)$ instead of the conditional mean $\text{E}(y|x_1, \ldots, x_k)$. This makes LAD a special case of quantile regression which studies general quantiles of which the median (=0.5 quantile) is just a special case. In R, general quantile regression (and LAD as the default special case) can easily be implemented with the command **rq** from the package **quantreg**. It works very similar to **lm** for OLS estimation.

Script 9.10 (LAD.R) demonstrates its application using the example from Wooldridge (2016, Example 9.8) and Script 9.9. Note that LAD inferences are only valid asymptotically, so the results in this example with $n = 32$ should be taken with a grain of salt.

_____ **Output of Script 9.10:** LAD.R _____

```
> library(foreign)

> rdchem <- read.dta("http://fmwww.bc.edu/ec-p/data/wooldridge/rdchem.dta")

> # OLS Regression
> ols <- lm(rdintens ~ I(sales/1000) +profmarg, data=rdchem)

> # LAD Regression
> library(quantreg)

> lad <- rq(rdintens ~ I(sales/1000) +profmarg, data=rdchem)

> # regression table
> library(stargazer)

> stargazer(ols,lad,  type = "text")


===================================================
                         Dependent variable:
                     ------------------------------
                                 rdintens
                        OLS          quantile
                                     regression
                        (1)             (2)
---------------------------------------------------
I(sales/1000)          0.054           0.019
                      (0.044)         (0.059)

profmarg               0.045          0.118**
                      (0.046)         (0.049)

Constant              2.623***        1.621***
                      (0.585)         (0.510)


---------------------------------------------------
Observations            32              32
R2                     0.076
Adjusted R2            0.013
Residual Std. Error 1.862 (df = 29)
F Statistic         1.201 (df = 2; 29)
===================================================
Note:                   *p<0.1; **p<0.05; ***p<0.01
```

Part II.

Regression Analysis with Time Series Data

10. Basic Regression Analysis with Time Series Data

Time series differ from cross-sectional data in that each observation (i.e. row in a data frame) corresponds to one point or period in time. Section 10.1 introduces the most basic static time series models. In Section 10.2, we look into more technical details how to deal with time series data in R. Other aspects of time series models such as dynamics, trends, and seasonal effects are treated in Section 10.3.

10.1. Static Time Series Models

Static time series regression models describe the contemporaneous relation between the dependent variable y and the regressors $z_1, \ldots, z_k$. For each observation $t = 1, \ldots, n$, a static equation has the form

$$y_t = \beta_0 + \beta_1 z_{1t} + \cdots + \beta_k z_{kt} + u_t. \tag{10.1}$$

For the estimation of these models, the fact that we have time series does not make any practical difference. We can still use `lm` to estimate the parameters and the other tools for statistical inference. We only have to be aware that the assumptions needed for unbiased estimation and valid inference differ somewhat. Important differences to cross-sectional data are that we have to assume *strict* exogeneity (Assumption TS.3) for unbiasedness and no serial correlation (Assumption TS.5) for the usual variance-covariance formula to be valid, see Wooldridge (2016, Section 10.3).

Wooldridge, Example 10.2: Effects of Inflation and Deficits on Interest Rates

The data set `INTDEF.dta` contains yearly information on interest rates and related time series between 1948 and 2003. Script 10.1 (`Example-10-2.R`) estimates a static model explaining the interest rate `i3` with the inflation rate `inf` and the federal budget deficit `def`. There is nothing different in the implementation than for cross-sectional data. Both regressors are found to have a statistically significant relation to the interest rate.

Output of Script 10.1: `Example-10-2.R`

```
> library(foreign)

> intdef <- read.dta("http://fmwww.bc.edu/ec-p/data/wooldridge/intdef.dta")

> # Linear regression of static model:
> summary( lm(i3~inf+def,data=intdef)  )

Call:
lm(formula = i3 ~ inf + def, data = intdef)

Residuals:
    Min      1Q  Median      3Q     Max
-3.9948 -1.1694  0.1959  0.9602  4.7224

Coefficients:
            Estimate Std. Error t value Pr(>|t|)
(Intercept)  1.73327    0.43197   4.012  0.00019 ***
inf          0.60587    0.08213   7.376 1.12e-09 ***
def          0.51306    0.11838   4.334 6.57e-05 ***
---
Signif. codes:  0 '***' 0.001 '**' 0.01 '*' 0.05 '.' 0.1 ' ' 1

Residual standard error: 1.843 on 53 degrees of freedom
Multiple R-squared:  0.6021,      Adjusted R-squared:  0.5871
F-statistic: 40.09 on 2 and 53 DF,  p-value: 2.483e-11
```

10.2. Time Series Data Types in *R*

For calculations specific to times series such as lags, trends, and seasonal effects, we will have to explicitly define the structure of our data. In *R*, there are several variable types specific to time series data. The most important distinction is whether or not the data are equispaced. The observations of **equispaced** time series are collected at regular points in time. Typical examples are monthly, quarterly, or yearly data. In *R*, these data are efficiently stored in the standard **ts** variable type which is introduced in Section 10.2.1.

Observations of **irregular** time series have varying distances. An important example are daily financial data which are unavailable on weekends and bank holidays. Another example is financial tick data which contain a record each time a trade is completed which obviously does not happen at regular points in time. Although we will mostly work with equispaced data, we will briefly introduce these types in Section 10.2.2.

10.2.1. Equispaced Time Series in *R*

A convenient way to deal with equispaced time series in *R* is to store them as **ts** objects. Suppose we have stored our data in the object `mydata`. It can be one variable stored in a vector or several variables in a matrix or data frame. A **ts** version of our data can be stored in object `myts` using

```
myts <- ts(mydata, ...)
```

The options of this command describe the time structure of the data. The most important ones are

Figure 10.1. Time series plot: Imports of barium chloride from China

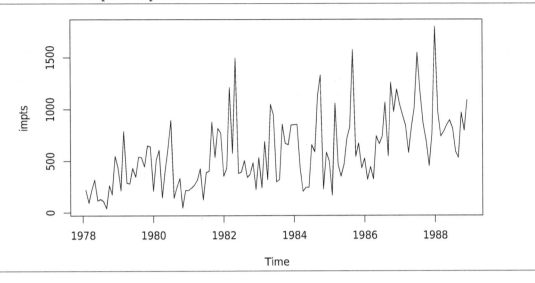

- **start**: Time of first observation. Examples:
  - **start=1**: Time units are numbered starting at 1 (the default if left out).
  - **start=1948**: Data start at (the beginning of) 1948.
  - **start=c(1978,2)**: Data start at year 1978, second month/quarter/...
- **frequency**: Number of observations per time unit (usually per year). Examples:
  - **frequency=1**: Yearly data (the default if left out)
  - **frequency=4**: Quarterly data
  - **frequency=12**: Monthly data

Because the data are equispaced, the time of each of the observations is implied.

As an example, consider the example data set named BARIUM.dta. It contains monthly data on imports of barium chloride from China between February 1978 and December 1988. Wooldridge (2016, Example 10.5) explains the data and background. As usual, the data are imported from the Stata data file into the data frame barium. The imports are stored as a variable barium$chnimp. An appropriate **ts** vector of the imports is therefore generated with

```
impts <- ts(barium$chnimp, start=c(1978,2), frequency=12)
```

Once we have defined this time series object, we can conveniently do additional analyses. A time series plot is simply generated with

```
plot(impts)
```

and is shown in Figure 10.1. The time axis is automatically formatted appropriately. The full *R* Script 10.2 (Example-Barium.R) for these calculations is shown in the appendix on page 314.

10.2.2. Irregular Time Series in *R*

For the remainder of this book, we will work with equispaced time series. But since irregular time series are important for example in finance, we will briefly introduce them here. There are several packages to deal with irregular time series. Probably the most important ones are **xts** and **zoo**.

The **zoo** objects are very useful for both regular and irregular time series. Because the data are not necessarily equispaced, each observation needs a time stamp provided in another vector. They can be measured in arbitrary time units such as years. For high frequency data, standard units such as the POSIX system are useful for pretty graphs and other outputs. Details are provided by Zeileis and Grothendieck (2005) and Ryan and Ulrich (2008).

We have already used the data set INTDEF.dta in example 10.2. It contains yearly data on interest rates and related time series. In Script 10.3 (Example-zoo.R), we define a **zoo** object containing all data using the variable year as the time measure. Simply plotting the variable i3 gives the time series plot shown in Figure 10.2.

—————— Output of Script 10.3: `Example-zoo.R` ——————

```
> library(foreign)

> intdef <- read.dta("http://fmwww.bc.edu/ec-p/data/wooldridge/intdef.dta")

> # Variable "year" as the time measure:
> intdef$year
 [1] 1948 1949 1950 1951 1952 1953 1954 1955 1956 1957 1958 1959 1960
[14] 1961 1962 1963 1964 1965 1966 1967 1968 1969 1970 1971 1972 1973
[27] 1974 1975 1976 1977 1978 1979 1980 1981 1982 1983 1984 1985 1986
[40] 1987 1988 1989 1990 1991 1992 1993 1994 1995 1996 1997 1998 1999
[53] 2000 2001 2002 2003

> # define "zoo" object containing all data, time measure=year:
> library(zoo)

> zoodata <- zoo(intdef, order.by=intdef$year)

> # Time series plot of inflation
> plot(zoodata$i3)
```

A useful package to obtain financial and other data is **pdfetch**. It automatically downloads time series data from different public sources:

- **pdfetch_BLS**: U.S. Bureau of Labor Statistics
- **pdfetch_BOE**: Bank of England Interactive Statistical Database
- **pdfetch_ECB**: European Central Bank's statistical data warehouse
- **pdfetch_EUROSTAT**: Eurostat
- **pdfetch_FRED**: St Louis Fed's FRED database
- **pdfetch_INSEE**: French National Institute of Statistics and Economic Studies (INSEE)
- **pdfetch_ONS**: UK Office of National Statistics
- **pdfetch_WB**: World Bank
- **pdfetch_YAHOO**: Yahoo Finance

The data are returned as **xts** objects with properly defined time stamps. They work essentially the same as **zoo** objects. As an example suppose we want to download stock market data from Yahoo Finance. The command is **pdfetch_YAHOO** with the options

Figure 10.2. Time series plot: Interest rate (3-month T-bills)

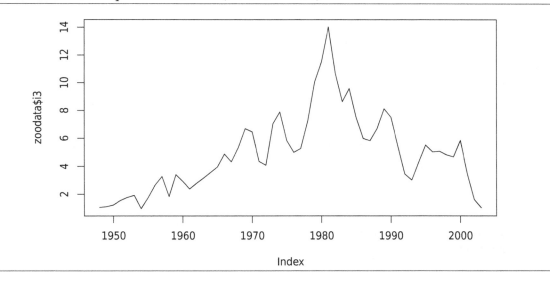

- (Vector of) the Yahoo ticker symbol(s). They can be found at
  `http://finance.yahoo.com/`.
- **fields**: Type(s) of information: `"open"`, `"high"`, `"low"`, `"close"`, `"volume"`, or `"adjclose"`
- **from**: Starting date. Can be supplied in the form `"2003-04-28"`.
- **to**: End date, same format. If omitted, the latest data will be included.

Script 10.4 (`Example-pdfetch.R`) downloads closing values for the S&P 500 index, the NASDAQ Composite index and the Apple stock from the beginning of 2000 through the latest available date. The script calls **Sys.Date()** to report the date it was run. Finally, the time series plot of the Apple stock in Figure 10.3 is generated.[1]

―――――― **Output of Script 10.4: Example-pdfetch.R** ――――――

```
> library(pdfetch)

> # Which Yahoo Finance symbols?
> # "^gspc"=S&P 500, "^ixic"=NASDAQ Composite, "AAPL"=Apple Inc.
> tickernames <- c("^gspc","^ixic", "AAPL")

> # Download data
> yahoo<-pdfetch_YAHOO(tickernames,fields="adjclose",from="2000-01-01")

> # The end date is left out, so we get the latest data. Today is...
> Sys.Date()
[1] "2016-01-19"

> # Number of obs., first and last rows of data
> nrow(yahoo)
[1] 4035
```

---

[1]Note that the option **las=2** of the **plot** command requests the axis labels to be perpendicular to the axis which is useful for the dates on the horizontal axis, see the help for **par**.

```
> head(yahoo)
             ^gspc    ^ixic     AAPL
2000-01-03 1455.22  4131.15  3.722380
2000-01-04 1399.42  3901.69  3.408544
2000-01-05 1402.11  3877.54  3.458425
2000-01-06 1403.45  3727.13  3.159138
2000-01-07 1441.47  3882.62  3.308782
2000-01-10 1457.60  4049.67  3.250587

> tail(yahoo)
             ^gspc    ^ixic     AAPL
2016-01-08 1922.03  4643.63  96.96
2016-01-11 1923.67  4637.99  98.53
2016-01-12 1938.68  4685.92  99.96
2016-01-13 1890.28  4526.06  97.39
2016-01-14 1921.84  4615.00  99.52
2016-01-15 1880.33  4488.42  97.13

> # Time series plot of Apple stock
> plot(yahoo$AAPL, las=2)
```

Figure 10.3. Time series plot: Stock price Apple Inc.

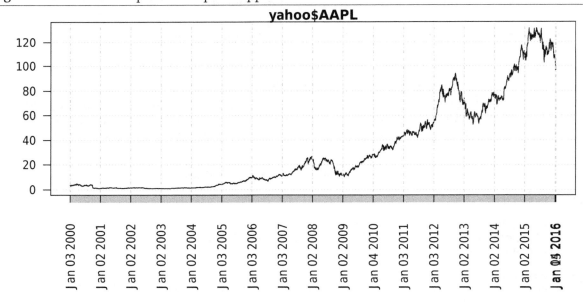

10.3. Other Time Series Models

10.3.1. The `dynlm` Package

In section 6.1, we have seen convenient ways to include arithmetic calculations like interactions, squares and logarithms directly into the `lm` formula. The package **dynlm** introduces the command **dynlm**. It is specifically designed for time-series data and accepts the data in the form of a **ts** or **zoo** object. The command **dynlm** works like **lm** but allows for additional formula expressions. For us, the important expressions are

- `L(x)`: Variable x, lagged by one time unit x_{t-1}.
- `L(x,k)`: Variable x, lagged by k time units x_{t-k}. The order k can also be a vector like `(0:3)`, see Section 10.3.2.
- `d(x)`: First difference $(x_t - x_{t-1})$, see Section 11.4.
- `trend(x)`: Linear time trends, see Section 10.3.3
- `season(x)`: Seasonal effects, see Section 10.3.4

10.3.2. Finite Distributed Lag Models

Finite distributed lag (FDL) models allow past values of regressors to affect the dependent variable. A FDL model of order q with an independent variable z can be written as

$$y_t = \alpha_0 + \delta_0 z_t + \delta_1 z_{t-1} + \cdots + \delta_q z_{t-q} + u_t \tag{10.2}$$

Wooldridge (2016, Section 10.2) discusses the specification and interpretation of such models. For the implementation, it is convenient not to have to generate the q additional variables that reflect the lagged values $z_{t-1}, \ldots, z_{t-q}$ but directly specify them in the model formula using **dynlm** instead of **lm**.

Wooldridge, Example 10.4: Effects of Personal Exemption on Fertility Rates

The data set `FERTIL3.dta` contains yearly information on the general fertility rate `gfr` and the personal tax exemption `pe` for the years 1913 through 1984. Dummy variables for the second world war `ww2` and the availability of the birth control pill `pill` are also included. Script 10.5 (`Example-10-4.R`) shows the distributed lag model including contemporaneous `pe` and two lags. All `pe` coefficients are insignificantly different from zero according to the respective t tests. A usual F test implemented with **linearHypothesis** reveals that they are jointly significantly different from zero at a significance level of $\alpha = 5\%$ with a p value of 0.012. As Wooldridge (2016) discusses, this points to a multicollinearity problem.

——————— **Output of Script 10.5:** `Example-10-4.R` ———————

```
> # Libraries for dynamic lm, regression table and F tests
> library(foreign);library(dynlm);library(lmtest);library(car)

> fertil3<-read.dta("http://fmwww.bc.edu/ec-p/data/wooldridge/fertil3.dta")

> # Define Yearly time series beginning in 1913
> tsdata <- ts(fertil3, start=1913)

> # Linear regression of model with lags:
> res <- dynlm(gfr ~ pe + L(pe) + L(pe,2) + ww2 + pill, data=tsdata)

> coeftest(res)

t test of coefficients:

              Estimate  Std. Error t value  Pr(>|t|)
(Intercept)  95.8704975   3.2819571 29.2114  < 2.2e-16 ***
pe            0.0726718   0.1255331  0.5789    0.5647
L(pe)        -0.0057796   0.1556629 -0.0371    0.9705
L(pe, 2)      0.0338268   0.1262574  0.2679    0.7896
ww2         -22.1264975  10.7319716 -2.0617    0.0433 *
pill        -31.3049888   3.9815591 -7.8625 5.634e-11 ***
---
Signif. codes:  0 '***' 0.001 '**' 0.01 '*' 0.05 '.' 0.1 ' ' 1


> # F test. H0: all pe coefficients are=0
> linearHypothesis(res, matchCoefs(res,"pe"))
Linear hypothesis test

Hypothesis:
pe = 0
L(pe) = 0
L(pe, 2) = 0

Model 1: restricted model
Model 2: gfr ~ pe + L(pe) + L(pe, 2) + ww2 + pill

  Res.Df   RSS Df Sum of Sq     F  Pr(>F)
1     67 15460
2     64 13033  3    2427.1 3.973 0.01165 *
---
Signif. codes:  0 '***' 0.001 '**' 0.01 '*' 0.05 '.' 0.1 ' ' 1
```

The long-run propensity (LRP) of FDL models measures the cumulative effect of a change in the independent variable z on the dependent variable y over time and is simply equal to the sum of the respective parameters

$$\text{LRP} = \delta_0 + \delta_1 + \cdots + \delta_q.$$

We can estimate it directly from the estimated Parameter vector **coef**(). For testing whether it is different from zero, we can again use the convenient **linearHypothesis** command.

Wooldridge, Example 10.4: (continued)

Script 10.6 (Example-10-4-contd.R) calculates the estimated LRP to be around 0.1. According to an F test, it is significantly different from zero with a p value of around 0.001.

——— **Output of Script 10.6: Example-10-4-contd.R** ———

```
> # Calculating the LRP
> b<-coef(res)

> b["pe"]+b["L(pe)"]+b["L(pe, 2)"]
       pe
0.1007191

> # F test. H0: LRP=0
> linearHypothesis(res,"pe + L(pe) + L(pe, 2) = 0")
Linear hypothesis test

Hypothesis:
pe  + L(pe)   + L(pe, 2) = 0

Model 1: restricted model
Model 2: gfr ~ pe + L(pe) + L(pe, 2) + ww2 + pill

  Res.Df    RSS Df Sum of Sq       F    Pr(>F)
1     65  15358
2     64  13033  1    2325.8  11.421  0.001241 **
---
Signif. codes:  0 '***' 0.001 '**' 0.01 '*' 0.05 '.' 0.1 ' ' 1
```

10.3.3. Trends

As pointed out by Wooldridge (2016, Section 10.5), deterministic linear (and exponential) time trends can be accounted for by adding the time measure as another independent variable. In a regression with **dynlm**, this can easily be done using the expression **trend(tsobj)** in the model formula with the time series object `tsobj`.

Wooldridge, Example 10.7: Housing Investment and Prices

The data set `HSEINV.dta` provides annual observations on housing investments `invpc` and housing prices `price` for the years 1947 through 1988. Using a double-logarithmic specification, Script 10.7 (`Example-10-7.R`) estimates a regression model with and without a linear trend. Forgetting to add the trend leads to the spurious finding that investments and prices are related.

Because of the logarithmic dependent variable, the trend in `invpc` (as opposed to log `invpc`) is exponential. The estimated coefficient implies a 1% yearly increase in investments.

─────── Output of Script 10.7: `Example-10-7.R` ───────

```
> library(foreign);library(dynlm);library(stargazer)

> hseinv <- read.dta("http://fmwww.bc.edu/ec-p/data/wooldridge/hseinv.dta")

> # Define Yearly time series beginning in 1947
> tsdata <- ts(hseinv, start=1947)

> # Linear regression of model with lags:
> res1 <- dynlm(log(invpc) ~ log(price)                , data=tsdata)

> res2 <- dynlm(log(invpc) ~ log(price) + trend(tsdata), data=tsdata)

> # Pretty regression table
> stargazer(res1,res2, type="text")

===============================================================
                                Dependent variable:
                        ---------------------------------------
                                      log(invpc)
                              (1)                 (2)
---------------------------------------------------------------
log(price)                  1.241***            -0.381
                            (0.382)             (0.679)

trend(tsdata)                                   0.010***
                                                (0.004)

Constant                   -0.550***           -0.913***
                            (0.043)             (0.136)

---------------------------------------------------------------
Observations                  42                  42
R2                           0.208               0.341
Adjusted R2                  0.189               0.307
Residual Std. Error   0.155 (df = 40)     0.144 (df = 39)
F Statistic         10.530*** (df = 1; 40) 10.080*** (df = 2; 39)
===============================================================
Note:                           *p<0.1; **p<0.05; ***p<0.01
```

10.3.4. Seasonality

To account for seasonal effects, we can add dummy variables for all but one (the reference) "season". So with monthly data, we can include eleven dummies, see Section 7 for a detailed discussion. The command **dynlm** automatically creates and adds the appropriate dummies when using the expression **season(tsobj)** in the model formula with the time series object `tsobj`.

Wooldridge, Example 10.11: Effects of Antidumping Filings

The data in BARIUM.dta were used in an antidumping case. They are monthly data on barium chloride imports from China between February 1978 and December 1988. Wooldridge (2016, Example 10.5) explains the data and background. When we estimate a model with monthly dummies, they do not have significant coefficients except the dummy for April which is marginally significant. An F test which is not reported reveals no joint significance.

—————— **Output of Script 10.8: Example-10-11.R** ——————

```
> library(foreign);library(dynlm);library(lmtest)

> barium <- read.dta("http://fmwww.bc.edu/ec-p/data/wooldridge/barium.dta")

> # Define monthly time series beginning in Feb. 1978
> tsdata <- ts(barium, start=c(1978,2), frequency=12)

> res <- dynlm(log(chnimp) ~ log(chempi)+log(gas)+log(rtwex)+befile6+
>                       affile6+afdec6+ season(tsdata) , data=tsdata )

> coeftest(res)

t test of coefficients:

                     Estimate Std. Error t value  Pr(>|t|)
(Intercept)        16.7792155 32.4286452  0.5174   0.60587
log(chempi)         3.2650621  0.4929302  6.6238 1.236e-09 ***
log(gas)           -1.2781403  1.3890083 -0.9202   0.35944
log(rtwex)          0.6630453  0.4713037  1.4068   0.16222
befile6             0.1397028  0.2668075  0.5236   0.60158
affile6             0.0126324  0.2786866  0.0453   0.96393
afdec6             -0.5213004  0.3019499 -1.7264   0.08700 .
season(tsdata)Feb  -0.4177110  0.3044444 -1.3720   0.17277
season(tsdata)Mar   0.0590520  0.2647307  0.2231   0.82389
season(tsdata)Apr  -0.4514830  0.2683864 -1.6822   0.09529 .
season(tsdata)May   0.0333090  0.2692425  0.1237   0.90176
season(tsdata)Jun  -0.2063315  0.2692515 -0.7663   0.44509
season(tsdata)Jul   0.0038366  0.2787666  0.0138   0.98904
season(tsdata)Aug  -0.1570645  0.2779927 -0.5650   0.57320
season(tsdata)Sep  -0.1341605  0.2676556 -0.5012   0.61718
season(tsdata)Oct   0.0516925  0.2668512  0.1937   0.84675
season(tsdata)Nov  -0.2462599  0.2628271 -0.9370   0.35077
season(tsdata)Dec   0.1328376  0.2714234  0.4894   0.62550
---
Signif. codes:  0 '***' 0.001 '**' 0.01 '*' 0.05 '.' 0.1 ' ' 1
```

11. Further Issues In Using OLS with Time Series Data

This chapter introduces important concepts for time series analyses. Section 11.1 discusses the general conditions under which asymptotic analyses work with time series data. An important requirement will be that the time series exhibit weak dependence. In Section 11.2, we study highly persistent time series and present some simulation excercises. One solution to this problem is first differencing as demonstrated in Section 11.3. How this can be done in the regression framework is the topic of Section 11.4.

11.1. Asymptotics with Time Series

As Wooldridge (2016, Section 11.2) discusses, asymptotic arguments also work with time series data under certain conditions. Importantly, we have to assume that the data are stationary and weakly dependent (Assumption TS.1). On the other hand, we can relax the strict exogeneity assumption TS.3 and only have to assume contemporaneous exogeneity (assumption TS.3'). Under the appropriate set of assumptions, we can use standard OLS estimation and inference.

Wooldridge, Example 11.4: Efficient Markets Hypothesis

The efficient markets hypothesis claims that we cannot predict stock returns from past returns. In a simple AR(1) model in which returns are regressed on lagged returns, this would imply a population slope coefficient of zero. The data set NYSE.dta contains data on weekly stock returns.
Script 11.1 (Example-11-4.R) shows the analyses. We transform the data frame into a **ts** object. Because we don't give any other information, the weeks are numbered from 1 to $n = 690$. Regression 1 is the AR(1) model also discussed by Wooldridge (2016). Models 2 and 3 add second and third lags to estimate higher-order AR(p) models. In all models, no lagged value has a significant coefficient and also the F tests for joint significance do not reject the efficient markets hypothesis.

——————————— Output of Script 11.1: `Example-11-4.R` ———————————

```
> library(foreign);library(dynlm);library(stargazer)

> nyse <- read.dta("http://fmwww.bc.edu/ec-p/data/wooldridge/nyse.dta")

> # Define time series (numbered 1,...,n)
> tsdata <- ts(nyse)

> # Linear regression of models with lags:
> reg1 <- dynlm(return~L(return)                         , data=tsdata)

> reg2 <- dynlm(return~L(return)+L(return,2)             , data=tsdata)

> reg3 <- dynlm(return~L(return)+L(return,2)+L(return,3), data=tsdata)

> # Pretty regression table
> stargazer(reg1, reg2, reg3, type="text",
>                             keep.stat=c("n","rsq","adj.rsq","f"))


===============================================================================
                                 Dependent variable:
                 --------------------------------------------------------------
                                        return
                      (1)                 (2)                 (3)
-------------------------------------------------------------------------------
L(return)            0.059               0.060               0.061
                    (0.038)             (0.038)             (0.038)

L(return, 2)                            -0.038              -0.040
                                        (0.038)             (0.038)

L(return, 3)                                                 0.031
                                                            (0.038)

Constant            0.180**             0.186**             0.179**
                    (0.081)             (0.081)             (0.082)

-------------------------------------------------------------------------------
Observations          689                 688                 687
R2                   0.003               0.005               0.006
Adjusted R2          0.002               0.002               0.001
F Statistic   2.399 (df = 1; 687) 1.659 (df = 2; 685) 1.322 (df = 3; 683)
===============================================================================
Note:                                         *p<0.1; **p<0.05; ***p<0.01
```

We can do a similar analysis for daily data. The **pdfetch_YAHOO** command from the package *pdfetch* introduced in Section 10.2.2 allows us to directly download daily stock prices from Yahoo Finance. Script 11.2 (`Example-EffMkts.R`) downloads daily stock prices of General Electric (ticker symbol GE) and stores them as a **zoo** object. From the prices p_t, the returns r_t are calculated using the standard formula

$$r_t = \log(p_t) - \log(p_{t-1}) \approx \frac{p_t - p_{t-1}}{p_{t-1}}.$$

Note that in the script, we calculate the difference using the function **diff**. It calculates the difference from trading day to trading day, ignoring the fact that some of them are separated by weekends or holidays. Figure 11.1 plots the returns of the GE stock. Even though we now have $n = 3520$ observations of daily returns, we cannot find any relation between current and past returns which supports (this version of) the efficient markets hypothesis.

———————— **Output of Script 11.2: Example-EffMkts.R** ————————

```
> # Download data from Yahoo Finance and store as "zoo" object
> library(zoo);library(pdfetch);library(dynlm);library(stargazer)

> dataset <- zoo( pdfetch_YAHOO("GE", fields="adjclose",
>                               from="2000-01-01", to="2013-12-31") )

> # Calculate return as the log difference
> ret <- diff( log(dataset$GE) )

> # Plot returns
> plot(ret)

> # Linear regression of models with lags:
> reg1 <- dynlm(ret~L(ret) )

> reg2 <- dynlm(ret~L(ret)+L(ret,2) )

> reg3 <- dynlm(ret~L(ret)+L(ret,2)+L(ret,3) )

> # Pretty regression table
> stargazer(reg1, reg2, reg3, type="text",
>                         keep.stat=c("n","rsq","adj.rsq","f"))
```

```
===============================================================================
                                       Dependent variable:
                        -------------------------------------------------------
                                               ret
                            (1)                 (2)                 (3)
-------------------------------------------------------------------------------
L(ret)                    -0.017              -0.017              -0.017
                          (0.017)             (0.017)             (0.017)

L(ret, 2)                                     -0.011              -0.011
                                              (0.017)             (0.017)

L(ret, 3)                                                         -0.006
                                                                  (0.017)

Constant                 -0.00003            -0.00003            -0.00004
                         (0.0003)            (0.0003)            (0.0003)

-------------------------------------------------------------------------------
Observations              3,519               3,518               3,517
R2                        0.0003              0.0004              0.0004
Adjusted R2              -0.00001             -0.0002             -0.0004
F Statistic  0.977 (df = 1; 3517) 0.718 (df = 2; 3515) 0.512 (df = 3; 3513)
===============================================================================
Note:                                     *p<0.1; **p<0.05; ***p<0.01
```

Figure 11.1. Time series plot: Daily stock returns, General Electric

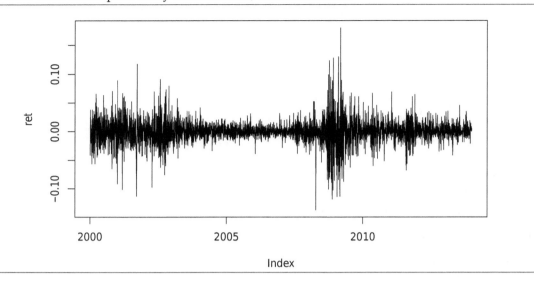

11.2. The Nature of Highly Persistent Time Series

The simplest model for highly persistent time series is a random walk. It can be written as

$$y_t = y_{t-1} + e_t \tag{11.1}$$
$$= y_0 + e_1 + e_2 + \cdots + e_{t-1} + e_t \tag{11.2}$$

where the shocks $e_1, \ldots, e_t$ are i.i.d with a zero mean. It is a special case of a unit root process. Random walk processes are strongly dependent and nonstationary, violating assumption TS1' required for the consistency of OLS parameter estimates. As Wooldridge (2016, Section 11.3) shows, the variance of y_t (conditional on y_0) increases linearly with t:

$$\text{Var}(y_t|y_0) = \sigma_e^2 \cdot t \tag{11.3}$$

This can be easily seen in a simulation exercise. Script 11.3 (`Simulate-RandomWalk.R`) draws 30 realizations from a random walk process with i.i.d. standard normal shocks e_t. After initializing the random number generator, an empty figure with the right dimensions is produced. Then, the realizations of the time series are drawn in a loop.[1] In each of the 30 draws, we first obtain a sample of the $n = 50$ shocks $e_1, \ldots, e_{50}$. The random walk is generated as the cumulative sum of the shocks according to Equation 11.2 with an initial value of $y_0 = 0$. The respective time series are then added to the plot. In the resulting Figure 11.2, the increasing variance can be seen easily.

---

[1]For a review of random number generation, see Section 1.6.4.

Figure 11.2. Simulations of a random walk process

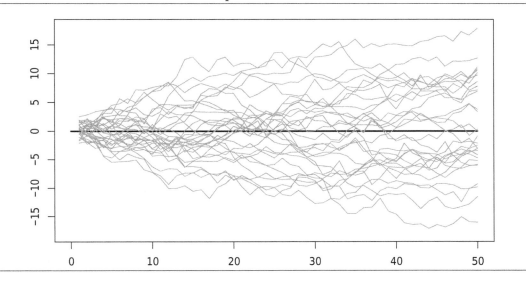

```
                     Script 11.3: Simulate-RandomWalk.R
# Initialize Random Number Generator
set.seed(348546)
# initial graph
plot(c(0,50),c(0,0),type="l",lwd=2,ylim=c(-18,18))

# loop over draws:
for(r in 1:30) {
  # i.i.d. standard normal shock
  e <- rnorm(50)
  # Random walk as cumulative sum of shocks
  y <- ts(cumsum(e))
  # Add line to graph
  lines(y, col=gray(.6))
}
```

A simple generalization is a random walk with drift:

$$y_t = \alpha_0 + y_{t-1} + e_t \tag{11.4}$$
$$= y_0 + \alpha_0 \cdot t + e_1 + e_2 + \cdots + e_{t-1} + e_t \tag{11.5}$$

Script 11.4 (Simulate-RandomWalkDrift.R) simulates such a process with $\alpha_0 = 2$ and i.i.d. standard normal shocks e_t. The resulting time series are plotted in Figure 11.3. The values fluctuate around the expected value $\alpha_0 \cdot t$. But unlike weakly dependent processes, they do not tend towards their mean, so the variance increases like for a simple random walk process.

Figure 11.3. Simulations of a random walk process with drift

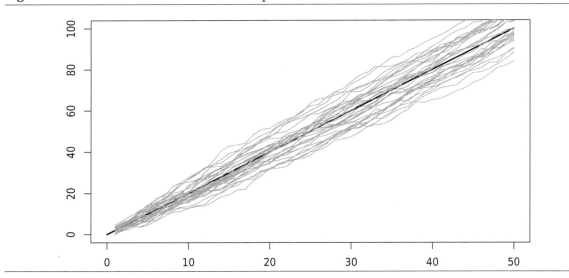

Script 11.4: Simulate-RandomWalkDrift.R

```
# Initialize Random Number Generator
set.seed(348546)
# initial empty graph with expected value
plot(c(0,50),c(0,100),type="l",lwd=2)

# loop over draws:
for(r in 1:30) {
  # i.i.d. standard normal shock
  e <- rnorm(50)
  # Random walk as cumulative sum of shocks
  y <- ts(cumsum(2+e))
  # Add line to graph
  lines(y, col=gray(.6))
}
```

An obvious question is whether a given sample is from a unit root process such as a random walk. We will cover test for unit roots in Section 18.2.

Figure 11.4. Simulations of a random walk process with drift: first differences

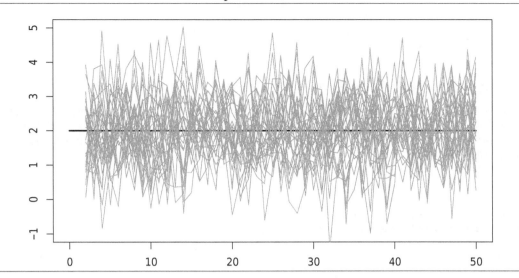

11.3. Differences of Highly Persistent Time Series

The simplest way to deal with highly persistent time series is to work with their differences rather than their levels. The first difference of the random walk with drift is

$$y_t = \alpha_0 + y_{t-1} + e_t \tag{11.6}$$

$$\Delta y_t = y_t - y_{t-1} = \alpha_0 + e_t \tag{11.7}$$

This is an i.i.d. process with mean α_0. Script 11.5 (`Simulate-RandomWalkDrift-Diff.R`) repeats the same simulation as Script 11.4 (`Simulate-RandomWalkDrift.R`) but calculates the differences using the function **diff**. The resulting series are shown in Figure 11.4. They have a constant mean of 2, a constant variance of $\sigma_e^2 = 1$, and are independent over time.

─────────── Script 11.5: `Simulate-RandomWalkDrift-Diff.R` ───────────

```
# Initialize Random Number Generator
set.seed(348546)
# initial empty graph with expected value
plot(c(0,50),c(2,2),type="l",lwd=2,ylim=c(-1,5))

# loop over draws:
for(r in 1:30) {
  # i.i.d. standard normal shock
  e <- rnorm(50)
  # Random walk as cumulative sum of shocks
  y <- ts(cumsum(2+e))
  # First difference
  Dy <- diff(y)
  # Add line to graph
  lines(Dy, col=gray(.6))
}
```

11.4. Regression with First Differences

Adding first differences to regression model formulas estimated with **dynlm** is straightforward. The dependent or independent variable var is specified as a first difference with **d(var)**. We can also combine **d()** and **L()** specifications. For example **L(d(var) ,3)** is the first difference, lagged by three time units. This is demonstrated in Example 11.6.

Wooldridge, Example 11.6: Fertility Equation

We continue Example 10-4 and specify the fertility equation in first differences. Script 11.6 (Example-11-6.R) shows the analyses. While the first difference of the tax exemptions has no significant effect, its second lag has a significantly positive coefficient in the second model. This is consistent with fertility reacting two years after a change of the tax code.

─────── **Output of Script 11.6: Example-11-6.R** ───────

```
> # Libraries for dynamic lm and "stargazer" regression table
> library(foreign);library(dynlm);library(stargazer)

> fertil<-read.dta("http://fmwww.bc.edu/ec-p/data/wooldridge/fertil3.dta")

> # Define Yearly time series beginning in 1913
> tsdata <- ts(fertil, start=1913)

> # Linear regression of model with first differences:
> res1 <- dynlm( d(gfr) ~ d(pe), data=tsdata)

> # Linear regression of model with lagged differences:
> res2 <- dynlm( d(gfr) ~ d(pe) + L(d(pe)) + L(d(pe),2), data=tsdata)

> # Pretty regression table
> stargazer(res1,res2,type="text")
```

```
===========================================================
                           Dependent variable:
                    ---------------------------------------
                                    d(gfr)
                         (1)                    (2)
-----------------------------------------------------------
d(pe)                   -0.043                 -0.036
                        (0.028)                (0.027)

L(d(pe))                                       -0.014
                                               (0.028)

L(d(pe), 2)                                    0.110***
                                               (0.027)

Constant                -0.785                 -0.964**
                        (0.502)                (0.468)

-----------------------------------------------------------
Observations             71                     69
R2                      0.032                  0.232
Adjusted R2             0.018                  0.197
Residual Std. Error 4.221 (df = 69)     3.859 (df = 65)
F Statistic         2.263 (df = 1; 69) 6.563*** (df = 3; 65)
===========================================================
Note:                          *p<0.1; **p<0.05; ***p<0.01
```

12. Serial Correlation and Heteroscedasticity in Time Series Regressions

In Chapter 8, we discussed the consequences of heteroscedasticity in cross-sectional regressions. In the time series setting, similar consequences and strategies apply to both heteroscedasticity (with some specific features) and serial correlation of the error term. Unbiasedness and consistency of the OLS estimators are unaffected. But the OLS estimators are inefficient and the usual standard errors and inferences are invalid.

We first discuss how to test for serial correlation in Section 12.1. Section 12.2 introduces efficient estimation using feasible GLS estimators. As an alternative, we can still use OLS and calculate standard errors that are valid under both heteroscedasticity and autocorrelation as discussed in Section 12.3. Finally, Section 12.4 covers heteroscedasticity and autoregressive conditional heteroscedasticity (ARCH) models.

12.1. Testing for Serial Correlation of the Error Term

Suppose we are worried that the error terms $u_1, u_2, \ldots$ in a regression model of the form

$$y_t = \beta_0 + \beta_1 x_{t1} + \beta_2 x_{t2} + \cdots + \beta_k x_{tk} + u_t \tag{12.1}$$

are serially correlated. A straightforward and intuitive testing approach is described by Wooldridge (2016, Section 12.2). It is based on the fitted residuals $\hat{u}_t = y_t - \hat{\beta}_0 - \hat{\beta}_1 x_{t1} - \cdots - \hat{\beta}_k x_{tk}$ which can be obtained in R with the function **resid**, see Section 2.2.

To test for AR(1) serial correlation under strict exogeneity, we regress $\hat{u}_t$ on their lagged values $\hat{u}_{t-1}$. If the regressors are not necessarily strictly exogenous, we can adjust the test by adding the original regressors $x_{t1}, \ldots, x_{tk}$ to this regression. Then we perform the usual t test on the coefficient of $\hat{u}_{t-1}$.

For testing for higher order serial correlation, we add higher order lags $\hat{u}_{t-2}, \hat{u}_{t-3}, \ldots$ as explanatory variables and test the joint hypothesis that they are all equal to zero using either an F test or a Lagrange multiplier (LM) test. Especially the latter version is often called Breusch-Godfrey test.

Wooldridge, Example 12.1: Testing for AR(1) Serial Correlation

We use this example to demonstrate the "pedestrian" way to test for autocorrelation which is actually straightforward and instructive. We estimate two versions of the Phillips curve: a static model

$$\mathrm{inf}_t = \beta_0 + \beta_1 \mathrm{unem}_t + u_t$$

and an expectation-augmented Phillips curve

$$\Delta \mathrm{inf}_t = \beta_0 + \beta_1 \mathrm{unem}_t + u_t.$$

Script 12.1 (Example-12-1.R) shows the analyses. After the estimation, the residuals are calculated with **resid** and regressed on their lagged values. We report standard errors and t statistics using the **coeftest** command. While there is strong evidence for autocorrelation in the static equation with a t statistic of 4.93, the null hypothesis of no autocorrelation cannot be rejected in the second model with a t statistic of -0.29.

―――――――――――――― Output of Script 12.1: **Example-12-1.R** ――――――――――――――

```
> library(foreign);library(dynlm);library(lmtest)

> phillips <-
>       read.dta("http://fmwww.bc.edu/ec-p/data/wooldridge/phillips.dta")

> # Define Yearly time series beginning in 1948
> tsdata <- ts(phillips, start=1948)

> # Estimation of static Phillips curve:
> reg.s <- dynlm( inf ~ unem, data=tsdata, end=1996)

> # residuals and AR(1) test:
> residual.s <- resid(reg.s)

> coeftest( dynlm(residual.s ~ L(residual.s)) )

t test of coefficients:

               Estimate Std. Error t value  Pr(>|t|)
(Intercept)    -0.11340    0.35940 -0.3155    0.7538
L(residual.s)   0.57297    0.11613  4.9337 1.098e-05 ***
---
Signif. codes:  0 '***' 0.001 '**' 0.01 '*' 0.05 '.' 0.1 ' ' 1


> # Same with expectations-augmented Phillips curve:
> reg.ea <- dynlm( d(inf) ~ unem, data=tsdata, end=1996)

> residual.ea <- resid(reg.ea)

> coeftest( dynlm(residual.ea ~ L(residual.ea)) )

t test of coefficients:

                Estimate Std. Error t value Pr(>|t|)
(Intercept)     0.194166   0.300384  0.6464   0.5213
L(residual.ea) -0.035593   0.123891 -0.2873   0.7752
```

This class of tests can also be performed automatically using the command **bgtest** from the package **lmtest**. Given the regression results are stored in a variable res, the LM version of a test of AR(1) serial correlation can simply be tested using

```
bgtest(res)
```

Using different options, the test can be fine tuned:

- **order=q**: Test for serial correlation of order q instead of order 1.
- **type="F"**: Use an *F* test instead of an LM test.

Wooldridge, Example 12.3: Testing for AR(3) Serial Correlation

We already used the monthly data set BARIUM.dta and estimated a model for barium chloride imports in Example 10.11. Script 12.2 (Example-12-3.R) estimates the model and tests for AR(3) serial correlation using the manual regression approach and the command **bgtest**. The manual approach gives exactly the results reported by Wooldridge (2016) while the built-in command differs very slightly because of details of the implementation, see the documentation.

―――――――― Output of Script 12.2: `Example-12-3.R` ――――――――

```
> library(foreign);library(dynlm);library(car);library(lmtest)

> barium<-read.dta("http://fmwww.bc.edu/ec-p/data/wooldridge/barium.dta")

> tsdata <- ts(barium, start=c(1978,2), frequency=12)

> reg <- dynlm(log(chnimp)~log(chempi)+log(gas)+log(rtwex)+
>                             befile6+affile6+afdec6, data=tsdata )

> # Pedestrian test:
> residual <- resid(reg)

> resreg <- dynlm(residual ~ L(residual)+L(residual,2)+L(residual,3)+
>                             log(chempi)+log(gas)+log(rtwex)+befile6+
>                                     affile6+afdec6, data=tsdata )

> linearHypothesis(resreg,
>                 c("L(residual)","L(residual, 2)","L(residual, 3)"))
Linear hypothesis test

Hypothesis:
L(residual) = 0
L(residual, 2) = 0
L(residual, 3) = 0

Model 1: restricted model
Model 2: residual ~ L(residual) + L(residual, 2) + L(residual, 3) + log(chempi) +
    log(gas) + log(rtwex) + befile6 + affile6 + afdec6

  Res.Df    RSS Df Sum of Sq      F  Pr(>F)
1    121 43.394
2    118 38.394  3    5.0005 5.1229 0.00229 **
---
Signif. codes:  0 '***' 0.001 '**' 0.01 '*' 0.05 '.' 0.1 ' ' 1
```

```
> # Automatic test:
> bgtest(reg, order=3, type="F")

        Breusch-Godfrey test for serial correlation of order up to 3

data:  reg
LM test = 5.1247, df1 = 3, df2 = 121, p-value = 0.002264
```

Another popular test is the Durbin-Watson test for AR(1) serial correlation. While the test statistic is pretty straightforward to compute, its distribution is non-standard and depends on the data. Package **lmtest** offers the command **dwtest**. It is convenient because it reports p values which can be interpreted in the standard way (given the necessary CLM assumptions hold).

Script 12.3 (Example-DWtest.R) repeats Example 12.1 but conducts DW tests instead of the t tests. The conclusions are the same: For the static model, no serial correlation is clearly rejected with a test statistic of $DW = 0.8027$ and $p < 10^{-6}$. For the expectation augmented Phillips curve, the null hypothesis is not rejected at usual significance levels ($DW = 1.7696, p = 0.1783$).

—————————————— **Output of Script 12.3:** **Example-DWtest.R** ——————————————

```
> library(foreign); library(dynlm); library(lmtest)

> phillips <-
>     read.dta("http://fmwww.bc.edu/ec-p/data/wooldridge/phillips.dta")

> tsdata <- ts(phillips, start=1948)

> # Estimation of both Phillips curve models:
> reg.s <- dynlm( inf ~ unem, data=tsdata, end=1996)

> reg.ea <- dynlm( d(inf) ~ unem, data=tsdata, end=1996)

> # DW tests
> dwtest(reg.s)

        Durbin-Watson test

data:  reg.s
DW = 0.8027, p-value = 7.552e-07
alternative hypothesis: true autocorrelation is greater than 0


> dwtest(reg.ea)

        Durbin-Watson test

data:  reg.ea
DW = 1.7696, p-value = 0.1783
alternative hypothesis: true autocorrelation is greater than 0
```

12.2. FGLS Estimation

There are several ways to implement the FGLS methods for serially correlated error terms in *R*. A simple way is provided by the package **orcutt** with its command **cochrane.orcutt**. It expects a fitted OLS model and reports the Cochrane-Orcutt estimator as demonstrated in Example 12.4. As an alternative approach, the **arima** command offers maximum likelihood estimation of a rich class of models including regression models with general ARMA(p,q) errors.

Wooldridge, Example 12.4: Cochrane-Orcutt Estimation

We once again use the monthly data set BARIUM.dta and the same model as before. Script 12.4 (Example-12-4.R) estimates the model with OLS and then calls **cochrane.orcutt**. As expected, the results are very close to the Prais-Winsten estimates reported by Wooldridge (2016).

```
──────── Output of Script 12.4: Example-12-4.R ────────

> library(foreign);library(dynlm);library(car);library(orcutt)

> barium<-read.dta("http://fmwww.bc.edu/ec-p/data/wooldridge/barium.dta")

> tsdata <- ts(barium, start=c(1978,2), frequency=12)

> # OLS estimation
> olsres <- dynlm(log(chnimp)~log(chempi)+log(gas)+log(rtwex)+
>         befile6+affile6+afdec6, data=tsdata)

> # Cochrane-Orcutt estimation
> cochrane.orcutt(olsres)
$Cochrane.Orcutt

Call:
lm(formula = YB ~ XB - 1)

Residuals:
    Min      1Q  Median      3Q     Max
-2.0103 -0.3955  0.0704  0.3584  1.3511

Coefficients:
               Estimate Std. Error t value Pr(>|t|)
XB(Intercept) -37.32224   23.22141  -1.607   0.1106
XBlog(chempi)   2.94743    0.64556   4.566 1.19e-05 ***
XBlog(gas)      1.05486    0.99090   1.065   0.2892
XBlog(rtwex)    1.13692    0.51351   2.214   0.0287 *
XBbefile6      -0.01637    0.32072  -0.051   0.9594
XBaffile6      -0.03308    0.32315  -0.102   0.9186
XBafdec6       -0.57716    0.34345  -1.680   0.0954 .
---
Signif. codes:  0 '***' 0.001 '**' 0.01 '*' 0.05 '.' 0.1 ' ' 1

Residual standard error: 0.5756 on 123 degrees of freedom
Multiple R-squared:  0.9839,     Adjusted R-squared:  0.983
F-statistic:  1075 on 7 and 123 DF,  p-value: < 2.2e-16


$rho
[1] 0.2933617

$number.interaction
[1] 8
```

12.3. Serial Correlation-Robust Inference with OLS

Unbiasedness and consistency of OLS are not affected by heteroscedasticity or serial correlation, but the standard errors are. Similar to the heteroscedasticity-robust standard errors discussed in Section 8.1, we can use a formula for the variance-covariance matrix, often referred to as Newey-West standard errors. The package *sandwich* provides the formula as the command **vcovHAC**.We again use **coeftest** command from the **lmtest** package to generate a regression table with robust standard errors, *t* statistics and their *p* values.

Wooldridge, Example 12.7: The Puerto Rican Minimum Wage

Script 12.5 (Example-12-7.R) estimates a model for the employment rate depending on the minimum wage as well as the GNP in Puerto Rico and the US. After the model has been fitted by OLS, **coeftest** without additional arguments provides the regression table using the usual variance-covariance formula. With the option **vcovHAC** provided by *sandwich*, we get the results for the HAC variance-covariance formula. Both results imply a significantly negative relation between the minimum wage and employment.

─────────── Output of Script 12.5: `Example-12-7.R` ───────────

```
> library(foreign); library(dynlm); library(lmtest); library(sandwich)

> minwg<-read.dta("http://fmwww.bc.edu/ec-p/data/wooldridge/prminwge.dta")

> tsdata <- ts(minwg, start=1950)

> # OLS regression
> reg<-dynlm(log(prepop)~log(mincov)+log(prgnp)+log(usgnp)+trend(tsdata),
>                                                         data=tsdata )

> # results with usual SE
> coeftest(reg)

t test of coefficients:

               Estimate Std. Error t value  Pr(>|t|)
(Intercept)   -6.6634416  1.2578286 -5.2976 7.667e-06 ***
log(mincov)   -0.2122612  0.0401523 -5.2864 7.924e-06 ***
log(prgnp)     0.2852380  0.0804921  3.5437  0.001203 **
log(usgnp)     0.4860482  0.2219825  2.1896  0.035731 *
trend(tsdata) -0.0266633  0.0046267 -5.7629 1.940e-06 ***
---
Signif. codes:  0 '***' 0.001 '**' 0.01 '*' 0.05 '.' 0.1 ' ' 1


> # results with HAC SE
> coeftest(reg, vcovHAC)

t test of coefficients:

               Estimate Std. Error t value  Pr(>|t|)
(Intercept)   -6.6634416  1.6856887 -3.9529 0.0003845 ***
log(mincov)   -0.2122612  0.0460683 -4.6075 5.835e-05 ***
log(prgnp)     0.2852380  0.1034900  2.7562 0.0094497 **
log(usgnp)     0.4860482  0.3108939  1.5634 0.1275013
trend(tsdata) -0.0266633  0.0054301 -4.9103 2.402e-05 ***
---
Signif. codes:  0 '***' 0.001 '**' 0.01 '*' 0.05 '.' 0.1 ' ' 1
```

12.4. Autoregressive Conditional Heteroscedasticity

In time series, especially in financial data, a specific form of heteroscedasticity is often present. Autoregressive conditional heteroscedasticity (ARCH) and related models try to capture these effects.

Consider a basic linear time series equation

$$y_t = \beta_0 + \beta_1 x_{t1} + \beta_2 x_{t2} + \cdots + \beta_k x_{tk} + u_t. \tag{12.2}$$

The error term u follows a ARCH process if

$$E(u_t^2 | u_{t-1}, u_{t-2}, ...) = \alpha_0 + \alpha_1 u_{t-1}^2. \tag{12.3}$$

As the equation suggests, we can estimate α_0 and α_1 by an OLS regression of the residuals $\hat{u}_t^2$ on $\hat{u}_{t-1}^2$.

Wooldridge, Example 12.9: ARCH in Stock Returns

Script 12.6 (`Example-12-9.R`) estimates a simple AR(1) model for weekly NYSE stock returns, already studied in Example 11.4. After the squared residuals are obtained, they are regressed on their lagged values. The coefficients from this regression are estimates for α_0 and α_1.

—————— Output of Script 12.6: `Example-12-9.R` ——————

```
> library(foreign);library(dynlm);library(lmtest)

> nyse <- read.dta("http://fmwww.bc.edu/ec-p/data/wooldridge/nyse.dta")

> tsdata <- ts(nyse)

> # Linear regression of model:
> reg <- dynlm(return ~ L(return), data=tsdata)

> # squared residual
> residual.sq <- resid(reg)^2

> # Model for squared residual:
> ARCHreg <- dynlm(residual.sq ~ L(residual.sq))

> coeftest(ARCHreg)

t test of coefficients:

                Estimate Std. Error t value  Pr(>|t|)
(Intercept)     2.947434   0.440234  6.6951 4.485e-11 ***
L(residual.sq)  0.337062   0.035947  9.3767 < 2.2e-16 ***
---
Signif. codes:  0 '***' 0.001 '**' 0.01 '*' 0.05 '.' 0.1 ' ' 1
```

As a second example, let us reconsider the daily stock returns from Script 11.2 (Example-EffMkts.R). We again download the daily stock prices for General Electric from Yahoo Finance and calculate their returns. Figure 11.1 on page 182 plots them. They show a very typical pattern for an ARCH-type of model: there are periods with high (such as 2008–2009) and other periods with low volatility (such as 2004–2007). In Script 12.7 (Example-ARCH.R), we estimate an AR(1) process for the squared residuals. The t statistic is larger than 15, so there is very strong evidence for autoregressive conditional heteroscedasticity.

—————————— Output of Script 12.7: `Example-ARCH.R` ——————————

```
> # Libraries
> library(zoo);library(pdfetch);library(dynlm);library(lmtest)

> # Download GE stock prices from Yahoo Finance and store as "zoo" object
> dataset <- zoo( pdfetch_YAHOO("GE", fields="adjclose",
>                               from="2000-01-01", to="2013-12-31") )

> # Calculate return as the log difference
> GE.ret <- diff( log(dataset$GE) )

> # AR(1) model for returns
> reg <- dynlm( GE.ret ~ L(GE.ret) )

> # squared residual
> residual.sq <- resid(reg)^2

> # Model for squared residual:
> ARCHreg <- dynlm(residual.sq ~ L(residual.sq))

> summary(ARCHreg)

Time series regression with "zoo" data:
Start = 2000-01-06, End = 2013-12-31

Call:
dynlm(formula = residual.sq ~ L(residual.sq))

Residuals:
     Min        1Q    Median        3Q       Max
-0.006851 -0.000326 -0.000284 -0.000086  0.031715

Coefficients:
               Estimate Std. Error t value Pr(>|t|)
(Intercept)    3.192e-04  2.278e-05   14.02   <2e-16 ***
L(residual.sq) 2.510e-01  1.632e-02   15.37   <2e-16 ***
---
Signif. codes:  0 '***' 0.001 '**' 0.01 '*' 0.05 '.' 0.1 ' ' 1

Residual standard error: 0.001286 on 3516 degrees of freedom
Multiple R-squared:  0.06298,	Adjusted R-squared:  0.06272
F-statistic: 236.3 on 1 and 3516 DF,  p-value: < 2.2e-16
```

There are many generalizations of ARCH models. The packages ***tseries*** and ***rugarch*** provide automated maximum likelihood estimation for many models of this class.

Part III.

Advanced Topics

13. Pooling Cross-Sections Across Time: Simple Panel Data Methods

Pooled cross sections consist of random samples from the same population at different points in time. Section 13.1 introduces this type of data set and how to use it for estimating changes over time. Section 13.2 covers difference-in-differences estimators, an important application of pooled cross-sections for identifying causal effects.

Panel data resemble pooled cross sectional data in that we have observations at different points in time. The key difference is that we observe the *same* cross-sectional units, for example individuals or firms. Panel data methods require the data to be organized in a systematic way, as discussed in Section 13.3. This allows specific calculations used for panel data analyses that are presented in Section 13.4. Section 13.5 introduces the first panel data method, first differenced estimation.

13.1. Pooled Cross-Sections

If we have random samples at different points in time, this does not only increase the overall sample size and thereby the statistical precision of our analyses. It also allows to study changes over time and shed additional light on relationships between variables.

Wooldridge, Example 13.2: Changes to the Return to Education and the Gender Wage Gap

The data set `CPS78_85.RData` includes two pooled cross-sections for the years 1978 and 1985. The dummy variable `y85` is equal to one for observations in 1985 and to zero for 1978. We estimate a model for the log wage `lwage` of the form

$$\texttt{lwage} = \beta_0 + \delta_0 \texttt{y85} + \beta_1 \texttt{educ} + \delta_1(\texttt{y85} \cdot \texttt{educ}) + \beta_2 \texttt{exper} + \beta_3 \frac{\texttt{exper}^2}{100}$$
$$+ \beta_4 \texttt{union} + \beta_5 \texttt{female} + \delta_5(\texttt{y85} \cdot \texttt{female}) + u$$

Note that we divide $\texttt{exper}^2$ by 100 and thereby multiply β_3 by 100 compared to the results reported in Wooldridge (2016). The parameter β_1 measures the return to education in 1978 and δ_1 is the *difference* of the return to education in 1985 relative to 1978. Likewise, β_5 is the gender wage gap in 1978 and δ_5 is the change of the wage gap.

Script 13.1 (`Example-13-2.R`) estimates the model. The return to education is estimated to have increased by $\hat{\delta}_1 = 0.018$ and the gender wage gap decreased in absolute value from $\hat{\beta}_5 = -0.317$ to $\hat{\beta}_5 + \hat{\delta}_5 = -0.232$, even though this change is only marginally significant. The interpretation and implementation of interactions were covered in more detail in Section 6.1.5.

```
                ——————————— Output of Script 13.1: Example-13-2.R ———————————

> library(foreign)

> cps <- read.dta("http://fmwww.bc.edu/ec-p/data/wooldridge/cps78_85.dta")

> # Detailed OLS results including interaction terms
> summary( lm(lwage ~ y85*(educ+female) +exper+ I((exper^2)/100) + union,
>                                                            data=cps) )

Call:
lm(formula = lwage ~ y85 * (educ + female) + exper + I((exper^2)/100) +
    union, data = cps)

Residuals:
     Min      1Q   Median      3Q      Max
-2.56098 -0.25828  0.00864  0.26571  2.11669

Coefficients:
                 Estimate Std. Error t value Pr(>|t|)
(Intercept)      0.458933   0.093449   4.911 1.05e-06 ***
y85              0.117806   0.123782   0.952   0.3415
educ             0.074721   0.006676  11.192  < 2e-16 ***
female          -0.316709   0.036621  -8.648  < 2e-16 ***
exper            0.029584   0.003567   8.293 3.27e-16 ***
I((exper^2)/100) -0.039943   0.007754  -5.151 3.08e-07 ***
union            0.202132   0.030294   6.672 4.03e-11 ***
y85:educ         0.018461   0.009354   1.974   0.0487 *
y85:female       0.085052   0.051309   1.658   0.0977 .
---
Signif. codes:  0 '***' 0.001 '**' 0.01 '*' 0.05 '.' 0.1 ' ' 1

Residual standard error: 0.4127 on 1075 degrees of freedom
Multiple R-squared:  0.4262,        Adjusted R-squared:  0.4219
F-statistic:  99.8 on 8 and 1075 DF,  p-value: < 2.2e-16
```

13.2. Difference-in-Differences

Wooldridge (2016, Section 13.2) discusses an important type of applications for pooled cross-sections. Difference-in-differences (DiD) estimators estimate the effect of a policy intervention (in the broadest sense) by comparing the change over time of an outcome of interest between an affected and an unaffected group of observations.

In a regression framework, we regress the outcome of interest on a dummy variable for the affected ("treatment") group, a dummy indicating observations after the treatment and an interaction term between both. The coefficient of this interaction term can then be a good estimator for the effect of interest, controlling for initial differences between the groups and contemporaneous changes over time.

Wooldridge, Example 13.3: Effect of a Garbage Incinerator's Location on Housing Prices

We are interested in whether and how much the construction of a new garbage incinerator affected the value of nearby houses. Script 13.2 (Example-13-3-1.R) uses the data set KIELMC.dta. We first estimate separate models for 1978 (before there were any rumors about the new incinerator) and 1981 (when the construction began). In 1981, the houses close to the construction site were cheaper by an average of $30,688.27. But this was not only due to the new incinerator since even in 1978, nearby houses were cheaper by an average of $18,824.37. The difference of these differences $\hat{\delta} = \$30,688.27 - \$18,824.37 = \$11,863.90$ is the DiD estimator and is arguably a better indicator of the actual effect.

The DiD estimator can be obtained more conveniently using a joint regression model with the interaction term as described above. The estimator $\hat{\delta} = \$11,863.90$ can be directly seen as the coefficient of the interaction term. Conveniently, standard regression tables include t tests of the hypothesis that the actual effect is equal to zero. For a one-sided test, the p value is $\frac{1}{2} \cdot 0.112 = 0.056$, so there is some statistical evidence of a negative impact.

The DiD estimator can be improved. A logarithmic specification is more plausible since it implies a constant *percentage* effect on the house values. We can also add additional regressors to control for incidental changes in the composition of the houses traded. Script 13.3 (Example-13-3-2.R) implements both improvements. The model including features of the houses implies an estimated decrease in the house values of about 13.2%. This effect is also significantly different from zero.

_____ Output of Script 13.2: `Example-13-3-1.R` _____

```
> library(foreign)

> kielmc <- read.dta("http://fmwww.bc.edu/ec-p/data/wooldridge/kielmc.dta")

> # Separate regressions for 1978 and 1981: report coeeficients only
> coef( lm(rprice~nearinc, data=kielmc, subset=(year==1978)) )
(Intercept)      nearinc
   82517.23    -18824.37

> coef( lm(rprice~nearinc, data=kielmc, subset=(year==1981)) )
(Intercept)      nearinc
  101307.51    -30688.27

> # Joint regression including an interaction term
> library(lmtest)

> coeftest( lm(rprice~nearinc*y81, data=kielmc) )

t test of coefficients:

             Estimate Std. Error t value  Pr(>|t|)
(Intercept)   82517.2     2726.9 30.2603 < 2.2e-16 ***
nearinc      -18824.4     4875.3 -3.8612 0.0001368 ***
y81           18790.3     4050.1  4.6395 5.117e-06 ***
nearinc:y81  -11863.9     7456.6 -1.5911 0.1125948
---
Signif. codes:  0 '***' 0.001 '**' 0.01 '*' 0.05 '.' 0.1 ' ' 1
```

```
───────── Output of Script 13.3: Example-13-3-2.R ─────────

> DiD       <- lm(log(rprice)~nearinc*y81                      , data=kielmc)

> DiDcontr <- lm(log(rprice)~nearinc*y81+age+I(age^2)+log(intst)+
>                          log(land)+log(area)+rooms+baths, data=kielmc)

> library(stargazer)

> stargazer(DiD,DiDcontr,type="text")
```

```
================================================================
                               Dependent variable:
                       -----------------------------------------
                                      log(rprice)
                           (1)                     (2)
----------------------------------------------------------------
nearinc                 -0.340***                 0.032
                         (0.055)                 (0.047)

y81                      0.193***                0.162***
                         (0.045)                 (0.028)

age                                             -0.008***
                                                 (0.001)

I(age2)                                         0.00004***
                                                (0.00001)

log(intst)                                       -0.061*
                                                 (0.032)

log(land)                                        0.100***
                                                 (0.024)

log(area)                                        0.351***
                                                 (0.051)

rooms                                            0.047***
                                                 (0.017)

baths                                            0.094***
                                                 (0.028)

nearinc:y81              -0.063                  -0.132**
                         (0.083)                 (0.052)

Constant                11.285***                7.652***
                         (0.031)                 (0.416)

----------------------------------------------------------------
Observations               321                     321
R2                        0.246                   0.733
Adjusted R2               0.239                   0.724
Residual Std. Error  0.338 (df = 317)        0.204 (df = 310)
F Statistic        34.470*** (df = 3; 317) 84.915*** (df = 10; 310)
================================================================
Note:                          *p<0.1; **p<0.05; ***p<0.01
```

13.3. Organizing Panel Data

A panel data set includes several observations at different points in time t for the same (or at least an overlapping) set of cross-sectional units i. A simple "pooled" regression model could look like

$$y_{it} = \beta_0 + \beta_1 x_{it1} + \beta_2 x_{it2} + \cdots + \beta_k x_{itk} + v_{it}; \qquad t = 1, \ldots, T; \qquad i = 1, \ldots, n, \qquad (13.1)$$

where the double subscript now indicates values for individual (or other cross-sectional unit) i at time t. We could estimate this model by OLS, essentially ignoring the panel structure. But at least the assumption that the error terms are unrelated is very hard to justify since they contain unobserved individual traits that are likely to be constant or at least correlated over time. Therefore, we need specific methods for panel data.

For the calculations used by panel data methods, we have to make sure that the data set is systematically organized and the estimation routines understand its structure. Usually, a panel data set comes in a "long" form where each row of data corresponds to one combination of i and t. We have to define which observations belong together by introducing an index variable for the cross-sectional units i and preferably also the time index t.

The package **plm** (for panel linear models) is a comprehensive collection of commands dealing with panel data. Similar to specific data types for time series, it offers a data type named **pdata.frame**. It essentially corresponds to a standard **data.frame** but has additional attributes that describe the individual and time dimensions. Suppose we have our data in a standard data frame named mydf. It includes a variable ivar indicating the cross-sectional units and a variable tvar indicating the time. Then we can create a panel data frame with the command

```
mypdf <- pdata.frame( mydf, index=c("ivar","tvar") )
```

If we have a balanced panel (i.e. the same number of observations T for each "individual" $i = 1, \ldots, n$) and the observations are first sorted by i and then by t, we can alternatively call

```
mypdf <- pdata.frame( mydf, index=n )
```

In this case, the new variables id and time are generated as the index variables.

Once we have defined our data set, we can check the dimensions with **pdim(mypdf)**. It will report whether the panel is balanced, the number of cross-sectional units n, the number of time units T, and the total number of observations N (which is $n \cdot T$ in balanced panels).

Let's apply this to the data set CRIME2.dta discussed by Wooldridge (2016, Section 13.3). It is a balanced panel of 46 cities, properly sorted. Script 13.4 (PDataFrame.R) imports the the data set. We define our new panel data frame crime2.p and check its dimensions. Apparently, R understood us correctly and reports a balanced panel with two observations on 46 cities each. We also display the first six rows of data for the new id and time index variables and other selected variables. Now we're ready to work with this data set.

―――――――――――――― Output of Script 13.4: `PDataFrame.R` ――――――――――――――

```
> library(foreign);library(plm)

> crime2 <- read.dta("http://fmwww.bc.edu/ec-p/data/wooldridge/crime2.dta")

> # Define panel data frame
> crime2.p <- pdata.frame(crime2, index=46 )

> # Panel dimensions:
> pdim(crime2.p)
Balanced Panel: n=46, T=2, N=92

> # Observation 1-6: new "id" and "time" and some other variables:
> crime2.p[1:6,c("id","time","year","pop","crimes","crmrte","unem")]
    id time year     pop crimes   crmrte unem
1-1  1    1   82  229528  17136 74.65756  8.2
1-2  1    2   87  246815  17306 70.11729  3.7
2-1  2    1   82  814054  75654 92.93487  8.1
2-2  2    2   87  933177  83960 89.97221  5.4
3-1  3    1   82  374974  31352 83.61113  9.0
3-2  3    2   87  406297  31364 77.19476  5.9
```

13.4. Panel-specific computations

Once we have defined our panel data set, we can do useful computations specific to panel data. They will be used by the estimators discussed below. While we will see that for much of applied panel data regressions, the canned routines will take care of these calculations, it is still instructive and gives us more flexibility to be able to implement them ourselves.

Consider a panel data set with the cross-sectional units (individuals,...) $i = 1, ..., n$. There are T_i observations for individual i. The total number of observations is $N = \sum_{i=1}^{n} T_i$. In the special case of a balanced panel, all individuals have the same $T_i = T$ and $N = n \cdot T$.

Table 13.1 lists the most important special functions. We can calculate lags and first differences using **lag** and **diff**, respectively. Unlike in pure time series data, the lags and differences are calculated for the individuals separately, so the first observations for each $i = 1, ..., n$ is **NA**. Higher-order lags can be specified as a second argument.

The individual averages $\bar{x}_i = \frac{1}{T_i} \sum_{t=1}^{T_i} x_{it}$ are calculated using the function **between** which returns one value for each *individual* in a vector of length n. Often, we need this value for each of the N *observations*. The command **Between** returns this vector of length N where each $\bar{x}_i$ is repeated T_i times. The within transformation conveniently calculated with **Within** subtracts the individual mean $\bar{x}_i$ from observation x_{it}. These "demeaned" variables play an important role in Chapter 14.

Table 13.1. Panel-specific computations

l=lag(x)	Lag:	$l_{it} = x_{it-1}$
d=diff(x)	Difference Δx_{it}	$d_{it} = x_{it} - x_{it-1}$
b=between(x)	Between transformation $\bar{x}_i$ (length n):	$b_i = \frac{1}{T_i} \sum_{t=1}^{T_i} x_{it}$
B=Between(x)	Between transformation $\bar{x}_i$ (length N):	$B_{it} = b_i$
w=Within(x)	Within transformation (demeaning) $\ddot{x}_{it}$:	$w_{it} = x_{it} - B_{it}$

Script 13.5 (Example-PLM-Calcs.R) demonstrates these functions. The data set CRIME4.dta has data on 90 counties for seven years. The data set includes the index variables county and year which are used in the definition of our **pdata.frame**. We calculate lags, differences, between and within transformations of the crime rate (crmrte). The results are stored back into the panel data frame. The first rows of data are then presented for illustration.

The lagged variable vcr.l is just equal to crmrte but shifted down one row. The difference between these two variables is cr.d. The average crmrte within the first seven rows (i.e. for county 1) is given as the first seven values of cr.B and cr.W is the difference between crmrte and cr.B.

```
——————— Output of Script 13.5: Example-PLM-Calcs.R ———————
> library(foreign);library(plm)

> crime4 <- read.dta("http://fmwww.bc.edu/ec-p/data/wooldridge/crime4.dta")

> # Generate pdata.frame:
> crime4.p <- pdata.frame(crime4, index=c("county","year") )

> # Calculations within the pdata.frame:
> crime4.p$cr.l <- lag(crime4.p$crmrte)

> crime4.p$cr.d <- diff(crime4.p$crmrte)

> crime4.p$cr.B <- Between(crime4.p$crmrte)

> crime4.p$cr.W <- Within(crime4.p$crmrte)

> # Display selected variables for observations 1-16:
> crime4.p[1:16,c("county","year","crmrte","cr.l","cr.d","cr.B","cr.W")]
      county year   crmrte        cr.l            cr.d          cr.B           cr.W
1-81       1   81 0.0398849          NA              NA 0.03574136   0.0041435414
1-82       1   82 0.0383449   0.0398849  -0.0015399978 0.03574136   0.0026035437
1-83       1   83 0.0303048   0.0383449  -0.0080401003 0.03574136  -0.0054365567
1-84       1   84 0.0347259   0.0303048   0.0044211000 0.03574136  -0.0010154567
1-85       1   85 0.0365730   0.0347259   0.0018470995 0.03574136   0.0008316429
1-86       1   86 0.0347524   0.0365730  -0.0018206015 0.03574136  -0.0009889587
1-87       1   87 0.0356036   0.0347524   0.0008512028 0.03574136  -0.0001377559
3-81       3   81 0.0163921          NA              NA 0.01493636   0.0014557433
3-82       3   82 0.0190651   0.0163921   0.0026730001 0.01493636   0.0041287434
3-83       3   83 0.0151492   0.0190651  -0.0039159004 0.01493636   0.0002128430
3-84       3   84 0.0136621   0.0151492  -0.0014871005 0.01493636  -0.0012742575
3-85       3   85 0.0120346   0.0136621  -0.0016275002 0.01493636  -0.0029017577
3-86       3   86 0.0129982   0.0120346   0.0009636004 0.01493636  -0.0019381573
3-87       3   87 0.0152532   0.0129982   0.0022550002 0.01493636   0.0003168429
5-81       5   81 0.0093372          NA              NA 0.01256721  -0.0032300143
5-82       5   82 0.0123229   0.0093372   0.0029857000 0.01256721  -0.0002443143
```

13.5. First Differenced Estimator

Wooldridge (2016, Sections 13.3 – 13.5) discusses basic unobserved effects models and their estimation by first-differencing (FD). Consider the model

$$y_{it} = \beta_0 + \beta_1 x_{it1} + \cdots + \beta_k x_{itk} + a_i + u_{it}; \qquad t = 1, \ldots, T; \qquad i = 1, \ldots, n, \qquad (13.2)$$

which differs from Equation 13.1 in that it explicitly involves an unobserved effect a_i that is constant over time (since it has no t subscript). If it is correlated with one or more of the regressors $x_{it1}, \ldots, x_{itk}$, we cannot simply ignore a_i, leave it in the composite error term $v_{it} = a_i + u_{it}$ and estimate the equation by OLS. The error term v_{it} would be related to the regressors, violating assumption MLR.4 (and MLR.4') and creating biases and inconsistencies. Note that this problem is not unique to panel data, but possible solutions are.

The first differenced (FD) estimator is based on the first difference of the whole equation:

$$\begin{aligned} \Delta y_{it} &\equiv y_{it} - y_{it-1} \\ &= \beta_1 \Delta x_{it1} + \cdots + \beta_k \Delta x_{itk} + \Delta u_{it}; \qquad t = 2, \ldots, T; \qquad i = 1, \ldots, n. \qquad (13.3) \end{aligned}$$

Note that we cannot evaluate this equation for the first observation $t = 1$ for any i since the lagged values are unknown for them. The trick is that a_i drops out of the equation by differencing since it does not change over time. No matter how badly it is correlated with the regressors, it cannot hurt the estimation anymore. This estimating equation is then analyzed by OLS. We simply regress the differenced dependent variable Δy_{it} on the differenced independent variables $\Delta x_{it1}, \ldots, \Delta x_{itk}$.

Script 13.6 (Example-FD.R) opens the data set CRIME2.dta already used above. Within a **pdata.frame**, we use the function **diff** to calculate first differences of the dependent variable crime rate (crmrte) and the independent variable unemployment rate (unem) within our data set.

A list of the first six observations reveals that the differences are unavailable (**NA**) for the first year of each city. The other differences are also calculated as expected. For example the change of the crime rate for city 1 is $70.11729 - 74.65756 = -4.540268$ and the change of the unemployment rate for city 2 is $5.4 - 8.1 = -2.7$.

The FD estimator can now be calculated by simply applying OLS to these differenced values. The observations for the first year with missing information are automatically dropped from the estimation sample. The results show a significantly positive relation between unemployment and crime.

Output of Script 13.6: Example-FD.R

```
> library(foreign);library(plm); library(lmtest)

> crime2 <- read.dta("http://fmwww.bc.edu/ec-p/data/wooldridge/crime2.dta")

> crime2.p <- pdata.frame(crime2, index=46 )

> # manually calculate first differences:
> crime2.p$dcrmrte <- diff(crime2.p$crmrte)

> crime2.p$dunem    <- diff(crime2.p$unem)
```

```
> # Display selected variables for observations 1-6:
> crime2.p[1:6,c("id","time","year","crmrte","dcrmrte","unem","dunem")]
    id time year    crmrte   dcrmrte unem dunem
1-1  1    1   82 74.65756        NA  8.2    NA
1-2  1    2   87 70.11729 -4.540276  3.7  -4.5
2-1  2    1   82 92.93487        NA  8.1    NA
2-2  2    2   87 89.97221 -2.962654  5.4  -2.7
3-1  3    1   82 83.61113        NA  9.0    NA
3-2  3    2   87 77.19476 -6.416367  5.9  -3.1

> # Estimate FD model with lm on differenced data:
> coeftest( lm(dcrmrte~dunem, data=crime2.p) )

t test of coefficients:

            Estimate Std. Error t value Pr(>|t|)
(Intercept) 15.40219    4.70212  3.2756  0.00206 **
dunem        2.21800    0.87787  2.5266  0.01519 *
---
Signif. codes:  0 '***' 0.001 '**' 0.01 '*' 0.05 '.' 0.1 ' ' 1


> # Estimate FD model with plm on original data:
> coeftest( plm(crmrte~unem, data=crime2.p, model="fd") )

t test of coefficients:

            Estimate Std. Error t value Pr(>|t|)
(intercept) 15.40219    4.70212  3.2756  0.00206 **
unem         2.21800    0.87787  2.5266  0.01519 *
---
Signif. codes:  0 '***' 0.001 '**' 0.01 '*' 0.05 '.' 0.1 ' ' 1
```

Generating the differenced values and using **lm** on them is actually unnecessary. Package **plm** provide the versatile command **plm** which implements FD and other estimators, some of which we will use in chapter 14. It works just like **lm** but is directly applied to the original variables and does the necessary calculations internally. With the option **model="pooling"**, the pooled OLS estimator is requested, option **model="fd"** produces the FD estimator. As the output of Script Example-FD shows, the parameter estimates are exactly the same as our pedestrian calculations.

Wooldridge, Example 13.9: County Crime Rates in North Carolina

Script 13.7 (Example-13-9.R) analyzes the data CRIME4.dta already used in Script 13.5 (Example-PLM-Calcs.R). Just for illustration, we calculate the first difference of crmrte and display the first nine rows of data. The first difference is **NA** for the first year for each county. Then we estimate the model in first differences using **plm**.

Note that in this specification, all variables are automatically differenced, so they have the intuitive interpretation in the level equation. In the results reported by Wooldridge (2016), the year dummies are not differenced which only makes a difference for the interpretation of the year coefficients. To reproduce the exact same results as Wooldridge (2016), we could use a pooled OLS estimator and explicitly difference the other variables:

```
plm(diff(log(crmrte)) ~ d83+d84+d85+d86+d87+diff(lprbarr)+diff(lprbconv)+
                        diff(lprbpris)+diff(lavgsen)+diff(lpolpc),
                        data=pdata, model="pooling")
```

We will repeat this example with "robust" standard errors in Section 14.4.

Output of Script 13.7: `Example-13-9.R`

```
> library(foreign);library(plm)

> crime4<-read.dta("http://fmwww.bc.edu/ec-p/data/wooldridge/crime4.dta")

> crime4.p <- pdata.frame(crime4, index=c("county","year") )

> pdim(crime4.p)
Balanced Panel: n=90, T=7, N=630

> # manually calculate first differences of crime rate:
> crime4.p$dcrmrte <- diff(crime4.p$crmrte)

> # Display selected variables for observations 1-9:
> crime4.p[1:9, c("county","year","crmrte","dcrmrte")]
      county year    crmrte          dcrmrte
1-81       1   81 0.0398849              NA
1-82       1   82 0.0383449  -0.0015399978
1-83       1   83 0.0303048  -0.0080401003
1-84       1   84 0.0347259   0.0044211000
1-85       1   85 0.0365730   0.0018470995
1-86       1   86 0.0347524  -0.0018206015
1-87       1   87 0.0356036   0.0008512028
3-81       3   81 0.0163921              NA
3-82       3   82 0.0190651   0.0026730001

> # Estimate FD model:
> coeftest( plm(log(crmrte)~d83+d84+d85+d86+d87+lprbarr+lprbconv+
>                     lprbpris+lavgsen+lpolpc,data=crime4.p, model="fd") )

t test of coefficients:

            Estimate Std. Error  t value  Pr(>|t|)
(intercept) 0.007713   0.017058   0.4522 0.6513343
d83        -0.099865   0.023895  -4.1793 3.421e-05 ***
d84        -0.147802   0.041279  -3.5805 0.0003745 ***
d85        -0.152413   0.058400  -2.6098 0.0093157 **
d86        -0.124899   0.076004  -1.6433 0.1009124
d87        -0.084071   0.094000  -0.8944 0.3715287
lprbarr    -0.327495   0.029980 -10.9237 < 2.2e-16 ***
lprbconv   -0.238106   0.018234 -13.0583 < 2.2e-16 ***
lprbpris   -0.165046   0.025969  -6.3555 4.488e-10 ***
lavgsen    -0.021761   0.022091  -0.9851 0.3250460
lpolpc      0.398426   0.026882  14.8213 < 2.2e-16 ***
---
Signif. codes:  0 '***' 0.001 '**' 0.01 '*' 0.05 '.' 0.1 ' ' 1
```

14. Advanced Panel Data Methods

In this chapter, we look into additional panel data models and methods. We start with the widely used fixed effects (FE) estimator in Section 14.1, followed by random effects (RE) in Section 14.2. The dummy variable regression and correlated random effects approaches presented in Section 14.3 can be used as alternatives and generalizations of FE. Finally, we cover robust formulas for the variance-covariance matrix and the implied "clustered" standard errors in Section 14.4. We will come back to panel data in combination with instrumental variables in Section 15.6.

14.1. Fixed Effects Estimation

We start from the same basic unobserved effects models as Equation 13.2. Instead of first differencing, we get rid of the unobserved individual effect a_i using the within transformation:

$$
\begin{aligned}
y_{it} &= \beta_0 + \beta_1 x_{it1} + \cdots + \beta_k x_{itk} + a_i + u_{it}; & t = 1, \ldots, T; \quad i = 1, \ldots, n, \\
\bar{y}_i &= \beta_0 + \beta_1 \bar{x}_{i1} + \cdots + \beta_k \bar{x}_{ik} + a_i + \bar{u}_i \\
\ddot{y}_{it} = y_{it} - \bar{y}_i &= \quad\;\; \beta_1 \ddot{x}_{it1} + \cdots + \beta_k \ddot{x}_{itk} \qquad\;\, + \ddot{u}_{it},
\end{aligned}
\tag{14.1}
$$

where $\bar{y}_i$ is the average of y_{it} over time for cross-sectional unit i and for the other variables accordingly. The within transformation subtracts these individual averages from the respective observations y_{it}. We already know how to conveniently calculate these demeaned variables like $\ddot{y}_{it}$ using the command **Within** from Section 13.4.

The fixed effects (FE) estimator simply estimates the demeaned Equation 14.1 using pooled OLS. Instead of applying the within transformation to all variables and running **lm**, we can simply use **plm** on the original data with the option **model="within"**. This has the additional advantage that the degrees of freedom are adjusted to the demeaning and the variance-covariance matrix and standard errors are adjusted accordingly. We will come back to different ways to get the same estimates in Section 14.3.

Wooldridge, Example 14.2: Has the Return to Education Changed over Time?

We estimate the change of the return to education over time using a fixed effects estimator. Script 14.1 (Example-14-2.R) shows the implementation. The data set WAGEPAN.dta is a balanced panel for $n = 545$ individuals over $T = 8$ years. It includes the index variables nr and year for individuals and years, respectively. Since educ does not change over time, we cannot estimate its overall impact. However, we can interact it with time dummies to see how the impact changes over time.

──────────── **Output of Script 14.1: `Example-14-2.R`** ────────────

```
> library(foreign);library(plm)

> wagepan<-read.dta("http://fmwww.bc.edu/ec-p/data/wooldridge/wagepan.dta")

> # Generate pdata.frame:
> wagepan.p <- pdata.frame(wagepan, index=c("nr","year") )

> pdim(wagepan.p)
Balanced Panel: n=545, T=8, N=4360

> # Estimate FE model
> summary( plm(lwage~married+union+factor(year)*educ,
>                                    data=wagepan.p, model="within") )
Oneway (individual) effect Within Model

Call:
plm(formula = lwage ~ married + union + factor(year) * educ,
    data = wagepan.p, model = "within")

Balanced Panel: n=545, T=8, N=4360

Residuals :
   Min. 1st Qu.  Median 3rd Qu.    Max.
-4.1500 -0.1260  0.0109  0.1610  1.4800

Coefficients :
                    Estimate Std. Error t-value  Pr(>|t|)
married            0.0548205  0.0184126  2.9773  0.002926 **
union              0.0829785  0.0194461  4.2671 2.029e-05 ***
factor(year)1981  -0.0224159  0.1458885 -0.1537  0.877893
factor(year)1982  -0.0057613  0.1458558 -0.0395  0.968494
factor(year)1983   0.0104296  0.1458579  0.0715  0.942999
factor(year)1984   0.0843743  0.1458518  0.5785  0.562966
factor(year)1985   0.0497251  0.1458602  0.3409  0.733191
factor(year)1986   0.0656064  0.1458917  0.4497  0.652958
factor(year)1987   0.0904447  0.1458505  0.6201  0.535217
factor(year)1981:educ 0.0115854  0.0122625  0.9448  0.344827
factor(year)1982:educ 0.0147905  0.0122635  1.2061  0.227871
factor(year)1983:educ 0.0171182  0.0122633  1.3959  0.162829
factor(year)1984:educ 0.0165839  0.0122657  1.3521  0.176437
factor(year)1985:educ 0.0237086  0.0122738  1.9316  0.053479 .
factor(year)1986:educ 0.0274123  0.0122740  2.2334  0.025583 *
factor(year)1987:educ 0.0304332  0.0122723  2.4798  0.013188 *
---
Signif. codes:  0 '***' 0.001 '**' 0.01 '*' 0.05 '.' 0.1 ' ' 1

Total Sum of Squares:    572.05
Residual Sum of Squares: 474.35
R-Squared      :  0.1708
     Adj. R-Squared :  0.14882
F-statistic: 48.9068 on 16 and 3799 DF, p-value: < 2.22e-16
```

14.2. Random Effects Models

We again base our analysis on the basic unobserved effects model in Equation 13.2. The random effects (RE) model assumes that the unobserved effects a_i are independent of (or at least uncorrelated with) the regressors x_{itj} for all t and $j = 1, \ldots, k$. Therefore, our main motivation for using FD or FE disappears: OLS consistently estimates the model parameters under this additional assumption.

However, like the situation with heteroscedasticity (see Section 8.3) and autocorrelation (see Section 12.2), we can obtain more efficient estimates if we take into account the structure of the variances and covariances of the error term. Wooldridge (2016, Section 14.2) shows that the GLS transformation that takes care of their special structure implied by the RE model leads to a quasi-demeaned specification

$$\mathring{y}_{it} = y_{it} - \theta \bar{y}_i = \beta_0(1 - \theta) + \beta_1 \mathring{x}_{it1} + \cdots + \beta_k \mathring{x}_{itk} + \mathring{v}_{it}, \tag{14.2}$$

where $\mathring{y}_{it}$ is similar to the demeaned $\ddot{y}_{it}$ from Equation 14.1 but subtracts only a fraction θ of the individual averages. The same holds for the regressors x_{itj} and the composite error term $v_{it} = a_i + u_{it}$.

The parameter $\theta = 1 - \sqrt{\frac{\sigma_u^2}{\sigma_u^2 + T\sigma_a^2}}$ depends on the variances of u_{it} and a_i and the length of the time series dimension T. It is unknown and has to be estimated. Given our experience with FD and FE estimation, it should not come as a surprise that we can estimate the RE model parameters using the command **plm** with the option **model="random"**. Different versions of estimating the random effects parameter θ are implemented and can be chosen with the option **random.method**, see Croissant and Millo (2008) for details.

Unlike with FD and FE estimators, we can include variables in our model that are constant over time for each cross-sectional unit. The command **pvar** provides a list of these variables as well as of those that do not vary within each point in time.

Wooldridge, Example 14.4: A Wage Equation Using Panel Data

The data set WAGEPAN.dta was already used in Example 14.2. Script 14.2 (Example-14-4-1.R) loads the data set and defines the panel structure. Then, we check the panel dimensions and get a list of time-constant variables using **pvar**. With these preparations, we get estimates using OLS, RE, and FE estimators in Script 14.3 (Example-14-4-2.R). We use **plm** with the options **pooling**, **random**, and **within**, respectively. We once again use **stargazer** to display the results, with additional options for labeling the estimates (**column.labels**), and selecting variables (**keep**) and statistics (**keep.stat**).

──────── Output of Script 14.2: `Example-14-4-1.R` ────────

```
> library(foreign);library(plm);library(stargazer)

> wagepan<-read.dta("http://fmwww.bc.edu/ec-p/data/wooldridge/wagepan.dta")

> # Generate pdata.frame:
> wagepan.p <- pdata.frame(wagepan, index=c("nr","year") )

> pdim(wagepan.p)
Balanced Panel: n=545, T=8, N=4360

> # Check variation of variables within individuals
> pvar(wagepan.p)
no time variation   :  nr black hisp educ
no individual variation :  year d81 d82 d83 d84 d85 d86 d87
```

—————— **Output of Script 14.3:** `Example-14-4-2.R` ——————

```
> # Estimate different models
> wagepan.p$yr<-factor(wagepan.p$year)

> reg.ols<- (plm(lwage~educ+black+hisp+exper+I(exper^2)+married+union+yr,
>                                    data=wagepan.p, model="pooling") )

> reg.re <- (plm(lwage~educ+black+hisp+exper+I(exper^2)+married+union+yr,
>                                    data=wagepan.p, model="random") )

> reg.fe <- (plm(lwage~                    I(exper^2)+married+union+yr,
>                                    data=wagepan.p, model="within") )

> # Pretty table of selected results (not reporting year dummies)
> stargazer(reg.ols,reg.re,reg.fe, type="text",
>         column.labels=c("OLS","RE","FE"),keep.stat=c("n","rsq"),
>         keep=c("ed","bl","hi","exp","mar","un"))
```

```
==========================================
                 Dependent variable:
                -----------------------------
                           lwage
                 OLS        RE         FE
                 (1)        (2)        (3)
------------------------------------------
educ             0.091***   0.092***
                (0.005)    (0.011)

black           -0.139***  -0.139***
                (0.024)    (0.048)

hisp             0.016      0.022
                (0.021)    (0.043)

exper            0.067***   0.106***
                (0.014)    (0.015)

I(exper2)       -0.002***  -0.005***  -0.005***
                (0.001)    (0.001)    (0.001)

married          0.108***   0.064***   0.047**
                (0.016)    (0.017)    (0.018)

union            0.182***   0.106***   0.080***
                (0.017)    (0.018)    (0.019)

------------------------------------------
Observations     4,360      4,360      4,360
R2               0.189      0.181      0.181
==========================================
Note:           *p<0.1; **p<0.05; ***p<0.01
```

The RE estimator needs stronger assumptions to be consistent than the FE estimator. On the other hand, it is more efficient if these assumptions hold and we can include time constant regressors. A widely used test of this additional assumption is the Hausman test. It is based on the comparison between the FE and RE parameter estimates. Package **plm** offers the simple command **phtest** for automated testing. It expects both estimates and reports test results including the appropriate p values.

Script 14.4 (`Example-HausmTest.R`) uses the estimates obtained in Script 14.3 (`Example-14-4-2.R`) and stored in variables `reg.re` and `reg.fe` to run the Hausman test for this model. With the p value of 0.0033, the null hypothesis that the RE model is consistent is clearly rejected with sensible significance levels like $\alpha = 5\%$ or $\alpha = 1\%$.

─────────── **Output of Script 14.4: `Example-HausmTest.R`** ───────────

```
> # Note that the estimates "reg.fe" and "reg.re" are calculated in
> # Example 14.4. The scripts have to be run first.
>
> # Hausman test of RE vs. FE:
> phtest(reg.fe, reg.re)

        Hausman Test

data:  lwage ~ I(exper^2) + married + union + yr
chisq = 26.361, df = 10, p-value = 0.003284
alternative hypothesis: one model is inconsistent
```

14.3. Dummy Variable Regression and Correlated Random Effects

It turns out that we can get the FE parameter estimates in two other ways than the within transformation we used in Section 14.1. The dummy variable regression uses OLS on the original variables in Equation 13.2 instead of the transformed ones. But it adds $n - 1$ dummy variables (or n dummies and removes the constant), one for each cross-sectional unit $i = 1, \ldots, n$. The simplest (although not the computationally most efficient) way to implement this in R is to use the cross-sectional index as another **factor** variable.

The third way to get the same results is the correlated random effects (CRE) approach. Instead of assuming that the individual affects a_i are independent of the regressors x_{itj}, we assume that they only depend on the averages over time $\bar{x}_{ij} = \frac{1}{T_i} \sum_{i=1}^{2} T_i$:

$$a_i = \gamma_0 + \gamma_1 \bar{x}_{i1} + \cdots + \gamma_k \bar{x}_{ik} + r_i \tag{14.3}$$

$$y_{it} = \beta_0 + \beta_1 x_{it1} + \cdots + \beta_k x_{itk} + a_i + u_{it}$$

$$= \beta_0 + \gamma_0 + \beta_1 x_{it1} + \cdots + \beta_k x_{itk} + \gamma_1 \bar{x}_{i1} + \cdots + \gamma_k \bar{x}_{ik} + r_i + u_{it} \tag{14.4}$$

If r_i is uncorrelated with the regressors, we can consistently estimate the parameters of this model using the RE estimator. In addition to the original regressors, we include their averages over time. Remember from Section 13.4 that these averages are computed with the function **Between**.

Script 14.5 (Example-Dummy-CRE-1.R) uses WAGEPAN.dta again. We estimate the FE parameters using the within transformation (reg.fe), the dummy variable approach (reg.dum), and the CRE approach (reg.cre). We also estimate the RE version of this model (reg.re). Script 14.6 (Example-Dummy-CRE-2.R) produces the regression table using **stargazer**. The results confirm that the first three methods deliver exactly the same parameter estimates, while the RE estimates differ.

─────── Script 14.5: **Example-Dummy-CRE-1.R** ───────

```
library(foreign);library(plm);library(stargazer)
wagepan<-read.dta("http://fmwww.bc.edu/ec-p/data/wooldridge/wagepan.dta")

# Generate pdata.frame:
wagepan.p <- pdata.frame(wagepan, index=c("nr","year") )

# Estimate FE parameter in 3 different ways:
wagepan.p$yr<-factor(wagepan.p$year)
reg.fe <-(plm(lwage~married+union+yr*educ,data=wagepan.p, model="within"))
reg.dum<-( lm(lwage~married+union+yr*educ+factor(nr), data=wagepan.p))
reg.re <-(plm(lwage~married+union+yr*educ,data=wagepan.p, model="random"))
reg.cre<-(plm(lwage~married+union+yr*educ+Between(married)+Between(union)
                                      ,data=wagepan.p, model="random"))
```

────── **Output of Script 14.6:** `Example-Dummy-CRE-2.R` ──────

```
> stargazer(reg.fe,reg.dum,reg.cre,reg.re,type="text",model.names=FALSE,
>           keep=c("married","union",":educ"),keep.stat=c("n","rsq"),
>           column.labels=c("Within","Dummies","CRE","RE"))
```

```
======================================================
                         Dependent variable:
                  ------------------------------------
                                  lwage
                  Within   Dummies    CRE       RE
                   (1)       (2)      (3)       (4)
------------------------------------------------------
married           0.055*** 0.055*** 0.055*** 0.078***
                  (0.018)  (0.018)  (0.018)  (0.017)

union             0.083*** 0.083*** 0.083*** 0.108***
                  (0.019)  (0.019)  (0.019)  (0.018)

Between(married)                    0.127***
                                    (0.044)

Between(union)                      0.160***
                                    (0.050)

yr1981:educ        0.012    0.012    0.012    0.011
                  (0.012)  (0.012)  (0.012)  (0.012)

yr1982:educ        0.015    0.015    0.015    0.014
                  (0.012)  (0.012)  (0.012)  (0.012)

yr1983:educ        0.017    0.017    0.017    0.017
                  (0.012)  (0.012)  (0.012)  (0.012)

yr1984:educ        0.017    0.017    0.017    0.016
                  (0.012)  (0.012)  (0.012)  (0.012)

yr1985:educ        0.024*   0.024*   0.024*   0.023*
                  (0.012)  (0.012)  (0.012)  (0.012)

yr1986:educ        0.027**  0.027**  0.027**  0.026**
                  (0.012)  (0.012)  (0.012)  (0.012)

yr1987:educ        0.030**  0.030**  0.030**  0.030**
                  (0.012)  (0.012)  (0.012)  (0.012)

------------------------------------------------------
Observations      4,360    4,360    4,360    4,360
R2                0.171    0.616    0.174    0.170
======================================================
Note:                     *p<0.1; **p<0.05; ***p<0.01
```

Given we have estimated the CRE model, it is easy to test the null hypothesis that the RE estimator is consistent. The additional assumptions needed are $\gamma_1 = \cdots = \gamma_k = 0$. They can easily be tested using an F test as demonstrated in Script 14.7 (`Example-CRE-test-RE.R`). Like the Hausman test, we clearly reject the null hypothesis that the RE model is appropriate with a tiny p value of about 0.00005.

Output of Script 14.7: `Example-CRE-test-RE.R`

```
> # Note that the estimates "reg.cre" are calculated in
> # Script "Example-Dummy-CRE-1.R" which has to be run first.
>
> # RE test as an F test on the "Between" coefficients
> library(car)

> linearHypothesis(reg.cre, matchCoefs(reg.cre,"Between"))
Linear hypothesis test

Hypothesis:
Between(married) = 0
Between(union) = 0

Model 1: restricted model
Model 2: lwage ~ married + union + yr * educ + Between(married) + Between(union)

  Res.Df Df  Chisq Pr(>Chisq)
1   4342
2   4340  2 19.814  4.983e-05 ***
---
Signif. codes:  0 '***' 0.001 '**' 0.01 '*' 0.05 '.' 0.1 ' ' 1
```

Another advantage of the CRE approach is that we can add time-constant regressors to the model. Since we cannot control for average values $\bar{x}_{ij}$ for these variables, they have to be uncorrelated with a_i for consistent estimation of *their* coefficients. For the other coefficients of the time-varying variables, we still don't need these additional RE assumptions.

Script 14.8 (`Example-CRE2.R`) estimates another version of the wage equation using the CRE approach. The variables `married` and `union` vary over time, so we can control for their between effects. The variables `educ`, `black`, and `hisp` do not vary. For a causal interpretation of *their* coefficients, we have to rely on uncorrelatedness with a_i. Given a_i includes intelligence and other labor market success factors, this uncorrelatedness is more plausible for some variables (like gender or race) than for other variables (like education).

────── **Output of Script 14.8:** `Example-CRE2.R` ──────

```
> library(foreign);library(plm)

> wagepan<-read.dta("http://fmwww.bc.edu/ec-p/data/wooldridge/wagepan.dta")

> # Generate pdata.frame:
> wagepan.p <- pdata.frame(wagepan, index=c("nr","year") )

> # Estimate CRE parameters
> wagepan.p$yr<-factor(wagepan.p$year)

> summary(plm(lwage~married+union+educ+black+hisp+Between(married)+
>                     Between(union), data=wagepan.p, model="random"))
Oneway (individual) effect Random Effect Model
   (Swamy-Arora's transformation)

Call:
plm(formula = lwage ~ married + union + educ + black + hisp +
    Between(married) + Between(union), data = wagepan.p, model = "random")

Balanced Panel: n=545, T=8, N=4360

Effects:
                var std.dev share
idiosyncratic 0.1426  0.3776 0.577
individual    0.1044  0.3231 0.423
theta:  0.6182

Residuals :
   Min. 1st Qu.  Median 3rd Qu.    Max.
-4.5300 -0.1620  0.0266  0.2030  1.6500

Coefficients :
                  Estimate Std. Error t-value  Pr(>|t|)
(Intercept)      0.6325629  0.1081545  5.8487 5.317e-09 ***
married          0.2416845  0.0176735 13.6750 < 2.2e-16 ***
union            0.0700438  0.0207240  3.3798 0.0007316 ***
educ             0.0760374  0.0087787  8.6616 < 2.2e-16 ***
black           -0.1295163  0.0488981 -2.6487 0.0081094 **
hisp             0.0116700  0.0428188  0.2725 0.7852172
Between(married) -0.0797385  0.0442674 -1.8013 0.0717258 .
Between(union)   0.1918545  0.0506522  3.7877 0.0001541 ***
---
Signif. codes:  0 '***' 0.001 '**' 0.01 '*' 0.05 '.' 0.1 ' ' 1

Total Sum of Squares:    668.91
Residual Sum of Squares: 620.38
R-Squared    :  0.072556
    Adj. R-Squared :  0.072423
F-statistic: 48.638 on 7 and 4352 DF, p-value: < 2.22e-16
```

14.4. Robust (Clustered) Standard Errors

We argued above that under the RE assumptions, OLS is inefficient but consistent. Instead of using RE, we could simply use OLS but would have to adjust the standard errors for the fact that the composite error term $v_{it} = a_i + u_{it}$ is correlated over time because of the constant individual effect a_i. In fact, the variance-covariance matrix could be more complex than the RE assumption with i.i.d. u_{it} implies. These error terms could be serially correlated and/or heteroscedastic. This would invalidate the standard errors not only of OLS but also of FD, FE, RE, and CRE.

There is an elegant solution, especially in panels with a large cross-sectional dimension. Similar to standard errors that are robust with respect to heteroscedasticity in cross-sectional data (Section 8.1) and serial correlation in time series (Section 12.3), there are formulas for the variance-covariance matrix for panel data that are robust with respect to heteroscedasticity and *arbitrary* correlations of the error term within a cross-sectional unit (or "cluster").

These "clustered" standard errors are mentioned in Wooldridge (2016, Section 14.4 and Example 13.9). Different versions of the clustered variance-covariance matrix can be computed with the command **vcovHC** from the package *plm*, see Croissant and Millo (2008) for details.[1] It works for all estimates obtained by **plm** and can be used like as an input for regression tables using **coeftest** or **stargazer** or testing commands like **linearHypothesis**.

Script 14.9 (Example-13-9-ClSE.R) repeats the FD regression from Example 13.9 but also reports the regression table with clustered standard errors and respective t statistics in addition to the usual standard errors.

---

[1]Don't confuse this with **vcovHC** from the package *sandwich* which only gives heteroscedasticity-robust results and unfortunately has the same name.

Output of Script 14.9: `Example-13-9-ClSE.R`

```
> library(foreign);library(plm);library(lmtest)

> crime4<-read.dta("http://fmwww.bc.edu/ec-p/data/wooldridge/crime4.dta")

> # Generate pdata.frame:
> crime4.p <- pdata.frame(crime4, index=c("county","year") )

> # Estimate FD model:
> reg <- ( plm(log(crmrte)~d83+d84+d85+d86+d87+lprbarr+lprbconv+
>                   lprbpris+lavgsen+lpolpc,data=crime4.p, model="fd") )

> # regression table with standard SE
> coeftest(reg)

t test of coefficients:

            Estimate Std. Error  t value  Pr(>|t|)
(intercept)  0.007713  0.017058   0.4522 0.6513343
d83         -0.099865  0.023895  -4.1793 3.421e-05 ***
d84         -0.147802  0.041279  -3.5805 0.0003745 ***
d85         -0.152413  0.058400  -2.6098 0.0093157 **
d86         -0.124899  0.076004  -1.6433 0.1009124
d87         -0.084071  0.094000  -0.8944 0.3715287
lprbarr     -0.327495  0.029980 -10.9237 < 2.2e-16 ***
lprbconv    -0.238106  0.018234 -13.0583 < 2.2e-16 ***
lprbpris    -0.165046  0.025969  -6.3555 4.488e-10 ***
lavgsen     -0.021761  0.022091  -0.9851 0.3250460
lpolpc       0.398426  0.026882  14.8213 < 2.2e-16 ***
---
Signif. codes:  0 '***' 0.001 '**' 0.01 '*' 0.05 '.' 0.1 ' ' 1


> # regression table with "clustered" SE:
> coeftest(reg,vcovHC)

t test of coefficients:

            Estimate Std. Error t value  Pr(>|t|)
(intercept)  0.007713  0.013580  0.5680 0.5702980
d83         -0.099865  0.021926 -4.5546 6.520e-06 ***
d84         -0.147802  0.035566 -4.1557 3.781e-05 ***
d85         -0.152413  0.050541 -3.0157 0.0026874 **
d86         -0.124899  0.062383 -2.0021 0.0457803 *
d87         -0.084071  0.077337 -1.0871 0.2774950
lprbarr     -0.327495  0.055591 -5.8912 6.828e-09 ***
lprbconv    -0.238106  0.038997 -6.1058 1.982e-09 ***
lprbpris    -0.165046  0.045113 -3.6585 0.0002791 ***
lavgsen     -0.021761  0.025437 -0.8555 0.3926720
lpolpc       0.398426  0.101407  3.9290 9.662e-05 ***
---
Signif. codes:  0 '***' 0.001 '**' 0.01 '*' 0.05 '.' 0.1 ' ' 1
```

15. Instrumental Variables Estimation and Two Stage Least Squares

Instrumental variables are potentially powerful tools for the identification and estimation of causal effects. We start the discussion in Section 15.1 with the simplest case of one endogenous regressor and one instrumental variable. Section 15.2 shows how to implement models with additional exogenous regressors. In Section 15.3, we will introduce two stage least squares which efficiently deals with several endogenous variables and several instruments.

Tests of the exogeneity of the regressors and instruments are presented in Sections 15.4 and 15.5, respectively. Finally, Section 15.6 shows how to conveniently combine panel data estimators with instrumental variables.

15.1. Instrumental Variables in Simple Regression Models

We start the discussion of instrumental variables (IV) regression with the most straightforward case of only one regressor and only one instrumental variable. Consider the simple linear regression model for cross-sectional data

$$y = \beta_0 + \beta_1 x + u. \tag{15.1}$$

The OLS estimator for the slope parameter is $\hat{\beta}_1^{\text{OLS}} = \frac{\text{Cov}(x,y)}{\text{Var}(x)}$, see Equation 2.3. Suppose the regressor x is correlated with the error term u, so OLS parameter estimators will be biased and inconsistent.

If we have a valid instrumental variable z, we can consistently estimate β_1 using the IV estimator

$$\hat{\beta}_1^{\text{IV}} = \frac{\text{Cov}(z,y)}{\text{Cov}(z,x)}. \tag{15.2}$$

A valid instrument is correlated with the regressor x ("relevant"), so the denominator of Equation 15.2 is nonzero. It is also uncorrelated with the error term u ("exogenous"). Wooldridge (2016, Section 15.1) provides more discussion and examples.

To implement IV regression in R, the package **AER** offers the convenient command **ivreg**. It works similar to **lm**. In the formula specification, the regressor(s) are separated from the instruments with a vertical line | (like in "conditional on z"):

```
ivreg( y ~ x | z )
```

Note that we can easily deal with heteroscedasticity: Results obtained by **ivreg** can be directly used with robust standard errors from **hccm** (Package *car*) or **vcovHC** (package *sandwich*), see Section 8.1.

Wooldridge, Example 15.1: Return to education for married women

Script 15.1 (Example-15-1.R) uses data from MROZ.dta. We only analyze women with non-missing wage, so we extract a **subset** from our data. We want to estimate the return to education for these women. As an instrumental variable for educations, we use the education of her father fatheduc. First, we calculate the OLS and IV slope parameters according to Equations 2.3 and 15.2, respectively. Remember that the **with** command defines that all variables names refer to our data frame oursample. Then, the full OLS and IV estimates are calculated using the boxed routines **lm** and **ivreg**, respectively. The results are once again displayed using **stargazer**. Not surprisingly, the slope parameters match the manual results.

─────────────── Output of Script 15.1: `Example-15-1.R` ───────────────

```
> library(foreign);library(AER);library(stargazer)

> mroz <- read.dta("http://fmwww.bc.edu/ec-p/data/wooldridge/mroz.dta")

> # restrict to non-missing wage observations
> oursample <- subset(mroz, !is.na(wage))

> # OLS slope parameter manually
> with(oursample, cov(log(wage),educ) / var(educ) )
[1] 0.1086487

> # IV slope parameter manually
> with(oursample, cov(log(wage),fatheduc) / cov(educ,fatheduc) )
[1] 0.05917348

> # OLS automatically
> reg.ols <-    lm(log(wage) ~ educ, data=oursample)

> # IV automatically
> reg.iv <- ivreg(log(wage) ~ educ | fatheduc, data=oursample)

> # Pretty regression table
> stargazer(reg.ols,reg.iv, type="text")
```

```
=================================================================
                                    Dependent variable:
                          ---------------------------------------
                                         log(wage)
                              OLS            instrumental
                                               variable
                              (1)               (2)
-----------------------------------------------------------------
educ                        0.109***           0.059*
                            (0.014)            (0.035)

Constant                    -0.185             0.441
                            (0.185)            (0.446)

-----------------------------------------------------------------
Observations                  428               428
R2                           0.118             0.093
Adjusted R2                  0.116             0.091
Residual Std. Error (df = 426)   0.680         0.689
F Statistic         56.929*** (df = 1; 426)
=================================================================
Note:                            *p<0.1; **p<0.05; ***p<0.01
```

15.2. More Exogenous Regressors

The IV approach can easily be generalized to include additional exogenous regressors, i.e. regressors that are assumed to be unrelated to the error term. In **ivreg**, we have to include these variables both to the list of regressors left of the | symbol and to the list of exogenous instrument to the right of the | symbol.

Wooldridge, Example 15.4: Using college proximity as an IV for education

In Script 15.2 (`Example-15-4.R`), we use CARD.dta to estimate the return to education. Education is allowed to be endogenous and instrumented with the dummy variable nearc4 which indicates whether the individual grew up close to a college. In addition, we control for experience, race, and regional information. These variables are assumed to be exogenous and act as their own instruments.
We first check for relevance by regressing the endogenous independent variable educ on all exogenous variables including the instrument nearc4. Its parameter is highly significantly different from zero, so relevance is supported. We then estimate the log wage equation with OLS and IV. All results are displayed in one table with **stargazer**.

─────────── Output of Script 15.2: `Example-15-4.R` ───────────

```
> library(foreign);library(AER);library(stargazer)

> card <- read.dta("http://fmwww.bc.edu/ec-p/data/wooldridge/card.dta")

> # Checking for relevance: reduced form
> redf<-lm(educ ~ nearc4+exper+I(exper^2)+black+smsa+south+smsa66+reg662+
>           reg663+reg664+reg665+reg666+reg667+reg668+reg669, data=card)

> # OLS
> ols<-lm(log(wage)~educ+exper+I(exper^2)+black+smsa+south+smsa66+reg662+
>           reg663+reg664+reg665+reg666+reg667+reg668+reg669, data=card)

> # IV estimation
> iv <-ivreg(log(wage)~educ+exper+I(exper^2)+black+smsa+south+smsa66+
>             reg662+reg663+reg664+reg665+reg666+reg667+reg668+reg669
>        | nearc4+exper+I(exper^2)+black+smsa+south+smsa66+
>             reg662+reg663+reg664+reg665+reg666+reg667+reg668+reg669
>        , data=card)

> # Pretty regression table of selected coefficients
> stargazer(redf,ols,iv,type="text",
>           keep=c("ed","near","exp","bl"),keep.stat=c("n","rsq"))

===============================================
                    Dependent variable:
              ---------------------------------
               educ          log(wage)
               OLS       OLS    instrumental
                                  variable
               (1)       (2)       (3)
-----------------------------------------------
nearc4        0.320***
              (0.088)

educ                    0.075***   0.132**
                        (0.003)   (0.055)
```

```
exper              -0.413***  0.085***     0.108***
                    (0.034)   (0.007)      (0.024)

I(exper2)           0.001    -0.002***    -0.002***
                    (0.002)   (0.0003)     (0.0003)

black              -0.936*** -0.199***    -0.147***
                    (0.094)   (0.018)      (0.054)

--------------------------------------------------
Observations   3,010        3,010         3,010
R2             0.477        0.300         0.238
==================================================
Note:                  *p<0.1;  **p<0.05;  ***p<0.01
```

15.3. Two Stage Least Squares

Two stage least squares (2SLS) is a general approach for IV estimation when we have one or more endogenous regressors and at least as many additional instrumental variables. Consider the regression model

$$y_1 = \beta_0 + \beta_1 y_2 + \beta_2 y_3 + \beta_3 z_1 + \beta_4 z_2 + \beta_5 z_3 + u_1 \tag{15.3}$$

The regressors y_2 and y_3 are potentially correlated with the error term u_1, the regressors z_1, z_2, and z_3 are assumed to be exogenous. Because we have two endogenous regressors, we need at least two additional instrumental variables, say z_4 and z_5.

The name of 2SLS comes from the fact that it can be performed in two stages of OLS regressions:

(1) Separately regress y_2 and y_3 on z_1 through z_5. Obtain fitted values $\hat{y}_2$ and $\hat{y}_3$.

(2) Regress y_1 on $\hat{y}_2$, $\hat{y}_3$, and z_1 through z_3.

If the instruments are valid, this will give consistent estimates of the parameters β_0 through β_5. Generalizing this to more endogenous regressors and instrumental variables is obvious.

This procedure can of course easily be implemented in *R*, remembering that fitted values are obtained with **fitted** which can be directly called from the **formula** of **lm**. One of the problems of this manual approach is that the resulting variance-covariance matrix and analyses based on them are invalid. Conveniently, **ivreg** will automatically do these calculations and calculate correct standard errors and the like.

Wooldridge, Example 15.5: Return to education for working women

We continue Example 15.1 and still want to estimate the return to eduction for women using the data in MROZ.dta. Now, we use both mother's and father's education as instruments for the own education. In Script 15.3 (Example-15-5.R), we obtain 2SLS estimates in two ways: First, we do both stages manually, including fitted education as **fitted(stage1)** as a regressors in the second stage. **ivreg** does this automatically and delivers the same parameter estimates as the output table reveals. But the standard errors differ slightly because the manual two stage version did not correct them.

─────── **Output of Script 15.3:** `Example-15-5.R` ───────

```
> library(foreign);library(AER);library(stargazer)

> mroz <- read.dta("http://fmwww.bc.edu/ec-p/data/wooldridge/mroz.dta")

> # restrict to non-missing wage observations
> oursample <- subset(mroz, !is.na(wage))

> # 1st stage: reduced form
> stage1 <- lm(educ~exper+I(exper^2)+motheduc+fatheduc, data=oursample)

> # 2nd stage
> man.2SLS<-lm(log(wage)~fitted(stage1)+exper+I(exper^2), data=oursample)

> # Automatic 2SLS estimation
> aut.2SLS<-ivreg(log(wage)~educ+exper+I(exper^2)
>                | motheduc+fatheduc+exper+I(exper^2) , data=oursample)

> # Pretty regression table
> stargazer(stage1,man.2SLS,aut.2SLS,type="text",keep.stat=c("n","rsq"))
```

```
============================================
              Dependent variable:
          ----------------------------------
            educ          log(wage)
            OLS      OLS     instrumental
                             variable
            (1)      (2)        (3)
--------------------------------------------
fitted(stage1)       0.061*
                    (0.033)

educ                            0.061*
                               (0.031)

exper       0.045   0.044***   0.044***
           (0.040)  (0.014)    (0.013)

I(exper2)  -0.001   -0.001**   -0.001**
           (0.001)  (0.0004)   (0.0004)

motheduc   0.158***
           (0.036)

fatheduc   0.190***
           (0.034)

Constant   9.103***  0.048      0.048
           (0.427)  (0.420)    (0.400)

--------------------------------------------
Observations 428     428        428
R2          0.211    0.050      0.136
============================================
Note:          *p<0.1; **p<0.05; ***p<0.01
```

15.4. Testing for Exogeneity of the Regressors

There is another way to get the same IV parameter estimates as with 2SLS. In the same setup as above, this "control function approach" also consists of two stages:

(1) Like in 2SLS, regress y_2 and y_3 on z_1 through z_5. Obtain residuals $\hat{v}_2$ and $\hat{v}_3$ instead of fitted values $\hat{y}_2$ and $\hat{y}_3$.

(2) Regress y_1 on y_2, y_3, z_1, z_2, z_3, and the first stage residuals $\hat{v}_2$ and $\hat{v}_3$.

This approach is as simple to implement as 2SLS and will also result in the same parameter estimates and invalid OLS standard errors in the second stage (unless the dubious regressors y_2 and y_3 are in fact exogenous).

After this second stage regression, we can test for exogeneity in a simple way assuming the instruments are valid. We just need to do a t or F test of the null hypothesis that the parameters of the first-stage residuals are equal to zero. If we reject this hypothesis, this indicates endogeneity of y_2 and y_3.

Wooldridge, Example 15.7: Return to education for working women

In Script 15.4 (`Example-15-7.R`), we continue Example 15.5 using the control function approach. Again, we use both mother's and father's education as instruments. The first stage regression is identical as in Script 15.3 (`Example-15-5.R`). The second stage adds the first stage residuals to the original list of regressors. The parameter estimates are identical to both the manual 2SLS and the automatic **ivreg** results. We can directly interpret the t test from the regression table as a test for exogeneity. Here, $t = 1.6711$ with a two-sided p value of $p = 0.095$, indicating a marginally significant evidence for endogeneity.

―――――――――― **Output of Script 15.4: `Example-15-7.R`** ――――――――――

```
> library(foreign);library(AER);library(lmtest)

> mroz <- read.dta("http://fmwww.bc.edu/ec-p/data/wooldridge/mroz.dta")

> # restrict to non-missing wage observations
> oursample <- subset(mroz, !is.na(wage))

> # 1st stage: reduced form
> stage1<-lm(educ~exper+I(exper^2)+motheduc+fatheduc, data=oursample)

> # 2nd stage
> stage2<-lm(log(wage)~educ+exper+I(exper^2)+resid(stage1),data=oursample)

> # results including t tests
> coeftest(stage2)

t test of coefficients:

                 Estimate  Std. Error t value  Pr(>|t|)
(Intercept)    0.04810030  0.39457526  0.1219 0.9030329
educ           0.06139663  0.03098494  1.9815 0.0481824 *
exper          0.04417039  0.01323945  3.3363 0.0009241 ***
I(exper^2)    -0.00089897  0.00039591 -2.2706 0.0236719 *
resid(stage1)  0.05816661  0.03480728  1.6711 0.0954406 .
---
Signif. codes:  0 '***' 0.001 '**' 0.01 '*' 0.05 '.' 0.1 ' ' 1
```

15.5. Testing Overidentifying Restrictions

If we have more instruments than endogenous variables, we can use either all or only some of them. If are all valid, using all improves the accuracy of the 2SLS estimator and reduces its standard errors. If the exogeneity of some is dubious, including them might cause inconsistency. It is therefore useful to test for the exogeneity of a set of dubious instruments if we have another (large enough) set that is undoubtedly exogenous. The procedure is described by Wooldridge (2016, Section 15.5):

(1) Estimate the model by 2SLS and obtain residuals $\hat{u}_1$.

(2) Regress $\hat{u}_1$ on all exogenous variables and calculate R_1^2.

(3) The test statistic nR_1^2 is asymptotically distributed as χ_q^2, where q is the number of *overidentifying* restrictions, i.e. number of instruments minus number of endogenous regressors.

Wooldridge, Example 15.8: Return to education for working women

We will again use the data and model of Examples 15.5 and 15.7. Script 15.5 (`Example-15-8.R`) estimates the model using **ivreg**. The results are stored in variable `res.2sls` and their **summary** is printed. We then run the auxiliary regression (2) and compute its R^2 as `r2`. The test statistic is computed to be `teststat=0.378`. We also compute the p value from the χ_1^2 distribution. We cannot reject exogeneity of the instruments using this test. But be aware of the fact that the underlying assumption that at least one instrument is valid might be violated here.

15.6. Instrumental Variables with Panel Data

Instrumental variables can be used for panel data, too. In this way, we can get rid of time-constant individual heterogeneity by first differencing or within transformations and then fix remaining endogeneity problems with instrumental variables.

We know how to get panel data estimates using OLS on the transformed data, so we can easily use IV as before. But we can do it even more conveniently: The **plm** command from the *plm* package allows to directly enter instruments. As with **ivreg**, we can simply add a list of instruments after the | sign in the formula.

Wooldridge, Example 15.10: Return to education for working women

We use the data set `JTRAIN`.dta to estimate the effect of job training `hrsemp` on the scrap rate. In Script 15.6 (`Example-15-10.R`), we load the data, choose a **subset** of the years 1987 and 1988 and store the data as a **pdata.frame** using the index variables `fcode` and `year`, see Section 13.3. Then we estimate the parameters using first-differencing with the instrumental variable `grant`.

Output of Script 15.5: `Example-15-8.R`

```
> library(foreign);library(AER)

> mroz <- read.dta("http://fmwww.bc.edu/ec-p/data/wooldridge/mroz.dta")

> # restrict to non-missing wage observations
> oursample <- subset(mroz, !is.na(wage))

> # IV regression
> summary( res.2sls <- ivreg(log(wage) ~ educ+exper+I(exper^2)
>                       | exper+I(exper^2)+motheduc+fatheduc,data=oursample) )

Call:
ivreg(formula = log(wage) ~ educ + exper + I(exper^2) | exper +
    I(exper^2) + motheduc + fatheduc, data = oursample)

Residuals:
     Min      1Q  Median      3Q     Max
 -3.0986 -0.3196  0.0551  0.3689  2.3493

Coefficients:
              Estimate Std. Error t value Pr(>|t|)
(Intercept)  0.0481003  0.4003281   0.120  0.90442
educ         0.0613966  0.0314367   1.953  0.05147 .
exper        0.0441704  0.0134325   3.288  0.00109 **
I(exper^2)  -0.0008990  0.0004017  -2.238  0.02574 *
---
Signif. codes:  0 '***' 0.001 '**' 0.01 '*' 0.05 '.' 0.1 ' ' 1

Residual standard error: 0.6747 on 424 degrees of freedom
Multiple R-Squared: 0.1357,        Adjusted R-squared: 0.1296
Wald test: 8.141 on 3 and 424 DF,  p-value: 2.787e-05


> # Auxiliary regression
> res.aux <-  lm(resid(res.2sls) ~ exper+I(exper^2)+motheduc+fatheduc
>                     , data=oursample)

> # Calculations for test
> ( r2 <- summary(res.aux)$r.squared )
[1] 0.0008833444

> ( n <- nobs(res.aux) )
[1] 428

> ( teststat <- n*r2 )
[1] 0.3780714

> ( pval <- 1-pchisq(teststat,1) )
[1] 0.5386372
```

Output of Script 15.6: Example-15-10.R

```
> library(foreign);library(plm)

> jtrain <- read.dta("http://fmwww.bc.edu/ec-p/data/wooldridge/jtrain.dta")

> # Define panel data (for 1987 and 1988 only)
> jtrain.87.88 <- subset(jtrain,year<=1988)

> jtrain.p<-pdata.frame(jtrain.87.88, index=c("fcode","year"))
series d89, xgrant_1, xcgrant_1 are constants and have been removed

> # IV FD regression
> summary( plm(log(scrap)~hrsemp|grant, model="fd",data=jtrain.p) )
Oneway (individual) effect First-Difference Model
Instrumental variable estimation
    (Balestra-Varadharajan-Krishnakumar's transformation)

Call:
plm(formula = log(scrap) ~ hrsemp | grant, data = jtrain.p, model = "fd")

Unbalanced Panel: n=47, T=1-2, N=92

Residuals :
    Min.  1st Qu.   Median  3rd Qu.     Max.
-2.31000 -0.21900 -0.00893  0.26700  2.43000

Coefficients :
              Estimate Std. Error t-value Pr(>|t|)
(intercept) -0.0326684  0.1269512 -0.2573  0.79815
hrsemp      -0.0141532  0.0079147 -1.7882  0.08079 .
---
Signif. codes:  0 '***' 0.001 '**' 0.01 '*' 0.05 '.' 0.1 ' ' 1

Total Sum of Squares:     17.29
Residual Sum of Squares: 17.015
R-Squared      :  0.061927
    Adj. R-Squared :  0.059175
F-statistic: 0.694855 on 1 and 43 DF, p-value: 0.40912
```

16. Simultaneous Equations Models

In simultaneous equations models (SEM), both the dependent variable and at least one regressor are determined jointly. This leads to an endogeneity problem and inconsistent OLS parameter estimators. The main challenge for successfully using SEM is to specify a sensible model and make sure it is identified, see Wooldridge (2016, Sections 16.1–16.3). We briefly introduce a general model and the notation in Section 16.1.

As discussed in Chapter 15, 2SLS regression can solve endogeneity problems if there are enough exogenous instrumental variables. This also works in the setting of SEM, an example is given in Section 16.2. For estimating the whole system simultaneously, specialized commands such as **systemfit** in R can be handy. It is demonstrated in Section 16.3. Using this package, more advanced estimation commands are straightforward to implement. We will show this for three-stage-least-squares (3SLS) estimation in Section 16.4.

16.1. Setup and Notation

Consider the general SEM with q endogenous variables $y_1, \ldots, y_q$ and k exogenous variables $x_1, \ldots, x_k$. The system of equations is

$$y_1 = \alpha_{12} y_2 + \alpha_{13} y_3 + \cdots + \alpha_{1q} y_q \qquad + \beta_{10} + \beta_{11} x_1 + \cdots + \beta_{1k} x_k + u_1$$
$$y_2 = \alpha_{21} y_1 + \alpha_{23} y_3 + \cdots + \alpha_{2q} y_q \qquad + \beta_{20} + \beta_{21} x_1 + \cdots + \beta_{2k} x_k + u_2$$

$$\vdots$$

$$y_q = \alpha_{q1} y_1 + \alpha_{q2} y_2 + \cdots + \alpha_{qq-1} y_{q-1} + \beta_{q0} + \beta_{q1} x_1 + \cdots + \beta_{qk} x_k + u_q$$

As discussed in more detail in Wooldridge (2016, Section 16), this system is not identified without restrictions on the parameters. The order condition for identification of any equation is that if we have m included endogenous regressors (i.e. α parameters that are not restricted to 0), we need to exclude at least m exogenous regressors (i.e. restrict their β parameters to 0). They can then be used as instrumental variables.

Wooldridge, Example 16.3: Labor supply of married, working women

We have the two endogenous variables hours and wage which influence each other.

$$\text{hours} = \alpha_{12} \log(\text{wage}) + \beta_{10} + \beta_{11}\text{educ} + \beta_{12}\text{age} + \beta_{13}\text{kidslt6} + \beta_{14}\text{nwifeinc}$$
$$+ \beta_{15}\text{exper} + \beta_{16}\text{exper}^2 + u_1$$
$$\log(\text{wage}) = \alpha_{21}\text{hours} \quad + \beta_{20} + \beta_{21}\text{educ} + \beta_{22}\text{age} + \beta_{23}\text{kidslt6} + \beta_{24}\text{nwifeinc}$$
$$+ \beta_{25}\text{exper} + \beta_{26}\text{exper}^2 + u_2$$

For both equations to be identified, we have to exclude at least one exogenous regressor from each equation. Wooldridge (2016) discusses a model in which we restrict $\beta_{15} = \beta_{16} = 0$ in the first and $\beta_{22} = \beta_{23} = \beta_{24} = 0$ in the second equation.

16.2. Estimation by 2SLS

Estimation of each equation separately by 2SLS is straightforward once we have set up the system and ensured identification. The excluded regressors in each equation serve as instrumental variables. As shown is Chapter 15, the command **ivreg** from the package **AER** provides convenient 2SLS estimation.

Wooldridge, Example 16.5: Labor supply of married, working women

Script 16.1 (`Example-16-5-ivreg.R`) estimates the parameters of the two equations from Example 16.3 separately using **ivreg**.

--------- Output of Script 16.1: `Example-16-5-ivreg.R` ---------

```
> library(foreign);library(AER)

> mroz <- read.dta("http://fmwww.bc.edu/ec-p/data/wooldridge/mroz.dta")

> oursample <- subset(mroz,!is.na(wage))

> # 2SLS regressions
> summary( ivreg(hours~log(wage)+educ+age+kidslt6+nwifeinc
>                |educ+age+kidslt6+nwifeinc+exper+I(exper^2), data=oursample))

Call:
ivreg(formula = hours ~ log(wage) + educ + age + kidslt6 + nwifeinc |
    educ + age + kidslt6 + nwifeinc + exper + I(exper^2), data = oursample)

Residuals:
     Min       1Q   Median       3Q      Max
-4570.13  -654.08   -36.94   569.86  8372.91

Coefficients:
            Estimate Std. Error t value Pr(>|t|)
(Intercept) 2225.662    574.564   3.874 0.000124 ***
log(wage)   1639.556    470.576   3.484 0.000545 ***
educ        -183.751     59.100  -3.109 0.002003 **
age           -7.806      9.378  -0.832 0.405664
kidslt6     -198.154    182.929  -1.083 0.279325
nwifeinc     -10.170      6.615  -1.537 0.124942
---
Signif. codes:  0 '***' 0.001 '**' 0.01 '*' 0.05 '.' 0.1 ' ' 1

Residual standard error: 1354 on 422 degrees of freedom
Multiple R-Squared: -2.008,      Adjusted R-squared: -2.043
Wald test: 3.441 on 5 and 422 DF,  p-value: 0.004648
```

```
> summary( ivreg(log(wage)~hours+educ+exper+I(exper^2)
>            |educ+age+kidslt6+nwifeinc+exper+I(exper^2), data=oursample))

Call:
ivreg(formula = log(wage) ~ hours + educ + exper + I(exper^2) |
    educ + age + kidslt6 + nwifeinc + exper + I(exper^2), data = oursample)

Residuals:
     Min      1Q   Median      3Q     Max
-3.49800 -0.29307  0.03208  0.36486  2.45912

Coefficients:
             Estimate Std. Error t value Pr(>|t|)
(Intercept) -0.6557254  0.3377883  -1.941   0.0529 .
hours        0.0001259  0.0002546   0.494   0.6212
educ         0.1103300  0.0155244   7.107 5.08e-12 ***
exper        0.0345824  0.0194916   1.774   0.0767 .
I(exper^2)  -0.0007058  0.0004541  -1.554   0.1209
---
Signif. codes:  0 '***' 0.001 '**' 0.01 '*' 0.05 '.' 0.1 ' ' 1

Residual standard error: 0.6794 on 423 degrees of freedom
Multiple R-Squared: 0.1257,       Adjusted R-squared: 0.1174
Wald test: 19.03 on 4 and 423 DF,  p-value: 2.108e-14
```

16.3. Joint Estimation of System

Instead of manual estimation of each equation by **ivreg**, we can make use of the specialized command **systemfit** from the package *systemfit*. It is more convenient to use and offers straightforward implementation of additional estimators. We define the system of equations as a **list** of formulas. Script 16.2 (Example-16-5-systemfit-prep.R) does this by first storing each equation as a formula and then combining them in the list eq.system. We also need to define the set of exogenous regressors and instruments using a formula with a right-hand side only. Script 16.2 (Example-16-5-systemfit-prep.R) stores this specification in the variable instrum.

With these preparations, **systemfit** is simply called with the equation system and the instrument set as arguments. Option **method="2SLS"** requests 2SLS estimation. As expected, the results produced by Script 16.3 (Example-16-5-systemfit.R) are the same as with the separate **ivreg** regressions seen previously.

———— Script 16.2: **Example-16-5-systemfit-prep.R** ————
```
library(foreign);library(systemfit)
mroz <- read.dta("http://fmwww.bc.edu/ec-p/data/wooldridge/mroz.dta")
oursample <- subset(mroz,!is.na(wage))

# Define system of equations and instruments
eq.hrs   <- hours     ~ log(wage)+educ+age+kidslt6+nwifeinc
eq.wage  <- log(wage)~ hours     +educ+exper+I(exper^2)
eq.system<- list(eq.hrs, eq.wage)
instrum  <- ~educ+age+kidslt6+nwifeinc+exper+I(exper^2)
```

```
─── Output of Script 16.3: Example-16-5-systemfit.R ───

> # 2SLS of whole system (run Example-16-5-systemfit-prep.R first!)
> summary(systemfit(eq.system,inst=instrum,data=oursample,method="2SLS"))

systemfit results
method: 2SLS

          N  DF       SSR  detRCov   OLS-R2  McElroy-R2
system  856 845 773893303   155089 -2.00762    0.748802

        N  DF       SSR        MSE      RMSE        R2    Adj R2
eq1   428 422 7.73893e+08 1.83387e+06 1354.204536 -2.007617 -2.043253
eq2   428 423 1.95266e+02 4.61621e-01    0.679427  0.125654  0.117385

The covariance matrix of the residuals
            eq1          eq2
eq1 1833869.924 -831.542688
eq2    -831.543    0.461621

The correlations of the residuals
          eq1       eq2
eq1  1.000000 -0.903769
eq2 -0.903769  1.000000


2SLS estimates for 'eq1' (equation 1)
Model Formula: hours ~ log(wage) + educ + age + kidslt6 + nwifeinc
Instruments: ~educ + age + kidslt6 + nwifeinc + exper + I(exper^2)

              Estimate  Std. Error  t value   Pr(>|t|)
(Intercept) 2225.66182   574.56411  3.87365 0.00012424 ***
log(wage)   1639.55560   470.57568  3.48415 0.00054535 ***
educ        -183.75128    59.09981 -3.10917 0.00200323 **
age           -7.80609     9.37801 -0.83238 0.40566402
kidslt6     -198.15430   182.92914 -1.08323 0.27932496
nwifeinc     -10.16959     6.61474 -1.53741 0.12494166
---
Signif. codes:  0 '***' 0.001 '**' 0.01 '*' 0.05 '.' 0.1 ' ' 1

Residual standard error: 1354.204536 on 422 degrees of freedom
Number of observations: 428 Degrees of Freedom: 422
SSR: 773893108.032133 MSE: 1833869.924247 Root MSE: 1354.204536
Multiple R-Squared: -2.007617 Adjusted R-Squared: -2.043253


2SLS estimates for 'eq2' (equation 2)
Model Formula: log(wage) ~ hours + educ + exper + I(exper^2)
Instruments: ~educ + age + kidslt6 + nwifeinc + exper + I(exper^2)

                Estimate    Std. Error  t value   Pr(>|t|)
(Intercept) -0.655725444  0.337788292 -1.94123   0.052894 .
hours        0.000125900  0.000254611  0.49448   0.621223
educ         0.110330004  0.015524358  7.10690 5.0768e-12 ***
exper        0.034582355  0.019491555  1.77422   0.076746 .
I(exper^2)  -0.000705769  0.000454080 -1.55428   0.120865
---
Signif. codes:  0 '***' 0.001 '**' 0.01 '*' 0.05 '.' 0.1 ' ' 1

Residual standard error: 0.679427 on 423 degrees of freedom
Number of observations: 428 Degrees of Freedom: 423
SSR: 195.26556 MSE: 0.461621 Root MSE: 0.679427
Multiple R-Squared: 0.125654 Adjusted R-Squared: 0.117385
```

16.4. Outlook: Estimation by 3SLS

The results of **systemfit** provides additional information, see the output of Script 16.3 (Example-16-5-systemfit.R). An interesting piece of information is the correlation between the residuals of the equations. In the example, it is reported to be a substantially negative -0.90. We can account for the correlation between the error terms to derive a potentially more efficient parameter estimator than 2SLS. Without going into details here, the three stage least squares (3SLS) estimator adds another stage to 2SLS by estimating the correlation and accounting for it using a FGLS approach. For a detailed discussion of this and related methods, see for example Wooldridge (2010, Chapter 8).

Using 3SLS in *R* is simple: Option **method="3SLS"** of **systemfit** is all we need to do as the output of Script 16.4 (Example-16-5-3sls.R) shows.

──────────── **Output of Script 16.4: Example-16-5-3sls.R** ────────────

```
> # 3SLS of whole system (run Example-16-5-systemfit-prep.R first!)
>
> summary(systemfit(eq.system,inst=instrum,data=oursample,method="3SLS"))

systemfit results
method: 3SLS

          N  DF       SSR detRCov   OLS-R2 McElroy-R2
system 856 845 873749822  102713 -2.39569     0.8498

     N  DF         SSR         MSE        RMSE         R2    Adj R2
eq1 428 422 8.73750e+08 2.07050e+06 1438.922072  -2.395695  -2.43593
eq2 428 423 2.02143e+02 4.77879e-01    0.691288   0.094859   0.08630

The covariance matrix of the residuals used for estimation
            eq1          eq2
eq1 1833869.924 -831.542688
eq2    -831.543    0.461621

The covariance matrix of the residuals
            eq1          eq2
eq1 2070496.729 -941.665440
eq2    -941.665    0.477879

The correlations of the residuals
          eq1         eq2
eq1  1.000000  -0.946674
eq2 -0.946674   1.000000
```

```
3SLS estimates for 'eq1' (equation 1)
Model Formula: hours ~ log(wage) + educ + age + kidslt6 + nwifeinc
Instruments: ~educ + age + kidslt6 + nwifeinc + exper + I(exper^2)

              Estimate    Std. Error   t value    Pr(>|t|)
(Intercept) 2305.857471   511.540684   4.50767   8.5013e-06 ***
log(wage)   1781.933408   439.884236   4.05091   6.0726e-05 ***
educ        -212.819501    53.727043  -3.96112   8.7558e-05 ***
age           -9.514997     7.960948  -1.19521   0.23268
kidslt6     -192.359056   150.917506  -1.27460   0.20315
nwifeinc      -0.176982     3.583623  -0.04939   0.96063
---
Signif. codes:  0 '***' 0.001 '**' 0.01 '*' 0.05 '.' 0.1 ' ' 1

Residual standard error: 1438.922072 on 422 degrees of freedom
Number of observations: 428 Degrees of Freedom: 422
SSR: 873749619.65837 MSE: 2070496.729048 Root MSE: 1438.922072
Multiple R-Squared: -2.395695 Adjusted R-Squared: -2.435928


3SLS estimates for 'eq2' (equation 2)
Model Formula: log(wage) ~ hours + educ + exper + I(exper^2)
Instruments: ~educ + age + kidslt6 + nwifeinc + exper + I(exper^2)

               Estimate     Std. Error   t value    Pr(>|t|)
(Intercept) -0.693920350   0.335995511  -2.06527   0.039506 *
hours        0.000190868   0.000247652   0.77071   0.441308
educ         0.112738573   0.015368872   7.33551  1.1364e-12 ***
exper        0.021428533   0.015383608   1.39295   0.164368
I(exper^2)  -0.000302959   0.000268028  -1.13033   0.258978
---
Signif. codes:  0 '***' 0.001 '**' 0.01 '*' 0.05 '.' 0.1 ' ' 1

Residual standard error: 0.691288 on 423 degrees of freedom
Number of observations: 428 Degrees of Freedom: 423
SSR: 202.142836 MSE: 0.477879 Root MSE: 0.691288
Multiple R-Squared: 0.094859 Adjusted R-Squared: 0.0863
```

17. Limited Dependent Variable Models and Sample Selection Corrections

A limited dependent variable (LDV) can only take a limited set of values. An extreme case are binary variables that can only take two values. We already used such dummy variables as regressors in Chapter 7. Section 17.1 discusses how to use them as dependent variables. Another example for LDV are counts that take only non-negative integers, they are covered in Section 17.2. Similarly, Tobit models discussed in Section 17.3 deal with dependent variables that can only take positive values (or are restricted in a similar way), but are otherwise continuous.

The dependent variables Sections 17.4 and 17.5 are concerned with are continuous but are not perfectly observed. For some units of the censored, truncated, or selected observations we only know that they are above or below a certain threshold or we don't know anything about them.

17.1. Binary Responses

Binary dependent variables are frequently studied in applied econometrics. Because a dummy variable y can only take the values 0 and 1, its (conditional) expected value is equal to the (conditional) probability that $y = 1$:

$$\begin{aligned} E(y|\mathbf{x}) &= 0 \cdot P(y = 0|\mathbf{x}) + 1 \cdot P(y = 1|\mathbf{x}) \\ &= P(y = 1|\mathbf{x}) \end{aligned} \quad (17.1)$$

So when we study the conditional mean, it makes sense to think about it as the probability of outcome $y = 1$. Likewise, the predicted value $\hat{y}$ should be thought of as a predicted probability.

17.1.1. Linear Probability Models

If a dummy variable is used as the dependent variable y, we can still use OLS to estimate its relation to the regressors $\mathbf{x}$. These linear probability models are covered by Wooldridge (2016) in Section 7.5. If we write the usual linear regression model

$$y = \beta_0 + \beta_1 x_1 + \cdots + \beta_k x_k \quad (17.2)$$

and make the usual assumptions, especially MLR.4: $E(u|\mathbf{x}) = 0$, this implies for the conditional mean (which is the probability that $y = 1$) and the predicted probabilities

$$P(y = 1|\mathbf{x}) = E(y|\mathbf{x}) = \beta_0 + \beta_1 x_1 + \cdots + \beta_k x_k \quad (17.3)$$

$$\hat{P}(y = 1|\mathbf{x}) = \quad \hat{y} \quad = \hat{\beta}_0 + \hat{\beta}_1 x_1 + \cdots + \hat{\beta}_k x_k \quad (17.4)$$

The interpretation of the parameters is straightforward: β_j is a measure of the average change in probability of a "success" ($y = 1$) as x_j increases by one unit and the other determinants remain constant. Linear probability models automatically suffer from heteroscedasticity, so with OLS, we should use heteroscedasticity-robust inference, see Section 8.1.

Wooldridge, Example 17.1: Labor supply of married, working women

We study the probability that a woman is in the labor force depending on socio-demographic characteristics. Script 17.1 (Example-17-1-1.R) estimates a linear probability model using the data set mroz.dta. The estimated coefficient of educ can be interpreted as: an additional year of schooling increases the probability that a woman is in the labor force *ceteris paribus* by 0.038 = 3.8% on average.

──────────── **Output of Script 17.1: Example-17-1-1.R** ────────────

```
> library(foreign);library(car); library(lmtest)   # for robust SE

> mroz <- read.dta("http://fmwww.bc.edu/ec-p/data/wooldridge/mroz.dta")

> # Estimate linear probability model
> linprob <- lm(inlf~nwifeinc+educ+exper+I(exper^2)+age+kidslt6+kidsge6,data=mroz)

> # Regression table with heteroscedasticity-robust SE and t tests:
> coeftest(linprob,vcov=hccm)

t test of coefficients:

              Estimate  Std. Error t value  Pr(>|t|)
(Intercept)  0.58551923  0.15358032  3.8125  0.000149 ***
nwifeinc    -0.00340517  0.00155826 -2.1852  0.029182 *
educ         0.03799530  0.00733982  5.1766 2.909e-07 ***
exper        0.03949239  0.00598359  6.6001 7.800e-11 ***
I(exper^2)  -0.00059631  0.00019895 -2.9973  0.002814 **
age         -0.01609081  0.00241459 -6.6640 5.183e-11 ***
kidslt6     -0.26181047  0.03215160 -8.1430 1.621e-15 ***
kidsge6      0.01301223  0.01366031  0.9526  0.341123
---
Signif. codes:  0 '***' 0.001 '**' 0.01 '*' 0.05 '.' 0.1 ' ' 1
```

One problem with linear probability models is that $P(y = 1|\mathbf{x})$ is specified as a linear function of the regressors. By construction, there are (more or less realistic) combinations of regressor values that yield $\hat{y} < 0$ or $\hat{y} > 1$. Since these are probabilities, this does not really make sense.

As an example, Script 17.2 (Example-17-1-2.R) calculates the predicted values for two women (see Section 6.2 for how to **predict** after OLS estimation): Woman 1 is 20 years old, has no work experience, 5 years of education, two children below age 6 and has additional family income of 100,000 USD. Woman 2 is 52 years old, has 30 years of work experience, 17 years of education, no children and no other source of income. The predicted "probability" for woman 1 is −41%, the probability for woman 2 is 104% as can also be easily checked with a calculator.

──────────── **Output of Script 17.2: Example-17-1-2.R** ────────────

```
> # predictions for two "extreme" women (run Example-17-1-1.R first!):
> xpred <- list(nwifeinc=c(100,0),educ=c(5,17),exper=c(0,30),
>               age=c(20,52),kidslt6=c(2,0),kidsge6=c(0,0))

> predict(linprob,xpred)
         1          2
-0.4104582  1.0428084
```

17.1.2. Logit and Probit Models: Estimation

Specialized models for binary responses make sure that the implied probabilities are restricted between 0 and 1. An important class of models specifies the success probability as

$$P(y = 1|\mathbf{x}) = G(\beta_0 + \beta_1 x_1 + \cdots + \beta_k x_k) = G(\mathbf{x}\boldsymbol{\beta}) \tag{17.5}$$

where the "link function" $G(z)$ always returns values between 0 and 1. In the statistics literature, this type of models is often called generalized linear model (GLM) because a linear part $\mathbf{x}\boldsymbol{\beta}$ shows up within the nonlinear function G.

For binary response models, by far the most widely used specifications for G are

- the **probit** model with $G(z) = \Phi(z)$, the standard normal cdf and
- the **logit** model with $G(z) = \Lambda(z) = \frac{\exp(z)}{1+\exp(z)}$, the cdf of the logistic distribution.

Wooldridge (2016, Section 17.1) provides useful discussions of the derivation and interpretation of these models. Here, we are concerned with the practical implementation. In R, many generalized linear models can be estimated with the command **glm** which works similar to **lm**. It accepts the additional option

- **family=binomial(link=logit)** for the logit model or
- **family=binomial(link=probit)** for the probit model.

Maximum likelihood estimation (MLE) of the parameters is done automatically and the **summary** of the results contains the most important regression table and additional information. Scripts 17.3 (Example-17-1-3.R) and 17.4 (Example-17-1-4.R) implement this for the logit and probit model, respectively. The log likelihood value $\mathscr{L}(\hat{\boldsymbol{\beta}})$ is not reported by default but can be requested with the function **logLik**. Instead, a statistic called Residual deviance is reported in the standard output. It is simply defined as $D(\hat{\boldsymbol{\beta}}) = -2\mathscr{L}(\hat{\boldsymbol{\beta}})$. Null deviance means $D_0 = -2\mathscr{L}_0$ where $\mathscr{L}_0$ is the likelihood of a model with an intercept only.

The two deviance statistics can be accessed for additional calculations from a stored result res with **res$deviance** and **res$null.deviance**. Scripts 17.3 (Example-17-1-3.R) and 17.4 (Example-17-1-4.R) demonstrate the calculation of different statistics derived from these results. McFadden's pseudo R-squared can be calculated as

$$\text{pseudo } R^2 = 1 - \frac{\mathscr{L}(\hat{\boldsymbol{\beta}})}{\mathscr{L}_0} = 1 - \frac{D(\hat{\boldsymbol{\beta}})}{D_0}. \tag{17.6}$$

─────────── **Output of Script 17.3:** `Example-17-1-3.R` ───────────

```
> library(foreign)

> mroz <- read.dta("http://fmwww.bc.edu/ec-p/data/wooldridge/mroz.dta")

> # Estimate logit model
> logitres<-glm(inlf~nwifeinc+educ+exper+I(exper^2)+age+kidslt6+kidsge6,
>                            family=binomial(link=logit),data=mroz)

> # Summary of results:
> summary(logitres)

Call:
glm(formula = inlf ~ nwifeinc + educ + exper + I(exper^2) + age +
    kidslt6 + kidsge6, family = binomial(link = logit), data = mroz)

Deviance Residuals:
    Min      1Q   Median       3Q      Max
-2.1770  -0.9063   0.4473   0.8561   2.4032

Coefficients:
             Estimate Std. Error z value Pr(>|z|)
(Intercept)  0.425452   0.860365   0.495  0.62095
nwifeinc    -0.021345   0.008421  -2.535  0.01126 *
educ         0.221170   0.043439   5.091 3.55e-07 ***
exper        0.205870   0.032057   6.422 1.34e-10 ***
I(exper^2)  -0.003154   0.001016  -3.104  0.00191 **
age         -0.088024   0.014573  -6.040 1.54e-09 ***
kidslt6     -1.443354   0.203583  -7.090 1.34e-12 ***
kidsge6      0.060112   0.074789   0.804  0.42154
---
Signif. codes:  0 '***' 0.001 '**' 0.01 '*' 0.05 '.' 0.1 ' ' 1

(Dispersion parameter for binomial family taken to be 1)

    Null deviance: 1029.75  on 752  degrees of freedom
Residual deviance:  803.53  on 745  degrees of freedom
AIC: 819.53

Number of Fisher Scoring iterations: 4


> # Log likelihood value:
> logLik(logitres)
'log Lik.' -401.7652 (df=8)

> # McFadden's pseudo R2:
> 1 - logitres$deviance/logitres$null.deviance
[1] 0.2196814
```

————— **Output of Script 17.4:** `Example-17-1-4.R` —————

```
> library(foreign)

> mroz <- read.dta("http://fmwww.bc.edu/ec-p/data/wooldridge/mroz.dta")

> # Estimate probit model
> probitres<-glm(inlf~nwifeinc+educ+exper+I(exper^2)+age+kidslt6+kidsge6,
>                            family=binomial(link=probit),data=mroz)

> # Summary of results:
> summary(probitres)

Call:
glm(formula = inlf ~ nwifeinc + educ + exper + I(exper^2) + age +
    kidslt6 + kidsge6, family = binomial(link = probit), data = mroz)

Deviance Residuals:
    Min       1Q   Median       3Q      Max
-2.2156  -0.9151   0.4315   0.8653   2.4553

Coefficients:
              Estimate Std. Error z value Pr(>|z|)
(Intercept)  0.2700736  0.5080782   0.532  0.59503
nwifeinc    -0.0120236  0.0049392  -2.434  0.01492 *
educ         0.1309040  0.0253987   5.154 2.55e-07 ***
exper        0.1233472  0.0187587   6.575 4.85e-11 ***
I(exper^2)  -0.0018871  0.0005999  -3.145  0.00166 **
age         -0.0528524  0.0084624  -6.246 4.22e-10 ***
kidslt6     -0.8683247  0.1183773  -7.335 2.21e-13 ***
kidsge6      0.0360056  0.0440303   0.818  0.41350
---
Signif. codes:  0 '***' 0.001 '**' 0.01 '*' 0.05 '.' 0.1 ' ' 1

(Dispersion parameter for binomial family taken to be 1)

    Null deviance: 1029.7  on 752  degrees of freedom
Residual deviance:  802.6  on 745  degrees of freedom
AIC: 818.6

Number of Fisher Scoring iterations: 4


> # Log likelihood value:
> logLik(probitres)
'log Lik.' -401.3022 (df=8)

> # McFadden's pseudo R2:
> 1 - probitres$deviance/probitres$null.deviance
[1] 0.2205805
```

17.1.3. Inference

The **summary** output of fitted **glm** results contains a standard regression table with parameters and (asymptotic) standard errors. The next column is labeled z value instead of t value in the output of **lm**. The interpretation is the same. The difference is that the standard errors only have an asymptotic foundation and the distribution used for calculating p values is the standard normal distribution (which is equal to the t distribution with very large degrees of freedom). The bottom line is that tests for single parameters can be done as before, see section 4.1.

For testing multiple hypotheses similar to the F test (see Section 4.3), the likelihood ratio test is popular. It is based on comparing the log likelihood values of the unrestricted and the restricted model. The test statistic is

$$LR = 2(\mathscr{L}_{ur} - \mathscr{L}_r) = D_r - D_{ur} \tag{17.7}$$

where $\mathscr{L}_{ur}$ and $\mathscr{L}_r$ are the log likelihood values of the unrestricted and restricted model, respectively, and D_{ur} and D_r are the corresponding reported deviance statistics. Under H_0, the LR test statistic is asymptotically distributed as χ^2 with the degrees of freedom equal to number of restrictions to be tested. The test of overall significance is a special case just like with F-tests. The null hypothesis is that all parameters except the constant are equal to zero. With the notation above, the test statistic is

$$LR = 2(\mathscr{L}(\hat{\beta}) - \mathscr{L}_0) = D_0 - D(\hat{\beta}). \tag{17.8}$$

Translated to R with fitted model results stored in res, this corresponds to
LR = res\$null.deviance − res\$deviance

The package *lmtest* also offers the LR test as the function **lrtest** including the convenient calculation of p values. The syntax is

- **lrtest(res)** for a test of overall significance for model res
- **lrtest(restr, unrestr)** for a test of the restricted model restr vs. the unrestricted model unrestr

Script 17.5 (Example-17-1-5.R) implements the test of overall significance for the probit model using both manual and and automatic calculations. It also tests the joint null hypothesis that experience and age are irrelevant by first estimating the restricted model and then running the automated LR test.

—————————— **Output of Script 17.5: Example-17-1-5.R** ——————————

```
> ##############################################################
> # Test of overall significance:
> # Manual calculation of the LR test statistic:
> probitres$null.deviance - probitres$deviance
[1] 227.142

> # Automatic calculations including p-values,...:
> library(lmtest)

> lrtest(probitres)
Likelihood ratio test

Model 1: inlf ~ nwifeinc + educ + exper + I(exper^2) + age + kidslt6 +
    kidsge6
Model 2: inlf ~ 1
  #Df  LogLik Df  Chisq Pr(>Chisq)
1   8 -401.30
2   1 -514.87 -7 227.14  < 2.2e-16 ***
---
Signif. codes:  0 '***' 0.001 '**' 0.01 '*' 0.05 '.' 0.1 ' ' 1
```

```
> ##############################################################
> # Test of HO: experience and age are irrelevant
> restr <- glm(inlf~nwifeinc+educ+ kidslt6+kidsge6,
>                         family=binomial(link=logit),data=mroz)

> lrtest(restr,probitres)
Likelihood ratio test

Model 1: inlf ~ nwifeinc + educ + kidslt6 + kidsge6
Model 2: inlf ~ nwifeinc + educ + exper + I(exper^2) + age + kidslt6 +
    kidsge6
  #Df  LogLik Df  Chisq Pr(>Chisq)
1   5 -464.92
2   8 -401.30  3 127.25  < 2.2e-16 ***
---
Signif. codes:  0 '***' 0.001 '**' 0.01 '*' 0.05 '.' 0.1 ' ' 1
```

17.1.4. Predictions

The command **predict** can calculate predicted values for the estimation sample ("fitted values") or arbitrary sets of regressor values also for binary response models estimated with **glm**. Given the results are stored in variable res, we can calculate

- $x_i\hat{\beta}$ for the estimation sample with **predict(res)**
- $x_i\hat{\beta}$ for the regressor values stored in xpred with **predict(res, xpred)**
- $\hat{y} = G(x_i\hat{\beta})$ for the estimation sample with **predict(res, type = "response")**
- $\hat{y} = G(x_i\hat{\beta})$ for the regressor values stored in xpred with **predict(res, xpred, type = "response")**

The predictions for the two hypothetical women introduced in Section 17.1.1 are repeated for the linear probability, logit, and probit models in Script 17.6 (Example-17-1-6.R). Unlike the linear probability model, the predicted probabilities from the logit and probit models remain between 0 and 1.

_____ Output of Script 17.6: **Example-17-1-6.R** _____

```
> # Predictions from linear probability, probit and logit model:
> # (run 17-1-1.R through 17-1-4.R first to define the variables!)
> predict(linprob,  xpred,type = "response")
         1         2
-0.4104582  1.0428084

> predict(logitres,  xpred,type = "response")
          1          2
0.005218002 0.950049117

> predict(probitres,xpred,type = "response")
          1          2
0.001065043 0.959869044
```

Figure 17.1. Predictions from binary response models (simulated data)

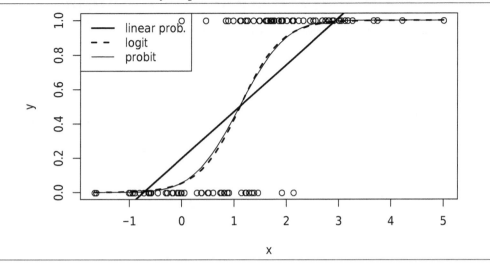

If we only have one regressor, predicted values can nicely be plotted against it. Figure 17.1 shows such a figure for a simulated data set. For interested readers, the script used for generating the data and the figure is printed as Script 17.7 (`Binary-Predictions.R`) in Appendix IV (p. 327). In this example, the linear probability model clearly predicts probabilities outside of the "legal" area between 0 and 1. The logit and probit models yield almost identical predictions. This is a general finding that holds for most data sets.

17.1.5. Partial Effects

The parameters of linear regression models have straightforward interpretations: β_j measures the *ceteris paribus* effect of x_j on $E(y|\mathbf{x})$. The parameters of nonlinear models like logit and probit have a less straightforward interpretation since the linear index $\mathbf{x}\boldsymbol{\beta}$ affects $\hat{y}$ through the link function G.

A useful measure of the influence is the partial effect (or marginal effect) which in a graph like Figure 17.1 is the slope and has the same interpretation as the parameters in the linear model. Because of the chain rule, it is

$$\frac{\partial \hat{y}}{\partial x_j} = \frac{\partial G(\hat{\beta}_0 + \hat{\beta}_1 x_1 + \cdots + \hat{\beta}_k x_k)}{\partial x_j} \tag{17.9}$$

$$= \hat{\beta}_j \cdot g(\hat{\beta}_0 + \hat{\beta}_1 x_1 + \cdots + \hat{\beta}_k x_k), \tag{17.10}$$

where $g(z)$ is the derivative of the link function $G(z)$. So
- for the probit model, the partial effect is
  $\frac{\partial \hat{y}}{\partial x_j} = \hat{\beta}_j \cdot \phi(\mathbf{x}\hat{\boldsymbol{\beta}})$
- for the logit model, it is
  $\frac{\partial \hat{y}}{\partial x_j} = \hat{\beta}_j \cdot \lambda(\mathbf{x}\hat{\boldsymbol{\beta}})$

where $\phi(z)$ and $\lambda(z)$ are the pdfs of the standard normal and the logistic distribution, respectively.

The partial effect depends on the value of $\mathbf{x}\hat{\boldsymbol{\beta}}$. The pdfs have the famous bell-shape with highest values in the middle and values close to zero in the tails. This is already obvious from Figure 17.1.

Figure 17.2. Partial effects for binary response models (simulated data)

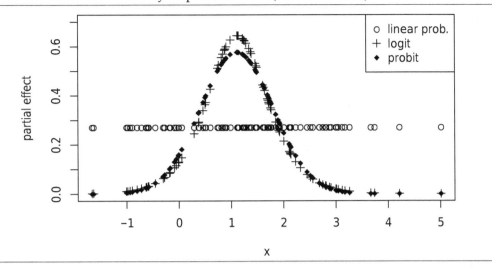

Depending on the value of x, the slope of the probability differs. For our simulated data set, Figure 17.2 shows the estimated partial effects for all 100 observed x values. Interested readers can see the complete code for this as Script 17.8 (`Binary-Margeff.R`) in Appendix IV (p. 328).

The fact that the partial effects differ by regressor values makes it harder to present the results in a concise and meaningful way. There are two common ways to aggregate the partial effects:

- Partial effects at the average: $PEA = \hat{\beta}_j \cdot g(\overline{\mathbf{x}}\hat{\beta})$

- Average partial effects: $APE = \frac{1}{n} \sum_{i=1}^{n} \hat{\beta}_j \cdot g(\mathbf{x}_i\hat{\beta}) = \hat{\beta}_j \cdot \overline{g(\mathbf{x}\hat{\beta})}$

where $\overline{\mathbf{x}}$ is the vector of sample averages of the regressors and $\overline{g(\mathbf{x}\hat{\beta})}$ is the sample average of g evaluated at the individual linear index $\mathbf{x}_i\hat{\beta}$. Both measures multiply each coefficient $\hat{\beta}_j$ with a constant factor.

Script 17.9 (`Example-17-1-7.R`) implements the APE calculations for our labor force participation example using already known *R* functions:

1. The linear indices $\mathbf{x}_i\hat{\beta}$ are calculated using **predict**

2. The factors $\overline{g(\mathbf{x}\hat{\beta})}$ are calculated by using the pdf functions **dlogis** and **dnorm** and then averaging over the sample with **mean**.

3. The APEs are calculated by multiplying the coefficient vector obtained with **coef** with the corresponding factor. Note that for the linear probability model, the partial effects are constant and simply equal to the coefficients.

The results for the constant do not not have a direct meaningful interpretation. The APEs for the other variables don't differ too much between the models. As a general observation, as long as we are interested in APEs only and not in individual predictions or partial effects and as long as not too many probabilities are close to 0 or 1, the linear probability model often works well enough.

```
──────── Output of Script 17.9: Example-17-1-7.R ────────
> # APEs (run 17-1-1.R through 17-1-4.R first to define the variables!)
>
> # Calculation of linear index at individual values:
> xb.log <- predict(logitres)

> xb.prob<- predict(probitres)

> # APE factors = average(g(xb))
> factor.log <- mean( dlogis(xb.log) )

> factor.prob<- mean( dnorm(xb.prob) )

> cbind(factor.log,factor.prob)
      factor.log factor.prob
[1,]  0.1785796   0.3007555

> # average partial effects = beta*factor:
> APE.lin <- coef(linprob) * 1

> APE.log <- coef(logitres) * factor.log

> APE.prob<- coef(probitres) * factor.prob

> # Table of APEs
> cbind(APE.lin, APE.log, APE.prob)
                    APE.lin         APE.log        APE.prob
(Intercept)    0.5855192287    0.0759771334    0.081226129
nwifeinc      -0.0034051689   -0.0038118134   -0.003616175
educ           0.0379953029    0.0394965237    0.039370095
exper          0.0394923894    0.0367641055    0.037097345
I(exper^2)    -0.0005963119   -0.0005632587   -0.000567546
age           -0.0160908062   -0.0157193607   -0.015895665
kidslt6       -0.2618104670   -0.2577536552   -0.261153464
kidsge6        0.0130122345    0.0107348185    0.010828887
```

A convenient package for calculating PEA and APE is ***mfx***. Among others, it provides the commands **logitmfx** and **probitmfx**. They estimate the corresponding model and display a regression table not with parameter estimates but with PEAs with the option **atmean=TRUE** and APEs with the option **atmean=FALSE**. Script 17.10 (Example-17-1-8.R) demonstrates this for the logit model of our labor force participation example. The reported APEs are the same as those manually calculated in Script 17.9 (Example-17-1-7.R).

―――――― **Output of Script 17.10: Example-17-1-8.R** ――――――

```
> # Automatic APE calculations with package mfx
> library(mfx)

> logitmfx(inlf~nwifeinc+educ+exper+I(exper^2)+age+kidslt6+kidsge6,
>                                          data=mroz, atmean=FALSE)
Call:
logitmfx(formula = inlf ~ nwifeinc + educ + exper + I(exper^2) +
    age + kidslt6 + kidsge6, data = mroz, atmean = FALSE)

Marginal Effects:
                  dF/dx    Std. Err.        z      P>|z|
nwifeinc     -0.00381181  0.00153898  -2.4769   0.013255 *
educ          0.03949652  0.00846811   4.6641 3.099e-06 ***
exper         0.03676411  0.00655577   5.6079 2.048e-08 ***
I(exper^2)   -0.00056326  0.00018795  -2.9968   0.002728 **
age          -0.01571936  0.00293269  -5.3600 8.320e-08 ***
kidslt6      -0.25775366  0.04263493  -6.0456 1.489e-09 ***
kidsge6       0.01073482  0.01339130   0.8016   0.422769
---
Signif. codes:  0 `***' 0.001 `**' 0.01 `*' 0.05 `.' 0.1 ` ' 1
```

17.2. Count Data: The Poisson Regression Model

Instead of just 0/1-coded binary data, count data can take any non-negative integer 0,1,2,... If they take very large numbers (like the number of students in a school), they can be approximated reasonably well as continuous variables in linear models and estimated using OLS. If the numbers are relatively small (like the number of children of a mother), this approximation might not work well. For example, predicted values can become negative.

The Poisson regression model is the most basic and convenient model explicitly designed for count data. The probability that y takes any value $h \in \{0, 1, 2, \dots\}$ for this model can be written as

$$P(y = h|\mathbf{x}) = \frac{e^{-e^{\mathbf{x}\beta}} \cdot e^{h \cdot \mathbf{x}\beta}}{h!} \tag{17.11}$$

The parameters of the Poisson model are much easier to interpret than those of a probit or logit model. In this model, the conditional mean of y is

$$E(y|\mathbf{x}) = e^{\mathbf{x}\beta}, \tag{17.12}$$

so each slope parameter β_j has the interpretation of a semi elasticity:

$$\frac{\partial E(y|\mathbf{x})}{\partial x_j} = \beta_j \cdot e^{\mathbf{x}\beta} = \beta_j \cdot E(y|\mathbf{x}) \tag{17.13}$$

$$\Leftrightarrow \beta_j = \frac{1}{E(y|\mathbf{x})} \cdot \frac{\partial E(y|\mathbf{x})}{\partial x_j}. \tag{17.14}$$

If x_j increases by one unit (and the other regressors remain the same), $E(y|\mathbf{x})$ will increase roughly by $100 \cdot \beta_j$ percent (the exact value is once again $100 \cdot (e^{\beta_j} - 1)$).

A problem with the Poisson model is that it is quite restrictive. The Poisson distribution implicitly restricts the variance of y to be equal to its mean. If this assumption is violated but the conditional mean is still correctly specified, the Poisson parameter estimates are consistent, but the standard errors and all inferences based on them are invalid. A simple solution is to interpret the Poisson estimators as quasi-maximum likelihood estimators (QMLE). Similar to the heteroscedasticity-robust inference for OLS discussed in Section 8.1, the standard errors can be adjusted.

Estimating Poisson regression models in R is straightforward. They also belong to the class of generalized linear models (GLM) and can be estimated using **glm**. The option to specify a Poisson model is **family=poisson**. For the more robust QMLE standard errors, we simply specify **family=quasipoisson**. For implementing more advanced count data models, see Kleiber and Zeileis (2008, Section 5.3).

Wooldridge, Example 17.3: Poisson Regression for Number of Arrests

We apply the Poisson regression model to study the number of arrests of young men in 1986. Script 17.11 (Example-17-3-1.R) imports the data and first estimates a linear regression model using OLS. Then, a Poisson model is estimated using **glm** with the **poisson** specification for the GLM family. Finally, we estimate the same model using the **quasipoisson** specification to adjust the standard errors for a potential violation of the Poisson distribution. We display the results jointly in Script 17.12 (Example-17-3-2.R) using the **stargazer** command for a joint table. By construction, the parameter estimates are the same, but the standard errors are larger for the QMLE.

```
───────────────── Script 17.11: Example-17-3-1.R ─────────────────
library(foreign)
crime1 <- read.dta("http://fmwww.bc.edu/ec-p/data/wooldridge/crime1.dta")

# Estimate linear model
lm.res      <-  lm(narr86~pcnv+avgsen+tottime+ptime86+qemp86+inc86+
                   black+hispan+born60, data=crime1)
# Estimate Poisson model
Poisson.res <- glm(narr86~pcnv+avgsen+tottime+ptime86+qemp86+inc86+
                   black+hispan+born60, data=crime1, family=poisson)
# Quasi-Poisson model
QPoisson.res<- glm(narr86~pcnv+avgsen+tottime+ptime86+qemp86+inc86+
                   black+hispan+born60, data=crime1, family=quasipoisson)
```

—————— **Output of Script 17.12:** `Example-17-3-2.R` ——————

```
> # Example 17.3: Regression table (run Example-17-3-1.R first!)
> library(stargazer) # package for regression output

> stargazer(lm.res,Poisson.res,QPoisson.res,type="text",keep.stat="n")
```

	Dependent variable:		
	narr86		
	OLS	Poisson	glm: quasipoisson link = log
	(1)	(2)	(3)
pcnv	-0.132***	-0.402***	-0.402***
	(0.040)	(0.085)	(0.105)
avgsen	-0.011	-0.024	-0.024
	(0.012)	(0.020)	(0.025)
tottime	0.012	0.024*	0.024
	(0.009)	(0.015)	(0.018)
ptime86	-0.041***	-0.099***	-0.099***
	(0.009)	(0.021)	(0.025)
qemp86	-0.051***	-0.038	-0.038
	(0.014)	(0.029)	(0.036)
inc86	-0.001***	-0.008***	-0.008***
	(0.0003)	(0.001)	(0.001)
black	0.327***	0.661***	0.661***
	(0.045)	(0.074)	(0.091)
hispan	0.194***	0.500***	0.500***
	(0.040)	(0.074)	(0.091)
born60	-0.022	-0.051	-0.051
	(0.033)	(0.064)	(0.079)
Constant	0.577***	-0.600***	-0.600***
	(0.038)	(0.067)	(0.083)
Observations	2,725	2,725	2,725
Note:		*p<0.1; **p<0.05; ***p<0.01	

Figure 17.3. Conditional means for the Tobit model

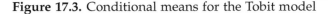

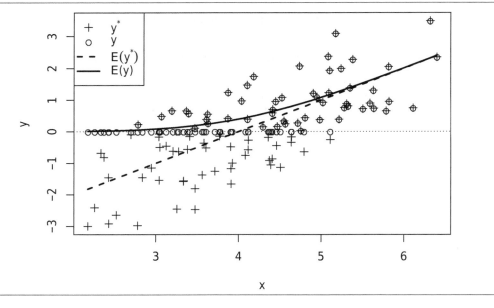

17.3. Corner Solution Responses: The Tobit Model

Corner solutions describe situations where the variable of interest is continuous but restricted in range. Typically, it cannot be negative. A significant share of people buy exactly zero amounts of alcohol, tobacco, or diapers. The Tobit model explicitly models dependent variables like this. It can be formulated in terms of a latent variable y^* that can take all real values. For it, the classical linear regression model assumptions MLR.1–MLR.6 are assumed to hold. If y^* is positive, we observe $y = y^*$. Otherwise, $y = 0$. Wooldridge (2016, Section 17.2) shows how to derive properties and the likelihood function for this model.

The problem of interpreting the parameters is similar to logit or probit models. While β_j measures the *ceteris paribus* effect of x_j on $\mathrm{E}(y^*|\mathbf{x})$, the interest is typically in y instead. The partial effect of interest can be written as

$$\frac{\partial \mathrm{E}(y|\mathbf{x})}{\partial x_j} = \beta_j \cdot \Phi\left(\frac{\mathbf{x}\boldsymbol{\beta}}{\sigma}\right) \tag{17.15}$$

and again depends on the regressor values $\mathbf{x}$. To aggregate them over the sample, we can either calculate the partial effects at the average (PEA) or the average partial effect (APE) just like with the binary variable models.

Figure 17.3 depicts these properties for a simulated data set with only one regressor. Whenever $y^* > 0$, $y = y^*$ and the symbols $\circ$ and $+$ are on top of each other. If $y^* < 0$, then $y = 0$. Therefore, the slope of $\mathrm{E}(y|x)$ gets close to zero for very low x values. The code that generated the data set and the graph is hidden as Script 17.13 (Tobit-CondMean.R) in Appendix IV (p. 329).

For the practical ML estimation in *R*, there are different options. Package **AER** provides the command **tobit** and package **censReg** offers the command **censReg**. Both work very similar and are easy to use. We will present an example using the latter. The command **censReg** can be used just like **lm** with the model formula and the data option. It will estimate the standard Tobit model discussed here. Other corner solutions ($y \geq a$ or $y \leq b$) can be specified using the options **left** and **right**. After storing the results from **censReg** in a variable res, the PEA can easily be calculated with **margEff(res)**.

Wooldridge, Example 17.2: Married Women's Annual Labor Supply

We have already estimated labor supply models for the women in the data set `mroz.dta`, ignoring the fact that the hours worked is necessarily non-negative. Script 17.14 (`Example-17-2.R`) estimates a Tobit model accounting for this fact. It also calculates the PEA using **margEff**.

─────────── **Output of Script 17.14:** `Example-17-2.R` ───────────

```
> library(foreign)

> mroz <- read.dta("http://fmwww.bc.edu/ec-p/data/wooldridge/mroz.dta")

> # Estimate Tobit model using censReg:
> library(censReg)

> TobitRes <- censReg(hours~nwifeinc+educ+exper+I(exper^2)+
>                                     age+kidslt6+kidsge6, data=mroz )

> summary(TobitRes)
Call:
censReg(formula = hours ~ nwifeinc + educ + exper + I(exper^2) +
    age + kidslt6 + kidsge6, data = mroz)

Observations:
          Total  Left-censored    Uncensored Right-censored
           753            325           428              0

Coefficients:
            Estimate Std. error t value  Pr(> t)
(Intercept) 965.30530  446.43625   2.162 0.030599 *
nwifeinc     -8.81424    4.45910  -1.977 0.048077 *
educ         80.64561   21.58324   3.736 0.000187 ***
exper       131.56430   17.27939   7.614 2.66e-14 ***
I(exper^2)   -1.86416    0.53766  -3.467 0.000526 ***
age         -54.40501    7.41850  -7.334 2.24e-13 ***
kidslt6    -894.02174  111.87803  -7.991 1.34e-15 ***
kidsge6     -16.21800   38.64139  -0.420 0.674701
logSigma      7.02289    0.03706 189.514  < 2e-16 ***
---
Signif. codes:  0 '***' 0.001 '**' 0.01 '*' 0.05 '.' 0.1 ' ' 1

Newton-Raphson maximisation, 7 iterations
Return code 1: gradient close to zero
Log-likelihood: -3819.095 on 9 Df


> # Partial Effects at the average x:
> margEff(TobitRes)
   nwifeinc        educ       exper  I(exper^2)         age
  -5.326442   48.734094   79.504231   -1.126509  -32.876918
     kidslt6     kidsge6
 -540.256832   -9.800526
```

Another alternative for estimating Tobit models is the command **survreg** from package **survival**. It is less straightforward to use but more flexible. We cannot comprehensively discuss all features but just show how to reproduce the same results for Example 17.2 in Script 17.15 (Example-17-2-survreg.R). We will come back to this command in the next section.

———————————— **Output of Script 17.15: Example-17-2-survreg.R** ————————————

```
> # Estimate Tobit model using survreg:
> library(survival)

> res <- survreg(Surv(hours, hours>0, type="left") ~ nwifeinc+educ+exper+
>               I(exper^2)+age+kidslt6+kidsge6, data=mroz, dist="gaussian")

> summary(res)

Call:
survreg(formula = Surv(hours, hours > 0, type = "left") ~ nwifeinc +
    educ + exper + I(exper^2) + age + kidslt6 + kidsge6, data = mroz,
    dist = "gaussian")
              Value Std. Error      z        p
(Intercept) 965.31    446.4361   2.16 3.06e-02
nwifeinc     -8.81      4.4591  -1.98 4.81e-02
educ         80.65     21.5832   3.74 1.87e-04
exper       131.56     17.2794   7.61 2.66e-14
I(exper^2)   -1.86      0.5377  -3.47 5.26e-04
age         -54.41      7.4185  -7.33 2.24e-13
kidslt6    -894.02    111.8780  -7.99 1.34e-15
kidsge6     -16.22     38.6414  -0.42 6.75e-01
Log(scale)    7.02      0.0371 189.51 0.00e+00

Scale= 1122

Gaussian distribution
Loglik(model)= -3819.1   Loglik(intercept only)= -3954.9
      Chisq= 271.59 on 7 degrees of freedom, p= 0
Number of Newton-Raphson Iterations: 4
n= 753
```

17.4. Censored and Truncated Regression Models

Censored regression models are closely related to Tobit models. In fact, their parameters can be estimated with the same software packages. General censored regression models also start from a latent variable y^*. The observed dependent variable y is equal to y^* for some (the uncensored) observations. For the other observations, we only know an upper or lower bound for y^*. In the basic Tobit model, we observe $y = y^*$ in the "uncensored" cases with $y^* > 0$ and we only know that $y^* \leq 0$ if we observe $y = 0$. The censoring rules can be much more general. There could be censoring from above or the thresholds can vary from observation to observation.

The main difference between Tobit and censored regression models is the interpretation. In the former case, we are interested in the observed y, in the latter case, we are interested in the underlying y^*.[1] Censoring is merely a data problem that has to be accounted for instead of a logical feature of the dependent variable. We already know how to estimate Tobit models. With censored regression, we can use the same tools. The problem of calculating partial effects does not exists in this case since we are interested in the linear $E(y^*|\mathbf{x})$ and the slope parameters are directly equal to the partial effects of interest.

Wooldridge, Example 17.4: Duration of Recidivism

We are interested in the criminal prognosis of individuals released from prison. We model the time it takes them to be arrested again. Explanatory variables include demographic characteristics as well as a dummy variable `workprg` indicating the participation in a work program during their time in prison. The 1445 former inmates observed in the data set `recid.dta` were followed for a while.

During that time, 893 inmates were not arrested again. For them, we only know that their true duration y^* is at least `durat`, which for them is the time between the release and the end of the observation period, so we have right censoring. The threshold of censoring differs by individual depending on when they were released.

Because of the more complicated selection rule, we use the command **survreg** for the estimation of the model in Script 17.16 (`Example-17-4.R`). We need to supply the dependent variable log(`durat`) as well as a dummy variable indicating *uncensored* observations. We generate a dummy variable `uncensored` within the data frame based on the existing variable `cens` that represents censoring.

The parameters can directly be interpreted. Because of the logarithmic specification, they represent semi-elasticities. For example do married individuals take around $100 \cdot \hat{\beta} = 34\%$ longer to be arrested again. (Actually, the accurate number is $100 \cdot (e^{\hat{\beta}} - 1) = 40\%$.) There is no significant effect of the work program.

---

[1]Wooldridge (2016, Section 7.4) uses the notation w instead of y and y instead of y^*.

―――――――――― **Output of Script 17.16: Example-17-4.R** ――――――――――

```
> library(foreign);library(survival)

> recid <- read.dta("http://fmwww.bc.edu/ec-p/data/wooldridge/recid.dta")

> # Define Dummy for UNcensored observations
> recid$uncensored <- recid$cens==0

> # Estimate censored regression model:
> res<-survreg(Surv(log(durat),uncensored, type="right") ~ workprg+priors+
>                    tserved+felon+alcohol+drugs+black+married+educ+age,
>                    data=recid, dist="gaussian")

> # Output:
> summary(res)

Call:
survreg(formula = Surv(log(durat), uncensored, type = "right") ~
    workprg + priors + tserved + felon + alcohol + drugs + black +
        married + educ + age, data = recid, dist = "gaussian")
               Value Std. Error       z        p
(Intercept)  4.09939   0.347535  11.796  4.11e-32
workprg     -0.06257   0.120037  -0.521  6.02e-01
priors      -0.13725   0.021459  -6.396  1.59e-10
tserved     -0.01933   0.002978  -6.491  8.51e-11
felon        0.44399   0.145087   3.060  2.21e-03
alcohol     -0.63491   0.144217  -4.402  1.07e-05
drugs       -0.29816   0.132736  -2.246  2.47e-02
black       -0.54272   0.117443  -4.621  3.82e-06
married      0.34068   0.139843   2.436  1.48e-02
educ         0.02292   0.025397   0.902  3.67e-01
age          0.00391   0.000606   6.450  1.12e-10
Log(scale)   0.59359   0.034412  17.249  1.13e-66

Scale= 1.81

Gaussian distribution
Loglik(model)= -1597.1   Loglik(intercept only)= -1680.4
        Chisq= 166.74 on 10 degrees of freedom, p= 0
Number of Newton-Raphson Iterations: 4
n= 1445
```

Truncation is a more serious problem than censoring since our observations are more severely affected. If the true latent variable y^* is above or below a certain threshold, the individual is not even sampled. We therefore do not even have any information. Classical truncated regression models rely on parametric and distributional assumptions to correct this problem. In *R*, they are available in the package ***truncreg***.

Figure 17.4 shows results for a simulated data set. Because it is simulated, we actually know the values for everybody (hollow dots). In our sample, we only observe those with $y > 0$ (solid dots). When applying OLS to this sample, we get a downward biased slope (dashed line). Truncated regression fixes this problem and gives a consistent slope estimator (solid line). Script 17.17 (TruncReg-Simulation.R) which generated the data set and the graph is shown in Appendix IV (p. 330).

Figure 17.4. Truncated regression: simulated example

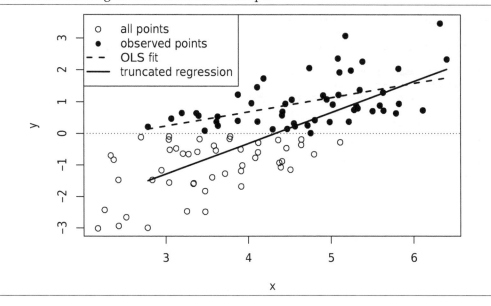

17.5. Sample Selection Corrections

Sample selection models are related to truncated regression models. We do have a random sample from the population of interest, but we do not observe the dependent variable y for a non-random sub-sample. The sample selection is not based on a threshold for y but on some other selection mechanism.

Heckman's selection model consists of a probit-like model for the binary fact whether y is observed and a linear regression-like model for y. Selection can be driven by the same determinants as y but should have at least one additional factor excluded from the equation for y. Wooldridge (2016, Section 17.5) discusses the specification and estimation of these models in more detail.

The classical Heckman selection model can be estimated either in two steps using software for probit and OLS as discussed by Wooldridge (2016) or by a specialized command using MLE. In *R*, the package ***sampleSelection*** offers automated estimation for both approaches.

Wooldridge, Example 17.5: Wage offer equation for married women

We once again look at the sample of women in the data set MROZ.dta. Of the 753 women, 428 worked (inlf=1) and the rest did not work (inlf=0). For the latter, we do not observe the wage they would have gotten had they worked. Script 17.18 (Example-17-5.R) estimates the Heckman selection model using the command **selection**. It expects two formulas: one for the selection and one for the wage equation. The option **method="2step"** requests implicit 2-step estimation to make the results comparable to those reported by Wooldridge (2016). With the option **method="ml"**, we would have gotten the more efficient MLE. The summary of the results gives a typical regression table for both equations and additional information.

—————— **Output of Script 17.18:** `Example-17-5.R` ——————

```
> library(foreign);library(sampleSelection)

> mroz <- read.dta("http://fmwww.bc.edu/ec-p/data/wooldridge/mroz.dta")

> # Estimate Heckman selection model (2 step version)
> res<-selection(inlf~educ+exper+I(exper^2)+nwifeinc+age+kidslt6+kidsge6,
>              log(wage)~educ+exper+I(exper^2), data=mroz, method="2step" )

> # Summary of results:
> summary(res)
--------------------------------------------
Tobit 2 model (sample selection model)
2-step Heckman / heckit estimation
753 observations (325 censored and 428 observed)
15 free parameters (df = 739)
Probit selection equation:
             Estimate Std. Error t value Pr(>|t|)
(Intercept)  0.270077   0.508593    0.531  0.59556
educ         0.130905   0.025254    5.183 2.81e-07 ***
exper        0.123348   0.018716    6.590 8.34e-11 ***
I(exper^2)  -0.001887   0.000600   -3.145  0.00173 **
nwifeinc    -0.012024   0.004840   -2.484  0.01320 *
age         -0.052853   0.008477   -6.235 7.61e-10 ***
kidslt6     -0.868328   0.118522   -7.326 6.21e-13 ***
kidsge6      0.036005   0.043477    0.828  0.40786
Outcome equation:
             Estimate Std. Error t value Pr(>|t|)
(Intercept) -0.5781032  0.3050062   -1.895  0.05843 .
educ         0.1090655  0.0155230    7.026 4.83e-12 ***
exper        0.0438873  0.0162611    2.699  0.00712 **
I(exper^2)  -0.0008591  0.0004389   -1.957  0.05068 .
Multiple R-Squared:0.1569,          Adjusted R-Squared:0.149
Error terms:
             Estimate Std. Error t value Pr(>|t|)
invMillsRatio 0.03226    0.13362    0.241    0.809
sigma         0.66363         NA       NA       NA
rho           0.04861         NA       NA       NA
--------------------------------------------
```

18. Advanced Time Series Topics

After we have introduced time series concepts in Chapters 10 – 12, this chapter touches on some more advanced topics in time series econometrics. Namely, we we look at infinite distributed lag models in Section 18.1, unit roots tests in Section 18.2, spurious regression in Section 18.3, cointegration in Section 18.4 and forecasting in Section 18.5.

18.1. Infinite Distributed Lag Models

We have covered finite distributed lag models in Section 10.3. We have estimated those and related models in *R* using the **dynlm** package. In *infinite* distributed lag models, shocks in the regressors z_t have an infinitely long impact on y_t, y_{t+1}, ... The long-run propensity is the overall future effect of increasing z_t by one unit and keeping it at that level.

Without further restrictions, infinite distributed lag models cannot be estimated. Wooldridge (2016, Section 18.1) discusses two different models. The **geometric (or Koyck)** distributed lag model boils down to a linear regression equation in terms of lagged dependent variables

$$y_t = \alpha_0 + \gamma z_t + \rho y_{t-1} + v_t \tag{18.1}$$

and has a long-run propensity of

$$LRP = \frac{\gamma}{1 - \rho}. \tag{18.2}$$

The **rational** distributed lag model can be written as a somewhat more general equation

$$y_t = \alpha_0 + \gamma_0 z_t + \rho y_{t-1} + \gamma_1 z_{t-1} + v_t \tag{18.3}$$

and has a long-run propensity of

$$LRP = \frac{\gamma_0 + \gamma_1}{1 - \rho}. \tag{18.4}$$

In terms of the implementation of these models, there is nothing really new compared to Section 10.3. The only difference is that we include lagged dependent variables as regressors.

Wooldridge, Example 18.1: Housing Investment and Residential Price Inflation

Script 18.1 (Example-18-1.R) implements the geometric and the rational distributed lag models for the housing investment equation. The dependent variable is detrended first by simply using the residual of a regression on a linear time trend. We store this detrended variable in the data frame which is then transformed into a time series object using **ts**, see Chapter 10.

The two models are estimated using **dynlm** and a regression table very similar to Wooldridge (2016, Table 18.1) is produced with **stargazer**. Finally, we estimate the LRP for both models using the formulas given above. We first extract the (named) coefficient vector as b and then do the calculations with the named indices. For example **b["gprice"]** is the coefficient with the label "gprice" which in our notation above corresponds to γ in the geometric distributed lag model.

—————— **Output of Script 18.1:** `Example-18-1.R` ——————

```
> library(foreign);library(dynlm); library(stargazer)

> hseinv<-read.dta("http://fmwww.bc.edu/ec-p/data/wooldridge/hseinv.dta")

> # detrended variable: residual from a regression on the obs. index:
> trendreg <- dynlm( log(invpc) ~ trend(hseinv), data=hseinv )

> hseinv$linv.detr <-  resid( trendreg )

> # ts data:
> hseinv.ts <- ts(hseinv)

> # Koyck geometric d.l.:
> gDL<-dynlm(linv.detr~gprice + L(linv.detr)                ,data=hseinv.ts)

> # rational d.l.:
> rDL<-dynlm(linv.detr~gprice + L(linv.detr) + L(gprice),data=hseinv.ts)

> stargazer(gDL,rDL, type="text", keep.stat=c("n","adj.rsq"))

===========================================
                  Dependent variable:
                -----------------------------
                        linv.detr
                   (1)           (2)
-------------------------------------------
gprice           3.095***       3.256***
                (0.933)        (0.970)

L(linv.detr)     0.340**        0.547***
                (0.132)        (0.152)

L(gprice)                      -2.936***
                               (0.973)

Constant        -0.010          0.006
                (0.018)        (0.017)

-------------------------------------------
Observations       41            40
Adjusted R2      0.375          0.504
===========================================
Note:           *p<0.1;  **p<0.05;  ***p<0.01

> # LRP geometric DL:
> b <- coef(gDL)

>  b["gprice"]                  / (1-b["L(linv.detr)"])
  gprice
4.688433

> # LRP rationalDL:
> b <- coef(rDL)

> (b["gprice"]+b["L(gprice)"]) / (1-b["L(linv.detr)"])
   gprice
0.7066858
```

18.2. Testing for Unit Roots

We have covered strongly dependent unit root processes in Chapter 11 and promised to supply tests for unit roots later. There are several tests available. Conceptually, the Dickey-Fuller (DF) test is the simplest. If we want to test whether variables y has a unit root, we regress Δy_t on y_{t-1}. The test statistic is the usual t-test statistic of the slope coefficient. One problem is that because of the unit root, this test statistic is *not t* or normally distributed, not even asymptotically. Instead, we have to use special distribution tables for the critical values. The distribution also depends on whether we allow for a time trend in this regression.

The augmented Dickey-Fuller (ADF) test is a generalization that allows for richer dynamics in the process of y. To implement it, we add lagged values $\Delta y_{t-1}, \Delta y_{t-2}, \ldots$ to the differenced regression equation.

Of course, working with the special (A)DF tables of critical values is somewhat inconvenient. In R, the package *tseries* offers automated DF and ADF tests for models with time trends. Command **adf.test(y)** performs an ADF test with automatically selecting the number of lags in Δy. **adf.test(y,k=1)** chooses one lag and **adf.test(y,k=0)** requests zero lags, i.e. a simple DF test. The package *urca* also offers different unit root tests, including the ADF test with and without trend using the command **ur.df**.

Wooldridge, Example 18.4: Unit Root in real GDP

Script 18.2 (Example-18-4.R) implements an ADF test for the logarithm of U.S. real GDP including a linear time trend. For a test with one lag in Δy and time trend, the equation to estimate is

$$\Delta y = \alpha + \theta y_{t-1} + \gamma_1 \Delta y_{t-1} + \delta_t t + e_t.$$

We already know how to implement such a regression. The different terms and their equivalent in **dynlm** syntax are:

- $\Delta y =$ **d(y)**
- $y_{t-1} =$ **L(y)**
- $\Delta y_{t-1} =$ **L(d(y))**
- $t =$ **trend(data)**

The relevant test statistic is $t = -2.421$ and the critical values are given in Wooldridge (2016, Table 18.3). More conveniently, the script also uses the automatic command **adf.test** which reports a p value of 0.41. So the null hypothesis of a unit root cannot be rejected with any reasonable significance level. Script 18.3 (Example-18-4-urca.R) repeats the same analysis but uses the package *urca*.

———————————— **Output of Script 18.2:** `Example-18-4.R` ————————————

```
> library(foreign);library(dynlm)

> inven <- read.dta("http://fmwww.bc.edu/ec-p/data/wooldridge/inven.dta")

> # variable to test: y=log(gdp)
> inven$y <- log(inven$gdp)

> inven.ts<- ts(inven)

> # summary output of ADF regression:
> summary(dynlm( d(y) ~ L(y) + L(d(y)) + trend(inven.ts), data=inven.ts))

Time series regression with "ts" data:
Start = 3, End = 37

Call:
dynlm(formula = d(y) ~ L(y) + L(d(y)) + trend(inven.ts), data = inven.ts)

Residuals:
     Min        1Q     Median        3Q        Max
-0.046332 -0.012563   0.004026   0.013572   0.030789

Coefficients:
                 Estimate Std. Error t value Pr(>|t|)
(Intercept)      1.650922   0.666399   2.477   0.0189 *
L(y)            -0.209621   0.086594  -2.421   0.0215 *
L(d(y))          0.263751   0.164739   1.601   0.1195
trend(inven.ts)  0.005870   0.002696   2.177   0.0372 *
---
Signif. codes:  0 '***' 0.001 '**' 0.01 '*' 0.05 '.' 0.1 ' ' 1

Residual standard error: 0.02011 on 31 degrees of freedom
Multiple R-squared:  0.268,        Adjusted R-squared:  0.1972
F-statistic: 3.783 on 3 and 31 DF,  p-value: 0.02015


> # automated ADF test using tseries:
> library(tseries)

> adf.test(inven$y, k=1)

        Augmented Dickey-Fuller Test

data:  inven$y
Dickey-Fuller = -2.4207, Lag order = 1, p-value = 0.4092
alternative hypothesis: stationary
```

———— **Output of Script 18.3:** `Example-18-4-urca.R` ————

```
> library(foreign);library(urca)

> inven <- read.dta("http://fmwww.bc.edu/ec-p/data/wooldridge/inven.dta")

> # automated ADF test using urca:
> summary( ur.df(log(inven$gdp) , type = c("trend"), lags = 1) )

###############################################
# Augmented Dickey-Fuller Test Unit Root Test #
###############################################

Test regression trend


Call:
lm(formula = z.diff ~ z.lag.1 + 1 + tt + z.diff.lag)

Residuals:
      Min       1Q    Median       3Q       Max
-0.046332 -0.012563  0.004026  0.013572  0.030789

Coefficients:
            Estimate Std. Error t value Pr(>|t|)
(Intercept)  1.656792   0.669068   2.476   0.0189 *
z.lag.1     -0.209621   0.086594  -2.421   0.0215 *
tt           0.005870   0.002696   2.177   0.0372 *
z.diff.lag   0.263751   0.164739   1.601   0.1195
---
Signif. codes:  0 `***' 0.001 `**' 0.01 `*' 0.05 `.' 0.1 ` ' 1

Residual standard error: 0.02011 on 31 degrees of freedom
Multiple R-squared:  0.268,      Adjusted R-squared:  0.1972
F-statistic: 3.783 on 3 and 31 DF,  p-value: 0.02015


Value of test-statistic is: -2.4207 8.2589 4.4035

Critical values for test statistics:
      1pct  5pct 10pct
tau3 -4.15 -3.50 -3.18
phi2  7.02  5.13  4.31
phi3  9.31  6.73  5.61
```

18.3. Spurious Regression

Unit roots generally destroy the usual (large sample) properties of estimators and tests. A leading example is spurious regression. Suppose two variables x and y are completely unrelated but both follow a random walk:

$$x_t = x_{t-1} + a_t$$
$$y_t = y_{t-1} + e_t,$$

where a_t and e_t are i.i.d. random innovations. If we want to test whether they are related from a random sample, we could simply regress y on x. A t test should reject the (true) null hypothesis that the slope coefficient is equal to zero with a probability of α, for example 5%. The phenomenon of spurious regression implies that this happens much more often.

Script 18.4 (`Simulate-Spurious-Regression-1.R`) simulates this model for one sample. Remember from Section 11.2 how to simulate a random walk in a simple way: with a starting value of zero, it is just the cumulative sum of the innovations. The time series for this simulated sample of size $n = 50$ are shown in Figure 18.1. When we regress y on x, the t statistic for the slope parameter is larger than 4 with a p value much smaller than 1%. So we would reject the (correct) null hypothesis that the variables are unrelated.

Figure 18.1. Spurious regression: simulated data from Script 18.4

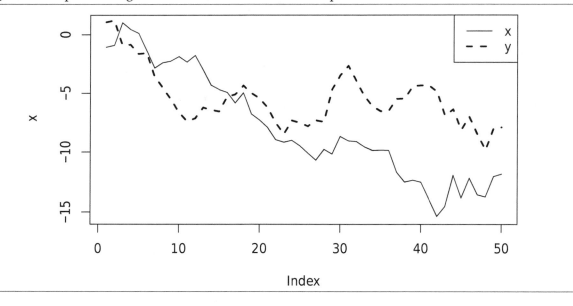

Index

_____ **Output of Script 18.4:** `Simulate-Spurious-Regression-1.R` _____

```
> # Initialize Random Number Generator
> set.seed(29846)

> # i.i.d. N(0,1) innovations
> n <- 50

> e <- rnorm(n)

> a <- rnorm(n)

> # independent random walks
> x <- cumsum(a)

> y <- cumsum(e)

> # plot
> plot(x,type="l",lty=1,lwd=1)

> lines(y        ,lty=2,lwd=2)

> legend("topright",c("x","y"), lty=c(1,2), lwd=c(1,2))

> # Regression of y on x
> summary( lm(y~x) )

Call:
lm(formula = y ~ x)

Residuals:
    Min      1Q  Median      3Q     Max
-3.5342 -1.4938 -0.2549  1.4803  4.6198

Coefficients:
            Estimate Std. Error t value Pr(>|t|)
(Intercept) -3.15050    0.56498  -5.576 1.11e-06 ***
x            0.29588    0.06253   4.732 2.00e-05 ***
---
Signif. codes:  0 '***' 0.001 '**' 0.01 '*' 0.05 '.' 0.1 ' ' 1

Residual standard error: 2.01 on 48 degrees of freedom
Multiple R-squared:  0.3181,    Adjusted R-squared:  0.3039
F-statistic: 22.39 on 1 and 48 DF,  p-value: 1.997e-05
```

We know that by definition, a valid test should reject a true null hypothesis with a probability of α, so maybe we were just unlucky with the specific sample we took. We therefore repeat the same analysis with 10,000 samples from the same data generating process in Script 18.5 (`Simulate-Spurious-Regression-2.R`). For each of the samples, we store the p value of the slope parameter in a vector named `pvals`. After these simulations are run, we simply check how often we would have rejected $H_0 : \beta_1 = 0$ by comparing these p values with 0.05.

We find that in 6,626 of the samples, so in 66% instead of $\alpha = 5\%$, we rejected H_0. So the t test seriously screws up the statistical inference because of the unit roots.

-------- **Output of Script 18.5:** `Simulate-Spurious-Regression-2.R` --------

```
> # Initialize Random Number Generator
> set.seed(29846)

> # generate 10,000 independent random walks
> # and store the p val of the t test
> pvals <- numeric(10000)

> for (r in 1:10000) {
>   # i.i.d. N(0,1) innovations
>   n <- 50
>   a <- rnorm(n)
>   e <- rnorm(n)
>   # independent random walks
>   x <- cumsum(a)
>   y <- cumsum(e)
>   # regression summary
>   regsum <- summary(lm(y~x))
>   # p value: 2nd row, 4th column of regression table
>   pvals[r] <- regsum$coef[2,4]
> }

> # How often is p<5% ?
> table(pvals<=0.05)

FALSE   TRUE
 3374   6626
```

18.4. Cointegration and Error Correction Models

In Section 18.3, we just saw that it is not a good idea to do linear regression with integrated variables. This is not generally true. If two variables are not only integrated (i.e. they have a unit root), but *cointegrated*, linear regression with them can actually make sense. Often, economic theory suggests a stable long-run relationship between integrated variables which implies cointegration. Cointegration implies that in the regression equation

$$y_t = \beta_0 + \beta_1 x_t + u_t,$$

the error term u does not have a unit root, while both y and x do. A test for cointegration can be based on this finding: We first estimate this model by OLS and then test for a unit root in the residuals $\hat{u}$. Again, we have to adjust the distribution of the test statistic and critical values. This approach is called Engle-Granger test in Wooldridge (2016, Section 18.4) or Phillips–Ouliaris (PO) test. It is implemented in package *tseries* as **po.test** and in package *urca* as **ca.po**.

If we find cointegration, we can estimate error correction models. In the Engle-Granger procedure, these models can be estimated in a two-step procedure using OLS. There are also powerful commands that automatically estimate different types of error correction models. Package *urca* provides **ca.jo** and for structural models, package *vars* offers the command **SVEC**.

18.5. Forecasting

One major goal of time series analysis is forecasting. Given the information we have today, we want to give our best guess about the future and also quantify our uncertainty. Given a time series model for y, the best guess for y_{t+1} given information I_t is the conditional mean of $E(y_{t+1}|I_t)$. For a model like

$$y_t = \delta_0 + \alpha_1 y_{t-1} + \gamma_1 z_{t-1} + u_t, \tag{18.5}$$

suppose we are at time t and know both y_t and z_t and want to predict y_{t+1}. Also suppose that $E(u_t|I_{t-1}) = 0$. Then,

$$E(y_{t+1}|I_t) = \delta_0 + \alpha_1 y_t + \gamma_1 z_t \tag{18.6}$$

and our prediction from an estimated model would be $\hat{y}_{t+1} = \hat{\delta}_0 + \hat{\alpha}_1 y_t + \hat{\gamma}_1 z_t$.

We already know how to get in-sample and (hypothetical) out-of-sample predictions including forecast intervals from linear models using the command **predict**. It can also be used for our purposes.

There are several ways how the performance of forecast models can be evaluated. It makes a lot of sense not to look at the model fit within the estimation sample but at the out-of-sample forecast performances. Suppose we have used observations $y_1, \ldots, y_n$ for estimation and additionally have observations $y_{n+1}, \ldots, y_{n+m}$. For this set of observations, we obtain out-of-sample forecasts $f_{n+1}, \ldots, f_{n+m}$ and calculate the m forecast errors

$$e_t = y_t - f_t \qquad \text{for } t = n+1, \ldots, n+m. \tag{18.7}$$

We want these forecast errors to be as small (in absolute value) as possible. Useful measures are the root mean squared error ($RMSE$) and the mean absolute error (MAE):

$$RMSE = \sqrt{\frac{1}{m} \sum_{h=1}^{m} e_{n+h}^2} \tag{18.8}$$

$$MAE = \frac{1}{m} \sum_{h=1}^{m} |e_{n+h}| \tag{18.9}$$

$$\tag{18.10}$$

Wooldridge, Example 18.8: Forecasting the U.S. Unemployment Rate

Script 18.6 (Example-18-8.R) estimates two simple models for forecasting the unemployment rate. The first one is a basic AR(1) model with only lagged unemployment as a regressor, the second one adds lagged inflation. We use the option **end** to restrict the estimation sample to years until 1996. After the estimation, we make predictions including 95% forecast intervals. Wooldridge (2016) explains how this can be done manually. We are somewhat lazy and simply use the command **predict**.

——————— **Output of Script 18.6:** `Example-18-8.R` ———————

```
> # load updataed data from URfIE Website since online file is incomplete
> # Adjust the path if needed!
> library(foreign);library(dynlm); library(stargazer)

> phillips <- read.dta("phillips.dta")

> tsdat=ts(phillips, start=1948)

> # Estimate models and display results
> res1 <- dynlm(unem ~ unem_1        , data=tsdat, end=1996)

> res2 <- dynlm(unem ~ unem_1+inf_1, data=tsdat, end=1996)

> stargazer(res1, res2 ,type="text", keep.stat=c("n","adj.rsq","ser"))

==================================================
                          Dependent variable:
                      ----------------------------
                                  unem
                          (1)             (2)
--------------------------------------------------
unem_1                  0.732***        0.647***
                        (0.097)         (0.084)

inf_1                                   0.184***
                                        (0.041)

Constant                1.572***        1.304**
                        (0.577)         (0.490)


--------------------------------------------------
Observations              48              48
Adjusted R2             0.544           0.677
Residual Std. Error 1.049 (df = 46) 0.883 (df = 45)
==================================================
Note:                    *p<0.1; **p<0.05; ***p<0.01

> # Predictions for 1997-2003 including 95% forecast intervals:
> predict(res1, newdata=window(tsdat,start=1997), interval="prediction")
       fit      lwr      upr
1 5.526452 3.392840 7.660064
2 5.160275 3.021340 7.299210
3 4.867333 2.720958 7.013709
4 4.647627 2.493832 6.801422
5 4.501157 2.341549 6.660764
6 5.087040 2.946509 7.227571
7 5.819394 3.686837 7.951950

> predict(res2, newdata=window(tsdat,start=1997), interval="prediction")
       fit      lwr      upr
1 5.348468 3.548908 7.148027
2 4.896451 3.090266 6.702636
3 4.509137 2.693393 6.324881
4 4.425175 2.607626 6.242724
5 4.516062 2.696384 6.335740
6 4.923537 3.118433 6.728641
7 5.350271 3.540939 7.159603
```

Wooldridge, Example 18.9: Comparing Out-of-Sample Forecast Performances

Script 18.7 (`Example-18-9.R`) calculates the forecast errors of the unemployment rate for the two models used in Example 18.8. The models are estimated using the sub sample until 1996 and the predictions are made for the other seven available years until 2003. The actual unemployment rate and the forecasts are plotted – the result is shown in Figure 18.2. Finally, we calculate the *RMSE* and *MAE* for both models. Both measures suggest that the second model including the lagged inflation performs better.

```
_____ Output of Script 18.7: Example-18-9.R _____

> # Note: run Example-18-8.R first to generate the results res1 and res2
>
> # Actual unemployment and forecasts:
> y   <- window(tsdat,start=1997)[,"unem"]

> f1 <- predict( res1, newdata=window(tsdat,start=1997) )

> f2 <- predict( res2, newdata=window(tsdat,start=1997) )

> # Plot unemployment and forecasts:
> matplot(time(y), cbind(y,f1,f2), type="l",  col="black",lwd=2,lty=1:3)

> legend("topleft",c("Unempl.","Forecast 1","Forecast 2"),lwd=2,lty=1:3)

> # Forecast errors:
> e1<- y - f1

> e2<- y - f2

> # RMSE:
> sqrt(mean(e1^2))
[1] 0.5761199

> sqrt(mean(e2^2))
[1] 0.5217543

> # MAE:
> mean(abs(e1))
[1] 0.542014

> mean(abs(e2))
[1] 0.4841945
```

Figure 18.2. Out-of-sample forecasts for unemployment

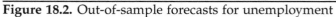

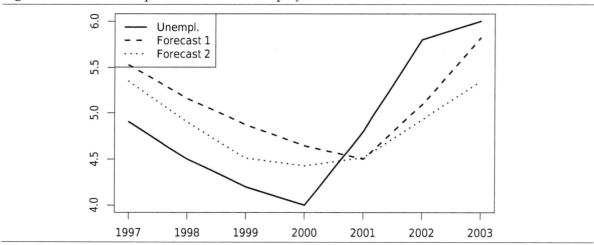

19. Carrying Out an Empirical Project

We are now ready for serious empirical work. Chapter 19 of Wooldridge (2016) discusses the formulation of interesting theories, collection of raw data, and the writing of research papers. We are concerned with the data analysis part of a research project and will cover some aspects of using *R* for real research.

This chapter is mainly about a few tips and tricks that might help to make our life easier by organizing the analyses and the output of *R* in a systematic way. While we have worked with *R* scripts throughout this book, Section 19.1 gives additional hints for using them effectively in larger projects. Section 19.2 shows how the results of our analyses can be written to a text file instead of just being displayed on the screen.

R Markdown is presented in Section 19.3. It is a straightforward markup language and is capable of generating anything between clearly laid out results documentations and complete little research papers that automatically include the analysis results. For heavy duty scientific writing, LATEX is a widely used system which was for example used to generate this book. *R* and LATEX can be used together efficiently and Section 19.4 shows how.

19.1. Working with *R* Scripts

We already argued in Section 1.1.2 that anything we do in *R* or any other statistical package should be done in scripts or the equivalent. In this way, it is always transparent how we generated our results. A typical empirical project has roughly the following steps:

1. Data Preparation: import raw data, recode and generate new variables, create sub-samples, ...

2. Generation of descriptive statistics, distribution of the main variables, ...

3. Estimation of the econometric models

4. Presentation of the results: tables, figures, ...

If we combine all these steps in one *R* script, it is very easy for us to understand how we came up with the regression results even a year after we have done the analysis. At least as important: It is also easy for our thesis supervisor, collaborators or journal referees to understand where the results came from and to reproduce them. If we made a mistake at some point or get an updated raw data set, it is easy to repeat the whole analysis to generate new results.

It is crucial to add helpful comments to the *R* scripts explaining what is done in each step. Scripts should start with an explanation like the following:

```
―――――――――――――――――――― Script 19.1: ultimate-calcs.R ――――――――――――――――――――
######################################################################
# Project X:
# "The Ultimate Question of Life, the Universe, and Everything"
# Project Collaborators: Mr. X, Mrs. Y
#
# R Script "ultimate-calcs"
# by: F Heiss
# Date of this version: February 08, 2016
######################################################################
```

```
# The main calculation using the method "square root"
# (http://mathworld.wolfram.com/SquareRoot.html)
sqrt(1764)
```

If a project requires many and/or time-consuming calculations, it might be useful to separate them into several *R* scripts. For example, we could have four different scripts corresponding to the steps listed above:

- data.R
- descriptives.R
- estimation.R
- results.R

So once the potentially time-consuming data cleaning is done, we don't have to repeat it every time we run regressions. To avoid confusion, it is highly advisable to document interdependencies. Both descriptives.R and estimation.R should at the beginning have a comment like

```
# Depends on data.R
```

And results.R could have a comment like

```
# Depends on estimation.R
```

Somewhere, we will have to document the whole work flow. The best way to do it is a master script that calls the separate scripts to reproduce the whole analyses from raw data to tables and figures. This can be done using the command **source(scriptfile)**.

For generating the familiar output, we should add the option **echo=TRUE**. To avoid abbreviated output, set **max.deparse.length=1000** or another large number. For our example, a master file could look like

Script 19.2: projecty-master.R
```
################################################################
# Bachelor Thesis Mr. Z
# "Best Practice in Using R Scripts"
#
# R Script "master"
# Date of this version: 2016-02-08
################################################################

# Some preparations:
setwd(~/bscthesis/r)
rm(list = ls())

# Call R scripts
source("data.R"         ,echo=TRUE,max=1000) # Data import and cleaning
source("descriptives.R",echo=TRUE,max=1000) # Descriptive statistics
source("estimation.R"   ,echo=TRUE,max=1000) # Estimation of model
source("results.R"      ,echo=TRUE,max=1000) # Tables and Figures
```

19.2. Logging Output in Text Files

Having the results appear on the screen and being able to copy and paste from there might work for small projects. For larger projects, this is impractical. A straightforward way for writing all results to a file is to use the command **sink**. If we want to write all output to a file logfile.txt, the basic syntax is

```
sink("logfile.txt")
# Do your calculations here
sink()
```

All output between starting the log file with **sink("logfile.txt")** and stopping it with **sink()** will be written to the file logfile.txt in the current working directory. We can of course use a different directory e.g. with **sink("~/mydir/logfile.txt")**. Note that comments, commands, and messages are not written to the file by default. The next section describes a more advanced way to store and display *R* results.

19.3. Formatted Documents and Reports with *R* Markdown

R Markdown is simple to use a system that allows to generate formatted HTML, Microsoft Word, and PDF documents which are automatically filled with results from *R*.

19.3.1. Basics

R Markdown can be used with the *R* package **rmarkdown**. An *R* Markdown file is a standard text file but should have the file name extension .Rmd. It includes normal text, formatting instructions, and *R* code. It is processed by *R* and generates a formatted documents. As a simple example, let's turn Script 19.1 into a basic *R* Markdown document. The file looks like this:[1]

─────────── **File ultimate-calcs-rmd.Rmd** ───────────
```
---
title: "Ultimate Question"
author: "F Heiss"
date: "February 08, 2016"
output: pdf_document
---

The main calculation using the method "square root"
(<http://mathworld.wolfram.com/SquareRoot.html>):

```{r}
sqrt(1764)
```
```

The file starts with a header between the two **---** that specifies a few standard properties like the author and the date. Then we see basic text and a URL. The only line that actually involves *R* code is framed by a ```{r} at the beginning and a ``` at the end.

Instead of running this file through *R* directly, we process it with tools from the package **rmarkdown**. If ultimate-calcs-rmd.Rmd is is the current working directory (otherwise, we need to add the path), we can simply create a HTML document with

───────────────────────────────

[1]This file can be downloaded along with all other files presented here at http://www.URfIE.net.

```
render("ultimate-calcs-rmd.Rmd")
```

The HTML document can be opened in any web browser, but also in word processors. Instead of HTML documents, we can create Microsoft Word documents with

```
render("ultimate-calcs-rmd.Rmd",output_format="word_document")
```

If the computer has a working LaTeX system installed, we can create a PDF file with

```
render("ultimate-calcs-rmd.Rmd",output_format="pdf_document")
```

With RStudio, R Markdown is even easier to use: When editing a R Markdown document, there is a `Knit HTML` button on top of the editor window. It will render the document properly. By default, the documents are created in the same directory and with the same file name (except the extension). We can also choose a different file name and/or a different directory with the options **output_file=...** and **output_path=...**, respectively.

All three formatted documents results look similar to each other and are displayed in Figure 19.1.

19.3.2. Advanced Features

There are countless possibilities to create useful and appealing *R* Markdown documents. We can only give a few examples for the most important formatting instructions:

- **# Header 1**, **## Header 2**, and **### Header 3** produce different levels of headers.
- ***word*** prints the word in *italics*.
- ****word**** prints the word in *bold*.
- **`word`** prints the word in code-like `typewriter font`.
- We can created lists with bullets using * at the beginning of a line.
- We can suppress *R* code and/or output for a code chunk with **echo=FALSE** and **include=FALSE**, respectively.
- If you are familiar with LaTeX, displayed and inline formulas can be inserted using $...$ and $$...$$ and the usual LaTeX syntax, respectively.
- Inside of the text, we can add *R* results using **`r someRexpression`**.

Figure 19.1. *R* Markdown example: different output formats

HTML output:

Ultimate Question

F Heiss

February 08, 2016

The main calculation using the method "square root" (http://mathworld.wolfram.com/SquareRoot.html):

```
sqrt(1764)
```

```
## [1] 42
```

Word output:

Ultimate Question

F Heiss

February 08, 2016

The main calculation using the method "square root" (http://mathworld.wolfram.com/SquareRoot.html):

```
sqrt(1764)
```

```
## [1] 42
```

PDF output:

Ultimate Question

F Heiss

February 08, 2016

The main calculation using the method "square root" (http://mathworld.wolfram.com/SquareRoot.html):

```
sqrt(1764)
```

```
## [1] 42
```

Different formatting options for text and code chunks are demonstrated in the following *R* Markdown script. Its HTML output is shown in Figure 19.2.

────────────────── **File rmarkdown-examples.Rmd** ──────────────────

```
---
title: "Different R Markdown Features"
author: "F. Heiss"
---

# Header 1: Hiding Input and/or Output

We can run *R* code but **hide**

* the  *input* with `echo=FALSE` and/or
* the  *results* with `include=FALSE`

```{r,echo=FALSE,include=FALSE}
require(foreign);require(stargazer)
gpa1 <- read.dta("http://fmwww.bc.edu/ec-p/data/wooldridge/gpa1.dta")
```

Header 2: Usual R Output

By *default*, both input commands and *R* output are displayed:
```{r}
table(gpa1$age)
olsres <- lm(colGPA ~ hsGPA, data=gpa1)
stargazer(olsres,type="text")
```

Header 3: Formulas and inline R results

We can also include formulas using LaTeX syntax if
we have LaTeX installed.
$$\overline x = \sum_{i=1}^n x_i$$

And we can use *R* results inside of the text like in
$\hat\beta_1=$ `r coef(olsres)[2]`.
```

19.3.3. Bottom Line

There are various situations in which *R* Markdown can be useful. It can simply be used to generate a structured log for all analyses and results. It can also be used for short research papers. While I can very well imagine a take-home assignment written in *R* Markdown, a Ph.D. thesis is likely to be too complex. For more information on *R* Markdown, see http://rmarkdown.rstudio.com.

Figure 19.2. *R* Markdown examples: HTML output

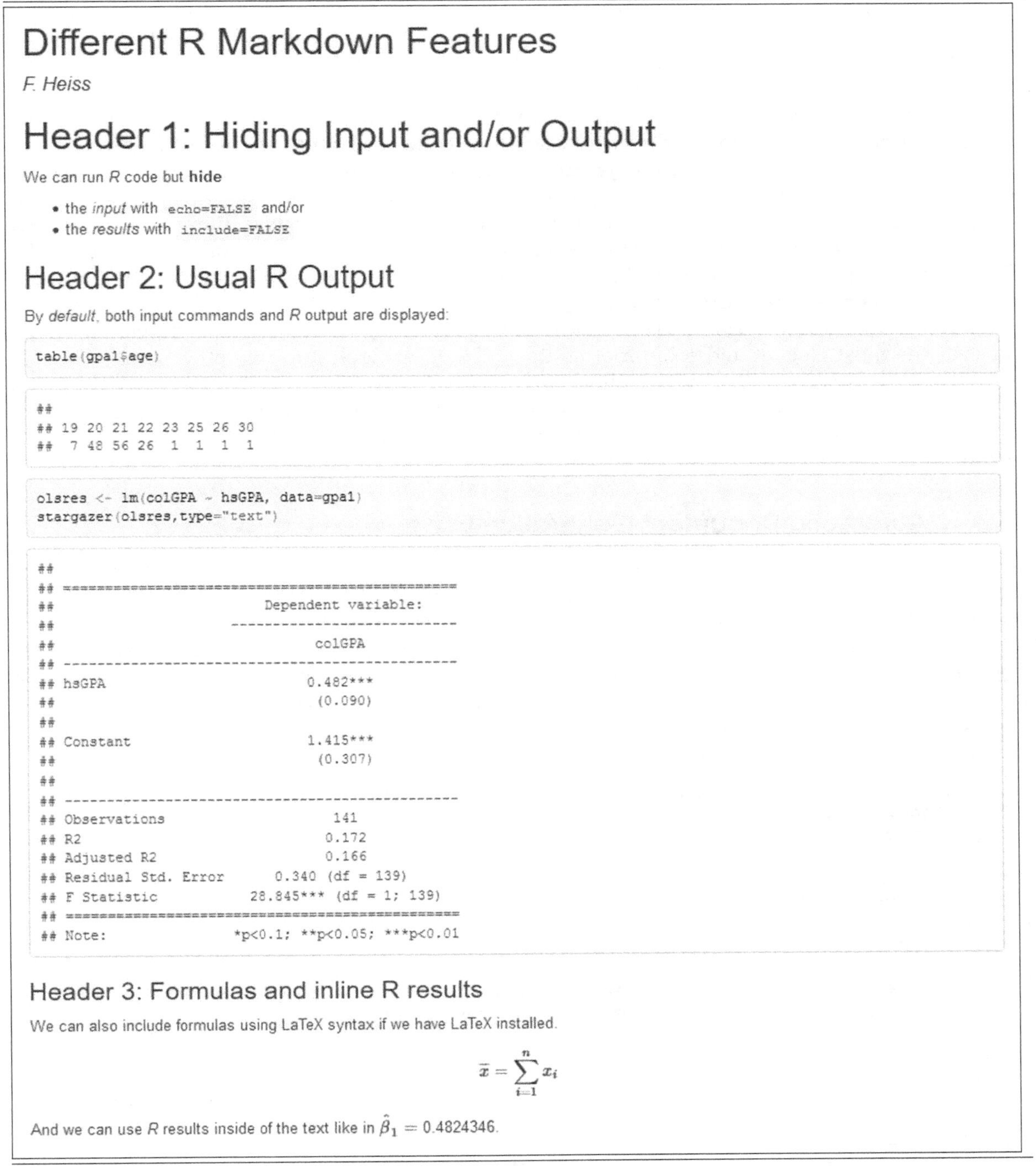

Different R Markdown Features

F. Heiss

Header 1: Hiding Input and/or Output

We can run *R* code but **hide**

- the *input* with `echo=FALSE` and/or
- the *results* with `include=FALSE`

Header 2: Usual R Output

By *default*, both input commands and *R* output are displayed:

```
table(gpa1$age)
```

```
##
## 19 20 21 22 23 25 26 30
##  7 48 56 26  1  1  1  1
```

```
olsres <- lm(colGPA ~ hsGPA, data=gpa1)
stargazer(olsres,type="text")
```

```
##
## =============================================
##                    Dependent variable:
##                  ---------------------------
##                            colGPA
## -------------------------------------------
## hsGPA                      0.482***
##                            (0.090)
##
## Constant                   1.415***
##                            (0.307)
##
## -------------------------------------------
## Observations                  141
## R2                           0.172
## Adjusted R2                  0.166
## Residual Std. Error    0.340 (df = 139)
## F Statistic          28.845*** (df = 1; 139)
## =============================================
## Note:            *p<0.1; **p<0.05; ***p<0.01
```

Header 3: Formulas and inline R results

We can also include formulas using LaTeX syntax if we have LaTeX installed.

$$\bar{x} = \sum_{i=1}^{n} x_i$$

And we can use *R* results inside of the text like in $\hat{\beta}_1 = 0.4824346$.

19.4. Combining *R* with LaTeX

If we need more typesetting power than *R* Markdown is capable of, we can resort to LaTeX. It is a powerful and free system for generating documents. In economics and other fields with a lot of maths involved, it is widely used – in many areas, it is the *de facto* standard. It is also popular for typesetting articles and books. This book is an example for a complex document created by LaTeX. At least basic knowledge of LaTeX as well as a working installation is needed to follow this section.

We show how *R* and LaTeX can be used jointly for convenient and automated document preparation. Several packages allow a direct translation of tables and other entities to LaTeX code. We have already seen the command **stargazer** for producing regression tables. So far, we have always used the option **type="text"** to generate directly readable results. With **type="latex"** instead, **stargazer** will generate LaTeX code for the table. For general tables, the command **xtable** from package **xtable** provides a flexible generation of LaTeX (and HTML) tables. Both are flexibly customizable to produce tailored results. There are also other packages to generate LaTeX output – examples are *memisc*, *texreg*, and *outreg*.

Now we have to get the generated code into our LaTeX file. Copy and paste from the console works but isn't the most elegant and fool-proof strategy. Here, we look into two other ones. First, we present **knitr** in Section 19.4.1 which allows to combine *R* with LaTeX code in one source document in a way similar to *R* Markdown. Section 19.4.2 briefly describes an approach that keeps *R* and LaTeX code separate but still automatically includes the up-to-date version of *R* results in the output document.

19.4.1. Automatic Document Generation using *Sweave* and *knitr*

The package *Sweave* implements a combination of LaTeX and *R* code in one source file and is in this sense similar to *R* Markdown. This file is first processed by *R* to generate a standard .tex file that combines the LaTeX part of the source file with the properly formatted results of the calculations, tables and figures generated in *R*. This file can then be processed like any other standard LaTeX file. The package **knitr** can be seen as a successor. It works very much like *Sweave* but is somewhat more flexible, convenient, and versatile. This section demonstrates basic usage of **knitr**.

A **knitr** file is a standard text file with the file name extension .Rnw. The basic "Ultimate Question" document from above translated to a **knitr** file is the following:

─────── File **ultimate-calcs-knitr.Rnw** ───────

```
\documentclass{article}
\begin{document}

\title{Ultimate Question}
\author{Florian Heiss}
\date{February 08, 2016}
\maketitle

The main calculation using the method ``square root''\\
(\texttt{http://mathworld.wolfram.com/SquareRoot.html}):

<<>>=
sqrt(1764)
@

\end{document}
```

The file contains standard LATEX code. It also includes an *R* code chunk which is started with `<<>>=` and ended with `@`. This file is processed ("knitted") by the **knitr** package using the command

```
knit("ultimate-calcs-knitr.Rnw")
```

to produce a pure LATEX file `ultimate-calcs-knitr.tex`. This file can in the next step be processed using a standard LATEX installation. *R* can also call any command line / shell commands appropriate for the operating system using the function **shell("some OS command")**. With a working `pdflatex` command installed on the system, we can therefore produce a .pdf from a .Rnw file with the *R* commands

```
knit("ultimate-calcs-knitr.Rnw")
shell("pdflatex ultimate-calcs-knitr.tex")
```

If we are using LATEX references and the like, pdflatex might have to be called repeatedly.

RStudio can be used to conveniently work with **knitr** including syntax highlighting for the LATEX code. By default, RStudio is set to work with **Sweave** instead, at least at the time of writing this. To use **knitr**, change the option `Tools → Global Options → Sweave → Weave Rnw files using` from `Sweave` to `knitr`. Then we can produce a .pdf file from a .Rnw file with a click of a "Compile PDF" button.

The *R* code chunks in a **knitr** can be customized with options by starting the chunk with `<<chunk-name, option 1, option 2, ...>>=` to change the way the *R* results are displayed. Important examples include

- **echo=FALSE**: Don't print include the *R* commands
- **results="hide"**: Don't print the *R* output
- **results="asis"**: The results are LATEX code, for example generated by **xtable** or **stargazer**.
- **error=FALSE**, **warning=FALSE**, **message=FALSE**: Don't print any errors, warnings, or messages from *R*.
- **fig=TRUE, width=..., height=...**: Include the generated figure with the respective width and height (in inches).

We can also display in-line results from *R* with **\Sexpr(...)**.

The following `.Rnw` file demonstrates some of these features. After running this file through **knit** and `pdflatex`, the resulting PDF file is shown in Figure 19.3. For more details on *knitr*, see Xie (2015).

─────────────────── **File knitr-example.Rnw** ───────────────────

```
\documentclass[fontsize=12pt,DIV=30]{scrartcl}
\begin{document}

\title{A Demonstration of Using \LaTeX\ with R}
\author{Florian Heiss}
\date{February 08, 2016}
\maketitle
\thispagestyle{empty}

<<prepare, echo=FALSE, results="hide", warning=FALSE, message=FALSE>>=
# Code chunk: Preparations. No code, output, warnings, or messages.
library(foreign);library(stargazer);library(xtable);library(knitr)
gpa1 <- read.dta("http://fmwww.bc.edu/ec-p/data/wooldridge/gpa1.dta")
gender <- factor(gpa1$male,labels=c("female","male"))
@

Our data set has \Sexpr{nrow(gpa1)} observations.
The distribution of gender is the following:
<<gendertab, echo=FALSE, results="asis">>=
# Code chunk: Table using xtable.
# No code, output "asis" since xtable generates LaTeX code.
xtable( table(gender) )
@

Table \ref{t:reg} shows the regression results.
<<regtab , echo=FALSE, results="asis">>=
# Code chunk: Regression table with stargazer.
# Table using xtable. No code, output "asis" since xtable generates LaTeX code.
res1 <- lm(colGPA ~ hsGPA        , data=gpa1)
res2 <- lm(colGPA ~         ACT, data=gpa1)
res3 <- lm(colGPA ~ hsGPA + ACT, data=gpa1)
stargazer(res1,res2,res3, keep.stat=c("n","rsq"), header=FALSE,
          type="latex",title="Regression Results",label="t:reg")
@

In model (1), $\hat\beta_1=\Sexpr{round(coef(res1)[2],3)}$.
Finally, here is our regression graph:

\centering
<<regfig, echo=FALSE, fig.width=3, fig.height=2>>=
# Code chunk: Plot.
# No code, figure dimensions given in inch.
par(mar=c(2,2,1,1))
plot(gpa1$hsGPA, gpa1$colGPA)
abline(res1)
@

\end{document}
```

Figure 19.3. PDF Result from `knitr-example.Rnw`

A Demonstration of Using LaTeX with R

Florian Heiss

February 08, 2016

Our data set has 141 observations. The distribution of gender is the following:

	gender
female	67
male	74

Table 1 shows the regression results.

Table 1: Regression Results

	Dependent variable:		
	colGPA		
	(1)	(2)	(3)
hsGPA	0.482***		0.453***
	(0.090)		(0.096)
ACT		0.027**	0.009
		(0.011)	(0.011)
Constant	1.415***	2.403***	1.286***
	(0.307)	(0.264)	(0.341)
Observations	141	141	141
R^2	0.172	0.043	0.176
Note:	*p<0.1; **p<0.05; ***p<0.01		

In model (1), $\hat{\beta}_1 = 0.482$. Finally, here is our regression graph:

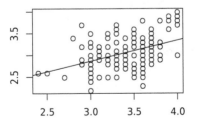

19.4.2. Separating *R* and LATEX code

When working with ***knitr*** or ***Sweave***, the calculations in *R* are performed whenever the document is "knitted" to a .tex file. In this way, we make sure that the resulting document is always up-to-date and the source file contains all *R* code for maximum transparency. This can also be a drawback: If the calculations in *R* are time-consuming, we typically don't want to repeat them over and over again whenever we want to typeset the document because of a small change in the text.

Here, we look at a simple approach to separate the calculations in *R* from the LATEX code. At the same time we want *R* to automatically change tables, figures, and even number in the text whenever we rerun the calculations. In Section 1.4.5, we have already discussed the automated generation and export of graphs. For use in combination with pdflatex, PDF files work best since they are scaled without any problems. In other setups, EPS or PNG files work well. In a similar way, we create tables and store them as text files. We can even write single numbers into text files. We already know that a straightforward way to write text into a file is **sink**. In the LATEX document, we simply include the graphics in a standard way and use \input{...} commands to add tables, number, and other results to the appropriate place.

Let's replicate the ***knitr*** example that generated Figure 19.3 using this approach. The following *R* code does all calculations and stores the results in the test files numb-n.txt, tab-gender.txt, tab-regr.txt, and numb-b1.txt, as well as the graphics file regr-graph.pdf:

Script 19.3: LaTeXwithR.R

```
library(foreign);library(stargazer);library(xtable)
gpa1 <- read.dta("http://fmwww.bc.edu/ec-p/data/wooldridge/gpa1.dta")


# Number of obs.
sink("numb-n.txt"); cat(nrow(gpa1)); sink()
# generate frequency table in file "tab-gender.txt"
gender <- factor(gpa1$male,labels=c("female","male"))
sink("tab-gender.txt")
xtable( table(gender) )
sink()

# calculate OLS results
res1 <- lm(colGPA ~ hsGPA        , data=gpa1)
res2 <- lm(colGPA ~         ACT, data=gpa1)
res3 <- lm(colGPA ~ hsGPA + ACT, data=gpa1)

# write regression table to file "tab-regr.txt"
sink("tab-regr.txt")
stargazer(res1,res2,res3, keep.stat=c("n","rsq"),
           type="latex",title="Regression Results",label="t:reg")
sink()

# b1 hat
sink("numb-b1.txt"); cat(round(coef(res1)[2],3)); sink()

# Generate graph as PDF file
pdf(file = "regr-graph.pdf", width = 3, height = 2)
par(mar=c(2,2,1,1))
plot(gpa1$hsGPA, gpa1$colGPA)
abline(res1)
dev.off()
```

After this script was run, the four text files have the following content:[2]

─────────────── File **numb-n.txt** ───────────────

```
141
```

─────────────── File **numb-b1.txt** ───────────────

```
0.482
```

─────────────── File **tab-gender.txt** ───────────────

```
% latex table generated in R 3.2.1 by xtable 1.7-4 package
% Mon Jan 25 15:10:25 2016
\begin{table}[ht]
\centering
\begin{tabular}{rr}
  \hline
 & gender \\
  \hline
female &  67 \\
  male &  74 \\
   \hline
\end{tabular}
\end{table}
```

─────────────── File **tab-regr.txt** ───────────────

```
% Table created by stargazer v.5.2 by Marek Hlavac, Harvard University.
% E-mail: hlavac at fas.harvard.edu
% Date and time: Mon, Jan 25, 2016 - 2:15:11 PM
\begin{table}[!htbp] \centering
  \caption{Regression Results}
  \label{t:reg}
\begin{tabular}{@{\extracolsep{5pt}}lccc}
\\[-1.8ex]\hline
\hline \\[-1.8ex]
 & \multicolumn{3}{c}{\textit{Dependent variable:}} \\
\cline{2-4}
\\[-1.8ex] & \multicolumn{3}{c}{colGPA} \\
\\[-1.8ex] & (1) & (2) & (3)\\
\hline \\[-1.8ex]
 hsGPA & 0.482$^{***}$ &  & 0.453$^{***}$ \\
  & (0.090) &  & (0.096) \\
  & & & \\
 ACT &  & 0.027$^{**}$ & 0.009 \\
  &  & (0.011) & (0.011) \\
  & & & \\
 Constant & 1.415$^{***}$ & 2.403$^{***}$ & 1.286$^{***}$ \\
  & (0.307) & (0.264) & (0.341) \\
  & & & \\
\hline \\[-1.8ex]
Observations & 141 & 141 & 141 \\
R$^{2}$ & 0.172 & 0.043 & 0.176 \\
\hline
\hline \\[-1.8ex]
\textit{Note:}  & \multicolumn{3}{r}{$^{*}$p$<$0.1; $^{**}$p$<$0.05;
$^{***}$p$<$0.01} \\
\end{tabular}
\end{table}
```

─────────────────────

[2] Make sure to use **setwd** first to choose the correct directory where we want to store the results.

Now we write a LaTeX file with the appropriate \input{...} commands to put tables and numbers into the right place. A file that generates the same document as the one in Figure 19.3 is the following:

```
——————— File LaTeXwithR.tex ———————
\documentclass[fontsize=12pt,DIV=30]{scrartcl}
\usepackage{graphicx}
\begin{document}

\title{A Demonstration of Using \LaTeX\ with R}
\author{Florian Heiss}
\date{February 08, 2016}
\maketitle
\thispagestyle{empty}

Our data set has \input{numb-n.txt} observations.
The distribution of gender is the following:
\input{tab-gender.txt}

Table \ref{t:reg} shows the regression results.
\input{tab-regr.txt}

In model (1), $\hat\beta_1=\input{numb-b1.txt}$.
Finally, here is our regression graph:

\centering\includegraphics{regr-graph.pdf}

\end{document}
```

Whenever we update the calculations, we rerun the *R* script and create updated tables, numbers, and graphs. Whenever we update the text in our document, LaTeX will use the latest version of the results to generate a publication-ready PDF document.

We have automatically generated exactly the same PDF document in two different ways in this and the previous section. Which one is better? It depends. In smaller projects with little and fast *R* computations, **knitr** is convenient because it combines everything in one file. This is also the ideal in terms of reproducibility. For larger projects with many or time-consuming *R* calculations, it is more convenient to separate calculations from the text, since **knitr** requires to redo all calculations whenever we compile the LaTeX code. This book was done in the separated spirit described in this section.

Part IV.

Appendices

R Scripts

1. Scripts Used in Chapter 01

─────────────── Script 1.1: `R-as-a-Calculator.R` ───────────────

```
1+1
5*(4-1)^2
sqrt( log(10) )
```

─────────────── Script 1.2: `Install-Packages.R` ───────────────

```
# This R script downloads and installs all packages used at some point.
# It needs to be run once for each computer/user only

install.packages("AER")
install.packages("car")
install.packages("censReg")
install.packages("dummies")
install.packages("dynlm")
install.packages("effects")
install.packages("ggplot2")
install.packages("lmtest")
install.packages("maps")
install.packages("mfx")
install.packages("orcutt")
install.packages("pdfetch")
install.packages("plm")
install.packages("sandwich")
install.packages("quantreg")
install.packages("rmarkdown")
install.packages("sampleSelection")
install.packages("stargazer")
install.packages("survival")
install.packages("systemfit")
install.packages("truncreg")
install.packages("tseries")
install.packages("urca")
install.packages("xtable")
install.packages("vars")
install.packages("xts")
install.packages("zoo")
```

─────────────── Script 1.3: `Objects.R` ───────────────

```
# generate object x (no output):
x <- 5

# display x & x^2:
x
x^2

# generate objects y&z with immediate display using ():
(y <- 3)
(z <- y^x)
```

─────────────────── Script 1.4: `Vectors.R` ───────────────────

```
# Define a with immediate output through parantheses:
(a <- c(1,2,3,4,5,6))
(b <- a+1)
(c <- a+b)
(d <- b*c)
sqrt(d)
```

─────────────────── Script 1.5: `Vector-Functions.R` ───────────────────

```
# Define vector
(a <- c(7,2,6,9,4,1,3))

# Basic functions:
sort(a)
length(a)
min(a)
max(a)
sum(a)
prod(a)

# Creating special vectors:
numeric(20)
rep(1,20)
seq(50)
5:15
seq(4,20,2)
```

─────────────────── Script 1.6: `Logical.R` ───────────────────

```
# Basic comparisons:
0 == 1
0 < 1

# Logical vectors:
( a <- c(7,2,6,9,4,1,3) )

( b <- a<3 | a>=6 )
```

─────────────────── Script 1.7: `Factors.R` ───────────────────

```
# Original ratings:
x <- c(3,2,2,3,1,2,3,2,1,2)
xf <- factor(x, labels=c("bad","okay","good"))
x
xf
```

─────────────────── Script 1.8: `Vector-Indices.R` ───────────────────

```
# Create a vector "avgs":
avgs <- c(.366, .358, .356, .349, .346)

# Create a string vector of names:
players <- c("Cobb","Hornsby","Jackson","O'Doul","Delahanty")

# Assign names to vector and display vector:
names(avgs) <- players
avgs

# Indices by number:
avgs[2]
```

```
avgs[1:4]

# Indices by name:
avgs["Jackson"]

# Logical indices:
avgs[ avgs>=0.35 ]
```

──────────── Script 1.9: `Matrices.R` ────────────

```
# Generating matrix A from one vector with all values:
v <- c(2,-4,-1,5,7,0)
( A <- matrix(v,nrow=2) )

# Generating matrix A from two vectors corresponding to rows:
row1 <- c(2,-1,7); row2 <- c(-4,5,0)
( A <- rbind(row1, row2) )

# Generating matrix A from three vectors corresponding to columns:
col1 <- c(2,-4); col2 <- c(-1,5); col3 <- c(7,0)
( A <- cbind(col1, col2, col3) )

# Giving names to rows and columns:
colnames(A) <- c("Alpha","Beta","Gamma")
rownames(A) <- c("Aleph","Bet")
A

# Diaginal and identity matrices:
diag( c(4,2,6) )
diag( 3 )

# Indexing for extracting elements (still using A from above):
A[2,1]
A[,2]
A[,c(1,3)]
```

──────────── Script 1.10: `Matrix-Operators.R` ────────────

```
A <- matrix( c(2,-4,-1,5,7,0), nrow=2)
B <- matrix( c(2,1,0,3,-1,5), nrow=2)
A
B
A*B

# Transpose:
(C <- t(B) )

# Matrix multiplication:
(D <- A %*% C )

# Inverse:
solve(D)
```

──────────── Script 1.11: `Lists.R` ────────────

```
# Generate a list object:
mylist <- list( A=seq(8,36,4), this="that", idm = diag(3))

# Print whole list:
mylist
```

```
# Vector of names:
names(mylist)

# Print component "A":
mylist$A
```

_____ Script 1.12: `Data-frames.R` _____
```
# Define one x vector for all:
year      <- c(2008,2009,2010,2011,2012,2013)
# Define a matrix of y values:
product1<-c(0,3,6,9,7,8); product2<-c(1,2,3,5,9,6); product3<-c(2,4,4,2,3,2)
sales_mat <- cbind(product1,product2,product3)
rownames(sales_mat) <- year
# The matrix looks like this:
sales_mat

# Create a data frame and display it:
sales <- as.data.frame(sales_mat)
sales
```

_____ Script 1.13: `Data-frames-vars.R` _____
```
# Accessing a single variable:
sales$product2

# Generating a new  variable in the data frame:
sales$totalv1 <- sales$product1 + sales$product2 + sales$product3

# The same but using "with":
sales$totalv2 <- with(sales, product1+product2+product3)

# The same but using "attach":
attach(sales)
sales$totalv3 <- product1+product2+product3
detach(sales)

# Result:
sales
```

_____ Script 1.14: `Data-frames-subsets.R` _____
```
# Full data frame (from Data-frames.R, has to be run first)
sales

# Subset: all years in which sales of product 3 were >=3
subset(sales, product3>=3)
```

_____ Script 1.15: `RData-Example.R` _____
```
# Note: "sales" is defined in Data-frames.R, so it has to be run first!
# save data frame as RData file (in the current working directory)
save(sales, file = "oursalesdata.RData")

# remove data frame "sales" from memory
rm(sales)

# Does variable "sales" exist?
exists("sales")
```

```
# Load data set   (in the current working directory):
load("oursalesdata.RData")

# Does variable "sales" exist?
exists("sales")

sales

# averages of the variables:
colMeans(sales)
```

_____ Script 1.16: `Example-Data.R` _____
```
# load package for dealing with Stata files:
library(foreign)
# download data and create data frame "affairs":
affairs<-read.dta("http://fmwww.bc.edu/ec-p/data/wooldridge/affairs.dta")

# first six rows:
head(affairs)

#averages:
colMeans(affairs)
```

_____ Script 1.17: `Plot-Overlays.R` _____
```
plot(x,y, main="Example for an Outlier")
points(8,1)
abline(a=0.31,b=0.97,lty=2,lwd=2)
text(7,2,"outlier",pos=3)
arrows(7,2,8,1,length=0.15)
```

_____ Script 1.18: `Plot-Matplot.R` _____
```
# Define one x vector for all:
year      <- c(2008,2009,2010,2011,2012,2013)
# Define a matrix of y values:
product1 <- c(0,3,6,9,7,8)
product2 <- c(1,2,3,5,9,6)
product3 <- c(2,4,4,2,3,2)
sales <- cbind(product1,product2,product3)
# plot
matplot(year,sales, type="b", lwd=c(1,2,3), col="black" )
```

_____ Script 1.19: `Plot-Legend.R` _____
```
curve( dnorm(x,0,1), -10, 10, lwd=1, lty=1)
curve( dnorm(x,0,2),add=TRUE, lwd=2, lty=2)
curve( dnorm(x,0,3),add=TRUE, lwd=3, lty=3)
# Add the legend
legend("topright",c("sigma=1","sigma=2","sigma=3"), lwd=1:3, lty=1:3)
```

_____ Script 1.20: `Plot-Legend2.R` _____
```
curve( dnorm(x,0,1), -10, 10, lwd=1, lty=1)
curve( dnorm(x,0,2),add=TRUE, lwd=2, lty=2)
curve( dnorm(x,0,3),add=TRUE, lwd=3, lty=3)
# Add the legend with greek sigma
legend("topleft",expression(sigma==1,sigma==2,sigma==3),lwd=1:3,lty=1:3)
# Add the text with the formula, centered at x=6 and y=0.3
text(6,.3,
     expression(f(x)==frac(1,sqrt(2*pi)*sigma)*e^{-frac(x^2,2*sigma^2)}))
```

──────────── Script 1.21: Maps-Example.R ────────────

```
library(maps)

# load unemployment data and FIPS county codes (included in maps)
data(unemp)
data(county.fips)

# match counties from unemployment data to counties plotted by FIPS code
plotdata <- unemp$unemp[match(county.fips$fips, unemp$fips)]
# transform data to color code: gray scale. max unemp=0 (black)
plotcol  <- gray(1-plotdata/max(plotdata))

# plot county map filled respective color (no boundary lines):
map("county", col=plotcol, fill=TRUE,resolution=0,lty = 0)

# add state boundaries as black lines:
map("state",add = TRUE)
```

──────────── Script 1.22: Descr-Tables.R ────────────

```
# load data set
library(foreign)
affairs<-read.dta("http://fmwww.bc.edu/ec-p/data/wooldridge/affairs.dta")

# Generate "Factors" to attach labels
haskids <- factor(affairs$kids,labels=c("no","yes"))
mlab <- c("very unhappy","unhappy","average","happy", "very happy")
marriage <- factor(affairs$ratemarr, labels=mlab)

# Frequencies for having kids:
table(haskids)
# Marriage ratings (share):
prop.table(table(marriage))

# Contigency table: counts (display & store in var.)
(countstab <- table(marriage,haskids))

# Share within "marriage" (i.e. within a row):
prop.table(countstab, margin=1)
# Share within "haskids"  (i.e. within a column):
prop.table(countstab, margin=2)
```

──────────── Script 1.23: Histogram.R ────────────

```
# Load data
library(foreign)
ceosal1<-read.dta("http://fmwww.bc.edu/ec-p/data/wooldridge/ceosal1.dta")

# Extract ROE to single vector
ROE <- ceosal1$roe

# Subfigure (a): histogram (counts)
hist(ROE)

# Subfigure (b): histogram (densities, explicit breaks)
hist(ROE, breaks=c(0,5,10,20,30,60) )
```

──────────── Script 1.24: KDensity.R ────────────

```
# Subfigure (c): kernel density estimate
plot( density(ROE) )
```

```
# Subfigure (d): overlay
hist(ROE, freq=FALSE, ylim=c(0,.07))
lines( density(ROE), lwd=3 )
```

———————————— Script 1.25: Descr-Stats.R ————————————
```
library(foreign)
ceosal1<-read.dta("http://fmwww.bc.edu/ec-p/data/wooldridge/ceosal1.dta")

# sample average:
mean(ceosal1$salary)
# sample median:
median(ceosal1$salary)
#standard deviation:
sd(ceosal1$salary)
# summary information:
summary(ceosal1$salary)

# correlation with ROE:
cor(ceosal1$salary, ceosal1$roe)
```

———————————— Script 1.26: PMF-example.R ————————————
```
# Values for x: all between 0 and 10
x <- seq(0,10)

# pmf for all these values
fx <- dbinom(x, 10, 0.2)

# Table(matrix) of values:
cbind(x, fx)
# Plot
plot(x, fx, type="h")
```

———————————— Script 1.27: Random-Numbers.R ————————————
```
# Sample from a standard normal RV with sample size n=5:
rnorm(5)
# A different sample from the same distribution:
rnorm(5)

# Set the seed of the random number generator and take two samples:
set.seed(6254137)
rnorm(5)
rnorm(5)

# Reset the seed to the same value to get the same samples again:
set.seed(6254137)
rnorm(5)
rnorm(5)
```

———————————— Script 1.28: Example-C-2.R ————————————
```
# Manually enter raw data from Wooldridge, Table C.3:
SR87<-c(10,1,6,.45,1.25,1.3,1.06,3,8.18,1.67,.98,1,.45,
                              5.03,8,9,18,.28,7,3.97)
SR88<-c(3,1,5,.5,1.54,1.5,.8,2,.67,1.17,.51,.5,.61,6.7,
                              4,7,19,.2,5,3.83)
# Calculate Change (the parentheses just display the results):
(Change <- SR88 - SR87)
```

```
# Ingredients to CI formula
(avgCh<- mean(Change))
(n     <- length(Change))
(sdCh <- sd(Change))
(se    <- sdCh/sqrt(n))
(c     <- qt(.975, n-1))

# Confidence intervall:
c( avgCh - c*se, avgCh + c*se )
```

_____ Script 1.29: `Example-C-3.R` _____

```
library(foreign)
audit <- read.dta("http://fmwww.bc.edu/ec-p/data/wooldridge/audit.dta")

# Ingredients to CI formula
(avgy<- mean(audit$y))
(n     <- length(audit$y))
(sdy <- sd(audit$y))
(se    <- sdy/sqrt(n))
(c     <- qnorm(.975))

# 95% Confidence intervall:
avgy + c * c(-se,+se)
# 99% Confidence intervall:
avgy + qnorm(.995) * c(-se,+se)
```

_____ Script 1.30: `Critical-Values-t.R` _____

```
# degrees of freedom = n-1:
df <- 19
# significance levels:
alpha.one.tailed = c(0.1, 0.05, 0.025, 0.01, 0.005, .001)
alpha.two.tailed = alpha.one.tailed * 2

# critical values & table:
CV <- qt(1 - alpha.one.tailed, df)
cbind(alpha.one.tailed, alpha.two.tailed, CV)
```

_____ Script 1.31: `Example-C-5.R` _____

```
# Note: we reuse variables from Example-C-3.R. It has to be run first!
# t statistic for H0: mu=0:
(t <- avgy/se)

# Critical values for t distribution with n-1=240 d.f.:
alpha.one.tailed = c(0.1, 0.05, 0.025, 0.01, 0.005, .001)
CV <- qt(1 - alpha.one.tailed, n-1)
cbind(alpha.one.tailed, CV)
```

_____ Script 1.32: `Example-C-6.R` _____

```
# Note: we reuse variables from Example-C-3.R. It has to be run first!
# t statistic for H0: mu=0:
(t <- avgCh/se)

# p value
(p <- pt(t,n-1))
```

──────────────── Script 1.33: `Example-C-7.R` ────────────────

```
# t statistic for H0: mu=0:
t <- -4.276816

# p value
(p <- pt(t,240))
```

──────────────── Script 1.34: `Examples-C2-C6.R` ────────────────

```
# data for the scrap rates examples:
SR87<-c(10,1,6,.45,1.25,1.3,1.06,3,8.18,1.67,.98,1,.45,5.03,8,9,18,.28,
                                                                 7,3.97)
SR88<-c(3,1,5,.5,1.54,1.5,.8,2,.67,1.17,.51,.5,.61,6.7,4,7,19,.2,5,3.83)
Change <- SR88 - SR87

# Example C.2: two-sided CI
t.test(Change)
# Example C.6: 1-sided test:
t.test(Change, alternative="less")
```

──────────────── Script 1.35: `Examples-C3-C5-C7.R` ────────────────

```
library(foreign)
audit <- read.dta("http://fmwww.bc.edu/ec-p/data/wooldridge/audit.dta")

# Example C.3: two-sided CI
t.test(audit$y)
# Examples C.5 & C.7: 1-sided test:
t.test(audit$y, alternative="less")
```

──────────────── Script 1.36: `Test-Results-List.R` ────────────────

```
library(foreign)
audit <- read.dta("http://fmwww.bc.edu/ec-p/data/wooldridge/audit.dta")

# store test results as a list "testres"
testres <- t.test(audit$y)

# print results:
testres

# component names: which results can be accessed?
names(testres)

# p-value
testres$p.value
```

──────────────── Script 1.37: `Simulate-Estimate.R` ────────────────

```
# Set the random seed
set.seed(123456)

# Draw a sample given the population parameters
sample <- rnorm(100,10,2)

# Estimate the population mean with the sample average
mean(sample)

# Draw a different sample and estimate again:
sample <- rnorm(100,10,2)
mean(sample)
```

```
# Draw a third sample and estimate again:
sample <- rnorm(100,10,2)
mean(sample)
```

──────────────────── Script 1.38: Simulation-Repeated.R ────────────────────

```
# Set the random seed
set.seed(123456)

# initialize ybar to a vector of length r=10000 to later store results:
ybar <- numeric(10000)

# repeat 10000 times:
for(j in 1:10000) {
  # Draw a sample and store the sample mean in pos. j=1,2,... of ybar:
  sample <- rnorm(100,10,2)
  ybar[j] <- mean(sample)
}
```

──────────────────── Script 1.39: Simulation-Repeated-Results.R ────────────────────

```
# The first 20 of 10000 estimates:
ybar[1:20]

# Simulated mean:
mean(ybar)

# Simulated variance:
var(ybar)

# Simulated density:
plot(density(ybar))
curve( dnorm(x,10,sqrt(.04)), add=TRUE,lty=2)
```

──────────────────── Script 1.40: Simulation-Inference.R ────────────────────

```
# Set the random seed
set.seed(123456)

# initialize vectors to later store results:
CIlower <- numeric(10000); CIupper <- numeric(10000)
pvalue1 <- numeric(10000); pvalue2 <- numeric(10000)

# repeat 10000 times:
for(j in 1:10000) {
  # Draw a sample
  sample <- rnorm(100,10,2)
  # test the (correct) null hypothesis mu=10:
  testres1 <- t.test(sample,mu=10)
  # store CI & p value:
  CIlower[j] <- testres1$conf.int[1]
  CIupper[j] <- testres1$conf.int[2]
  pvalue1[j] <- testres1$p.value
  # test the (incorrect) null hypothesis mu=9.5 & store the p value:
  pvalue2[j] <- t.test(sample,mu=9.5)$p.value
}

# Test results as logical value
reject1<-pvalue1<=0.05;   reject2<-pvalue2<=0.05
```

```
table(reject1)
table(reject2)
```

—————————————— Script 1.41: Simulation-Inference-Figure.R ——————————————
```
# Needs Simulation-Inference.R to be run first
# color vector:
color <- rep(gray(.5),100)
color[reject1[1:100]] <- "black"

# Prepare empty plot with correct axis limits & labels:
plot(0, xlim=c(9,11), ylim=c(1,100),
                    ylab="Sample No.", xlab="", main="Correct H0")
# Vertical line at 10:
abline(v=10, lty=2)
# Add the 100 first CIs (y is equal to j for both points):
for(j in 1:100) {
  lines(c(CIlower[j],CIupper[j]),c(j,j),col=color[j],lwd=2)
}
```

2. Scripts Used in Chapter 02

—————————————— Script 2.1: Example-2-3.R ——————————————
```
require(foreign)
ceosal1<-read.dta("http://fmwww.bc.edu/ec-p/data/wooldridge/ceosal1.dta")
attach(ceosal1)

# ingredients to the OLS formulas
cov(roe,salary)
var(roe)
mean(salary)
mean(roe)

# manual calculation of OLS coefficients
( b1hat <- cov(roe,salary)/var(roe) )
( b0hat <- mean(salary) - b1hat*mean(roe) )

# "detach" the data frame
detach(ceosal1)
```

—————————————— Script 2.2: Example-2-3-2.R ——————————————
```
require(foreign)
ceosal1<-read.dta("http://fmwww.bc.edu/ec-p/data/wooldridge/ceosal1.dta")

# OLS regression
lm( salary ~ roe, data=ceosal1 )
```

—————————————— Script 2.3: Example-2-3-3.R ——————————————
```
library(foreign)
ceosal1<-read.dta("http://fmwww.bc.edu/ec-p/data/wooldridge/ceosal1.dta")

# OLS regression
CEOregres <- lm( salary ~ roe, data=ceosal1 )

# Scatter plot (restrict y axis limits)
plot(ceosal1$roe, ceosal1$salary, ylim=c(0,4000))
```

```
# Add OLS regression line
abline(CEOregres)
```

_____ Script 2.4: `Example-2-4.R` _____
```
library(foreign)
wage1<-read.dta("http://fmwww.bc.edu/ec-p/data/wooldridge/wage1.dta")

# OLS regression:
lm(wage ~ educ, data=wage1)
```

_____ Script 2.5: `Example-2-5.R` _____
```
require(foreign)
vote1<-read.dta("http://fmwww.bc.edu/ec-p/data/wooldridge/vote1.dta")

# OLS regression (parentheses for immediate output):
( VOTEres <- lm(voteA ~ shareA, data=vote1) )

# scatter plot with regression line:
plot(vote1$shareA, vote1$voteA)
abline(VOTEres)
```

_____ Script 2.6: `Example-2-6.R` _____
```
require(foreign)
ceosal1<-read.dta("http://fmwww.bc.edu/ec-p/data/wooldridge/ceosal1.dta")

# extract variables as vectors:
sal <- ceosal1$salary
roe <- ceosal1$roe

# regression with vectors:
CEOregres <- lm( sal ~ roe  )

# obtain predicted values and residuals
sal.hat <- fitted(CEOregres)
u.hat <- resid(CEOregres)

# Wooldridge, Table 2.2:
cbind(roe, sal, sal.hat, u.hat)[1:15,]
```

_____ Script 2.7: `Example-2-7.R` _____
```
library(foreign)
wage1 <- read.dta("http://fmwww.bc.edu/ec-p/data/wooldridge/wage1.dta")

WAGEregres <- lm(wage ~ educ, data=wage1)

# obtain coefficients, predicted values and residuals
b.hat <- coef(WAGEregres)
wage.hat <- fitted(WAGEregres)
u.hat <- resid(WAGEregres)

# Confirm property (1):
mean(u.hat)

# Confirm property (2):
cor(wage1$educ , u.hat)
```

```
# Confirm property (3):
mean(wage1$wage)
b.hat[1] + b.hat[2] * mean(wage1$educ)
```

_____ Script 2.8: `Example-2-8.R` _____

```
library(foreign)
ceosal1<-read.dta("http://fmwww.bc.edu/ec-p/data/wooldridge/ceosal1.dta")

CEOregres <- lm( salary ~ roe, data=ceosal1 )

# Calculate predicted values & residuals:
sal.hat <- fitted(CEOregres)
u.hat <- resid(CEOregres)

# Calculate R^2 in three different ways:
sal <- ceosal1$salary
var(sal.hat) / var(sal)
1 - var(u.hat) / var(sal)
cor(sal, sal.hat)^2
```

_____ Script 2.9: `Example-2-9.R` _____

```
library(foreign)
vote1 <- read.dta("http://fmwww.bc.edu/ec-p/data/wooldridge/vote1.dta")

VOTEres <- lm(voteA ~ shareA, data=vote1)

# Summary of the regression results
summary(VOTEres)

# Calculate R^2 manually:
var( fitted(VOTEres) ) / var( vote1$voteA )
```

_____ Script 2.10: `Example-2-10.R` _____

```
require(foreign)
wage1 <- read.dta("http://fmwww.bc.edu/ec-p/data/wooldridge/wage1.dta")

# Estimate log-level model
lm( log(wage) ~ educ, data=wage1 )
```

_____ Script 2.11: `Example-2-11.R` _____

```
require(foreign)
ceosal1<-read.dta("http://fmwww.bc.edu/ec-p/data/wooldridge/ceosal1.dta")

# Estimate log-log model
lm( log(salary) ~ log(sales), data=ceosal1 )
```

_____ Script 2.12: `SLR-Origin-Const.R` _____

```
library(foreign)
ceosal1<-read.dta("http://fmwww.bc.edu/ec-p/data/wooldridge/ceosal1.dta")

# Usual OLS regression:
(reg1 <- lm( salary ~ roe, data=ceosal1))

# Regression without intercept (through origin):
(reg2 <- lm( salary ~ 0 + roe, data=ceosal1))
```

```
# Regression without slope (on a constant):
(reg3 <- lm( salary ~ 1 , data=ceosal1))

# average y:
mean(ceosal1$salary)

# Scatter Plot with all 3 regression lines
plot(ceosal1$roe, ceosal1$salary, ylim=c(0,4000))
abline(reg1, lwd=2, lty=1)
abline(reg2, lwd=2, lty=2)
abline(reg3, lwd=2, lty=3)
legend("topleft",c("full","through origin","const only"),lwd=2,lty=1:3)
```

—————————— Script 2.13: `Example-2-12.R` ——————————

```
library(foreign)
meap93<-read.dta("http://fmwww.bc.edu/ec-p/data/wooldridge/meap93.dta")

# Estimate the model and save the results as "results"
results <- lm(math10 ~ lnchprg, data=meap93)

# Number of obs.
( n <- nobs(results) )
# SER:
(SER <- sd(resid(results)) * sqrt((n-1)/(n-2)) )
# SE of b0hat & b1hat, respectively:
SER / sd(meap93$lnchprg) / sqrt(n-1) * sqrt(mean(meap93$lnchprg^2))
SER / sd(meap93$lnchprg) / sqrt(n-1)

# Automatic calculations:
summary(results)
```

—————————— Script 2.14: `SLR-Sim-Sample.R` ——————————

```
# Set the random seed
set.seed(1234567)

# set sample size
n<-1000

# set true parameters: betas and sd of u
b0<-1; b1<-0.5; su<-2

# Draw a sample of size n:
x <- rnorm(n,4,1)
u <- rnorm(n,0,su)
y <- b0 + b1*x + u

# estimate parameters by OLS
(olsres <- lm(y~x))

# features of the sample for the variance formula:
mean(x^2)
sum((x-mean(x))^2)

# Graph
plot(x, y, col="gray", xlim=c(0,8) )
abline(b0,b1,lwd=2)
abline(olsres,col="gray",lwd=2)
```

```
legend("topleft",c("pop. regr. fct.","OLS regr. fct."),
                          lwd=2,col=c("black","gray"))
```

—————————— Script 2.15: `SLR-Sim-Model.R` ——————————

```
# Set the random seed
set.seed(1234567)

# set sample size and number of simulations
n<-1000; r<-10000

# set true parameters: betas and sd of u
b0<-1; b1<-0.5; su<-2

# initialize b0hat and b1hat to store results later:
b0hat <- numeric(r)
b1hat <- numeric(r)

# repeat r times:
for(j in 1:r) {
  # Draw a sample of size n:
  x <- rnorm(n,4,1)
  u <- rnorm(n,0,su)
  y <- b0 + b1*x + u

  # estimate parameters by OLS and store them in the vectors
  bhat <- coefficients( lm(y~x) )
  b0hat[j] <- bhat["(Intercept)"]
  b1hat[j] <- bhat["x"]
}
```

—————————— Script 2.16: `SLR-Sim-Model-Condx.R` ——————————

```
# Set the random seed
set.seed(1234567)

# set sample size and number of simulations
n<-1000; r<-10000

# set true parameters: betas and sd of u
b0<-1; b1<-0.5; su<-2

# initialize b0hat and b1hat to store results later:
b0hat <- numeric(r)
b1hat <- numeric(r)

# Draw a sample of x, fixed over replications:
x <- rnorm(n,4,1)

# repeat r times:
for(j in 1:r) {
  # Draw a sample of y:
  u <- rnorm(n,0,su)
  y <- b0 + b1*x + u

  # estimate parameters by OLS and store them in the vectors
  bhat <- coefficients( lm(y~x) )
  b0hat[j] <- bhat["(Intercept)"]
  b1hat[j] <- bhat["x"]
}
```

_____ Script 2.17: `SLR-Sim-Results.R` _____

```
# MC estimate of the expected values:
mean(b0hat)
mean(b1hat)

# MC estimate of the variances:
var(b0hat)
var(b1hat)

# Initialize empty plot
plot( NULL, xlim=c(0,8), ylim=c(0,6), xlab="x", ylab="y")
# add OLS regression lines
for (j in 1:10) abline(b0hat[j],b1hat[j],col="gray")
# add population regression line
abline(b0,b1,lwd=2)
# add legend
legend("topleft",c("Population","OLS regressions"),
                        lwd=c(2,1),col=c("black","gray"))
```

_____ Script 2.18: `SLR-Sim-ViolSLR4.R` _____

```
# Set the random seed
set.seed(1234567)

# set sample size and number of simulations
n<-1000; r<-10000

# set true parameters: betas and sd of u
b0<-1; b1<-0.5; su<-2

# initialize b0hat and b1hat to store results later:
b0hat <- numeric(r)
b1hat <- numeric(r)

# Draw a sample of x, fixed over replications:
x <- rnorm(n,4,1)

# repeat r times:
for(j in 1:r) {
  # Draw a sample of y:
  u <- rnorm(n, (x-4)/5, su)
  y <- b0 + b1*x + u

  # estimate parameters by OLS and store them in the vectors
  bhat <- coefficients( lm(y~x) )
  b0hat[j] <- bhat["(Intercept)"]
  b1hat[j] <- bhat["x"]
}
```

_____ Script 2.19: `SLR-Sim-Results-ViolSLR4.R` _____

```
# MC estimate of the expected values:
mean(b0hat)
mean(b1hat)

# MC estimate of the variances:
var(b0hat)
var(b1hat)
```

―――――――――――――――― Script 2.20: `SLR-Sim-ViolSLR5.R` ――――――――――――――――

```
# Set the random seed
set.seed(1234567)

# set sample size and number of simulations
n<-1000; r<-10000

# set true parameters: betas and sd of u
b0<-1; b1<-0.5; su<-2

# initialize b0hat and b1hat to store results later:
b0hat <- numeric(r)
b1hat <- numeric(r)

# Draw a sample of x, fixed over replications:
x <- rnorm(n,4,1)

# repeat r times:
for(j in 1:r) {
  # Draw a sample of y:
  varu <- 4/exp(4.5) * exp(x)
  u <- rnorm(n, 0, sqrt(varu) )
  y <- b0 + b1*x + u

  # estimate parameters by OLS and store them in the vectors
  bhat <- coefficients( lm(y~x) )
  b0hat[j] <- bhat["(Intercept)"]
  b1hat[j] <- bhat["x"]
}
```

―――――――――――― Script 2.21: `SLR-Sim-Results-ViolSLR5.R` ――――――――――――

```
# MC estimate of the expected values:
mean(b0hat)
mean(b1hat)

# MC estimate of the variances:
var(b0hat)
var(b1hat)
```

3. Scripts Used in Chapter 03

―――――――――――――――― Script 3.1: `Example-3-1.R` ――――――――――――――――

```
library(foreign)
gpa1 <- read.dta("http://fmwww.bc.edu/ec-p/data/wooldridge/gpa1.dta")

# Just obtain parameter estimates:
lm(colGPA ~ hsGPA+ACT, data=gpa1)

# Store results under "GPAres" and display full table:
GPAres <- lm(colGPA ~ hsGPA+ACT, data=gpa1)
summary(GPAres)
```

―――――――――――――――― Script 3.2: `Example-3-2.R` ――――――――――――――――

```
library(foreign)
wage1 <- read.dta("http://fmwww.bc.edu/ec-p/data/wooldridge/wage1.dta")
```

```
# OLS regression:
summary( lm(log(wage) ~ educ+exper+tenure, data=wage1) )
```

────────────────── Script 3.3: **Example-3-3.R** ──────────────────
```
library(foreign)
d401k <- read.dta("http://fmwww.bc.edu/ec-p/data/wooldridge/401k.dta")

# OLS regression:
summary( lm(prate ~ mrate+age, data=d401k) )
```

────────────────── Script 3.4: **Example-3-5.R** ──────────────────
```
library(foreign)
crime1<-read.dta("http://fmwww.bc.edu/ec-p/data/wooldridge/crime1.dta")

# Model without avgsen:
summary( lm(narr86 ~ pcnv+ptime86+qemp86, data=crime1) )

# Model with avgsen:
summary( lm(narr86 ~ pcnv+avgsen+ptime86+qemp86, data=crime1) )
```

────────────────── Script 3.5: **Example-3-6.R** ──────────────────
```
library(foreign)
wage1 <- read.dta("http://fmwww.bc.edu/ec-p/data/wooldridge/wage1.dta")

# OLS regression:
summary( lm(log(wage) ~ educ, data=wage1) )
```

────────────────── Script 3.6: **OLS-Matrices.R** ──────────────────
```
library(foreign)
gpa1 <- read.dta("http://fmwww.bc.edu/ec-p/data/wooldridge/gpa1.dta")

# Determine sample size & no. of regressors:
n <- nrow(gpa1); k<-2

# extract y
y <- gpa1$colGPA

# extract X & add a column of ones
X <- cbind(1, gpa1$hsGPA, gpa1$ACT)

# Display first rows of X:
head(X)

# Parameter estimates:
( bhat <- solve( t(X)%*%X ) %*% t(X)%*%y )

# Residuals, estimated variance of u and SER:
uhat <- y - X %*% bhat
sigsqhat <- as.numeric( t(uhat) %*% uhat / (n-k-1) )
( SER <- sqrt(sigsqhat) )

# Estimated variance of the parameter estimators and SE:
Vbetahat <- sigsqhat * solve( t(X)%*%X )
( se <- sqrt( diag(Vbetahat) ) )
```

──────────── Script 3.7: Omitted–Vars.R ────────────

```
library(foreign)
gpa1 <- read.dta("http://fmwww.bc.edu/ec-p/data/wooldridge/gpa1.dta")

# Parameter estimates for full and simple model:
beta.hat <- coef( lm(colGPA ~ ACT+hsGPA, data=gpa1) )
beta.hat

# Relation between regressors:
delta.tilde <- coef( lm(hsGPA ~ ACT, data=gpa1) )
delta.tilde

# Omitted variables formula for beta1.tilde:
beta.hat["ACT"] + beta.hat["hsGPA"]*delta.tilde["ACT"]

# Actual regression with hsGPA omitted:
lm(colGPA ~ ACT, data=gpa1)
```

──────────── Script 3.8: MLR–SE.R ────────────

```
library(foreign)
gpa1 <- read.dta("http://fmwww.bc.edu/ec-p/data/wooldridge/gpa1.dta")

# Full estimation results including automatic SE :
res <- lm(colGPA ~ hsGPA+ACT, data=gpa1)
summary(res)

# Extract SER (instead of calculation via residuals)
( SER <- summary(res)$sigma )

# regressing hsGPA on ACT for calculation of R2 & VIF
( R2.hsGPA  <- summary( lm(hsGPA~ACT, data=gpa1) )$r.squared )
( VIF.hsGPA <- 1/(1-R2.hsGPA) )

# manual calculation of SE of hsGPA coefficient:
n <- nobs(res)
( SE.hsGPA <- 1/sqrt(n-1) * SER/sd(gpa1$hsGPA)  * sqrt(VIF.hsGPA) )
```

──────────── Script 3.9: MLR–VIF.R ────────────

```
library(foreign)
wage1 <- read.dta("http://fmwww.bc.edu/ec-p/data/wooldridge/wage1.dta")

# OLS regression:
lmres <- lm(log(wage) ~ educ+exper+tenure, data=wage1)

# Regression output:
summary(lmres)

# Load package "car" (has to be installed):
library(car)
# Automatically calculate VIF :
vif(lmres)
```

4. Scripts Used in Chapter 04

─────────── Script 4.1: **Example-4-3.R** ───────────
```
library(foreign)
gpa1 <- read.dta("http://fmwww.bc.edu/ec-p/data/wooldridge/gpa1.dta")

# Store results under "sumres" and display full table:
( sumres <- summary( lm(colGPA ~ hsGPA+ACT+skipped, data=gpa1) ) )

# Manually confirm the formulas: Extract coefficients and SE
regtable <- sumres$coefficients
bhat <- regtable[,1]
se   <- regtable[,2]

# Reproduce t statistic
( tstat <- bhat / se )
# Reproduce p value
( pval  <- 2*pt(-abs(tstat),137) )
```

─────────── Script 4.2: **Example-4-1.R** ───────────
```
library(foreign)
wage1 <- read.dta("http://fmwww.bc.edu/ec-p/data/wooldridge/wage1.dta")

# OLS regression:
summary( lm(log(wage) ~ educ+exper+tenure, data=wage1) )
```

─────────── Script 4.3: **Example-4-8.R** ───────────
```
library(foreign)
rdchem<-read.dta("http://fmwww.bc.edu/ec-p/data/wooldridge/rdchem.dta")

# OLS regression:
myres <- lm(log(rd) ~ log(sales)+profmarg, data=rdchem)

# Regression output:
summary(myres)

# 95% CI:
confint(myres)

# 99% CI:
confint(myres, level=0.99)
```

─────────── Script 4.4: **F-Test-MLB.R** ───────────
```
library(foreign)
mlb1 <- read.dta("http://fmwww.bc.edu/ec-p/data/wooldridge/mlb1.dta")

# Unrestricted OLS regression:
res.ur <- lm(log(salary) ~ years+gamesyr+bavg+hrunsyr+rbisyr, data=mlb1)

# Restricted OLS regression:
res.r <- lm(log(salary) ~ years+gamesyr, data=mlb1)

# R2:
( r2.ur <- summary(res.ur)$r.squared )
( r2.r <- summary(res.r)$r.squared )

# F statistic:
( F <- (r2.ur-r2.r) / (1-r2.ur) * 347/3 )
```

```
# p value = 1-cdf of the appropriate F distribution:
1-pf(F, 3,347)
```

──────────────── Script 4.5: `F-Test-MLB-auto.R` ────────────────
```
library(foreign)
mlb1 <- read.dta("http://fmwww.bc.edu/ec-p/data/wooldridge/mlb1.dta")

# Unrestricted OLS regression:
res.ur <- lm(log(salary) ~ years+gamesyr+bavg+hrunsyr+rbisyr, data=mlb1)

# Load package "car" (which has to be installed on the computer)
library(car)

# F test
myH0 <- c("bavg","hrunsyr","rbisyr")
linearHypothesis(res.ur, myH0)
```

──────────────── Script 4.6: `F-Test-MLB-auto2.R` ────────────────
```
# F test (F-Test-MLB-auto.R has to be run first!)
myH0 <- c("bavg", "hrunsyr=2*rbisyr")
linearHypothesis(res.ur, myH0)
```

──────────────── Script 4.7: `F-Test-MLB-auto3.R` ────────────────
```
# Note: Script "F-Test-MLB-auto.R" has to be run first to create res.ur.
# Which variables used in res.ur contain "yr" in their names?
myH0 <- matchCoefs(res.ur,"yr")
myH0

# F test (F-Test-MLB-auto.R has to be run first!)
linearHypothesis(res.ur, myH0)
```

──────────────── Script 4.8: `Example-4-10.R` ────────────────
```
library(foreign)
meap93<-read.dta("http://fmwww.bc.edu/ec-p/data/wooldridge/meap93.dta")

# define new variable within data frame
meap93$b_s <- meap93$benefits / meap93$salary

# Estimate three different models
model1<- lm(log(salary) ~ b_s                         , data=meap93)
model2<- lm(log(salary) ~ b_s+log(enroll)+log(staff), data=meap93)
model3<- lm(log(salary) ~ b_s+log(enroll)+log(staff)+droprate+gradrate
                                              , data=meap93)
# Load package and display table of results
library(stargazer)
stargazer(list(model1,model2,model3),type="text",keep.stat=c("n","rsq"))
```

5. Scripts Used in Chapter 05

──────────────── Script 5.1: `Sim-Asy-OLS-norm.R` ────────────────
```
# Set the random seed
set.seed(1234567)
# set true parameters: intercept & slope
b0<-1; b1<-0.5
```

```
# initialize b1hat to store 10000 results:
b1hat <- numeric(10000)

# Draw a sample of x, fixed over replications:
x <- rnorm(n,4,1)
# repeat r times:
for(j in 1:10000) {
  # Draw a sample of u (std. normal):
  u <- rnorm(n)
  # Draw a sample of y:
  y <- b0 + b1*x + u
  # regress y on x and store slope estimate at position j
  bhat <- coef( lm(y~x) )
  b1hat[j] <- bhat["x"]
}
```

———————————— Script 5.2: Sim–Asy–OLS–chisq.R ————————————

```
# Set the random seed
set.seed(1234567)
# set true parameters: intercept & slope
b0<-1; b1<-0.5
# initialize b1hat to store 10000 results:
b1hat <- numeric(10000)

# Draw a sample of x, fixed over replications:
x <- rnorm(n,4,1)
# repeat r times:
for(j in 1:10000) {
  # Draw a sample of u (standardized chi-squared[1]):
  u <- ( rchisq(n,1)-1 ) / sqrt(2)
  # Draw a sample of y:
  y <- b0 + b1*x + u
  # regress y on x and store slope estimate at position j
  bhat <- coef( lm(y~x) )
  b1hat[j] <- bhat["x"]
}
```

———————————— Script 5.3: Sim–Asy–OLS–uncond.R ————————————

```
# Set the random seed
set.seed(1234567)
# set true parameters: intercept & slope
b0<-1; b1<-0.5
# initialize b1hat to store 10000 results:
b1hat <- numeric(10000)

# repeat r times:
for(j in 1:10000) {
  # Draw a sample of x, varying over replications:
  x <- rnorm(n,4,1)
  # Draw a sample of u (std. normal):
  u <- rnorm(n)
  # Draw a sample of y:
  y <- b0 + b1*x + u
  # regress y on x and store slope estimate at position j
  bhat <- coef( lm(y~x) )
  b1hat[j] <- bhat["x"]
}
```

─────── Script 5.4: `Example-5-3.R` ───────

```
library(foreign)
crime1<-read.dta("http://fmwww.bc.edu/ec-p/data/wooldridge/crime1.dta")

# 1. Estimate restricted model:
restr <- lm(narr86 ~ pcnv+ptime86+qemp86, data=crime1)

# 2. Regression of residuals from restricted model:
utilde <- resid(restr)
LMreg <- lm(utilde ~ pcnv+ptime86+qemp86+avgsen+tottime, data=crime1)
# R-squared:
(r2 <- summary(LMreg)$r.squared )

# 3. Calculation of LM test statistic:
LM <- r2 * nobs(LMreg)
LM

# 4. Critical value from chi-squared distribution, alpha=10%:
qchisq(1-0.10, 2)

# Alternative to critical value: p value
1-pchisq(LM, 2)

# Alternative: automatic F test (see above)
library(car)
unrestr <- lm(narr86 ~ pcnv+ptime86+qemp86+avgsen+tottime, data=crime1)
linearHypothesis(unrestr, c("avgsen=0","tottime=0"))
```

6. Scripts Used in Chapter 06

─────── Script 6.1: `Data-Scaling.R` ───────

```
library(foreign)
bwght <- read.dta("http://fmwww.bc.edu/ec-p/data/wooldridge/bwght.dta")

# Basic model:
lm( bwght ~ cigs+faminc, data=bwght)

# Weight in pounds, manual way:
bwght$bwghtlbs <- bwght$bwght/16
lm( bwghtlbs ~ cigs+faminc, data=bwght)

# Weight in pounds, direct way:
lm( I(bwght/16) ~ cigs+faminc, data=bwght)

# Packs of cigarettes:
lm( bwght ~ I(cigs/20) +faminc, data=bwght)
```

─────── Script 6.2: `Example-6-1.R` ───────

```
library(foreign)
hprice2<-read.dta("http://fmwww.bc.edu/ec-p/data/wooldridge/hprice2.dta")

# Estimate model with standardized variables:
lm(scale(price) ~ 0+scale(nox)+scale(crime)+scale(rooms)+
                        scale(dist)+scale(stratio), data=hprice2)
```

──────── Script 6.3: `Formula-Logarithm.R` ────────

```
library(foreign)
hprice2<-read.dta("http://fmwww.bc.edu/ec-p/data/wooldridge/hprice2.dta")

# Estimate model with logs:
lm(log(price)~log(nox)+rooms, data=hprice2)
```

──────── Script 6.4: `Example-6-2.R` ────────

```
library(foreign)
hprice2<-read.dta("http://fmwww.bc.edu/ec-p/data/wooldridge/hprice2.dta")

res<- lm(log(price)~log(nox)+log(dist)+rooms+I(rooms^2)+
            stratio,data=hprice2)
summary(res)
```

──────── Script 6.5: `Example-6-3.R` ────────

```
library(foreign)
attend <- read.dta("http://fmwww.bc.edu/ec-p/data/wooldridge/attend.dta")

# Estimate model with interaction effect:
(myres<-lm(stndfnl~atndrte*priGPA+ACT+I(priGPA^2)+I(ACT^2), data=attend))

# Estimate for partial effect at priGPA=2.59:
b <- coef(myres)
b["atndrte"] + 2.59*b["atndrte:priGPA"]

# Test partial effect for priGPA=2.59:
library(car)
linearHypothesis(myres,c("atndrte+2.59*atndrte:priGPA"))
```

──────── Script 6.6: `Example-6-5.R` ────────

```
library(foreign)
gpa2 <- read.dta("http://fmwww.bc.edu/ec-p/data/wooldridge/gpa2.dta")

# Regress and report coefficients
reg <- lm(colgpa~sat+hsperc+hsize+I(hsize^2),data=gpa2)
reg

# Generate data set containing the regressor values for predictions
cvalues <- data.frame(sat=1200, hsperc=30, hsize=5)

# Point estimate of prediction
predict(reg, cvalues)

# Point estimate and 95% confidence interval
predict(reg, cvalues, interval = "confidence")

# Define three sets of regressor variables
cvalues <- data.frame(sat=c(1200,900,1400), hsperc=c(30,20,5),
                                            hsize=c(5,3,1))
cvalues
# Point estimates and 99% confidence intervals for these
predict(reg, cvalues, interval = "confidence", level=0.99)
```

─────── Script 6.7: `Example-6-6.R` ───────

```
library(foreign)
gpa2 <- read.dta("http://fmwww.bc.edu/ec-p/data/wooldridge/gpa2.dta")

# Regress (as before)
reg <- lm(colgpa~sat+hsperc+hsize+I(hsize^2),data=gpa2)

# Define three sets of regressor variables (as before)
cvalues <- data.frame(sat=c(1200,900,1400), hsperc=c(30,20,5),
                                             hsize=c(5,3,1))

# Point estimates and 95% prediction intervals for these
predict(reg, cvalues, interval = "prediction")
```

─────── Script 6.8: `Effects-Manual.R` ───────

```
# Repeating the regression from Example 6.2:
library(foreign)
hprice2<-read.dta("http://fmwww.bc.edu/ec-p/data/wooldridge/hprice2.dta")

res <- lm( log(price) ~ log(nox)+log(dist)+rooms+I(rooms^2)+stratio,
                                                    data=hprice2)

# Predictions: Values of the regressors:
# rooms = 4-8, all others at the sample mean:
X <- data.frame(rooms=seq(4,8),nox=5.5498,dist=3.7958,stratio=18.4593)

# Calculate predictions and confidence interval:
pred <- predict(res, X, interval = "confidence")

# Table of regressor values, predictions and CI:
cbind(X,pred)

# Plot
matplot(X$rooms, pred, type="l", lty=c(1,2,2))
```

─────── Script 6.9: `Effects-Automatic.R` ───────

```
# Repeating the regression from Example 6.2:
library(foreign)
hprice2<-read.dta("http://fmwww.bc.edu/ec-p/data/wooldridge/hprice2.dta")

res <- lm( log(price) ~ log(nox)+log(dist)+rooms+I(rooms^2)+stratio,
                                                    data=hprice2)

# Automatic effects plot using the package "effects"
library(effects)
plot( effect("rooms",res) )
```

7. Scripts Used in Chapter 07

─────── Script 7.1: `Example-7-1.R` ───────

```
library(foreign)
wage1 <- read.dta("http://fmwww.bc.edu/ec-p/data/wooldridge/wage1.dta")

lm(wage ~ female+educ+exper+tenure, data=wage1)
```

──────── Script 7.2: `Example-7-6.R` ────────

```
library(foreign)
wage1 <- read.dta("http://fmwww.bc.edu/ec-p/data/wooldridge/wage1.dta")

lm(log(wage)~married*female+educ+exper+I(exper^2)+tenure+I(tenure^2),
                                                            data=wage1)
```

──────── Script 7.3: `Example-7-1-logical.R` ────────

```
library(foreign)
wage1 <- read.dta("http://fmwww.bc.edu/ec-p/data/wooldridge/wage1.dta")

# replace "female" with logical variable
wage1$female <- as.logical(wage1$female)
table(wage1$female)

# regression with logical variable
lm(wage ~ female+educ+exper+tenure, data=wage1)
```

──────── Script 7.4: `Regr-Factors.R` ────────

```
data(CPS1985,package="AER")

# Table of categories and frequencies for two factor variables:
table(CPS1985$gender)
table(CPS1985$occupation)

# Directly using factor variables in regression formula:
lm(log(wage) ~ education+experience+gender+occupation, data=CPS1985)

# Manually redefine the  reference category:
CPS1985$gender <- relevel(CPS1985$gender,"female")
CPS1985$occupation <- relevel(CPS1985$occupation,"management")

# Rerun regression:
lm(log(wage) ~ education+experience+gender+occupation, data=CPS1985)
```

──────── Script 7.5: `Example-7-8.R` ────────

```
library(foreign)
lawsch85<-
    read.dta("http://fmwww.bc.edu/ec-p/data/wooldridge/lawsch85.dta")

# Define cut points for the rank
cutpts <- c(0,10,25,40,60,100,175)

# Create factor variable containing ranges for the rank
lawsch85$rankcat <- cut(lawsch85$rank, cutpts)

# Display frequencies
table(lawsch85$rankcat)

# Choose reference category
lawsch85$rankcat <- relevel(lawsch85$rankcat,"(100,175]")

# Run regression
lm(log(salary)~rankcat+LSAT+GPA+log(libvol)+log(cost), data=lawsch85)
```

─────────── Script 7.6: Dummy-Interact.R ───────────

```
library(foreign)
gpa3 <- read.dta("http://fmwww.bc.edu/ec-p/data/wooldridge/gpa3.dta")

# Model with full interactions with female dummy (only for spring data)
reg<-lm(cumgpa~female*(sat+hsperc+tothrs), data=gpa3, subset=(spring==1))
summary(reg)

# F-Test from package "car". H0: the interaction coefficients are zero
# matchCoefs(...) selects all coeffs with names containing "female"
library(car)
linearHypothesis(reg, matchCoefs(reg, "female"))
```

─────────── Script 7.7: Dummy-Interact-Sep.R ───────────

```
library(foreign)
gpa3 <- read.dta("http://fmwww.bc.edu/ec-p/data/wooldridge/gpa3.dta")

# Estimate model for males (& spring data)
lm(cumgpa~sat+hsperc+tothrs, data=gpa3, subset=(spring==1&female==0))

# Estimate model for females (& spring data)
lm(cumgpa~sat+hsperc+tothrs, data=gpa3, subset=(spring==1&female==1))
```

8. Scripts Used in Chapter 08

─────────── Script 8.1: Example-8-2.R ───────────

```
library(foreign)
gpa3 <- read.dta("http://fmwww.bc.edu/ec-p/data/wooldridge/gpa3.dta")

# load packages (which need to be installed!)
library(lmtest); library(car)

# Estimate model (only for spring data)
reg <- lm(cumgpa~sat+hsperc+tothrs+female+black+white,
                              data=gpa3, subset=(spring==1))
# Usual SE:
coeftest(reg)
# Refined White heteroscedasticity-robust SE:
coeftest(reg, vcov=hccm)
```

─────────── Script 8.2: Example-8-2-cont.R ───────────

```
# F-Tests using different variance-covariance formulas:
myH0 <- c("black","white")
# Ususal VCOV
linearHypothesis(reg, myH0)
# Refined White VCOV
linearHypothesis(reg, myH0, vcov=hccm)
# Classical White VCOV
linearHypothesis(reg, myH0, vcov=hccm(reg,type="hc0"))
```

─────────── Script 8.3: Example-8-4.R ───────────

```
library(foreign)
hprice1<-read.dta("http://fmwww.bc.edu/ec-p/data/wooldridge/hprice1.dta")

# Estimate model
```

```
reg <- lm(price~lotsize+sqrft+bdrms, data=hprice1)
reg

# Automatic BP test
library(lmtest)
bptest(reg)

# Manual regression of squared residuals
summary(lm( resid(reg)^2 ~ lotsize+sqrft+bdrms, data=hprice1))
```

────────────────── Script 8.4: Example-8-5.R ──────────────────

```
library(foreign)
hprice1<-read.dta("http://fmwww.bc.edu/ec-p/data/wooldridge/hprice1.dta")

# Estimate model
reg <- lm(log(price)~log(lotsize)+log(sqrft)+bdrms, data=hprice1)
reg

# BP test
library(lmtest)
bptest(reg)

# White test
bptest(reg, ~ fitted(reg) + I(fitted(reg)^2) )
```

────────────────── Script 8.5: Example-8-6.R ──────────────────

```
library(foreign)
d401k<-read.dta("http://fmwww.bc.edu/ec-p/data/wooldridge/401ksubs.dta")

# OLS (only for singles: fsize==1)
lm(nettfa ~ inc + I((age-25)^2) + male + e401k,
                                    data=d401k, subset=(fsize==1))

# WLS
lm(nettfa ~ inc + I((age-25)^2) + male + e401k, weight=1/inc,
                                    data=d401k, subset=(fsize==1))
```

────────────────── Script 8.6: WLS-Robust.R ──────────────────

```
library(foreign)
d401k<-read.dta("http://fmwww.bc.edu/ec-p/data/wooldridge/401ksubs.dta")

# WLS
wlsreg <- lm(nettfa ~ inc + I((age-25)^2) + male + e401k,
                            weight=1/inc, data=d401k, subset=(fsize==1))

# non-robust results
library(lmtest); library(car)
coeftest(wlsreg)

# robust results (Refined White SE:)
coeftest(wlsreg,hccm)
```

────────────────── Script 8.7: Example-8-7.R ──────────────────

```
library(foreign)
smoke <- read.dta("http://fmwww.bc.edu/ec-p/data/wooldridge/smoke.dta")

# OLS
```

```
olsreg<-lm(cigs~log(income)+log(cigpric)+educ+age+I(age^2)+restaurn,
                                                    data=smoke)
olsreg

# BP test
library(lmtest)
bptest(olsreg)

# FGLS: estimation of the variance function
logu2 <- log(resid(olsreg)^2)
varreg<-lm(logu2~log(income)+log(cigpric)+educ+age+I(age^2)+restaurn,
                                                    data=smoke)

# FGLS: WLS
w <- 1/exp(fitted(varreg))
lm(cigs~log(income)+log(cigpric)+educ+age+I(age^2)+restaurn,
                                          weight=w ,data=smoke)
```

9. Scripts Used in Chapter 09

──────── Script 9.1: Example-9-2-manual.R ────────

```
library(foreign)
hprice1<-read.dta("http://fmwww.bc.edu/ec-p/data/wooldridge/hprice1.dta")

# original linear regression
orig <- lm(price ~ lotsize+sqrft+bdrms, data=hprice1)

# regression for RESET test
RESETreg <- lm(price ~ lotsize+sqrft+bdrms+I(fitted(orig)^2)+
                                     I(fitted(orig)^3), data=hprice1)

RESETreg

# RESET test. H0: all coeffs including "fitted" are=0
library(car)
linearHypothesis(RESETreg, matchCoefs(RESETreg,"fitted"))
```

──────── Script 9.2: Example-9-2-automatic.R ────────

```
library(foreign)
hprice1<-read.dta("http://fmwww.bc.edu/ec-p/data/wooldridge/hprice1.dta")

# original linear regression
orig <- lm(price ~ lotsize+sqrft+bdrms, data=hprice1)

# RESET test
library(lmtest)
resettest(orig)
```

──────── Script 9.3: Nonnested-Test.R ────────

```
library(foreign)
hprice1<-read.dta("http://fmwww.bc.edu/ec-p/data/wooldridge/hprice1.dta")

# two alternative models
model1 <- lm(price ~      lotsize  +      sqrft  + bdrms, data=hprice1)
model2 <- lm(price ~ log(lotsize) + log(sqrft) + bdrms, data=hprice1)
```

```
# Test against comprehensive model
library(lmtest)
encomptest(model1,model2, data=hprice1)
```

─────────────────── Script 9.4: Sim-ME-Dep.R ───────────────────

```
# Set the random seed
set.seed(1234567)
# set true parameters: intercept & slope
b0<-1; b1<-0.5
# initialize b1hat to store 10000 results:
b1hat <- numeric(10000)
b1hat.me <- numeric(10000)

# Draw a sample of x, fixed over replications:
x <- rnorm(1000,4,1)
# repeat r times:
for(j in 1:10000) {
  # Draw a sample of u
  u <- rnorm(1000)
  # Draw a sample of ystar:
  ystar <- b0 + b1*x + u
  # regress ystar on x and store slope estimate at position j
  bhat <- coef( lm(ystar~x) )
  b1hat[j] <- bhat["x"]
  # Measurement error and mismeasured y:
  e0 <- rnorm(1000)
  y <- ystar+e0
  # regress y on x and store slope estimate at position j
  bhat.me <- coef( lm(y~x) )
  b1hat.me[j] <- bhat.me["x"]
}

# Mean with and without ME
c( mean(b1hat), mean(b1hat.me) )
# Variance with and without ME
c( var(b1hat), var(b1hat.me) )
```

─────────────────── Script 9.5: Sim-ME-Explan.R ───────────────────

```
# Set the random seed
set.seed(1234567)
# set true parameters: intercept & slope
b0<-1; b1<-0.5
# initialize b1hat to store 10000 results:
b1hat <- numeric(10000)
b1hat.me <- numeric(10000)

# Draw a sample of x, fixed over replications:
xstar <- rnorm(1000,4,1)
# repeat r times:
for(j in 1:10000) {
  # Draw a sample of u
  u <- rnorm(1000)
  # Draw a sample of ystar:
  y <- b0 + b1*xstar + u
  # regress y on xstar and store slope estimate at position j
  bhat <- coef( lm(y~xstar) )
  b1hat[j] <- bhat["xstar"]
  # Measurement error and mismeasured y:
```

```
  e1 <- rnorm(1000)
  x <- xstar+e1
  # regress y on x and store slope estimate at position j
  bhat.me <- coef( lm(y~x) )
  b1hat.me[j] <- bhat.me["x"]
}

# Mean with and without ME
c( mean(b1hat), mean(b1hat.me) )
# Variance with and without ME
c( var(b1hat), var(b1hat.me) )
```

─────────── Script 9.6: `NA-NaN-Inf.R` ───────────
```
x <- c(-1,0,1,NA,NaN,-Inf,Inf)
logx <- log(x)
invx <- 1/x
ncdf <- pnorm(x)
isna <- is.na(x)

data.frame(x,logx,invx,ncdf,isna)
```

─────────── Script 9.7: `Missings.R` ───────────
```
library(foreign)
lawsch<-read.dta("http://fmwww.bc.edu/ec-p/data/wooldridge/lawsch85.dta")

# extract LSAT
lsat <- lawsch$LSAT

# Create logical indicator for missings
missLSAT <- is.na(lawsch$LSAT)

# LSAT and indicator for Schools No. 120-129:
rbind(lsat,missLSAT)[,120:129]

# Frequencies of indicator
table(missLSAT)

# Missings for all variables in data frame (counts)
colSums(is.na(lawsch))

# Indicator for complete cases
compl <- complete.cases(lawsch)
table(compl)
```

─────────── Script 9.8: `Missings-Analyses.R` ───────────
```
library(foreign)
lawsch<-read.dta("http://fmwww.bc.edu/ec-p/data/wooldridge/lawsch85.dta")

# Mean of a variable with missings:
mean(lawsch$LSAT)
mean(lawsch$LSAT,na.rm=TRUE)

# Regression with missings
summary(lm(log(salary)~LSAT+cost+age, data=lawsch))
```

────────── Script 9.9: `Outliers.R` ──────────

```
library(foreign)
rdchem <- read.dta("http://fmwww.bc.edu/ec-p/data/wooldridge/rdchem.dta")

# Regression
reg <- lm(rdintens~sales+profmarg, data=rdchem)

# Studentized residuals for all observations:
studres <- rstudent(reg)

# Display extreme values:
min(studres)
max(studres)

# Histogram (and overlayed density plot):
hist(studres, freq=FALSE)
lines(density(studres), lwd=2)
```

────────── Script 9.10: `LAD.R` ──────────

```
library(foreign)
rdchem <- read.dta("http://fmwww.bc.edu/ec-p/data/wooldridge/rdchem.dta")

# OLS Regression
ols <- lm(rdintens ~ I(sales/1000) +profmarg, data=rdchem)
# LAD Regression
library(quantreg)
lad <- rq(rdintens ~ I(sales/1000) +profmarg, data=rdchem)

# regression table
library(stargazer)
stargazer(ols,lad,  type = "text")
```

10. Scripts Used in Chapter 10

────────── Script 10.1: `Example-10-2.R` ──────────

```
library(foreign)
intdef <- read.dta("http://fmwww.bc.edu/ec-p/data/wooldridge/intdef.dta")

# Linear regression of static model:
summary( lm(i3~inf+def,data=intdef)  )
```

────────── Script 10.2: `Example-Barium.R` ──────────

```
library(foreign)
barium <- read.dta("http://fmwww.bc.edu/ec-p/data/wooldridge/barium.dta")

# Imports from China: Variable "chnimp" from data frame "data"
# Monthly time series starting Feb. 1978
impts <- ts(barium$chnimp, start=c(1978,2), frequency=12)

# plot time series
plot(impts)
```

────────── Script 10.3: `Example-zoo.R` ──────────

```
library(foreign)
intdef <- read.dta("http://fmwww.bc.edu/ec-p/data/wooldridge/intdef.dta")
```

```
# Variable "year" as the time measure:
intdef$year

# define "zoo" object containing all data, time measure=year:
library(zoo)
zoodata <- zoo(intdef, order.by=intdef$year)

# Time series plot of inflation
plot(zoodata$i3)
```

_____ Script 10.4: Example-pdfetch.R _____

```
library(pdfetch)

# Which Yahoo Finance symbols?
# "^gspc"=S&P 500, "^ixic"=NASDAQ Composite, "AAPL"=Apple Inc.
tickernames <- c("^gspc","^ixic", "AAPL")

# Download data
yahoo<-pdfetch_YAHOO(tickernames,fields="adjclose",from="2000-01-01")

# The end date is left out, so we get the latest data. Today is...
Sys.Date()

# Number of obs., first and last rows of data
nrow(yahoo)
head(yahoo)
tail(yahoo)

# Time series plot of Apple stock
plot(yahoo$AAPL, las=2)
```

_____ Script 10.5: Example-10-4.R _____

```
# Libraries for dynamic lm, regression table and F tests
library(foreign);library(dynlm);library(lmtest);library(car)
fertil3<-read.dta("http://fmwww.bc.edu/ec-p/data/wooldridge/fertil3.dta")

# Define Yearly time series beginning in 1913
tsdata <- ts(fertil3, start=1913)

# Linear regression of model with lags:
res <- dynlm(gfr ~ pe + L(pe) + L(pe,2) + ww2 + pill, data=tsdata)
coeftest(res)

# F test. H0: all pe coefficients are=0
linearHypothesis(res, matchCoefs(res,"pe"))
```

_____ Script 10.6: Example-10-4-contd.R _____

```
# Calculating the LRP
b<-coef(res)
b["pe"]+b["L(pe)"]+b["L(pe, 2)"]

# F test. H0: LRP=0
linearHypothesis(res,"pe + L(pe) + L(pe, 2) = 0")
```

─────────────── Script 10.7: **Example-10-7.R** ───────────────
```
library(foreign);library(dynlm);library(stargazer)
hseinv <- read.dta("http://fmwww.bc.edu/ec-p/data/wooldridge/hseinv.dta")

# Define Yearly time series beginning in 1947
tsdata <- ts(hseinv, start=1947)

# Linear regression of model with lags:
res1 <- dynlm(log(invpc) ~ log(price)                , data=tsdata)
res2 <- dynlm(log(invpc) ~ log(price) + trend(tsdata), data=tsdata)

# Pretty regression table
stargazer(res1,res2, type="text")
```

─────────────── Script 10.8: **Example-10-11.R** ───────────────
```
library(foreign);library(dynlm);library(lmtest)
barium <- read.dta("http://fmwww.bc.edu/ec-p/data/wooldridge/barium.dta")

# Define monthly time series beginning in Feb. 1978
tsdata <- ts(barium, start=c(1978,2), frequency=12)

res <- dynlm(log(chnimp)  ~ log(chempi)+log(gas)+log(rtwex)+befile6+
                            affile6+afdec6+ season(tsdata) , data=tsdata )
coeftest(res)
```

11. Scripts Used in Chapter 11

─────────────── Script 11.1: **Example-11-4.R** ───────────────
```
library(foreign);library(dynlm);library(stargazer)
nyse <- read.dta("http://fmwww.bc.edu/ec-p/data/wooldridge/nyse.dta")

# Define time series (numbered 1,...,n)
tsdata <- ts(nyse)

# Linear regression of models with lags:
reg1 <- dynlm(return~L(return)                          , data=tsdata)
reg2 <- dynlm(return~L(return)+L(return,2)              , data=tsdata)
reg3 <- dynlm(return~L(return)+L(return,2)+L(return,3), data=tsdata)

# Pretty regression table
stargazer(reg1, reg2, reg3, type="text",
                    keep.stat=c("n","rsq","adj.rsq","f"))
```

─────────────── Script 11.2: **Example-EffMkts.R** ───────────────
```
# Download data from Yahoo Finance and store as "zoo" object
library(zoo);library(pdfetch);library(dynlm);library(stargazer)
dataset <- zoo( pdfetch_YAHOO("GE", fields="adjclose",
                      from="2000-01-01", to="2013-12-31") )

# Calculate return as the log difference
ret <- diff( log(dataset$GE) )

# Plot returns
plot(ret)
```

```
# Linear regression of models with lags:
reg1 <- dynlm(ret~L(ret) )
reg2 <- dynlm(ret~L(ret)+L(ret,2) )
reg3 <- dynlm(ret~L(ret)+L(ret,2)+L(ret,3) )

# Pretty regression table
stargazer(reg1, reg2, reg3, type="text",
                    keep.stat=c("n","rsq","adj.rsq","f"))
```

Script 11.3: Simulate-RandomWalk.R

```
# Initialize Random Number Generator
set.seed(348546)
# initial graph
plot(c(0,50),c(0,0),type="l",lwd=2,ylim=c(-18,18))

# loop over draws:
for(r in 1:30) {
  # i.i.d. standard normal shock
  e <- rnorm(50)
  # Random walk as cumulative sum of shocks
  y <- ts(cumsum(e))
  # Add line to graph
  lines(y, col=gray(.6))
}
```

Script 11.4: Simulate-RandomWalkDrift.R

```
# Initialize Random Number Generator
set.seed(348546)
# initial empty graph with expected value
plot(c(0,50),c(0,100),type="l",lwd=2)

# loop over draws:
for(r in 1:30) {
  # i.i.d. standard normal shock
  e <- rnorm(50)
  # Random walk as cumulative sum of shocks
  y <- ts(cumsum(2+e))
  # Add line to graph
  lines(y, col=gray(.6))
}
```

Script 11.5: Simulate-RandomWalkDrift-Diff.R

```
# Initialize Random Number Generator
set.seed(348546)
# initial empty graph with expected value
plot(c(0,50),c(2,2),type="l",lwd=2,ylim=c(-1,5))

# loop over draws:
for(r in 1:30) {
  # i.i.d. standard normal shock
  e <- rnorm(50)
  # Random walk as cumulative sum of shocks
  y <- ts(cumsum(2+e))
  # First difference
  Dy <- diff(y)
  # Add line to graph
  lines(Dy, col=gray(.6))
}
```

――――――――― Script 11.6: Example-11-6.R ―――――――――
```
# Libraries for dynamic lm and "stargazer" regression table
library(foreign);library(dynlm);library(stargazer)
fertil<-read.dta("http://fmwww.bc.edu/ec-p/data/wooldridge/fertil3.dta")

# Define Yearly time series beginning in 1913
tsdata <- ts(fertil, start=1913)

# Linear regression of model with first differences:
res1 <- dynlm( d(gfr) ~ d(pe), data=tsdata)

# Linear regression of model with lagged differences:
res2 <- dynlm( d(gfr) ~ d(pe) + L(d(pe)) + L(d(pe),2), data=tsdata)

# Pretty regression table
stargazer(res1,res2,type="text")
```

12. Scripts Used in Chapter 12

――――――――― Script 12.1: Example-12-1.R ―――――――――
```
library(foreign);library(dynlm);library(lmtest)
phillips <-
    read.dta("http://fmwww.bc.edu/ec-p/data/wooldridge/phillips.dta")

# Define Yearly time series beginning in 1948
tsdata <- ts(phillips, start=1948)

# Estimation of static Phillips curve:
reg.s <- dynlm( inf ~ unem, data=tsdata, end=1996)
# residuals and AR(1) test:
residual.s <- resid(reg.s)
coeftest( dynlm(residual.s ~ L(residual.s)) )

# Same with expectations-augmented Phillips curve:
reg.ea <- dynlm( d(inf) ~ unem, data=tsdata, end=1996)
residual.ea <- resid(reg.ea)
coeftest( dynlm(residual.ea ~ L(residual.ea)) )
```

――――――――― Script 12.2: Example-12-3.R ―――――――――
```
library(foreign);library(dynlm);library(car);library(lmtest)
barium<-read.dta("http://fmwww.bc.edu/ec-p/data/wooldridge/barium.dta")

tsdata <- ts(barium, start=c(1978,2), frequency=12)

reg <- dynlm(log(chnimp)~log(chempi)+log(gas)+log(rtwex)+
                                befile6+affile6+afdec6, data=tsdata )

# Pedestrian test:
residual <- resid(reg)
resreg <- dynlm(residual ~ L(residual)+L(residual,2)+L(residual,3)+
                            log(chempi)+log(gas)+log(rtwex)+befile6+
                                        affile6+afdec6, data=tsdata )
linearHypothesis(resreg,
                c("L(residual)","L(residual, 2)","L(residual, 3)"))
```

```
# Automatic test:
bgtest(reg, order=3, type="F")
```

—————————————— Script 12.3: Example-DWtest.R ——————————————
```
library(foreign);library(dynlm);library(lmtest)
phillips <-
    read.dta("http://fmwww.bc.edu/ec-p/data/woolridge/phillips.dta")

tsdata <- ts(phillips, start=1948)

# Estimation of both Phillips curve models:
reg.s <- dynlm( inf ~ unem, data=tsdata, end=1996)
reg.ea <- dynlm( d(inf) ~ unem, data=tsdata, end=1996)

# DW tests
dwtest(reg.s)
dwtest(reg.ea)
```

—————————————— Script 12.4: Example-12-4.R ——————————————
```
library(foreign);library(dynlm);library(car);library(orcutt)
barium<-read.dta("http://fmwww.bc.edu/ec-p/data/woolridge/barium.dta")

tsdata <- ts(barium, start=c(1978,2), frequency=12)

# OLS estimation
olsres <- dynlm(log(chnimp)~log(chempi)+log(gas)+log(rtwex)+
        befile6+affile6+afdec6, data=tsdata)

# Cochrane-Orcutt estimation
cochrane.orcutt(olsres)
```

—————————————— Script 12.5: Example-12-7.R ——————————————
```
library(foreign);library(dynlm);library(lmtest);library(sandwich)
minwg<-read.dta("http://fmwww.bc.edu/ec-p/data/woolridge/prminwge.dta")

tsdata <- ts(minwg, start=1950)

# OLS regression
reg<-dynlm(log(prepop)~log(mincov)+log(prgnp)+log(usgnp)+trend(tsdata),
                                                data=tsdata )
# results with usual SE
coeftest(reg)
# results with HAC SE
coeftest(reg, vcovHAC)
```

—————————————— Script 12.6: Example-12-9.R ——————————————
```
library(foreign);library(dynlm);library(lmtest)
nyse <- read.dta("http://fmwww.bc.edu/ec-p/data/woolridge/nyse.dta")

tsdata <- ts(nyse)

# Linear regression of model:
reg <- dynlm(return ~ L(return), data=tsdata)

# squared residual
residual.sq <- resid(reg)^2
```

```
# Model for squared residual:
ARCHreg <- dynlm(residual.sq ~ L(residual.sq))
coeftest(ARCHreg)
```

──────────────── Script 12.7: `Example-ARCH.R` ────────────────
```
# Libraries
library(zoo);library(pdfetch);library(dynlm);library(lmtest)
# Download GE stock prices from Yahoo Finance and store as "zoo" object
dataset <- zoo( pdfetch_YAHOO("GE", fields="adjclose",
                             from="2000-01-01", to="2013-12-31") )

# Calculate return as the log difference
GE.ret <- diff( log(dataset$GE) )

# AR(1) model for returns
reg <- dynlm( GE.ret ~ L(GE.ret) )

# squared residual
residual.sq <- resid(reg)^2

# Model for squared residual:
ARCHreg <- dynlm(residual.sq ~ L(residual.sq))
summary(ARCHreg)
```

13. Scripts Used in Chapter 13

──────────────── Script 13.1: `Example-13-2.R` ────────────────
```
library(foreign)
cps <- read.dta("http://fmwww.bc.edu/ec-p/data/wooldridge/cps78_85.dta")

# Detailed OLS results including interaction terms
summary( lm(lwage ~ y85*(educ+female) +exper+ I((exper^2)/100) + union,
                                                        data=cps) )
```

──────────────── Script 13.2: `Example-13-3-1.R` ────────────────
```
library(foreign)
kielmc <- read.dta("http://fmwww.bc.edu/ec-p/data/wooldridge/kielmc.dta")

# Separate regressions for 1978 and 1981: report coeeficients only
coef( lm(rprice~nearinc, data=kielmc, subset=(year==1978)) )
coef( lm(rprice~nearinc, data=kielmc, subset=(year==1981)) )

# Joint regression including an interaction term
library(lmtest)
coeftest( lm(rprice~nearinc*y81, data=kielmc) )
```

──────────────── Script 13.3: `Example-13-3-2.R` ────────────────
```
DiD      <- lm(log(rprice)~nearinc*y81                          , data=kielmc)
DiDcontr <- lm(log(rprice)~nearinc*y81+age+I(age^2)+log(intst)+
                          log(land)+log(area)+rooms+baths, data=kielmc)
library(stargazer)
stargazer(DiD,DiDcontr,type="text")
```

──────── Script 13.4: `PDataFrame.R` ────────

```
library(foreign);library(plm)
crime2 <- read.dta("http://fmwww.bc.edu/ec-p/data/wooldridge/crime2.dta")

# Define panel data frame
crime2.p <- pdata.frame(crime2, index=46 )

# Panel dimensions:
pdim(crime2.p)

# Observation 1-6: new "id" and "time" and some other variables:
crime2.p[1:6,c("id","time","year","pop","crimes","crmrte","unem")]
```

──────── Script 13.5: `Example-PLM-Calcs.R` ────────

```
library(foreign);library(plm)
crime4 <- read.dta("http://fmwww.bc.edu/ec-p/data/wooldridge/crime4.dta")

# Generate pdata.frame:
crime4.p <- pdata.frame(crime4, index=c("county","year") )

# Calculations within the pdata.frame:
crime4.p$cr.l <- lag(crime4.p$crmrte)
crime4.p$cr.d <- diff(crime4.p$crmrte)
crime4.p$cr.B <- Between(crime4.p$crmrte)
crime4.p$cr.W <- Within(crime4.p$crmrte)

# Display selected variables for observations 1-16:
crime4.p[1:16,c("county","year","crmrte","cr.l","cr.d","cr.B","cr.W")]
```

──────── Script 13.6: `Example-FD.R` ────────

```
library(foreign);library(plm); library(lmtest)
crime2 <- read.dta("http://fmwww.bc.edu/ec-p/data/wooldridge/crime2.dta")

crime2.p <- pdata.frame(crime2, index=46 )

# manually calculate first differences:
crime2.p$dcrmrte <- diff(crime2.p$crmrte)
crime2.p$dunem   <- diff(crime2.p$unem)

# Display selected variables for observations 1-6:
crime2.p[1:6,c("id","time","year","crmrte","dcrmrte","unem","dunem")]

# Estimate FD model with lm on differenced data:
coeftest( lm(dcrmrte~dunem, data=crime2.p) )

# Estimate FD model with plm on original data:
coeftest( plm(crmrte~unem, data=crime2.p, model="fd") )
```

──────── Script 13.7: `Example-13-9.R` ────────

```
library(foreign);library(plm)
crime4<-read.dta("http://fmwww.bc.edu/ec-p/data/wooldridge/crime4.dta")

crime4.p <- pdata.frame(crime4, index=c("county","year") )
pdim(crime4.p)

# manually calculate first differences of crime rate:
crime4.p$dcrmrte <- diff(crime4.p$crmrte)
```

```
# Display selected variables for observations 1-9:
crime4.p[1:9, c("county","year","crmrte","dcrmrte")]

# Estimate FD model:
coeftest( plm(log(crmrte)~d83+d84+d85+d86+d87+lprbarr+lprbconv+
                    lprbpris+lavgsen+lpolpc,data=crime4.p, model="fd") )
```

14. Scripts Used in Chapter 14

———————— Script 14.1: Example-14-2.R ————————
```
library(foreign);library(plm)
wagepan<-read.dta("http://fmwww.bc.edu/ec-p/data/wooldridge/wagepan.dta")

# Generate pdata.frame:
wagepan.p <- pdata.frame(wagepan, index=c("nr","year") )

pdim(wagepan.p)

# Estimate FE model
summary( plm(lwage~married+union+factor(year)*educ,
                                data=wagepan.p, model="within") )
```

———————— Script 14.2: Example-14-4-1.R ————————
```
library(foreign);library(plm);library(stargazer)
wagepan<-read.dta("http://fmwww.bc.edu/ec-p/data/wooldridge/wagepan.dta")

# Generate pdata.frame:
wagepan.p <- pdata.frame(wagepan, index=c("nr","year") )

pdim(wagepan.p)

# Check variation of variables within individuals
pvar(wagepan.p)
```

———————— Script 14.3: Example-14-4-2.R ————————
```
# Estimate different models
wagepan.p$yr<-factor(wagepan.p$year)

reg.ols<- (plm(lwage~educ+black+hisp+exper+I(exper^2)+married+union+yr,
                                data=wagepan.p, model="pooling") )
reg.re <- (plm(lwage~educ+black+hisp+exper+I(exper^2)+married+union+yr,
                                data=wagepan.p, model="random") )
reg.fe <- (plm(lwage~                    I(exper^2)+married+union+yr,
                                data=wagepan.p, model="within") )

# Pretty table of selected results (not reporting year dummies)
stargazer(reg.ols,reg.re,reg.fe, type="text",
        column.labels=c("OLS","RE","FE"),keep.stat=c("n","rsq"),
        keep=c("ed","bl","hi","exp","mar","un"))
```

———————— Script 14.4: Example-HausmTest.R ————————
```
# Note that the estimates "reg.fe" and "reg.re" are calculated in
# Example 14.4. The scripts have to be run first.
```

```
# Hausman test of RE vs. FE:
phtest(reg.fe, reg.re)
```

―――――――――― Script 14.5: **Example-Dummy-CRE-1.R** ――――――――――
```
library(foreign);library(plm);library(stargazer)
wagepan<-read.dta("http://fmwww.bc.edu/ec-p/data/wooldridge/wagepan.dta")

# Generate pdata.frame:
wagepan.p <- pdata.frame(wagepan, index=c("nr","year") )

# Estimate FE parameter in 3 different ways:
wagepan.p$yr<-factor(wagepan.p$year)
reg.fe <-(plm(lwage~married+union+yr*educ,data=wagepan.p, model="within"))
reg.dum<-( lm(lwage~married+union+yr*educ+factor(nr), data=wagepan.p))
reg.re <-(plm(lwage~married+union+yr*educ,data=wagepan.p, model="random"))
reg.cre<-(plm(lwage~married+union+yr*educ+Between(married)+Between(union)
                                    ,data=wagepan.p, model="random"))
```

―――――――――― Script 14.6: **Example-Dummy-CRE-2.R** ――――――――――
```
stargazer(reg.fe,reg.dum,reg.cre,reg.re,type="text",model.names=FALSE,
          keep=c("married","union",":educ"),keep.stat=c("n","rsq"),
          column.labels=c("Within","Dummies","CRE","RE"))
```

―――――――――― Script 14.7: **Example-CRE-test-RE.R** ――――――――――
```
# Note that the estimates "reg.cre" are calculated in
# Script "Example-Dummy-CRE-1.R" which has to be run first.

# RE test as an F test on the "Between" coefficients
library(car)
linearHypothesis(reg.cre, matchCoefs(reg.cre,"Between"))
```

―――――――――― Script 14.8: **Example-CRE2.R** ――――――――――
```
library(foreign);library(plm)
wagepan<-read.dta("http://fmwww.bc.edu/ec-p/data/wooldridge/wagepan.dta")

# Generate pdata.frame:
wagepan.p <- pdata.frame(wagepan, index=c("nr","year") )

# Estimate CRE parameters
wagepan.p$yr<-factor(wagepan.p$year)
summary(plm(lwage~married+union+educ+black+hisp+Between(married)+
                        Between(union), data=wagepan.p, model="random"))
```

―――――――――― Script 14.9: **Example-13-9-ClSE.R** ――――――――――
```
library(foreign);library(plm);library(lmtest)
crime4<-read.dta("http://fmwww.bc.edu/ec-p/data/wooldridge/crime4.dta")

# Generate pdata.frame:
crime4.p <- pdata.frame(crime4, index=c("county","year") )

# Estimate FD model:
reg <- ( plm(log(crmrte) ~d83+d84+d85+d86+d87+lprbarr+lprbconv+
                    lprbpris+lavgsen+lpolpc,data=crime4.p, model="fd") )
# regression table with standard SE
coeftest(reg)
# regression table with "clustered" SE:
coeftest(reg,vcovHC)
```

15. Scripts Used in Chapter 15

_____ Script 15.1: Example-15-1.R _____

```
library(foreign);library(AER);library(stargazer)
mroz <- read.dta("http://fmwww.bc.edu/ec-p/data/wooldridge/mroz.dta")

# restrict to non-missing wage observations
oursample <- subset(mroz, !is.na(wage))

# OLS slope parameter manually
with(oursample, cov(log(wage),educ) / var(educ) )
# IV slope parameter manually
with(oursample, cov(log(wage),fatheduc) / cov(educ,fatheduc) )


# OLS automatically
reg.ols <-   lm(log(wage) ~ educ, data=oursample)

# IV automatically
reg.iv <- ivreg(log(wage) ~ educ | fatheduc, data=oursample)

# Pretty regression table
stargazer(reg.ols,reg.iv, type="text")
```

_____ Script 15.2: Example-15-4.R _____

```
library(foreign);library(AER);library(stargazer)
card <- read.dta("http://fmwww.bc.edu/ec-p/data/wooldridge/card.dta")

# Checking for relevance: reduced form
redf<-lm(educ ~ nearc4+exper+I(exper^2)+black+smsa+south+smsa66+reg662+
         reg663+reg664+reg665+reg666+reg667+reg668+reg669, data=card)
# OLS
ols<-lm(log(wage)~educ+exper+I(exper^2)+black+smsa+south+smsa66+reg662+
         reg663+reg664+reg665+reg666+reg667+reg668+reg669, data=card)
# IV estimation
iv <-ivreg(log(wage)~educ+exper+I(exper^2)+black+smsa+south+smsa66+
           reg662+reg663+reg664+reg665+reg666+reg667+reg668+reg669
         | nearc4+exper+I(exper^2)+black+smsa+south+smsa66+
           reg662+reg663+reg664+reg665+reg666+reg667+reg668+reg669
         , data=card)

# Pretty regression table of selected coefficients
stargazer(redf,ols,iv,type="text",
          keep=c("ed","near","exp","bl"),keep.stat=c("n","rsq"))
```

_____ Script 15.3: Example-15-5.R _____

```
library(foreign);library(AER);library(stargazer)
mroz <- read.dta("http://fmwww.bc.edu/ec-p/data/wooldridge/mroz.dta")

# restrict to non-missing wage observations
oursample <- subset(mroz, !is.na(wage))

# 1st stage: reduced form
stage1 <- lm(educ~exper+I(exper^2)+motheduc+fatheduc, data=oursample)

# 2nd stage
man.2SLS<-lm(log(wage)~fitted(stage1)+exper+I(exper^2), data=oursample)
```

```
# Automatic 2SLS estimation
aut.2SLS<-ivreg(log(wage)~educ+exper+I(exper^2)
                | motheduc+fatheduc+exper+I(exper^2) , data=oursample)

# Pretty regression table
stargazer(stage1,man.2SLS,aut.2SLS,type="text",keep.stat=c("n","rsq"))
```

———————————— Script 15.4: **Example-15-7.R** ————————————
```
library(foreign);library(AER);library(lmtest)
mroz <- read.dta("http://fmwww.bc.edu/ec-p/data/wooldridge/mroz.dta")

# restrict to non-missing wage observations
oursample <- subset(mroz, !is.na(wage))

# 1st stage: reduced form
stage1<-lm(educ~exper+I(exper^2)+motheduc+fatheduc, data=oursample)

# 2nd stage
stage2<-lm(log(wage)~educ+exper+I(exper^2)+resid(stage1),data=oursample)

# results including t tests
coeftest(stage2)
```

———————————— Script 15.5: **Example-15-8.R** ————————————
```
library(foreign);library(AER)
mroz <- read.dta("http://fmwww.bc.edu/ec-p/data/wooldridge/mroz.dta")

# restrict to non-missing wage observations
oursample <- subset(mroz, !is.na(wage))

# IV regression
summary( res.2sls <- ivreg(log(wage) ~ educ+exper+I(exper^2)
                 | exper+I(exper^2)+motheduc+fatheduc,data=oursample) )

# Auxiliary regression
res.aux <-  lm(resid(res.2sls) ~ exper+I(exper^2)+motheduc+fatheduc
                       , data=oursample)

# Calculations for test
( r2 <- summary(res.aux)$r.squared )
( n <- nobs(res.aux) )
( teststat <- n*r2 )
( pval <- 1-pchisq(teststat,1) )
```

———————————— Script 15.6: **Example-15-10.R** ————————————
```
library(foreign);library(plm)
jtrain <- read.dta("http://fmwww.bc.edu/ec-p/data/wooldridge/jtrain.dta")

# Define panel data (for 1987 and 1988 only)
jtrain.87.88 <- subset(jtrain,year<=1988)
jtrain.p<-pdata.frame(jtrain.87.88, index=c("fcode","year"))

# IV FD regression
summary( plm(log(scrap)~hrsemp|grant, model="fd",data=jtrain.p) )
```

16. Scripts Used in Chapter 16

─────────── Script 16.1: `Example-16-5-ivreg.R` ───────────
```
library(foreign);library(AER)
mroz <- read.dta("http://fmwww.bc.edu/ec-p/data/wooldridge/mroz.dta")
oursample <- subset(mroz,!is.na(wage))

# 2SLS regressions
summary( ivreg(hours~log(wage)+educ+age+kidslt6+nwifeinc
           |educ+age+kidslt6+nwifeinc+exper+I(exper^2), data=oursample))
summary( ivreg(log(wage)~hours+educ+exper+I(exper^2)
           |educ+age+kidslt6+nwifeinc+exper+I(exper^2), data=oursample))
```

─────────── Script 16.2: `Example-16-5-systemfit-prep.R` ───────────
```
library(foreign);library(systemfit)
mroz <- read.dta("http://fmwww.bc.edu/ec-p/data/wooldridge/mroz.dta")
oursample <- subset(mroz,!is.na(wage))

# Define system of equations and instruments
eq.hrs   <- hours     ~ log(wage)+educ+age+kidslt6+nwifeinc
eq.wage  <- log(wage)~ hours     +educ+exper+I(exper^2)
eq.system<- list(eq.hrs, eq.wage)
instrum  <- ~educ+age+kidslt6+nwifeinc+exper+I(exper^2)
```

─────────── Script 16.3: `Example-16-5-systemfit.R` ───────────
```
# 2SLS of whole system (run Example-16-5-systemfit-prep.R first!)
summary(systemfit(eq.system,inst=instrum,data=oursample,method="2SLS"))
```

─────────── Script 16.4: `Example-16-5-3sls.R` ───────────
```
# 3SLS of whole system (run Example-16-5-systemfit-prep.R first!)

summary(systemfit(eq.system,inst=instrum,data=oursample,method="3SLS"))
```

17. Scripts Used in Chapter 17

─────────── Script 17.1: `Example-17-1-1.R` ───────────
```
library(foreign);library(car); library(lmtest)  # for robust SE
mroz <- read.dta("http://fmwww.bc.edu/ec-p/data/wooldridge/mroz.dta")

# Estimate linear probability model
linprob <- lm(inlf~nwifeinc+educ+exper+I(exper^2)+age+kidslt6+kidsge6,data=mroz)
# Regression table with heteroscedasticity-robust SE and t tests:
coeftest(linprob,vcov=hccm)
```

─────────── Script 17.2: `Example-17-1-2.R` ───────────
```
# predictions for two "extreme" women (run Example-17-1-1.R first!):
xpred <- list(nwifeinc=c(100,0),educ=c(5,17),exper=c(0,30),
             age=c(20,52),kidslt6=c(2,0),kidsge6=c(0,0))
predict(linprob,xpred)
```

─────────── Script 17.3: `Example-17-1-3.R` ───────────
```
library(foreign)
mroz <- read.dta("http://fmwww.bc.edu/ec-p/data/wooldridge/mroz.dta")
```

```
# Estimate logit model
logitres<-glm(inlf~nwifeinc+educ+exper+I(exper^2)+age+kidslt6+kidsge6,
                           family=binomial(link=logit),data=mroz)
# Summary of results:
summary(logitres)
# Log likelihood value:
logLik(logitres)
# McFadden's pseudo R2:
1 - logitres$deviance/logitres$null.deviance
```

_____ Script 17.4: Example-17-1-4.R _____
```
library(foreign)
mroz <- read.dta("http://fmwww.bc.edu/ec-p/data/wooldridge/mroz.dta")

# Estimate probit model
probitres<-glm(inlf~nwifeinc+educ+exper+I(exper^2)+age+kidslt6+kidsge6,
                           family=binomial(link=probit),data=mroz)
# Summary of results:
summary(probitres)
# Log likelihood value:
logLik(probitres)
# McFadden's pseudo R2:
1 - probitres$deviance/probitres$null.deviance
```

_____ Script 17.5: Example-17-1-5.R _____
```
################################################################
# Test of overall significance:
# Manual calculation of the LR test statistic:
probitres$null.deviance - probitres$deviance

# Automatic calculations including p-values,...:
library(lmtest)
lrtest(probitres)

################################################################
# Test of H0: experience and age are irrelevant
restr <- glm(inlf~nwifeinc+educ+ kidslt6+kidsge6,
                           family=binomial(link=logit),data=mroz)
lrtest(restr,probitres)
```

_____ Script 17.6: Example-17-1-6.R _____
```
# Predictions from linear probability, probit and logit model:
# (run 17-1-1.R through 17-1-4.R first to define the variables!)
predict(linprob,  xpred,type = "response")
predict(logitres, xpred,type = "response")
predict(probitres,xpred,type = "response")
```

_____ Script 17.7: Binary-Predictions.R _____
```
# Simulated data
set.seed(8237445)
y <- rbinom(100,1,0.5)
x <- rnorm(100) + 2*y

# Estimation
linpr.res <-  lm(y~x)
logit.res <- glm(y~x,family=binomial(link=logit))
```

```
probit.res<- glm(y~x,family=binomial(link=probit))

# Prediction for regular grid of x values
xp <- seq(from=min(x),to=max(x),length=50)
linpr.p <- predict( linpr.res, list(x=xp), type="response" )
logit.p <- predict( logit.res, list(x=xp), type="response" )
probit.p<- predict( probit.res,list(x=xp), type="response" )

# Graph
plot(x,y)
lines(xp,linpr.p, lwd=2,lty=1)
lines(xp,logit.p, lwd=2,lty=2)
lines(xp,probit.p,lwd=1,lty=1)
legend("topleft",c("linear prob.","logit","probit"),
                              lwd=c(2,2,1),lty=c(1,2,1))
```

_____ Script 17.8: Binary-Margeff.R _____

```
# Calculate partial effects
linpr.eff <- coef(linpr.res)["x"] * rep(1,100)
logit.eff <- coef(logit.res)["x"] * dlogis(predict(logit.res))
probit.eff <- coef(probit.res)["x"] * dnorm(predict(probit.res))

# Graph
plot(  x,linpr.eff, pch=1,ylim=c(0,.7),ylab="partial effect")
points(x,logit.eff, pch=3)
points(x,probit.eff,pch=18)
legend("topright",c("linear prob.","logit","probit"),pch=c(1,3,18))
```

_____ Script 17.9: Example-17-1-7.R _____

```
# APEs (run 17-1-1.R through 17-1-4.R first to define the variables!)

# Calculation of linear index at individual values:
xb.log <- predict(logitres)
xb.prob<- predict(probitres)
# APE factors = average(g(xb))
factor.log <- mean( dlogis(xb.log) )
factor.prob<- mean( dnorm(xb.prob) )
cbind(factor.log,factor.prob)

# average partial effects = beta*factor:
APE.lin <- coef(linprob) * 1
APE.log <- coef(logitres) * factor.log
APE.prob<- coef(probitres) * factor.prob

# Table of APEs
cbind(APE.lin, APE.log, APE.prob)
```

_____ Script 17.10: Example-17-1-8.R _____

```
# Automatic APE calculations with package mfx
library(mfx)
logitmfx(inlf~nwifeinc+educ+exper+I(exper^2)+age+kidslt6+kidsge6,
                                    data=mroz, atmean=FALSE)
```

_____ Script 17.11: Example-17-3-1.R _____

```
library(foreign)
crime1 <- read.dta("http://fmwww.bc.edu/ec-p/data/wooldridge/crime1.dta")
```

```
# Estimate linear model
lm.res        <-  lm(narr86~pcnv+avgsen+tottime+ptime86+qemp86+inc86+
                     black+hispan+born60, data=crime1)
# Estimate Poisson model
Poisson.res <- glm(narr86~pcnv+avgsen+tottime+ptime86+qemp86+inc86+
                     black+hispan+born60, data=crime1, family=poisson)
# Quasi-Poisson model
QPoisson.res<- glm(narr86~pcnv+avgsen+tottime+ptime86+qemp86+inc86+
                     black+hispan+born60, data=crime1, family=quasipoisson)
```

──────────────── Script 17.12: Example-17-3-2.R ────────────────

```
# Example 17.3: Regression table (run Example-17-3-1.R first!)
library(stargazer) # package for regression output
stargazer(lm.res,Poisson.res,QPoisson.res,type="text",keep.stat="n")
```

──────────────── Script 17.13: Tobit-CondMean.R ────────────────

```
# Simulated data
set.seed(93876553)
x           <- sort(rnorm(100)+4)
xb          <- -4 + 1*x
ystar       <- xb + rnorm(100)
y           <- ystar
y[ystar<0]<- 0

# Conditional means
Eystar <- xb
Ey <- pnorm(xb/1)*xb+1*dnorm(xb/1)

# Graph
plot(x,ystar,ylab="y", pch=3)
points(x,y, pch=1)
lines(x,Eystar, lty=2,lwd=2)
lines(x,Ey    , lty=1,lwd=2)
abline(h=0,lty=3)          # horizontal line at 0
legend("topleft",c(expression(y^"*"),"y",expression(E(y^"*")),"E(y)"),
       lty=c(NA,NA,2,1),pch=c(3,1,NA,NA),lwd=c(1,1,2,2))
```

──────────────── Script 17.14: Example-17-2.R ────────────────

```
library(foreign)
mroz <- read.dta("http://fmwww.bc.edu/ec-p/data/wooldridge/mroz.dta")

# Estimate Tobit model using censReg:
library(censReg)
TobitRes <- censReg(hours~nwifeinc+educ+exper+I(exper^2)+
                                age+kidslt6+kidsge6, data=mroz )

summary(TobitRes)

# Partial Effects at the average x:
margEff(TobitRes)
```

──────────────── Script 17.15: Example-17-2-survreg.R ────────────────

```
# Estimate Tobit model using survreg:
library(survival)
res <- survreg(Surv(hours, hours>0, type="left") ~ nwifeinc+educ+exper+
              I(exper^2)+age+kidslt6+kidsge6, data=mroz, dist="gaussian")
summary(res)
```

─────────────────── Script 17.16: `Example-17-4.R` ───────────────────
```
library(foreign);library(survival)
recid <- read.dta("http://fmwww.bc.edu/ec-p/data/wooldridge/recid.dta")

# Define Dummy for UNcensored observations
recid$uncensored <- recid$cens==0
# Estimate censored regression model:
res<-survreg(Surv(log(durat),uncensored, type="right") ~ workprg+priors+
                  tserved+felon+alcohol+drugs+black+married+educ+age,
                  data=recid, dist="gaussian")
# Output:
summary(res)
```

─────────────────── Script 17.17: `TruncReg-Simulation.R` ───────────────────
```
library(truncreg)
# Simulated data
set.seed(93876553)
x   <- sort(rnorm(100)+4)
y   <- -4 + 1*x + rnorm(100)

# complete observations and observed sample:
compl <- data.frame(x,y)
sample <- subset(compl, y>0)

# Predictions
pred.OLS   <- predict(       lm(y~x, data=sample) )
pred.trunc <- predict( truncreg(y~x, data=sample) )

# Graph
plot(    compl$x, compl$y,   pch= 1,xlab="x",ylab="y")
points(sample$x,sample$y,   pch=16)
lines( sample$x,pred.OLS,  lty=2,lwd=2)
lines( sample$x,pred.trunc,lty=1,lwd=2)
abline(h=0,lty=3)            # horizontal line at 0
legend("topleft", c("all points","observed points","OLS fit",
                  "truncated regression"),
       lty=c(NA,NA,2,1),pch=c(1,16,NA,NA),lwd=c(1,1,2,2))
```

─────────────────── Script 17.18: `Example-17-5.R` ───────────────────
```
library(foreign);library(sampleSelection)
mroz <- read.dta("http://fmwww.bc.edu/ec-p/data/wooldridge/mroz.dta")

# Estimate Heckman selection model (2 step version)
res<-selection(inlf~educ+exper+I(exper^2)+nwifeinc+age+kidslt6+kidsge6,
          log(wage)~educ+exper+I(exper^2), data=mroz, method="2step" )
# Summary of results:
summary(res)
```

18. Scripts Used in Chapter 18

─────────────────── Script 18.1: `Example-18-1.R` ───────────────────
```
library(foreign);library(dynlm); library(stargazer)
hseinv<-read.dta("http://fmwww.bc.edu/ec-p/data/wooldridge/hseinv.dta")
```

```
# detrended variable: residual from a regression on the obs. index:
trendreg <- dynlm( log(invpc) ~ trend(hseinv), data=hseinv )
hseinv$linv.detr <-  resid( trendreg )
# ts data:
hseinv.ts <- ts(hseinv)

# Koyck geometric d.l.:
gDL<-dynlm(linv.detr~gprice + L(linv.detr)              ,data=hseinv.ts)
# rational d.l.:
rDL<-dynlm(linv.detr~gprice + L(linv.detr) + L(gprice),data=hseinv.ts)

stargazer(gDL,rDL, type="text", keep.stat=c("n","adj.rsq"))

# LRP geometric DL:
b <- coef(gDL)
 b["gprice"]                    / (1-b["L(linv.detr)"])

# LRP rationalDL:
b <- coef(rDL)
 (b["gprice"]+b["L(gprice)"]) / (1-b["L(linv.detr)"])
```

──────── Script 18.2: Example-18-4.R ────────
```
library(foreign);library(dynlm)
inven <- read.dta("http://fmwww.bc.edu/ec-p/data/wooldridge/inven.dta")

# variable to test: y=log(gdp)
inven$y <- log(inven$gdp)
inven.ts<- ts(inven)

# summary output of ADF regression:
summary(dynlm( d(y) ~ L(y) + L(d(y)) + trend(inven.ts), data=inven.ts))

# automated ADF test using tseries:
library(tseries)
adf.test(inven$y, k=1)
```

──────── Script 18.3: Example-18-4-urca.R ────────
```
library(foreign);library(urca)
inven <- read.dta("http://fmwww.bc.edu/ec-p/data/wooldridge/inven.dta")

# automated ADF test using urca:
summary( ur.df(log(inven$gdp) , type = c("trend"), lags = 1) )
```

──────── Script 18.4: Simulate-Spurious-Regression-1.R ────────
```
# Initialize Random Number Generator
set.seed(29846)

# i.i.d. N(0,1) innovations
n <- 50
e <- rnorm(n)
a <- rnorm(n)
# independent random walks
x <- cumsum(a)
y <- cumsum(e)

# plot
plot(x,type="l",lty=1,lwd=1)
```

```
lines(y          ,lty=2,lwd=2)
legend("topright",c("x","y"), lty=c(1,2), lwd=c(1,2))

# Regression of y on x
summary( lm(y~x) )
```

───────────── Script 18.5: Simulate-Spurious-Regression-2.R ─────────────
```
# Initialize Random Number Generator
set.seed(29846)

# generate 10,000 independent random walks
# and store the p val of the t test
pvals <- numeric(10000)
for (r in 1:10000) {
  # i.i.d. N(0,1) innovations
  n <- 50
  a <- rnorm(n)
  e <- rnorm(n)
  # independent random walks
  x <- cumsum(a)
  y <- cumsum(e)
  # regression summary
  regsum <- summary(lm(y~x))
  # p value: 2nd row, 4th column of regression table
  pvals[r] <- regsum$coef[2,4]
}

# How often is p<5% ?
table(pvals<=0.05)
```

───────────── Script 18.6: Example-18-8.R ─────────────
```
# load updataed data from URfIE Website since online file is incomplete
# Adjust the path if needed!
library(foreign);library(dynlm); library(stargazer)
phillips <- read.dta("phillips.dta")
tsdat=ts(phillips, start=1948)

# Estimate models and display results
res1 <- dynlm(unem ~ unem_1        , data=tsdat, end=1996)
res2 <- dynlm(unem ~ unem_1+inf_1, data=tsdat, end=1996)
stargazer(res1, res2 ,type="text", keep.stat=c("n","adj.rsq","ser"))

# Predictions for 1997-2003 including 95% forecast intervals:
predict(res1, newdata=window(tsdat,start=1997), interval="prediction")
predict(res2, newdata=window(tsdat,start=1997), interval="prediction")
```

───────────── Script 18.7: Example-18-9.R ─────────────
```
# Note: run Example-18-8.R first to generate the results res1 and res2

# Actual unemployment and forecasts:
y  <- window(tsdat,start=1997)[,"unem"]
f1 <- predict( res1, newdata=window(tsdat,start=1997) )
f2 <- predict( res2, newdata=window(tsdat,start=1997) )

# Plot unemployment and forecasts:
matplot(time(y), cbind(y,f1,f2), type="l",  col="black",lwd=2,lty=1:3)
```

```
legend("topleft",c("Unempl.","Forecast 1","Forecast 2"),lwd=2,lty=1:3)

# Forecast errors:
e1<- y - f1
e2<- y - f2

# RMSE:
sqrt(mean(e1^2))
sqrt(mean(e2^2))

# MAE:
mean(abs(e1))
mean(abs(e2))
```

19. Scripts Used in Chapter 19

Script 19.1: ultimate-calcs.R
```
#########################################################################
# Project X:
# "The Ultimate Question of Life, the Universe, and Everything"
# Project Collaborators: Mr. X, Mrs. Y
#
# R Script "ultimate-calcs"
# by: F Heiss
# Date of this version: February 08, 2016
#########################################################################

# The main calculation using the method "square root"
# (http://mathworld.wolfram.com/SquareRoot.html)
sqrt(1764)
```

Script 19.2: projecty-master.R
```
#########################################################################
# Bachelor Thesis Mr. Z
# "Best Practice in Using R Scripts"
#
# R Script "master"
# Date of this version: 2016-02-08
#########################################################################

# Some preparations:
setwd(~/bscthesis/r)
rm(list = ls())

# Call R scripts
source("data.R"          ,echo=TRUE,max=1000) # Data import and cleaning
source("descriptives.R", echo=TRUE,max=1000) # Descriptive statistics
source("estimation.R"    ,echo=TRUE,max=1000) # Estimation of model
source("results.R"       ,echo=TRUE,max=1000) # Tables and Figures
```

Script 19.3: LaTeXwithR.R
```
library(foreign);library(stargazer);library(xtable)
gpa1 <- read.dta("http://fmwww.bc.edu/ec-p/data/wooldridge/gpa1.dta")
```

```
# Number of obs.
sink("numb-n.txt"); cat(nrow(gpa1)); sink()
# generate frequency table in file "tab-gender.txt"
gender <- factor(gpa1$male,labels=c("female","male"))
sink("tab-gender.txt")
xtable( table(gender) )
sink()

# calculate OLS results
res1 <- lm(colGPA ~ hsGPA       , data=gpa1)
res2 <- lm(colGPA ~        ACT, data=gpa1)
res3 <- lm(colGPA ~ hsGPA + ACT, data=gpa1)

# write regression table to file "tab-regr.txt"
sink("tab-regr.txt")
stargazer(res1,res2,res3, keep.stat=c("n","rsq"),
          type="latex",title="Regression Results",label="t:reg")
sink()

# b1 hat
sink("numb-b1.txt"); cat(round(coef(res1)[2],3)); sink()

# Generate graph as PDF file
pdf(file = "regr-graph.pdf", width = 3, height = 2)
par(mar=c(2,2,1,1))
plot(gpa1$hsGPA, gpa1$colGPA)
abline(res1)
dev.off()
```

Bibliography

CHANG, W. (2012): *R Graphics Cookbook*, O'Reilly Media.

CROISSANT, Y. AND G. MILLO (2008): "Panel Data Econometrics in R: The plm Package," *Journal of Statistical Software*, 27.

DALGAARD, P. (2008): *Introductory Statistics with R*, Springer.

FIELD, A., J. MILES, AND Z. FIELD (2012): *Discovering Statistics Using R*, Sage.

FOX, J. (2003): "Effect Displays in R for Generalised Linear Models," *Journal of Statistical Software*, 8.

FOX, J. AND S. WEISBERG (2011): *An R Companion to Applied Regression*, Sage.

HENNINGSEN, A. AND J. D. HAMANN (2007): "systemfit: A Package for Estimating Systems of Simultaneous Equations in R," *Journal of Statistical Software*, 23, 1–40.

HLAVAC, M. (2013): "Stargazer: LaTeX code and ASCII text for well-formatted regression and summary statistics tables." http://CRAN.R-project.org/package=stargazer.

HOTHORN, T. AND B. S. EVERITT (2014): *A Handbook of Statistical Analyses using R*, CRC Press, Chapman & Hall, 3 ed.

KLEIBER, C. AND A. ZEILEIS (2008): *Applied Econometrics with R*, Springer.

KOENKER, R. (2012): "Quantile Regression in R: A Vignette," http://CRAN.R-project.org/package=quantreg.

MATLOFF, N. (2011): *The Art of R Programming*, No Starch Press.

PFAFF, B. (2008): "VAR, SVAR and SVEC Models: Implementation Within R Package vars," *Journal of Statistical Software*, 27.

RYAN, J. A. AND J. M. ULRICH (2008): "xts: Extensible Time Series," http://CRAN.R-project.org/package=xts.

SILVERMAN, B. W. (1986): *Density Estimation for Statistics and Data Analysis*, Chapman & Hall.

TEETOR, P. (2011): *R Cookbook*, O'Reilly.

THERNEAU, T. M. AND P. M. GRAMBSCH (2000): *Modeling Survival Data: Extending the Cox Model*, Springer.

TOOMET, O. AND A. HENNINGSEN (2008): "Sample Selection Models in R: Package sampleSelection," *Journal of Statistical Software*, 27.

VERZANI, J. (2014): *Using R for Introductory Statistics*, CRC Press, Chapman & Hall.

WICKHAM, H. (2009): *ggplot2: Elegant Graphics for Data Analysis*, Springer.

——— (2014): *Advanced R*, CRC Press, Chapman & Hall.

WOOLDRIDGE, J. M. (2010): *Econometric Analysis of Cross Section and Panel Data*, MIT Press.

——— (2013): *Introductory Econometrics: A Modern Approach*, Cengage Learning, 5th ed.

——— (2014): *Introduction to Econometrics*, Cengage Learning.

——— (2016): *Introductory Econometrics: A Modern Approach*, Cengage Learning, 6th ed.

XIE, Y. (2015): *Dynamic Documents with R and knitr*, CRC Press, Chapman & Hall.

ZEILEIS, A. (2004): "Econometric Computing with HC and HAC Covariance Matrix Estimators," *Journal of Statistical Software*, 11.

ZEILEIS, A. AND G. GROTHENDIECK (2005): "zoo: S3 Infrastructure for Regular and Irregular Time Series," *Journal of Statistical Software*, 14.

List of Wooldridge (2016) examples

Index